iPhone 14 User Guide

The Easy-to-Follow Manual for Seniors and Beginners on How to Use iPhone 14, iPhone 14 Plus, iPhone 14 Pro, iPhone 14 Pro Max

Daniel Dean

3

Introduction to iPhone

Setup basics

iPhone has an easy setup process to help you get going when you first turn on your device. Whether you're just getting started or want to make sure you have the basics set up, you're in the right place.

Transfer your apps and info onto your new iPhone

When you first turn on your iPhone and begin the setup process, you can wirelessly transfer many of your apps, settings, and content from your previous iPhone directly to your new iPhone—just bring the two devices close together, then follow the onscreen instructions.

If you have an Android device, tap Move Data from Android on your iPhone during the setup process, then open the Move to iOS app on your Android device.

Set up cellular service and connect to Wi-Fi

Depending on your model, use an eSIM from your carrier or install a physical SIM card to connect to your cellular network. To check if your iPhone is connected to your cellular plan, go to Settings 🔘 > Cellular.

To connect your iPhone to your home Wi-Fi network, go to Settings 🔘 > Wi-Fi, turn on Wi-Fi, then choose your network. iPhone automatically connects to your Wi-Fi network whenever you're home.

Sign in with your Apple ID

Your Apple ID is the account you use to access Apple services such as Apple Music, FaceTime, iCloud, and iMessage. If you don't have an Apple ID, you can create one.

To sign in with your Apple ID, go to Settings 🔘 > Sign in to your iPhone. To verify that you're signed in, go to Settings 🔘 > [your name]; your Apple ID appears below your name.

Make your iPhone your own

You can tailor your iPhone to your own interests and preferences. Personalize your Lock Screen, change the sounds and vibrations for calls and messages, keep features like the flashlight or calculator handy, adjust the text size, and more.

Keep your favorite features handy

Some iPhone features—like the flashlight, timer, or calculator—are just a swipe away in Control Center. To quickly open Control Center on an iPhone with Face ID, swipe down from the top-right edge.

You can add more features—like the alarm or magnifier—to Control Center in Settings > Control Center.

Personalize your Lock Screen

You can showcase a favorite photo, add filters, and widgets, and even change the font of the date and time.

To get started, touch and hold the Lock Screen, then tap  at the bottom of the screen. Browse the gallery of options, then tap one to customize its appearance. When you've created a Lock Screen that you like, tap Add, then tap Set as Wallpaper Pair.

Add widgets to your Home Screen

Widgets let you easily see the information that's most important to you, like the current weather and upcoming calendar events.

To add a widget, touch and hold the background on any Home Screen page until the apps jiggle, then tap + .

Choose sounds and vibrations

iPhone can play different sounds and vibrations for phone calls, text messages, calendar alerts, and other notifications.

Go to Settings > Sounds & Haptics. You can also change the sounds iPhone plays for certain people; in the Contacts app , tap a person's name, tap Edit, then tap Ringtone or Text Tone.

Use built-in accessibility features

iPhone provides many accessibility features to support your vision, physical and motor, hearing, and learning needs. Change text size, make it easier to use the touchscreen, control your iPhone with just your voice, and more.

To customize these settings, go to Settings > Accessibility.

Check privacy settings

iPhone is designed to protect your privacy and information. You can grant or deny apps permission to track your activity across other companies' apps and websites. You can also use Safety Check to review and update which people and apps have access to your information. Go to Settings ⚙ > Privacy & Security, then tap Tracking or Safety Check.

Set up Face ID

You can use Face ID (face recognition) to securely unlock your iPhone, sign in to many apps, and make purchases. For your security, Face ID data doesn't leave your device and isn't saved anywhere else.

- Set up Face ID: Go to Settings ⚙ > Face ID & Passcode, tap Set up Face ID, then follow the onscreen instructions.

Turn on Find My iPhone

You can locate your iPhone if it's ever lost or stolen.

Go to Settings ⚙ > [your name] > Find My, tap Find My iPhone, then turn on Find My iPhone. You can see the location of your devices in the Find My app ⊙ . If you lose your iPhone and don't have access to the Find My app, you can locate your device using Find iPhone on iCloud.com.

Back up your data with iCloud

iCloud helps you keep your important info safe and in sync across your devices. If you replace or lose your iPhone, or it's damaged or stolen, your photos, videos, and more remain secure in iCloud.

To turn on or change the features you want to use with iCloud, go to Settings ⚙ > [your name] > iCloud.

Take great photos and videos

With your iPhone nearby, you'll never miss a chance to take a photo or video, snap a selfie, or capture scenes in low light. After you take photos, use the iPhone editing tools to crop, adjust the light and color, and much more.

Capture the moment

To quickly open Camera, just swipe left on the Lock Screen. Camera automatically focuses the shot and adjusts the exposure. Tap the Shutter button to take a photo.

Quickly switch to video

You can record videos without switching out of Photo mode. Just touch and hold the Shutter button and Camera begins recording a QuickTake video. Release the button to stop recording. QuickTake is available on iPhone XS, iPhone XR, and later.

Take the perfect selfie

To take a selfie, open Camera, then tap ⟳ or ⟳ (depending on your model). Hold your iPhone in front of you, then tap the Shutter button or either volume button to take the shot.

Shoot photos in low light

Night mode automatically takes bright, detailed photos in low-light settings. When ⊚ turns yellow, Night mode is on. Tap the Shutter button, then hold your iPhone still to capture the shot.

To experiment with Night mode, tap ⊚, then move the slider below the frame to adjust the exposure time.

Night mode is available with the front camera, and when you toggle between 0.5x, 1x, 2x, 2.5x, or 3x.

Keep in touch with friends and family

iPhone makes it easy to reach the people important to you—so you can catch up with phone or video calls and quickly text your group of friends.

A smarter address book

Enter phone numbers, email addresses, birthdays, and more in the Contacts app ⊡ once, and you have them everywhere you need them—from Messages to FaceTime to Mail.

You can also add contact information from another account (like Google or Yahoo). Go to Settings ⚙ > Contacts > Accounts, then tap Add Account.

Choose your favorites

Add the people you talk to frequently to your Favorites list in the Phone app 📞 to make them easier to reach.

In the Phone app, tap Favorites, tap ✛ , then choose a contact. To call a Favorite, just tap their name.

Start a group conversation

You can send messages to a group of people you want to talk to all at the same time, like members of your family.

In the Messages app ⬤ , tap ✐ , type the names of the people you want to send a message to, then send the first message.

Share features with your family

There are special features you and your family can use to share purchases, stay connected, and protect your data. If you have children, you can also set up parental controls to manage how your children use their Apple devices.

Set up Family Sharing

With Family Sharing, you and your family members can share purchases, subscriptions, your location, and more. Everyone uses their own device and Apple ID, but iCloud storage, subscriptions (including to services like Apple Music and Apple Arcade), and other content is shared.

To get started, go to Settings ⚙ > [your name] > Family Sharing.

Share your location with Find My

When you set up Family Sharing, you can share your location with members of your family and help them find lost devices with the Find My app ⬤ .

To share your location with family members, go to Settings ⚙ > [your name] > Family Sharing, then scroll down and tap Location. Tap the name of a family member you want to share your location with. After you share your location with members of your Family Sharing group, they can help locate a missing device.

Share your health data

You can use the Health app ❤ to share your health data—such as your activity, mobility, and health trends—with family members.

In the Health app, tap Sharing at the bottom of the screen, then tap Share with Someone. You can choose what you want to share, and if you want the people you're sharing with to be notified about significant trends, like a steep decline in activity.

Just in case

You can add family members and other trusted people as Account Recovery Contacts to help you regain access to your account if you ever get locked out. The Digital Legacy program allows you to designate people as Legacy Contacts so they can access your account and personal information in the event of your death.

To add people, go to Settings ⚙ > [your name] > Password & Security, then choose Account Recovery or Legacy Contact.

Use iPhone for your daily routines

While you're going about your day, you can use the apps on your iPhone to get directions, make purchases, and control accessories in your home. You can also silence notifications while you're driving or working, or allow only specific notifications related to what you're focused on.

Get directions to your favorite places

Whether you're walking, driving, or biking, you can use the Maps app 🧭 to get directions to places you visit frequently, like your home or your favorite café, without entering the address every time.

In the Maps app, tap ╋ in the row of Favorites, then add a location.

Set up a virtual wallet

Keep your credit cards, transit passes, vaccination cards, and more in the Wallet app 💳 on your iPhone. When you add a credit or debit card to Wallet, you can use it to make secure payments in stores and online, and send and receive money from friends and family.

To add your first card, open the Wallet app, tap ➕, then follow the onscreen instructions.

Stay focused

Whether you're driving, working, or just need to step away from your iPhone, you can set up a Focus to temporarily silence notifications that don't match your task—and let other people know you're busy.

Go to Settings ⚙ > Focus, then choose the Focus you want to use, or tap ╋ to create your own.

Reminders when you need them

You can use the Reminders app ⋮ to make to-do lists for tasks around the house and projects at work. You can even get a reminder about something when you arrive at a certain location.

To create your first reminder, open the Reminders app, then tap New Reminder.

Forgot to turn off the lights?

With the Home app ⌂ on iPhone, you can securely control HomeKit-enabled accessories, such as lights, smart TVs, and thermostats from anywhere. You can also create automations that simplify your normal routines, like automatically turning on your entryway lights when you arrive home at night.

To add your first Works with HomeKit accessory, open the Home app, tap ＋ , then tap Add Accessory.

Make a video call

You can use FaceTime to make video calls with your friends and family.

In the FaceTime app 🎥 , tap New FaceTime near the top of the screen, type the name of the person you want to call, then tap 🎥 . During the call, you can tap the screen to show the FaceTime controls (in case you want to mute yourself, for example).

Add people to a FaceTime call

You can add more people to a FaceTime call—friends and family can join at any time. Tap the screen to show the controls, tap ⓘ

Add the final touches

After you take a photo or video, use the editing tools in the Photos app to make it even better. Open a photo or video, tap Edit, then tap the buttons at the bottom of the screen to adjust lighting, add a filter, crop, or rotate. As you make edits, tap the photo to compare your changes to the original.

Your iPhone

Identify your iPhone model and iOS version

Go to Settings > General > About.

Get iOS updates

To update your iPhone to the latest iOS software compatible with your model, go to Settings > General > Software Update.

iPhone 14

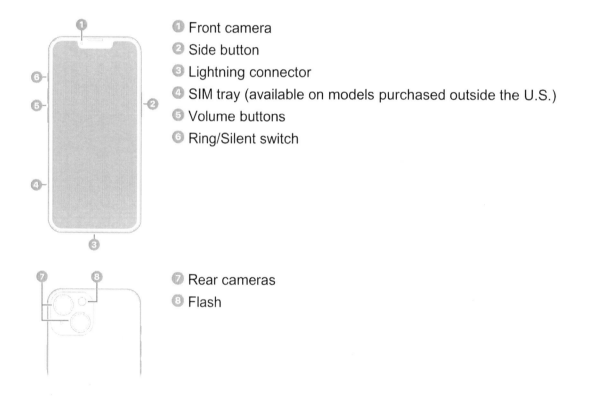

1 Front camera
2 Side button
3 Lightning connector
4 SIM tray (available on models purchased outside the U.S.)
5 Volume buttons
6 Ring/Silent switch

7 Rear cameras
8 Flash

iPhone 14 Plus

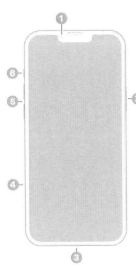

1 Front camera
2 Side button
3 Lightning connector
4 SIM tray (available on models purchased outside the U.S.)
5 Volume buttons
6 Ring/Silent switch

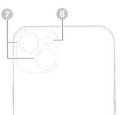

7 Rear cameras
8 Flash

iPhone 14 Pro

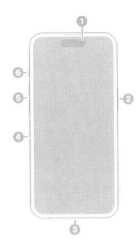

1 Front camera
2 Side button
3 Lightning connector
4 SIM tray (available on models purchased outside the U.S.)
5 Volume buttons
6 Ring/Silent switch

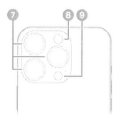 ⑦ Rear cameras
⑧ Flash
⑨ LiDAR Scanner

iPhone 14 Pro Max

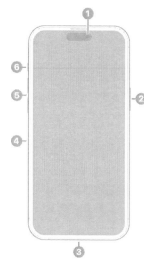
① Front camera
② Side button
③ Lightning connector
④ SIM tray (available on models purchased outside the U.S.)
⑤ Volume buttons
⑥ Ring/Silent switch

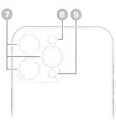
⑦ Rear cameras
⑧ Flash
⑨ LiDAR Scanner

Set up and get started

Turn on and set up iPhone

You can turn on and set up your new iPhone with an internet connection. You can also set up an iPhone by connecting it to your computer. If you have another iPhone, an iPad, or an Android device, you can transfer your data to your new iPhone.

Note: If your iPhone is deployed or managed by a company or other organization, see an administrator for setup instructions.

Prepare for setup

To make setup as smooth as possible, have the following items available:

- An internet connection through a Wi-Fi network (you may need the name and password of the network)
- Your Apple ID and password; if you don't have an Apple ID, you can create one during setup
- Your credit or debit card account information, if you want to add a card to Apple Pay during setup
- Your previous iPhone or a backup of your device, if you're transferring your data to your new device
  Tip: If you don't have sufficient storage space to back up your device, iCloud will grant you as much as you need to complete a temporary backup, free of charge, for up to three weeks from the purchase of your iPhone. On your previous device, go to Settings > General > Transfer or Reset [device]. Tap Get Started, then follow the onscreen instructions.
- Your Android device, if you're transferring your Android content

Turn on and set up your iPhone

1. Press and hold the side button until the Apple logo appears.

   If iPhone doesn't turn on, you might need to charge the battery.
2. Do one of the following:
    - Tap Set Up Manually, then follow the onscreen setup instructions.

o   If you have another iPhone, iPad, or iPod touch with iOS 11, iPadOS 13, or later, you can use Quick Start to automatically set up your new device. Bring the two devices close together, then follow the onscreen instructions to securely copy many of your settings, preferences, and iCloud Keychain. You can then restore the rest of your data and content to your new device from your iCloud backup. Or, if both devices have iOS 12.4, iPadOS 13, or later, you can transfer all your data wirelessly from your previous device to your new one. Keep your devices near each other and plugged into power until the migration process is complete. You can also transfer your data using a wired connection between your devices.

o   During setup, if you're blind or have low vision, you can triple-click the side button to turn on VoiceOver, the screen reader. You can also double-tap the screen with three fingers to turn on Zoom.

Move from an Android device to iPhone

If you have an Android device, you can transfer your data with the Move to iOS app when you first set up your new iPhone.

Note: If you already completed setup and want to use Move to iOS, you must erase your iPhone and start over, or move your data manually.

1.   On your device with Android version 4.0 or later and download the Move to iOS app.
2.   On your iPhone, do the following:
     o   Follow the setup assistant.
     o   On the Apps & Data screen, tap Move Data from Android.
3.   On the Android device, do the following:
     o   Turn on Wi-Fi.
     o   Open the Move to iOS app.
     o   Follow the onscreen instructions.

Wake and unlock iPhone

iPhone turns off the display to save power, locks for security, and goes to sleep when you're not using it. You can quickly wake and unlock iPhone when you want to use it again.

Wake iPhone

To wake iPhone, do one of the following:

- Press the side button.

- Raise iPhone.

Note: To turn off Raise to Wake, go to Settings  > Display & Brightness.
- Tap the screen.

Unlock iPhone with Face ID

If you didn't turn on Face ID during setup, see Set up Face ID on iPhone.

1. Tap the screen or raise iPhone to wake it, then glance at your iPhone.
   The lock icon animates from closed to open to indicate that iPhone is unlocked.
2. Swipe up from the bottom of the screen.

To lock iPhone again, press the side button. iPhone locks automatically if you don't touch the

screen for a minute or so. However, if Attention Aware Features is turned on in Settings >
Face ID & Passcode, iPhone won't dim or lock as long as it detects attention.

Unlock iPhone with Apple Watch

When you're wearing your Apple Watch (Series 3 and later), you can use it to securely unlock iPhone when you're wearing a face mask (models with Face ID; watchOS 7.4 or later required).

Unlock iPhone with a passcode

If you didn't create a passcode when you set up iPhone, see Set a passcode on iPhone.
1. Swipe up from the bottom of the Lock Screen.
2. Enter the passcode.

To lock iPhone again, press the side button. iPhone locks automatically if you don't touch the screen for a minute or so.

Set up cellular service on iPhone

Your iPhone needs a physical SIM or an eSIM to connect to a cellular network. (Not all options are available on all models or in all countries and regions. On iPhone 14 models purchased in the US, you can only use eSIM.) Contact your carrier to get a SIM and set up cellular service.

Set up an eSIM

Supported models can digitally store an eSIM provided by your carrier. If your carrier supports either eSIM Carrier Activation or eSIM Quick Transfer, you can turn on your iPhone and follow the instructions to activate your eSIM during setup.

If you already completed setup, you can do any of the following:

- **eSIM Carrier Activation**: Some carriers can assign a new eSIM directly to your iPhone; contact your carrier to initiate this process. When you receive the "Finish Setting Up Cellular" notification, tap it. Or go to Settings ⚙ > Cellular, then tap Set Up Cellular or Add eSIM.
- **eSIM Quick Transfer**: Some carriers support transferring a phone number from your previous iPhone to your new iPhone without needing to contact them. Make sure you're signed in with your Apple ID on both devices, or make sure your previous iPhone is unlocked, nearby with Bluetooth turned on, and running iOS 16 or later.
  On your new iPhone, go to Settings > Cellular, tap Set Up Cellular or Add eSIM, then tap Transfer From Nearby iPhone or choose a phone number. On your previous iPhone, follow the instructions to confirm the transfer.
  Note: After your phone number is transferred to your new iPhone, it stops working on your previous iPhone.
- **Scan a QR Code provided by your carrier**: Go to Settings > Cellular, tap Set Up Cellular or Add eSIM, then tap Use QR Code. (You may need to tap Other Options first.) Position iPhone so the QR code appears in the frame, or enter the details manually. You may be asked to enter a confirmation code provided by your carrier.

- **Transfer from a different smartphone**: If your previous phone isn't an Apple iPhone, contact your carrier to transfer the phone number.
- **Activate service through a participating carrier's app**: Go to the App Store, download the carrier's app, then use the app to activate cellular service.

Note: If prompted, connect your iPhone to an available Wi-Fi or cellular network. eSIM setup requires an internet connection.

Install a physical SIM

You can get a nano-SIM card from a carrier or move it from your previous iPhone.

Note: Physical SIM isn't compatible with iPhone 14 models purchased in the US.

1. Insert a paper clip or SIM eject tool into the small hole of the SIM tray, then push in toward iPhone to eject the tray.

   Note: The shape and orientation of the SIM tray depend on the iPhone model and your country or region.
2. Remove the tray from iPhone.
3. Place the SIM in the tray. The angled corner determines the correct orientation.

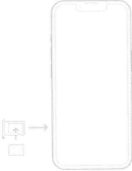

4. Insert the tray back into iPhone.
5. If you previously set up a PIN on the SIM, carefully enter the PIN when prompted. WARNING: Never try to guess a SIM PIN. An incorrect guess can permanently lock your SIM, and you won't be able to make phone calls or use cellular data through your carrier until you get a new SIM.

Convert a physical SIM to an eSIM

23

If your carrier supports it, you can convert a physical SIM to an eSIM.

1. Go to Settings ⚙ > Cellular, tap Set Up Cellular or Add eSIM, then choose the phone number with a physical SIM.
2. Tap Convert to eSIM, then follow the onscreen instructions.

Important: The availability of cellular capabilities depends on the wireless network, your iPhone model, and your location.

Consider applicable data, voice, and roaming charges when managing your cellular plans, especially when you travel with iPhone.

Some carriers let you unlock iPhone for use with another carrier (additional fees may apply). Contact your carrier for authorization and setup information.

Use Dual SIM on iPhone

Note: eSIM isn't available in certain countries or regions.

Here are some of the many ways you can use Dual SIM:

- Use one number for business and another number for personal calls.
- Add a local data plan when you travel to another country or region.
- Have separate voice and data plans.

Note: To use two different carriers, your iPhone must be unlocked.

Set up Dual SIM

1. Go to Settings ⚙ > Cellular, then make sure you have at least two lines (below SIMs).
2. Turn on two lines—tap a line, then tap Turn On this Line.
   You can also change settings such as Cellular Plan Label, Wi-Fi Calling (if available from your carrier), Calls on Other Devices, or SIM PIN. The label appears in Phone, Messages, and Contacts.
3. Choose the default line for cellular data—tap Cellular Data, then tap a line. To use either line depending on coverage and availability, turn on Allow Cellular Data Switching.
   You may incur roaming charges if Data Roaming is on and you're outside the country or region covered by the carrier's network.
4. Choose the default line for voice calls—tap Default Voice Line, then tap a line.

When using Dual SIM, note the following:

- Wi-Fi Calling must be turned on for a line to enable that line to receive calls while the other line is in use for a call. If you receive a call on one line while the other is in use for a call, and no Wi-Fi connection is available, iPhone uses the cellular data of the line that is in use for the call to receive the other line's call. Charges may apply. The line that is in use for the call must be permitted for data use in your Cellular Data settings (either as the default line, or as the non-default line with Allow Cellular Data Switching turned on) to receive the other line's call.
- If you don't turn on Wi-Fi Calling for a line, any incoming phone calls on that line (including calls from emergency services) go directly to voicemail (if available from your

carrier) when the other line is in use; you won't receive missed call notifications.

If you set up conditional call forwarding (if available from your carrier) from one line to another when a line is busy or not in service, the calls don't go to voicemail; contact your carrier for setup information.

- If you make a phone call from another device, such as your Mac, by relaying it through your iPhone with Dual SIM, the call is made using your default voice line.
- If you start an SMS/MMS Messages conversation using one line, you can't switch the conversation to your other line; you need to delete the conversation and start a new conversation using the other line. Also, you may incur additional charges if you send SMS/MMS attachments on the line that's not selected for cellular data.
- Instant Hotspot and Personal Hotspot use the line selected for cellular data.

Connect iPhone to the internet

Connect your iPhone to the internet by using an available Wi-Fi or cellular network.

Connect iPhone to a Wi-Fi network

1. Go to Settings ⚙ > Wi-Fi, then turn on Wi-Fi.
2. Tap one of the following:
   o A network: Enter the password, if required.
   o Other: To join a hidden network, enter the name of the network, security type, and password.

If 🛜 appears at the top of the screen, iPhone is connected to a Wi-Fi network. (To verify this, open Safari to view a webpage.) iPhone reconnects when you return to the same location.

Join a Personal Hotspot

If an iPad (Wi-Fi + Cellular) or another iPhone is sharing a Personal Hotspot, you can use its cellular internet connection.

1. Go to Settings ⚙ > Wi-Fi, then choose the name of the device sharing the Personal Hotspot.
2. If asked for a password on your iPhone, enter the password shown in Settings > Cellular > Personal Hotspot on the device sharing the Personal Hotspot.

Connect iPhone to a cellular network

Your iPhone automatically connects to your carrier's cellular data network if a Wi-Fi network isn't available. If iPhone doesn't connect, check the following:

1. Verify that your SIM is activated and unlocked.
2. Go to Settings ⚙ > Cellular.

3. Verify that Cellular Data is turned on. If you're using Dual SIM, tap Cellular Data, then verify the selected line. (You can choose only one line for cellular data.)

When you need an internet connection, iPhone does the following, in order, until the connection is made:

- Tries to connect to the most recently used available Wi-Fi network
- Shows a list of Wi-Fi networks in range and connects to the one you choose
- Connects to your carrier's cellular data network
  On an iPhone that supports 5G, iPhone may use your 5G cellular data instead of Wi-Fi. If so, you see Using 5G Cellular For Internet below the Wi-Fi network's name. To switch back to Wi-Fi, tap ⓘ next to the network name, then tap Use Wi-Fi for Internet.

Note: If a Wi-Fi connection to the internet isn't available, apps and services may transfer data over your carrier's cellular network, which may result in additional fees. Contact your carrier for information about your cellular data rates.

Apple ID and iCloud

Manage Apple ID settings on iPhone

Your Apple ID is the account you use to access Apple services such as the App Store, the iTunes Store, Apple Books, Apple Music, FaceTime, iCloud, iMessage, and more.

Sign in with your Apple ID

If you didn't sign in during setup, do the following:

1. Go to Settings 🔘 .
2. Tap Sign in to your iPhone.
3. Enter your Apple ID and password.
   If you don't have an Apple ID, you can create one.
4. If you protect your account with two-factor authentication, enter the six-digit verification code.

Change your Apple ID settings

1. Go to Settings 🔘 > [your name].
2. Do any of the following:
   - Update your contact information
   - Change your password
   - Add or remove Account Recovery Contacts
   - View and manage your subscriptions
   - Update your payment methods or billing address
   - Manage Family Sharing

Use iCloud on iPhone

iCloud securely stores your photos, videos, documents, backups, and more—and keeps them updated across all your devices—automatically. With iCloud, you can also share photos, calendars, notes, folders, and files with friends and family. iCloud provides you with an email account and 5 GB of free storage for your data. For more storage and additional features, you can subscribe to iCloud+.

Note: Some iCloud features have minimum system requirements. The availability of iCloud and its features varies by country or region.

Change your iCloud settings

Sign in with your Apple ID, then do the following:

1. Go to Settings ⚙ > [your name] > iCloud.
2. Do any of the following:
   - See your iCloud storage status.
   - Turn on the features you want to use, such as Photos, iCloud Drive, and iCloud Backup.

Ways to use iCloud on iPhone

iCloud can keep your iPhone backed up automatically.

You can also keep the following information stored in iCloud and kept up to date across your iPhone and other Apple devices:

- Photos and videos
- Files and documents
- iCloud Mail
- Contacts, Calendars, Notes, and Reminders
- Data from compatible third-party apps and games
- Messages threads
- Passwords and payment methods
- Safari bookmarks and open tabs
- News, Stocks, and Weather settings
- Home and Health data
- Voice memos
- Map favorites

You can also do the following:

- Share your photos and videos.
- Share folders and documents with iCloud Drive.
- Use Find My to locate a missing device or share locations with friends and family.

For additional storage and access to iCloud Private Relay (beta), Hide My Email, and HomeKit Secure Video support, you can subscribe to iCloud+.

Subscribe to iCloud+ on iPhone

iCloud+ gives you everything iCloud offers plus premium features including iCloud Private Relay (beta), Hide My Email, HomeKit Secure Video support, and all the storage you need for your photos, files, and more.

You can subscribe to iCloud+ or to Apple One, which includes iCloud+ and other Apple services.

Note: Some iCloud+ features have minimum system requirements. The availability of iCloud+ and its features varies by country or region.

What's included with iCloud+

When you subscribe to iCloud+, you can do the following on iPhone:

- Get 50 GB, 200 GB, or 2 TB of storage.
- Create unique, random email addresses that forward to your personal inbox with Hide My Email.
- Browse the web in an even more secure and private way with iCloud Private Relay (beta).
- Set up home security cameras with HomeKit Secure Video so you can view your footage from anywhere while keeping it private and secure.
- Use a custom email domain to personalize iCloud Mail.

Upgrade, change, or cancel your iCloud+ subscription

1. Go to Settings ⚙ > [your name] > iCloud.
2. Tap Manage Account Storage, tap Change Storage Plan, select an option, then follow the onscreen instructions.

Note: If you cancel your iCloud+ subscription, you lose access to the additional iCloud storage and iCloud+ features.

Share iCloud+

You can use Family Sharing to share iCloud+ with up to five other family members. When your family members accept your invitation to share iCloud+, they have instant access to the additional storage and features.

Note: To stop sharing iCloud+ with a family group, you can cancel the subscription, leave the family group, or leave or turn off Family Sharing.

Find settings on iPhone

In the Settings app ⚙, you can search for iPhone settings you want to change, such as your passcode, notification sounds, and more.

1. Tap Settings on the Home Screen (or in the App Library).
2. Swipe down to reveal the search field, tap the search field, enter a term—"volume," for example—then tap a setting.

Set up mail, contacts, and calendar accounts on iPhone

In addition to the apps that come with iPhone and that you use with iCloud, iPhone works with Microsoft Exchange and many of the most popular internet-based mail, contacts, and calendar services. You can set up accounts for these services.

Set up a mail account

1. Go to Settings ⚙ > Mail > Accounts > Add Account.
2. Do one of the following:
   - Tap a service—for example, iCloud or Microsoft Exchange—then enter your account information.
   - Tap Other, tap Add Mail Account, then enter your account information.

Set up a contacts account

1. Go to Settings ⚙ > Contacts > Accounts > Add Account.
2. Do one of the following:
   - Tap a service—for example, iCloud or Microsoft Exchange—then enter your account information.
   - Tap Other, tap Add LDAP Account or Add CardDAV Account (if your organization supports it), then enter the server and account information.

Set up a calendar account

1. Go to Settings ⚙ > Calendar > Accounts > Add Account.
2. Do one of the following:
   - **Choose a service**: Tap a service—for example, iCloud or Microsoft Exchange—then enter your account information.
   - **Add a calendar account**: Tap Other, tap Add CalDAV Account, then enter your server and account information.
   - **Subscribe to iCal (.ics) calendars**: Tap Other, tap Add Subscribed Calendar, then enter the URL of the .ics file to subscribe to; or import an .ics file from Mail.

If you turn on iCloud Keychain on your iPhone, your accounts stay up to date on all your devices that have iCloud Keychain turned on.

Learn the meaning of the iPhone status icons

The icons in the status bar at the top of the screen provide information about iPhone. On an iPhone with Face ID, there are additional status icons at the top of Control Center.

Note: If you turn on a Focus, its icon appears in the status bar.

Status icon	What it means
📶	**Wi-Fi**. iPhone is connected to the internet over a Wi-Fi network.

.ıll	**Cell signal**. The number of bars indicates the signal strength of your cellular service. If there's no signal, "No Service" appears.
.:!!	**Dual cell signals**. On models with Dual SIM, the upper row of bars indicates the signal strength of the line you use for cellular data. The lower row of bars indicates the signal strength of your other line. If there's no signal, "No Service" appears.
✈	**Airplane mode**. Airplane mode is on—you can't make phone calls, and other wireless functions may be disabled.
5G	**5G**. Your carrier's 5G network is available, and supported models can connect to the internet over that network (not available in all countries or regions).
5G$_C^U$	**5G UC**. Your carrier's 5G UC network is available, which can include your carrier's higher frequency version of 5G. Supported models can connect to the internet over that network (not available in all countries or regions).
5G+	**5G+**. Your carrier's 5G+ network is available, which can include your carrier's higher frequency version of 5G. Supported models can connect to the internet over that network (not available in all countries or regions).
5G$_W^U$	**5G UW**. Your carrier's 5G UW network is available, which can include your carrier's higher frequency version of 5G. Supported models can connect to the internet over that network (not available in all countries or regions).
5G$_E$	**5G E**. Your carrier's 5G E network is available, and iPhone can connect to the internet over that network (supported on iPhone 8 and later; not available in all countries or regions).
LTE	**LTE**. Your carrier's LTE network is available, and iPhone can connect to the internet over that network (not available in all countries or regions).
4G	**UMTS**. Your carrier's 4G UMTS (GSM) or LTE network (depending on the carrier) is available, and iPhone can connect to the internet over that network (not available in all countries or regions).
3G	**UMTS/EV-DO**. Your carrier's 3G UMTS (GSM) or EV-DO (CDMA) network is available, and iPhone can connect to the internet over that network.
E	**EDGE**. Your carrier's EDGE (GSM) network is available, and iPhone can connect to the internet over that network.
G	**GPRS/1xRTT**. Your carrier's GPRS (GSM) or 1xRTT (CDMA) network is available, and iPhone can connect to the internet over that network.

Wi-Fi	**Wi-Fi calling**. iPhone is set up for Wi-Fi calling. iPhone also displays a carrier name next to the icon.
	Personal Hotspot connection. iPhone is connected to the internet through the Personal Hotspot of another device.
VPN	**VPN**. iPhone is connected to a network using VPN.
	Navigation. iPhone is providing turn-by-turn directions.
	Personal Hotspot. iPhone is providing a Personal Hotspot.
	Phone call. iPhone is on a phone call.
	FaceTime. iPhone is on a FaceTime call.
	Screen recording. iPhone is recording your screen.
	Camera in use. An app is using your camera.
	Microphone in use. An app is using your microphone.
	Syncing. iPhone is syncing with your computer.
	Network activity. Shows that there's network activity. Some third-party apps may also use it to show an active process.
	Call forwarding. Call forwarding is set up.
	Lock. iPhone is locked.
	Do Not Disturb. Do Not Disturb is turned on.
	Portrait orientation lock. The iPhone screen is locked in portrait orientation.
	Location services. An app is using Location Services.
	Alarm. An alarm is set.

⌒	**Headphones connected**. iPhone is paired with Bluetooth headphones that are turned on and within Bluetooth range.
▭	**Battery**. Shows the iPhone battery level. When the icon is yellow, Low Power Mode is on.
⚡	**Battery charging**. Shows the iPhone battery is charging.
▯	**Bluetooth battery.** Shows the battery level of a paired Bluetooth device.
◻	**AirPlay.** AirPlay is on.
◍	**Voice Control**. Voice Control is turned on in Settings > Accessibility.
☎	**TTY.** Software RTT / TTY or Hardware TTY is turned on.
⊙	**CarPlay.** iPhone is connected to CarPlay.
⍦	**Siri Eyes Free.** You can ask a question or make a request to Siri in your car.

Charge and monitor the battery

Charge the iPhone battery

iPhone has an internal, lithium-ion rechargeable battery, which currently provides the best performance for your device. Compared with traditional battery technology, lithium-ion batteries are lighter, charge faster, last longer, and have a higher power density for more battery life.

About charging the battery

The battery icon in the top-right corner shows the battery level or charging status. When you're syncing or using iPhone, it may take longer to charge the battery.

If iPhone is very low on power, it may display an image of a nearly depleted battery, indicating that it needs to charge for up to 10 minutes before you can use it. If iPhone is extremely low on power when you begin to charge it, the display may be blank for up to 2 minutes before the low-battery image appears.

Charge the battery

To charge iPhone, do any of the following:

- Connect iPhone to a power outlet using the charging cable (included) and an Apple USB power adapter (sold separately).

- Place iPhone face up on MagSafe Charger or MagSafe Duo Charger (connected to Apple 20W USB-C power adapter or other compatible power adapter) or on a Qi-certified charger. (MagSafe Charger, MagSafe Duo Charger, power adapters, and Qi-certified chargers are sold separately.)

Note: You can also use third-party power adapters and Qi-certified chargers that are compliant with applicable country regulations and international and regional safety standards.

Make sure your computer is turned on—if iPhone is connected to a computer that's turned off, the battery may drain instead of charge. Look for ⚡ on the battery icon to make sure your iPhone is charging.

Note: Don't try to charge your iPhone by connecting it to your keyboard, unless your keyboard has a high-power USB port.

Connecting iPhone to a power outlet or placing it on a wireless charger can start an iCloud backup or wireless computer syncing.

WARNING: If you suspect there may be liquid in the charging port of iPhone, don't plug the charging cable into it.

Turn on Low Power Mode

Low Power Mode reduces the amount of power that your iPhone uses when the battery gets low. It optimizes performance for essential tasks like making and receiving calls; sending and receiving email and messages; accessing the internet; and more. On models with ProMotion display technology, Low Power Mode limits the display refresh rate to 60 frames per second. Your iPhone might perform some tasks more slowly when in Low Power Mode.

Note: If iPhone switches to Low Power Mode automatically, it turns off Low Power Mode after charging to 80%.

To manually turn Low Power Mode on or off, use any of the following methods:

- In Settings: Go to Settings ⚙ > Battery.
- In Control Center: Go to Settings > Control Center, then choose Low Power Mode to add it to Control Center.

Optimize iPhone battery charging

iPhone has a setting that helps slow the rate of your battery's aging by reducing the time it spends fully charged. This setting uses machine learning to understand your daily charging routine, then waits to finish charging past 80% until you need it.

1. Go to Settings ⚙ > Battery, then tap Battery Health.
2. Turn on Optimized Battery Charging.

Battery life and charge cycles vary with use and settings. The iPhone battery should be serviced or recycled by Apple or an Apple Authorized Service Provider.

Show the iPhone battery percentage

You can view how much charge remains in your iPhone battery in the status bar. You can also add a widget to the Home Screen to monitor the battery levels of your iPhone and connected accessories (including AirPods and other devices).

See the iPhone battery percentage in the status bar

Swipe down from the top-right corner.

Add a Batteries widget to your Home Screen

1. Touch and hold the Home Screen background until the apps begin to jiggle.
2. Tap ＋ at the top of the screen, then scroll down and tap Batteries.
3. Swipe left and right through the widgets to view the size options.
   The different sizes show different information.
4. When you see the size you want, tap Add Widget, then tap Done.

Check the iPhone battery health and usage

You can view information about your iPhone battery health and learn how your iPhone usage affects the battery level.

Review your iPhone battery health

1. Go to Settings ⚙ > Battery.
2. Tap Battery Health.
   iPhone displays information about your battery's capacity, peak performance, and whether your battery needs to be serviced.

View your battery usage information

Go to Settings ⚙ > Battery.

Information about your battery usage and activity appears for the last 24 hours and up to the last 10 days.

- **Insights and suggestions**: You might see insights about conditions or usage patterns that cause iPhone to consume energy. You might also see suggestions for lowering energy consumption. If a suggestion appears, you can tap it to go to the corresponding setting.
- **Last Charged**: Indicates how fully the battery was last charged and the time it was disconnected.
- **Battery Level graph (in Last 24 Hours)**: Shows the battery level, charging intervals, and periods when iPhone was in Low Power Mode or the battery was critically low.

- **Battery Usage graph (in Last 10 Days)**: Shows the percentage of battery used each day.
- **Activity graph**: Shows activity over time, split by whether the screen was on or off.
- **Screen On and Screen Off**: Shows total activity for the selected time interval, for when the screen was on and when it was off. The Last 10 Days view shows the average per day.
- **Battery Usage by App**: Shows the proportion of the battery used by each app in the selected time interval.
- **Activity by App**: Shows the amount of time each app was used in the selected time interval.

Note: To see battery information for a specific hour or day, tap that time interval in the graph. To deselect it, tap outside the graph.

Battery life and charge cycles vary with use and settings. The iPhone battery should be serviced or recycled by Apple or an Apple Authorized Service Provider

Download or bookmark the iPhone User Guide

You can view the iPhone User Guide in the Safari app , or download it to the Books app so you can read it even when you're offline.

View and bookmark the user guide in Safari

In Safari, go to https://support.apple.com/guide/iphone.

To view the user guide in a different language, scroll down to the bottom of the page, tap the country or region link (United States, for example), then choose a country or region.

Tip: For quick access, add the guide as a shortcut on your Home Screen or as a bookmark in Safari. Tap , then choose any of the following:

- **Add to Home Screen**: The shortcut appears as a new icon on the Home Screen.
- **Add Bookmark**: The bookmark appears when you tap in Safari.

Download the user guide from Apple Books

If you download the guide from Apple Books (where available), you can read it even when iPhone isn't connected to the internet.

1. Open the Books app .
2. Tap Search, tap the search field, then enter "iPhone User Guide."
3. Tap Get, then wait for the book to download.

Basics

Learn gestures for iPhone

Learn basic gestures to interact with iPhone

Control iPhone and its apps using a few simple gestures—tap, touch and hold, swipe, scroll, and zoom.

Symbol	Gesture
	Tap. Touch one finger lightly on the screen.
	Touch and hold. Touch and hold items in an app or in Control Center to preview contents and perform quick actions. On the Home Screen or in App Library, touch and hold an app icon briefly to open a quick actions menu.
	Swipe. Move one finger across the screen quickly.
	Scroll. Move one finger across the screen without lifting. For example, in Photos, you can drag a list up or down to see more. Swipe to scroll quickly; touch the screen to stop scrolling.
	Zoom. Place two fingers on the screen near each other. Spread them apart to zoom in, or move them toward each other to zoom out. You can also double-tap a photo or webpage to zoom in, and double-tap again to zoom out. In Maps, double-tap and hold, then drag up to zoom in or drag down to zoom out.

Learn gestures for Face ID

Here's a handy reference to the gestures you use for interacting with an iPhone that has Face ID.

Gesture	Description

	Go Home. Swipe up from the bottom edge of the screen to return to the Home Screen at any time.
	Quickly access controls. Swipe down from the top-right corner to open Control Center; touch and hold a control to reveal more options. To add or remove controls, go to Settings > Control Center.
	Open the App Switcher. Swipe up from the bottom edge, pause in the center of the screen, then lift your finger. To browse the open apps, swipe right, then tap the app you want to use.
	Switch between open apps. Swipe right or left along the bottom edge of the screen to quickly switch between open apps.
	Use Siri. Just say, "Hey Siri." Or hold down the side button while you ask a question or make a request, then release the button.
	Use Apple Pay. Double-click the side button to display your default credit card, then glance at iPhone to authenticate with Face ID.
	Use Accessibility Shortcut. Triple-click the side button.
	Use Emergency SOS (all countries or regions except India). Simultaneously press and hold the side button and either volume button until the sliders appear, then drag Emergency SOS.

	Use Emergency SOS (in India). Triple-click the side button. If you've turned on Accessibility Shortcut, simultaneously press and hold the side button and either volume button until the sliders appear, then drag Emergency SOS.
	Turn off. Simultaneously press and hold the side button and either volume button until the sliders appear, then drag the top slider to power off. Or go to Settings > General > Shut Down.
	Force restart. Press and release the volume up button, press and release the volume down button, then press and hold the side button until the Apple logo appears.

Adjust the volume on iPhone

When you're on the phone or listening to songs, movies, or other media on iPhone, you can use the buttons on the side of your device to adjust the audio volume. Otherwise, the buttons control the volume for the ringer, alerts, and other sound effects. You can also use Siri to turn the volume up or down.

Siri: Say something like: "Turn up the volume" or "Turn down the volume."

Lock the ringer and alert volumes in Settings

1. Go to Settings .
2. Tap Sounds & Haptics.
3. Turn off Change with Buttons.

Adjust the volume in Control Center

When iPhone is locked or when you're using an app, you can adjust the volume in Control Center.

Open Control Center, then drag .

Temporarily silence calls, alerts, and notifications

Open Control Center, tap Focus, then tap Do Not Disturb.

Put iPhone in silent mode

To put iPhone in silent mode 🔕, set the Ring/Silent switch so that the switch shows orange. To turn off silent mode, set the switch back.

When silent mode is off, iPhone plays all sounds. When silent mode is on, iPhone doesn't ring or play alerts or other sound effects (but iPhone may still vibrate).

Important: Clock alarms, audio apps such as Music, and many games play sounds through the built-in speaker, even when silent mode is on. In some countries or regions, the sound effects for Camera, Voice Memos, and Emergency Alerts are played, even when the Ring/Silent switch is set to silent.

Use your apps

Open apps on iPhone

You can quickly open apps from your Home Screen pages or your App Library.

1. To go to the Home Screen, swipe up from the bottom edge of the screen.
2. Swipe left to browse apps on other Home Screen pages.
3. Swipe left past all your Home Screen pages to see App Library, where your apps are organized by category.
4. To open an app, tap its icon.
5. To return to App Library, swipe up from the bottom edge of the screen.

Find your apps in App Library on iPhone

App Library shows your apps organized into categories, such as Creativity, Social, and Entertainment. The apps you use most are near the top of the screen and at the top level of their categories, so you can easily locate and open them.

Note: The apps in App Library are organized in categories intelligently, based on how you use your apps. You can add apps in App Library to the Home Screen, but you can't move them to another category in App Library.

Find and open an app in App Library

1. Go to the Home Screen, then swipe left past all your Home Screen pages to get to App Library.
2. Tap the search field at the top of the screen, then enter the name of the app you're looking for. Or scroll up and down to browse the alphabetical list.
3. To open an app, tap it.

If a category has a few small app icons, you can tap them to expand the category and see all the apps in it.

Hide and show Home Screen pages

Because you can find all of your apps in App Library, you might not need as many Home Screen pages for apps. You can hide some Home Screen pages, which brings App Library closer to your first Home Screen page. (When you want to see the hidden pages again, you can show them.)

1. Touch and hold the Home Screen until the apps begin to jiggle.
2. Tap the dots at the bottom of the screen.
   Thumbnail images of your Home Screen pages appear with checkmarks below them.
3. To hide pages, tap to remove the checkmarks.
   To show hidden pages, tap to add the checkmarks.
4. Tap Done twice.

With the extra Home Screen pages hidden, you can go from the first page of the Home Screen to App Library (and back) with only one or two swipes.

Note: When Home Screen pages are hidden, new apps you download from the App Store may be added to App Library instead of the Home Screen.

Reorder Home Screen pages

If you have multiple Home Screen pages, you change their order. For example, you can gather together your favorite apps on one Home Screen page, and then make that your first Home Screen page.

1. Touch and hold the Home Screen background until the apps begin to jiggle.
2. Tap the dots at the bottom of the screen.
   Thumbnail images of your Home Screen pages appear with checkmarks below them.
3. To move each Home Screen page, touch and hold it, then drag it to a new position.
4. Tap Done twice.

Change where new apps get downloaded

When you download new apps from the App Store, you can add them to the Home Screen and App Library, or to App Library only.

1. Go to Settings ⚙ > Home Screen.
2. Choose whether to add new apps to both your Home Screen and App Library, or to App Library only.

Note: To allow app notification badges to appear on apps in App Library, turn on Show in App Library.

Move an app from App Library to the Home Screen

You can add an app in App Library to the Home Screen, unless it's already there.

Touch and hold the app, then tap Add to Home Screen (available only if the app isn't already on the Home Screen).

The app appears on the Home Screen and in App Library.

Switch between open apps on iPhone

Open the App Switcher to quickly switch from one open app to another on your iPhone. When you switch back, you can pick up right where you left off.

Use the App Switcher

1. To see all your open apps in the App Switcher, do one of the following:
   ○ Swipe up from the bottom of the screen, then pause in the center of the screen.
2. To browse the open apps, swipe right, then tap the app you want to use.

Switch between open apps

To quickly switch between open apps on an iPhone with Face ID, swipe right or left along the bottom edge of the screen.

Quit and reopen an app on iPhone

If an app isn't responding, you can quit it and then reopen it to try and resolve the issue. (Typically, there's no reason to quit an app; quitting it doesn't save battery power, for example.)

1. To quit the app, open the App Switcher, swipe right to find the app, then swipe up on the app.
2. To reopen the app, go to the Home Screen (or App Library), then tap the app.

If quitting and reopening the app doesn't resolve the issue, try restarting iPhone.

Enter, select, and revise text

Dictate text on iPhone

With Dictation on iPhone, you can dictate text anywhere you can type it. You can also use typing and Dictation together—the keyboard stays open during Dictation so you can easily switch between voice and touch to enter text. For example, you can select text with touch and replace it with your voice.

General text Dictation (for example, composing messages and notes, but not dictating in a search field) are processed on your device in many languages—no internet connection is required. When you dictate in a search field, your dictated text may be sent to the search provider in order to process the search. When you use Dictation on a device, you can dictate text of any length without a timeout. You can stop Dictation manually, or it stops automatically when you stop speaking for 30 seconds.

Note: Dictation may not be available in all languages or in all countries or regions, and features may vary. Cellular data charges may apply.

Note: iPhone needs to download Siri speech models before it can process dictation on device.

To check whether your device processes dictation on device, go to Settings ⚙ > Siri & Search. If the text below Siri & Dictation History reads "Voice input is processed on iPhone," the Siri speech models have been downloaded.

Turn on Dictation

1. Go to Settings ⚙ > General > Keyboard.
2. Turn on Enable Dictation.

Dictate text

1. Tap to place the insertion point where you want to insert text.

2. Tap 🎤 on the onscreen keyboard or in any text field where it appears (as in Messages, for example). Then speak.

   If you don't see 🎤, make sure Enable Dictation is turned on in Settings ⚙ > General > Keyboard.

As you speak to insert text, iPhone automatically inserts punctuation for you. You can insert emoji by saying their names (for example, "mind blown emoji" or "happy emoji").

Note: You can turn this setting off by going to Settings ⚙ > General > Keyboard and turning off Auto-Punctuation.

3. When you finish, tap 🎤.

Type with the onscreen keyboard on iPhone

In apps on iPhone, you can use the onscreen keyboard to enter and edit text. You can also use Magic Keyboard and Dictation to enter text.

Enter text using the onscreen keyboard

In any app that allows text editing, open the onscreen keyboard by tapping a text field. Tap individual keys to type, or use QuickPath to type a word by sliding from one letter to the next without lifting your finger (not available for all languages). To end a word, lift your finger. You can use either method as you type, and even switch in the middle of a sentence. (If you tap ⌫ after sliding to type a word, it deletes the whole word.)

Note: As you slide to type, you see suggested alternatives to the word you're entering, rather than predictions for your next word.

While entering text, you can do any of the following:

- **Type uppercase letters**: Tap ⇧, or touch ⇧, then slide to a letter.
- Turn on Caps Lock: Double-tap ⇧.

- Quickly end a sentence with a period and a space: Double-tap the Space bar.
- **Correct spelling**: Tap a misspelled word (underlined in red) to see suggested corrections, then tap a suggestion to replace the word, or type the correction.
- Enter numbers, punctuation, or symbols: Tap 123 or #+=.
- **Undo the last edit**: Swipe left with three fingers, then tap Undo at the top of the screen.
- **Redo the last edit**: Swipe right with three fingers, then tap Redo at the top of the screen.
- **Enter emoji**: Tap 😃 or 🌐 to switch to the emoji keyboard. You can search for an emoji by entering a commonly used word—such as "heart" or "smiley face"—in the search field above the emoji keyboard, then swipe through the emoji that appear. To return to the regular keyboard, tap ABC in the lower-left corner.

Turn the onscreen keyboard into a trackpad

1. Touch and hold the Space bar with one finger until the keyboard turns light gray.
2. Move the insertion point by dragging around the keyboard.

Drag around the keyboard to move the insertion point.

3. To select text, touch and hold the keyboard with a second finger, then adjust the selection by moving the first finger around the keyboard.

Enter accented letters or other characters while typing

While typing, touch and hold the letter, number, or symbol on the keyboard that's related to the character you want.

For example, to enter é, touch and hold the e key, then slide to choose a variant.

You can also do any of the following:

- **On a Thai keyboard**: To choose native numbers, touch and hold the related Arabic number.
- **On a Chinese, Japanese, or Arabic keyboard**: Tap a suggested character or candidate at the top of the keyboard to enter it, or swipe left to see more candidates. Note: To view the full candidate list, tap the up arrow on the right. To return to the short list, tap the down arrow.

Move text

1. In a text editing app, select the text you want to move.
2. Touch and hold the selected text until it lifts up, then drag it to another location within the app.

If you drag to the bottom or top of a long document, the document automatically scrolls.

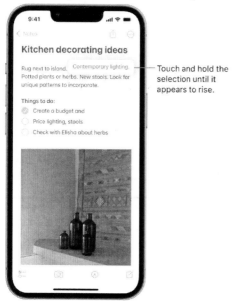

Touch and hold the selection until it appears to rise.

If you change your mind about moving the text, lift your finger before dragging, or drag the text off the screen.

Set typing options

You can turn on special typing features—such as predictive text and auto-correction—that assist you when you type on iPhone.

1. While typing text using the onscreen keyboard, touch and hold 😃 or 🌐, then tap Keyboard Settings. You can also go to Settings ⚙ > General > Keyboard.
2. In the list, turn the typing features (below All Keyboards) on or off.

Type with one hand

To make it easier to type with one hand, you can move the keys closer to your thumb.

1. Touch and hold 😃 or 🌐.

2. Tap one of the keyboard layouts. (For example, choose ▶⌨ to move the keyboard to the right side of the screen.)
   To center the keyboard again, tap the right or left edge of the keyboard.

Select, cut, copy, and paste text on iPhone

In apps on iPhone, you can use the onscreen keyboard to select and edit text in text fields. You can also use an external keyboard or Dictation.

Select and edit text

1. To select text, do any of the following:
   - **Select a word**: Double-tap with one finger.
   - **Select a paragraph**: Triple-tap with one finger.
   - **Select a block of text**: Double-tap and hold the first word in the block, then drag to the last word.
2. After selecting the text you want to revise, you can type, or tap the selection to see editing options:
   - **Cut**: Tap Cut or pinch closed with three fingers two times.
   - **Copy**: Tap Copy or pinch closed with three fingers.
   - **Paste**: Tap Paste or pinch open with three fingers.
   - **Select All**: Select all the text in the document.
   - **Replace**: View suggested replacement text, or have Siri suggest alternative text.
   - **Format**: Format the selected text.
   - ⟩: View more options.

Insert or edit text by typing

1. Place the insertion point where you want to insert or edit text by doing any of the following:
   - Tap where you want to add or edit text.
   - Touch and hold to magnify the text, then move the insertion point by dragging it.

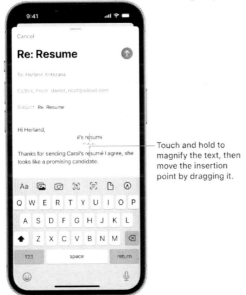

Touch and hold to magnify the text, then move the insertion point by dragging it.

2.
   Note: To navigate a long document, touch and hold the right edge of the document, then drag the scroller to locate the text you want to revise.
3. Type the text you want to insert.
   You can also insert text you cut or copied from another place in the document.

With Universal Clipboard, you can cut or copy something on one Apple device and paste it to another. You can also move selected text within an app.

Use predictive text on iPhone

As you type text on the iPhone keyboard, you see predictions for your next word, emoji that could take the place of your word, and other suggestions based on your recent activity and information from your apps (not available for all languages). In Messages, for example, when you type something like:

- "I'm at" followed by a space, your current location appears as an option
- "My number is" followed by a space, your phone number appears as an option

Accept or reject a predictive text suggestion

While typing text, you can do either of the following:

- Accept a suggested word or emoji by tapping it; accept a highlighted suggestion by entering a space or punctuation.
  When you tap a suggested word, a space appears after the word. If you enter a comma, period, or other punctuation, the space is deleted.
- Reject the suggestions by tapping your original word (shown as the predictive text option with quotation marks).

Turn off predictive text

1. While editing text, touch and hold ☺ or ⊕.
2. Tap Keyboard Settings, then turn off Predictive.

When you turn off predictive text, iPhone may still try to suggest corrections for misspelled words. To accept a correction, enter a space or punctuation, or tap Return. To reject a correction, tap the "x." If you reject the same suggestion a few times, iPhone stops suggesting it.

Save keystrokes with text replacements on iPhone

Set up a text replacement you can use to enter a word or phrase by typing just a few characters. For example, type "omw" to enter "On my way!" That one's already set up for you, but you can also add your own.

Create a text replacement

1. While typing in a text field, touch and hold ☺ or ⊕.
2. Tap Keyboard Settings, then tap Text Replacement.
3. Tap ＋ at the top right.
4. Type a phrase in the Phrase field and the text shortcut you want to use for it in the Shortcut field.

Have a word or phrase you use and don't want it corrected?

1. Go to Settings ⚙ > General > Keyboard, then tap Text Replacement.
2. Tap ＋ at the top right, then enter your word or phrase in the Phrase field, but leave the Shortcut field blank.

Create a text replacement for word and input pairs

When using certain Chinese or Japanese keyboards, you can create a text replacement for word and input pairs. The text replacement is added to your personal dictionary. When you type the text shortcut for a word or input while using a supported keyboard, the paired word or input is substituted for the typed shortcut.

Shortcuts are available for the following:

- Simplified Chinese: Pinyin
- Traditional Chinese: Pinyin and Zhuyin
- Japanese: Romaji and Kana

Use iCloud to keep your personal dictionary up to date on your other devices

Go to Settings ⊚ > [your name] > iCloud, then turn on iCloud Drive.

Reset your personal dictionary

1. Go to Settings ⊚ > General > Reset.
2. Tap Reset Keyboard Dictionary.
   All custom words and shortcuts are deleted, and the keyboard dictionary returns to its default state.

Add or change keyboards on iPhone

You can turn typing features, such as spell checking, on or off; add keyboards for writing in different languages; and change the layout of your onscreen or wireless keyboard.

If you add keyboards for other languages, you can type in two languages without having to switch between keyboards. Your keyboard automatically switches between the two languages you use most often. (Not available for all languages.)

Add or remove a keyboard for another language

1. Go to Settings ⊚ > General > Keyboard.
2. Tap Keyboards, then do any of the following:
   - **Add a keyboard**: Tap Add New Keyboard, then choose a keyboard from the list. Repeat to add more keyboards.
   - **Remove a keyboard**: Tap Edit, tap ⊖ next to the keyboard you want to remove, tap Delete, then tap Done.
   - **Reorder your keyboard list**: Tap Edit, drag ≡ next to a keyboard to a new place in the list, then tap Done.

If you add a keyboard for a different language, the corresponding language is automatically added to the Preferred Language Order list. You can view this list and add languages directly to it in Settings > General > Language & Region. You can also reorder the list to change how apps and websites display text.

Switch to another keyboard

1. While typing text, touch and hold ☺ or ⊕.
2. Tap the name of the keyboard you want to switch to.

You can also tap 😊 or 🌐 to switch from one keyboard to another. Continue tapping to access other enabled keyboards.

You can also switch between Magic Keyboard and other keyboards.

Assign an alternative layout to a keyboard

You can use an alternative keyboard layout that doesn't match the keys on your keyboard.

1. Go to Settings ⚙ > General > Keyboard > Keyboards.
2. Tap a language at the top of the screen, then select an alternative layout from the list.

Multitask with Picture in Picture on iPhone

With Picture in Picture, you can watch a video or use FaceTime while you use other apps.

While watching a video, tap 🔲.

The video window scales down to a corner of your screen so you can see the Home Screen and open other apps. With the video window showing, you can do any of the following:

- **Resize the video window**: To make the small video window larger, pinch open. To shrink it again, pinch closed.
- **Show and hide controls**: Tap the video window.
- **Move the video window**: Drag it to a different corner of the screen.
- **Hide the video window**: Drag it off the left or right edge of the screen.
- Close the video window: Tap ⊗.
- **Return to a full video screen**: Tap 🔲 in the small video window.

Access features from the iPhone Lock Screen

The Lock Screen—which shows the current time and date, your most recent notifications, and a photo or any custom widgets you've added—appears when you turn on or wake iPhone. From the Lock Screen, you can see notifications, open Camera and Control Center, get information from your favorite apps at a glance, and more.

Access features and information from the Lock Screen

You can quickly access useful features and information from the Lock Screen, even while iPhone is locked. From the Lock Screen, do any of the following:

- **Open Camera**: Swipe left. You can touch and hold 📷, then lift your finger.
- **Open Control Center**: Swipe down from the top-right corner.
- **See earlier notifications**: Swipe up from the center.
- **View widgets**: Swipe right.

Show notification previews on the Lock Screen

1. Go to Settings  > Notifications.
2. Tap Show Previews, then tap Always.
3. Choose how you want notifications displayed on the Lock Screen:
    o View just the number of notifications: Select Count.
    o View the notifications grouped into stacks by app: Select Stack.
    o View the notifications in a list: Select List.
4. You can pinch the notifications on the Lock Screen to change the layout.

Notification previews can include text from Messages, lines from Mail messages, and details about Calendar invitations.

View activities in the Dynamic Island on iPhone

On iPhone 14 Pro and iPhone 14 Pro Max, you can check alerts and current activity in progress—such as music that's playing, your timer, an AirDrop connection, and directions from Maps—in the Dynamic Island on the Home Screen or in any app. The Dynamic Island appears whenever your iPhone is unlocked.

A Voice Memos recording showing in the Dynamic Island

Touch and hold the Dynamic Island to expand it and see more details about the activity.

Perform quick actions on iPhone

On the Home Screen, in App Library, in Control Center, and in apps, you can use quick actions menus, see previews, and more.

Perform quick actions from the Home Screen and App Library

On the Home Screen and in App Library, touch and hold apps to open quick actions menus.

For example:

49

- Touch and hold Camera 📷, then choose Take Selfie.
- Touch and hold Maps 🗺️, then choose Send My Location.
- Touch and hold Notes 📝, then choose New Note.

Note: If you touch and hold an app for too long before choosing a quick action, all of the apps begin to jiggle. Tap Done, then try again.

See previews and other quick actions menus

- In Photos, touch and hold an image to preview it and see a list of options.
- In Mail, touch and hold a message in a mailbox to preview the message contents and see a list of options.
- Open Control Center, then touch and hold an item like Camera or the brightness control to see options.
- On the Lock Screen, touch and hold a notification to respond to it.
- When typing, touch and hold the Space bar with one finger to turn your keyboard into a trackpad.

Search from the iPhone Home Screen or Lock Screen

In Spotlight on iPhone, you can search for apps and contacts, content inside apps like Mail, Messages, and Photos, and even text in your photos using Live Text. You can also check stock and currency information and perform calculations, including unit conversions. You can find and open webpages, open apps, and find images in your photo library, across your system, and on the web. Spotlight returns rich results in a full, scrollable window—including contacts, musicians, actors, TV shows, movies, businesses, and sports leagues and teams.

In Settings > Siri & Search, you can choose which apps you want to include in search results. Search offers suggestions based on your app usage, and updates results as you type.

Choose which apps to include in Search

1. Go to Settings ⚙️ > Siri & Search.
2. Scroll down, tap an app, then turn Show App in Search on or off.

Search with iPhone

1. Tap 🔍 Search at the bottom of the Home Screen or swipe down on the Home Screen or the Lock Screen.
2. Enter what you're looking for in the search field.
3. Do any of the following:
   - Hide the keyboard and see more results on the screen: Tap Search.
   - Open a suggested app: Tap it.

- **Take quick action**: Start a timer, turn on a Focus, find the name of a song with Shazam, run any shortcut, and more. Search for an app's name to see shortcuts available for the app, or create your own using the Shortcuts app.
- Check a suggested website: Tap it.
- **Get more information about a search suggestion**: Tap it, then tap one of the results to open it.
- **Start a new search**: Tap ⊗ in the search field.

Turn off Location-Based Suggestions

1. Go to Settings ⚙ > Privacy & Security > Location Services.
2. Tap System Services, then turn off Location-Based Suggestions.

Search in apps

Many apps include a search field or a search button so you can find something within the app. For example, in the Maps app, you can search for a specific location.

1. In an app, tap the search field or 🔍.
   If you don't see a search field or button, swipe down from the top.
2. Type your search, then tap Search.

Add a dictionary

On iPhone, you can add dictionaries, which can be used in searches.

1. Go to Settings ⚙ > General > Dictionary.
2. Select a dictionary.

Use AirDrop on iPhone to send items to nearby devices

With AirDrop, you can wirelessly send your photos, videos, websites, locations, and more to other nearby devices and Mac computers (iOS 7, iPadOS 13, OS X 10.10, or later required). AirDrop transfers information using Wi-Fi and Bluetooth—both must be turned on. To use AirDrop, you need to be signed in with your Apple ID. Transfers are encrypted for security.

Send an item using AirDrop

1. Open the item, then tap 📤, Share, AirDrop, •••, or another button that displays the app's sharing options.
2. Tap ◉ in the row of share options, then tap the profile picture of a nearby AirDrop user.

If the person doesn't appear as a nearby AirDrop user, ask them to open Control Center on iPhone, iPad, or iPod touch and allow AirDrop to receive items. To send to someone on a Mac, ask them to allow themselves to be discovered in AirDrop in the Finder.

To send an item using a method other than AirDrop, choose the method—for example, Messages or Mail—from the row of sharing options (options vary by app). Siri may also suggest ways to share with the people you know by displaying their profile pictures and icons representing sharing methods.

You can also use AirDrop to securely share app and website passwords with someone using an iPhone, iPad, iPod touch, or a Mac.

Allow others to send items to your iPhone using AirDrop

1. Open Control Center, touch and hold the top-left group of controls, then tap 📶.
2. Tap Contacts Only or Everyone to choose who you want to receive items from.
   You can accept or decline each request as it arrives.

Note: The Contacts Only option is available on devices with iOS 10, iPadOS, macOS 10.12, or later. If AirDrop is set to Contacts Only on your device with an earlier software version, select the Everyone option in Control Center to receive items by AirDrop. You can choose the Everyone option when using AirDrop and disable it when not in use.

Take a screenshot or screen recording on iPhone

You can take a picture of the screen, just as it appears, or a recording of actions on the screen, to share with others or use in documents.

Take a screenshot

1. Simultaneously press and then release the side button and volume up button.
2. Tap the screenshot in the lower-left corner, then tap Done.
3. Choose Save to Photos, Save to Files, or Delete Screenshot.

If you choose Save to Photos, you can view it in the Screenshots album in the Photos app, or in the All Photos album if iCloud Photos is turned on in Settings 🔘 > Photos.

Save a full-page screenshot as a PDF

You can take a full-page, scrolling screenshot of a webpage, document, or email that exceeds the length of your iPhone screen, then save it as a PDF.

1. Simultaneously press and then release the side button and volume up button.
2. Tap the screenshot in the lower-left corner, then tap Full Page.
3. Do any of the following:
   - **Save the screenshot**: Tap Done, choose Save PDF to Files, choose a location, then tap Save.

○ **Share the screenshot**: Tap ⬆️, choose a sharing option (for example AirDrop, Messages, or Mail), enter any other requested information, then send the PDF.

Create a screen recording

You can create a screen recording and capture sound on your iPhone.

1. Go to Settings ⚙️ > Control Center, then tap ➕ next to Screen Recording.
2. Open Control Center, tap ⏺️, then wait for the three-second countdown.
3. To stop recording, open Control Center, tap ⏺️ or the red status bar at the top of the screen, then tap Stop.

Go to Photos 🌸, then select your screen recording.

Mark up files and photos

Draw in apps with Markup on iPhone

In supported apps such as Mail, Messages, Notes, and Books, you can annotate photos, screenshots, PDFs, and more using built-in drawing tools.

Draw with Markup

1. In a supported app, tap Ⓐ or Markup.
2. In the Markup toolbar, tap the pen, marker, or pencil tool, then write or draw with your finger.
3. To hide the Markup toolbar, tap Ⓐ or Done.

While drawing, do any of the following:

- **Change the line weight**: Tap the selected drawing tool in the toolbar, then choose an option.
- **Change the opacity**: Tap the selected drawing tool in the toolbar, then drag the slider.
- **Change the color**: Tap ⚫ in the toolbar, then choose a color.
- Undo a mistake: Tap ↺.
- Draw a straight line: Tap the ruler tool in the toolbar, then draw a line along the edge of the ruler.
    - To change the angle of the ruler, touch and hold the ruler with two fingers, then rotate your fingers.
    - To move the ruler without changing its angle, drag it with one finger.
    - To hide the ruler, tap the ruler tool in the toolbar again.

Erase a mistake

Tap the eraser tool in the Markup toolbar in a supported app, then do one of the following:

- **Erase with the pixel eraser**: Scrub over the mistake with your finger.
- **Erase with the object eraser**: Touch the object with your finger.

- **Switch between the pixel and the object erasers**: Tap the eraser tool again, then choose Pixel Eraser or Object Eraser.

Note: If you don't see the Markup toolbar, tap Ⓐ or Markup. If the toolbar is minimized, tap its minimized version.

Move elements of your drawing

1. In the Markup toolbar, tap the lasso tool (between the eraser and ruler tools), then drag around the elements to make a selection.

   Note: If you don't see the Markup toolbar in a supported app, tap Ⓐ or Markup. If the toolbar is minimized, tap its minimized version.
2. Lift your finger, then drag your selection to a new location.

Tip: To mark up a screenshot right after you take it, tap the thumbnail that appears for a few moments in the bottom-left corner of the screen. (To share a screenshot after you mark it up, tap ⬆️.)

Add text, shapes, and signatures with Markup on iPhone

In supported apps, you can use Markup to add text, speech bubbles, shapes, and signatures.

Add text

1. In the Markup toolbar in a supported app, tap ⊕, then tap Text.

   Note: If you don't see the Markup toolbar, tap Ⓐ or Markup. If the toolbar is minimized, tap its minimized version.
2. Double-tap the text box.
3. Use the keyboard to enter text.

To change text after you add it, tap the text to select it, then do any of the following:

- **Change the font, size, or layout**: Tap A A in the toolbar, then choose an option.
- Delete, edit, or duplicate the text: Tap Edit, then choose an option.
- Move the text: Drag it.

To hide the Markup toolbar when you finish, tap Ⓐ or Done.

Add a shape

In the Markup toolbar in a supported app, tap ⊕, then choose a shape.

Note: If you don't see the Markup toolbar, tap Ⓐ or Markup. If the toolbar is minimized, tap its minimized version.

To adjust the shape, do any of the following:

- Move the shape: Drag it.
- **Resize the shape**: Drag any blue dot along the shape's outline.
- **Change the outline color**: Tap a color in the color picker.
- Fill the shape with color or change the line thickness: Tap 🔲, then choose an option.
- Adjust the form of an arrow or speech bubble shape: Drag a green dot.

- **Delete or duplicate a shape**: Tap it, then choose an option.

To hide the Markup toolbar when you finish, tap ⓐ or Done.

Draw a shape

You can use Markup to draw geometrically perfect shapes—lines, arcs, and more—to use in diagrams and sketches.

1. In the Markup toolbar in a supported app, tap the pen, marker, or pencil tool.

   Note: If you don't see the Markup toolbar, tap ⓐ or Markup. If the toolbar is minimized, tap its minimized version.

2. Draw a shape in one stroke with your finger, then pause.
   A perfect version of the shape snaps into place, replacing the drawing. (If you prefer to keep the freehand shape, tap ↰.)

The shapes you can draw include straight lines, arrows, arcs, continuous lines with 90-degree turns, squares, circles, rectangles, triangles, pentagons, chat bubbles, hearts, stars, and clouds.

Add your signature

1. In the Markup toolbar in a supported app, tap ⊕, then choose Signature.

   Note: If you don't see the Markup toolbar, tap ⓐ or Markup. If the toolbar is minimized, tap its minimized version.

2. Do one of the following:

   ○ **Add a new signature**: Tap Add or Remove Signature, tap +, then use your finger to sign your name.
   To use the signature, tap Done, or to draw a new one, tap Clear.
   ○ **Add an existing signature**: Tap the one you want.
   To see all of your signatures, scroll down the list.

3. Drag your signature where you want it.

To hide the Markup toolbar when you finish, tap ⓐ or Done.

Zoom in or magnify in Markup on iPhone

In Markup in supported apps, you can zoom in when you need to draw the details. Use the magnifier when you only need to see the details.

Zoom in

While using Markup in a supported app, pinch open so you can draw, adjust shapes, and more, up close.

To pan when you're zoomed in, drag two fingers. To zoom back out, pinch closed.

Magnify

In the Markup toolbar in a supported app, tap ⊕, then tap Magnifier.

Note: If you don't see the Markup toolbar, tap ⓐ or Markup. If the toolbar is minimized, tap its minimized version.

To change the magnifier's characteristics, do any of the following:

- **Change the magnification level**: Drag the green dot on the magnifier.
- **Change the size of the magnifier**: Drag the blue dot on the magnifier.
- Move the magnifier: Drag it.

- Change the outline thickness of the magnifier: Tap 🔲, then choose an option.
- **Change the outline color of the magnifier**: Choose an option from the color picker.
- **Remove or duplicate the magnifier**: Tap its outline, then tap Delete or Duplicate.

To hide the Markup toolbar when you finish, tap Ⓐ or Done.

Get information about your iPhone

View overall storage availability and storage used per app

Go to Settings ⚙ > General > iPhone Storage.

See battery usage

Go to Settings ⚙ > Battery to see the elapsed time since iPhone was charged as well as battery usage by app.

You can also display battery level as a percentage, turn Low Power Mode on or off, and check your battery's health.

View call time and cellular usage

Go to Settings ⚙ > Cellular.

See more information about iPhone

Go to Settings ⚙ > General > About. The items you can view include:

- Name
- iOS software version
- Model name
- Part and model numbers. To the right of Model, the part number appears. To see the model number, tap the part number.
- Serial number
- Number of songs, videos, photos, and apps
- Capacity and available storage space
- Wi-Fi and Bluetooth addresses
- Cellular network

- Carrier settings. To the right of Carrier, the carrier settings version number appears. To see additional carrier-specific information, tap the version number. Contact your carrier for more details.
- IMEI (International Mobile Equipment Identity)
- ICCID (Integrated Circuit Card Identifier, or Smart Card) for GSM networks
- MEID (Mobile Equipment Identifier) for CDMA networks
- Modem firmware

To copy the serial number and other identifiers, touch and hold the identifier until Copy appears.

To see Legal & Regulatory information (including legal notices and license, warranty, and RF exposure information) and regulatory marks, go to Settings > General > Legal & Regulatory.

You can also find the IMEI on the SIM card tray and the model number in the SIM tray opening.

View or turn off diagnostic information

Go to Settings ⚙ > Privacy & Security > Analytics & Improvements.

To help Apple improve products and services, iPhone sends diagnostic and usage data. This data doesn't personally identify you, but may include location information.

View or change cellular data settings on iPhone

You can turn cellular data and roaming on or off, set which apps and services use cellular data, see cellular data usage, and set other cellular data options.

Note: For help with cellular network services, voicemail, and billing, contact your wireless service provider.

If iPhone is connected to the internet using the cellular data network, an icon identifying the cellular network appears in the status bar.

5G, LTE, 4G, and 3G service on GSM cellular networks support simultaneous voice and data communications. For all other cellular connections, you can't use internet services while you're talking on the phone unless iPhone also has a Wi-Fi connection to the internet.

Depending on your network connection, you may not be able to receive calls while iPhone transfers data over the cellular network—when downloading a webpage, for example.

- **GSM networks**: On an EDGE or GPRS connection, incoming calls may go directly to voicemail during data transfers. For incoming calls that you answer, data transfers are paused.
- **CDMA networks**: On EV-DO connections, data transfers are paused when you answer incoming calls. On 1xRTT connections, incoming calls may go directly to voicemail during data transfers. For incoming calls that you answer, data transfers are paused.

Data transfer resumes when you end the call.

If Cellular Data is off, all data services—including email, web browsing, and push notifications—use Wi-Fi only. If Cellular Data is on, carrier charges may apply. For example, using certain features and services that transfer data, such as Siri and Messages, could result in charges to your data plan.

Choose cellular data options for data usage, performance, battery life, and more

To turn Cellular Data on or off, go to Settings ⚙ > Cellular.

To set options when Cellular Data is on, go to Settings > Cellular > Cellular Data Options, then do any of the following:

- **Reduce cellular usage**: Turn on Low Data Mode, or tap Data Mode, then choose Low Data Mode. This mode pauses automatic updates and background tasks when iPhone isn't connected to Wi-Fi.
- **Turn Data Roaming on or off**: Data Roaming permits internet access over a cellular data network when you're in a region not covered by your carrier's network. When you're traveling, you can turn off Data Roaming to avoid roaming charges.

Depending on your iPhone model, carrier, and region, the following options may be available:

- **Turn Voice Roaming on or off**: (CDMA) Turn Voice Roaming off to avoid charges from using other carrier's networks. When your carrier's network isn't available, iPhone won't have cellular (data or voice) service.
- **Enable or disable 4G/LTE**: Using 4G or LTE loads internet data faster in some cases but may decrease battery performance. There may be options for turning off 4G/LTE or for selecting Voice & Data (VoLTE) or Data Only.

On iPhone models with a 5G data plan, you can do the following:

- **Enable Smart Data mode to optimize battery life**: Tap Voice & Data, then choose 5G Auto. In this mode, your iPhone automatically switches to LTE when 5G speeds don't provide noticeably better performance.
- Use higher-quality video and FaceTime HD on 5G networks: Tap Data Mode, then choose Allow More Data on 5G.

Set up a Personal Hotspot to begin sharing the cellular internet connection from iPhone

1. Go to Settings ⚙ > Cellular, then turn on Cellular Data.
2. Tap Set up Personal Hotspot, then follow the instructions in Share your internet connection from iPhone.

Set cellular data use for apps and services

Go to Settings ⚙ > Cellular, then turn Cellular Data on or off for any app (such as Maps) or service (such as Wi-Fi Assist) that can use cellular data.

If a setting is off, iPhone uses only Wi-Fi for that service.

Note: Wi-Fi Assist is on by default. If Wi-Fi connectivity is poor, Wi-Fi Assist automatically switches to cellular data to boost the signal. Because you stay connected to the internet over cellular when you have a poor Wi-Fi connection, you might use more cellular data, which may incur additional charges depending on your data plan.

Lock your SIM card

If your device uses a SIM card for phone calls or cellular data, you can lock the card with a personal identification number (PIN) to prevent others from using the card. Then, every time you restart your device or remove the SIM card, your card locks automatically, and you're required to enter your PIN.

Choose iPhone settings for travel

When you travel with iPhone, choose settings that comply with airline requirements. Some airlines let you keep your iPhone turned on if you switch to airplane mode. By default, Wi-Fi and Bluetooth are disabled in airplane mode—you can't make calls, but you can listen to music, play games, watch videos, and use other apps that don't require network or phone connections.

Turn on airplane mode

Open Control Center, then tap ✈.

Tap to turn on airplane mode.

You can also turn airplane mode on or off in Settings ⚙. When airplane mode is on, ✈ appears in the status bar.

Turn on Wi-Fi or Bluetooth while in airplane mode

If your airline allows it, you can use Wi-Fi or Bluetooth while in airplane mode.

1. Open Control Center, then turn on airplane mode.

2. Tap to turn on Wi-Fi or to turn on Bluetooth.

If you turn on Wi-Fi or Bluetooth while in airplane mode, it may be on the next time you return to airplane mode. You can turn it off again in Control Center.

Personalize your iPhone

Change iPhone sounds and vibrations

In Settings ⚙, change the sounds iPhone plays when you get a call, text, voicemail, email, reminder, or other type of notification.

You feel a tap—called haptic feedback—after you perform some actions, such as when you touch and hold the Camera icon on the Home Screen.

Set sound and vibration options

1. Go to Settings ⚙ > Sounds & Haptics.
2. To set the volume for all sounds, drag the slider below Ringtone and Alert Volume.
3. To set the tones and vibration patterns for sounds, tap a sound type, such as ringtone or text tone.
4. Do any of the following:
   - Choose a tone (scroll to see them all).
     Ringtones play for incoming calls, clock alarms, and the clock timer; text tones are used for text messages, new voicemail, and other alerts.
   - Tap Vibration, then choose a vibration pattern, or tap Create New Vibration to create your own.

You can also change the sounds iPhone plays for certain people. Go to Contacts 👤, tap a person's name, tap Edit, then choose a ringtone and text tone.

Turn haptic feedback off or on

1. Go to Settings ⚙ > Sounds & Haptics.
2. Turn System Haptics off or on.
   When System Haptics is off, you won't hear or feel vibrations for incoming calls and alerts.

Tip: If you're not receiving incoming calls and alerts when you expect them, open Control Center, then check whether Do Not Disturb is on. If 🌙 is highlighted, tap it to turn off Do Not Disturb. (When Do Not Disturb is on, 🌙 also appears in the status bar.)

Personalize your iPhone Lock Screen

You can personalize your Lock Screen by adding wallpaper, customizing the colors and fonts, layering photos in front of the time, and much more. You can also add widgets with information from your favorite apps to your Lock Screen, such as today's headlines, the weather, and calendar events.

You can create more than one Lock Screen and switch between them. Since each Lock Screen can be linked to a Focus, you can switch your Focus by switching to a different Lock Screen.

Tip: It's easier to create a custom Lock Screen if you set up Face ID.

Create a custom Lock Screen

1. Touch and hold the Lock Screen until the Customize button appears at the bottom of the screen.
   If the Customize button doesn't appear, touch and hold the Lock Screen again, then enter your passcode.
2. Tap ⊕ at the bottom of the screen.
   The Lock Screen wallpaper gallery appears.
3. Tap one of the wallpaper options to select it as your Lock Screen.
   For some wallpaper choices, you can swipe left or right to try different color filters, patterns, and fonts that complement each other.
4. Tap Add, then do one of the following:
   - Choose whether to use the wallpaper on both the Lock Screen and Home Screen: Tap Set as Wallpaper Pair.
   - **Make further changes to the Home Screen**: Tap Customize Home Screen. Tap a color to change the wallpaper color, tap 🖼 to use a custom photo, or select Blur to blur the wallpaper so the apps stand out.

Add a photo to your Lock Screen

You can add a photo to your Lock Screen by selecting one from your photo library or letting iPhone intelligently suggest a photo that complements your other Lock Screen settings.

1. Touch and hold the Lock Screen until the Customize button appears at the bottom of the screen.
   If the Customize button doesn't appear, touch and hold the Lock Screen again, then enter your passcode.
2. Tap ⊕ at the bottom of the screen, then choose one of the photo options (Photos or Photo Shuffle) at the top of the screen.
3. If you choose Photos and want to create a multilayered effect, tap ⋯ at the bottom right, then choose Depth Effect.

Note: This option may not be available for all photos. Layering is not available on wallpapers with widgets. The multilayered effect is available on supported models. Layering is available only on images with people, pets, or the sky, and isn't available on every image in those categories. Layering may not be available if the subject is too high, too low, or obscures too much of the clock.

4. To reposition your selected image, pinch open to zoom in on it, drag the image with two fingers to move it to the position you want, then pinch closed to zoom out. You can also swipe left or right to try different photo styles that include color filters and fonts that complement each other.

5. If you choose Photo Shuffle, you can preview the photos by tapping ⣿, and set the shuffle frequency by tapping ⊙, then selecting an option below Shuffle Frequency.

Tip: Alternatively, you can add a photo directly from your photo library to your Home Screen and Lock Screen. In the Photos app ✿, tap Library, select a photo, then tap ⬆. Scroll down and select Use as Wallpaper, tap Done, then choose whether to show it on both your Home Screen and Lock Screen.

Add widgets to your Lock Screen

You can add widgets to your Lock Screen to get information at a glance—for example, the temperature, battery level, or upcoming calendar events.

1. Touch and hold the Lock Screen until the Customize button appears at the bottom of the screen, then tap Customize.
   If the Customize button doesn't appear, touch and hold the Lock Screen again, then enter your passcode.
2. Tap Customize, then tap the box below the time to add widgets to your Lock Screen.

3. Tap or drag the widgets you want to add.
   If there's not enough room for a new widget, you can tap ⊖ to remove a widget and make room for a new one.

Tip: On iPhone 14 Pro and iPhone 14 Pro Max, you can set your Lock Screen to stay on so you can glance at it at any time to check the date, time, and information in your widgets.

Link a Focus to your Lock Screen

Focus helps you concentrate on a task by minimizing notifications, or distractions. You can set up a Focus to temporarily silence all notifications, or allow only specific notifications (ones that apply to your task, for example). By linking a Focus to your Lock Screen, you have access to the features of the Focus when you use that Lock Screen.

1. Touch and hold the Lock Screen until the Customize button appears at the bottom of the screen.
   If the Customize button doesn't appear, touch and hold the Lock Screen again, then enter your passcode.
2. Tap Focus near the bottom of the wallpaper to see the Focus options—for example, Do Not Disturb, Personal, Sleep, and Work.
3. Select a Focus, then tap ✕.

Switch between Lock Screens

You can create multiple custom Lock Screens and switch between them throughout the day. If a Lock Screen links to a specific Focus, switching from that Lock Screen to another also switches your Focus.

1. Touch and hold the Lock Screen until the Customize button appears at the bottom of the screen.
   If the Customize button doesn't appear, touch and hold the Lock Screen again, then enter your passcode.
2. Swipe to the Lock Screen you want to use, then tap it.

Edit a Lock Screen

After you create a custom Lock Screen, you can make changes to it.

1. Touch and hold the Lock Screen until the Customize button appears at the bottom of the screen.
   If the Customize button doesn't appear, touch and hold the Lock Screen again, then enter your passcode.
2. Swipe to the Lock Screen you want to edit, then tap ⊕.
3. Do any of the following:
   - **Choose a wallpaper**: Tap an option in one of the categories (for example, Featured, Suggested Photos, or Photo Shuffle) or tap a button at the top of the screen (Photos, People, Photo Shuffle, Emoji, or Weather).
   - **Add widgets**: Tap the box below the time, then tap the widgets you want to add.
   - **Select a photo style for a Lock Screen with a photo**: Swipe to change the color filter (for example, Vibrant, Tone, Deep, and Vapor), the background for the photo (Natural, Black & White, Duotone, Color Wash, and so on), and the font for the time.
   - **Add a multilayered effect for a Lock Screen with a photo**: Tap ⋯ at the bottom right, then choose Depth Effect (not available for all photos).
   - **Change the Focus**: Tap Focus near the bottom of the wallpaper, then choose another Focus from the list.
   - **Change the style of the time**: Tap Customize, tap the time, then select a font, color, and shade by tapping .

Note: You can also add new wallpaper in Settings ⚙.

Delete a Lock Screen

You can delete Lock Screens you no longer need.

1. Touch and hold the Lock Screen until the Customize button appears at the bottom of the screen.
   If the Customize button doesn't appear, touch and hold the Lock Screen again, then enter your passcode.

2. Swipe to go to the Lock Screen you want to delete, swipe up on the screen, then tap 🗑.

Change the wallpaper on iPhone

On iPhone, you can change the wallpaper on the Lock Screen and the Home Screen. You can set your wallpaper in Settings or through the wallpaper gallery from your Lock Screen.

Change the wallpaper

1. Go to Settings ⚙ > Wallpaper, then tap Add New Wallpaper.
   The wallpaper gallery appears.
2. Do one of the following:
   - Tap a button at the top of the wallpaper gallery—for example, Photos, People, Photo Shuffle, Emoji, or Weather—to design your wallpaper with a photo, an emoji pattern, a picture of your local weather, and more.
   - Tap a wallpaper option in one of the categories—for example, Featured, Suggested Photos, or Photo Shuffle.
3. Tap Add, then do one of the following:
   - Choose whether to use the wallpaper on both the Lock Screen and Home Screen: Tap Set as Wallpaper Pair.
   - **Make further changes to the Home Screen**: Tap Customize Home Screen. Tap a color to change the wallpaper color, tap 🖼 to use a custom photo, or select Blur to blur the wallpaper so the apps stand out.

Adjust the screen brightness and color on iPhone

On iPhone, you can make your screen dimmer or brighter (dimming the screen extends battery life). You can also adjust the screen brightness and color manually or automatically with Dark Mode, True Tone, and Night Shift.

Adjust the screen brightness manually

To make your iPhone screen dimmer or brighter, do one of the following:

- Open Control Center, then drag ☀.
- Go to Settings ⚙ > Display & Brightness, then drag the slider.

Adjust the screen brightness automatically

iPhone adjusts the screen brightness for current light conditions using the built-in ambient light sensor.

1. Go to Settings ⚙ > Accessibility.
2. Tap Display & Text Size, then turn on Auto-Brightness.

Turn Dark Mode on or off

Dark Mode gives the entire iPhone experience a dark color scheme that's perfect for low-light environments. With Dark Mode on, you can use your iPhone while, for example, reading in bed, without disturbing the person next to you.

Do any of the following:

- Open Control Center, touch and hold ☀, then tap 🌓 to turn Dark Mode on or off.
- Go to Settings ⚙ > Display & Brightness, then select Dark to turn on Dark Mode, or select Light to turn it off.

Schedule Dark Mode to turn on and off automatically

You can set Dark Mode to turn on automatically at night (or on a custom schedule) in Settings.

1. Go to Settings ⚙ > Display & Brightness.
2. Turn on Automatic, then tap Options.
3. Select either Sunset to Sunrise or Custom Schedule.
   If you choose Custom Schedule, tap the options to schedule the times you want Dark Mode to turn on and off.
   If you select Sunset to Sunrise, iPhone uses the data from your clock and geolocation to determine when it's nighttime for you.

Turn Night Shift on or off

You can turn on Night Shift manually, which is helpful when you're in a darkened room during the day.

Open Control Center, touch and hold ☀, then tap ☀.

Schedule Night Shift to turn on and off automatically

Schedule Night Shift to shift the colors in your display to the warmer end of the spectrum at night and make viewing the screen easier on your eyes.

1. Go to Settings ⊚ > Display & Brightness > Night Shift.
2. Turn on Scheduled.
3. To adjust the color balance for Night Shift, drag the slider below Color Temperature toward the warmer or cooler end of the spectrum.
4. Tap From, then select either Sunset to Sunrise or Custom Schedule.
   If you choose Custom Schedule, tap the options to schedule the times you want Night Shift to turn on and off.

If you select Sunset to Sunrise, iPhone uses the data from your clock and geolocation to determine when it's nighttime for you.

Note: The Sunset to Sunrise option isn't available if you turned off Location Services in Settings ⊚ > Privacy & Security, or if you turned off Setting Time Zone in Settings > Privacy & Security > Location Services > System Services.

Turn True Tone on or off

True Tone automatically adapts the color and intensity of the display to match the light in your environment.

Do any of the following:

- Open Control Center, touch and hold ☀, then tap ☀ to turn True Tone on or off.
- Go to Settings ⊚ > Display & Brightness, then turn True Tone on or off.

Keep the iPhone display on longer

The iPhone display stays on while you're looking at it, but it dims and eventually locks (for your security) when you look away for a while. If you need the display to stay on longer (for example, when you're navigating with Maps), you can change how long it takes iPhone to automatically dim and lock.

Change when iPhone automatically locks

You can set how long it takes iPhone to automatically lock.

Go to Settings ⊚ > Display & Brightness > Auto-Lock, then choose a length of time.

Keep your Lock Screen visible

On iPhone 14 Pro and iPhone 14 Pro Max, the Always On setting allows a dimmed version of your Lock Screen to stay visible, even when your iPhone is locked, so you can glance at your Lock Screen to check essential information, like alerts, the date, time, and information in your widgets.

The display automatically turns off when iPhone is face down or obstructed from view, not near a paired Apple Watch, when a CarPlay session begins, while Continuity Camera is in use, while Low Power Mode is on, while Sleep Focus is on, or at your usual bedtime.

Always On is on by default. To turn it off, go to Settings ⚙ > Display & Brightness, then turn off Always On.

Magnify the iPhone screen with Display Zoom

You can see larger onscreen controls on an iPhone with Display Zoom.

1. Go to Settings ⚙ > Display & Brightness > Display Zoom.
2. Select Larger Text to make all the text on iPhone larger.
3. Tap Done, then tap Use Zoomed.

Change the name of your iPhone

You can change the name of your iPhone, which is used by iCloud, AirDrop, your Personal Hotspot, and your computer.

1. Go to Settings ⚙ > General > About > Name.
2. Tap ⊗, enter a new name, then tap Done.

Change the date and time on iPhone

By default, the date and time, visible on the Lock Screen, are set automatically based on your location. If you want to change them—for example, when you're traveling—you can adjust them.

1. Go to Settings ⚙ > General > Date & Time.
2. Turn on any of the following:
    - **Set Automatically**: iPhone gets the correct time over the network and updates it for the time zone you're in. Some networks don't support network time, so in some countries or regions, iPhone may not be able to automatically determine the local time.
    - **24-Hour Time**: (not available in all countries or regions) iPhone displays the hours from 0 to 23.

To change the default date and time, turn off Set Automatically, then change the date and time displayed.

Change the language and region on iPhone

You choose the language and region of your iPhone during setup. If you travel or move, you can change the language or region.

1. Go to Settings ⚙ > General > Language & Region.
2. Set the following:

- The language for iPhone
- The region
- The calendar format
- The temperature unit (Celsius or Fahrenheit)
- The measurement system (metric, U.S., or UK)
- The first day of the week
- Live Text (text you can select in images to copy or take action on)

3. To add another language and keyboard to your iPhone, tap Add Language, then select a language.

Customize the Home Screen

Organize your apps in folders on iPhone

You can organize your apps into folders to make them easier to find on your Home Screen pages.

Create folders

1. Touch and hold the Home Screen background until the apps begin to jiggle.
2. To create a folder, drag an app onto another app.
3. Drag other apps into the folder.
   You can have multiple pages of apps in the folder.
4. To rename the folder, touch and hold it, tap Rename, then enter a new name.
   If the apps begin to jiggle, tap the Home Screen background and try again.
5. When you're finished, tap Done, then tap the Home Screen background twice.

To delete a folder, tap the folder to open it, then drag all the apps out of it. The folder is automatically deleted.

Note: Organizing your apps on the Home Screen doesn't affect the organization of apps in the App Library.

Move an app from a folder to the Home Screen

You can move an app from a folder to the Home Screen to make it easier to locate and open.

1. Go to the Home Screen page with the folder that contains the app, then tap the folder to open it.
2. Touch and hold the app until the apps begin to jiggle.
3. Drag the app from the folder to the Home Screen.

Add widgets on iPhone

Widgets show you current information from your favorite apps at a glance—today's headlines, weather, calendar events, battery levels, and more. You can view widgets in Today View. You can also add widgets to your Home Screen and Lock Screen to keep this information at your fingertips.

View widgets

To view widgets, swipe right from the left edge of the Home Screen or the Lock Screen, then scroll up and down.

View widgets when iPhone is locked

1. Go to Settings ⚙ > Face ID & Passcode.
2. Enter your passcode.
3. Turn on Today View and Search (below Allow Access When Locked).

Add a widget to your Home Screen

1. Go to the Home Screen page where you want to add the widget, then touch and hold the Home Screen background until the apps begin to jiggle.
2. Tap + at the top of the screen to open the widget gallery.
3. Scroll or search to find the widget you want, tap it, then swipe left and right through the size options.
   The different sizes display different information.
4. When you see the size you want, tap Add Widget.
5. While the apps are still jiggling, move the widget where you want it on the screen, then tap Done.

Tip: A Smart Stack (with dots next to it) is a set of widgets that uses information such as the time, your location, and activity to automatically display the most relevant widget at the appropriate time in your day. You can add a Smart Stack to the Home Screen, then swipe through it to see the widgets it contains.

Edit a widget

You can customize most widgets right from your Home Screen so they display the information you want to see. For example, for a Mail widget, you can tap the mailbox shown in the widget, then choose a different mailbox so the messages in that mailbox are displayed in the widget. Or you can customize a Smart Stack to rotate through its widgets based on your activity, your location, the time of day, and so on.

1. On your Home Screen, touch and hold a widget to open the quick actions menu.
2. Tap Edit Widget if it appears (or Edit Stack, if it's a Smart Stack), then choose options.
   For a Smart Stack, you can turn Smart Rotate or Widget Suggestions off or on, reorder widgets by dragging them within the stack, drag a widget from the Smart Stack to the Home Screen, or remove a widget by tapping – in the upper-left corner.
   When you turn on Widget Suggestions, suggested widgets for apps you already use automatically appear in your Smart Stack at the right time based on your past activity. An option lets you add the widget to your stack so it's always there when you need it.
3. Tap Done.

Remove a widget from the Home Screen

1. Touch and hold the widget to open the quick actions menu.
2. Tap Remove Widget (or Remove Stack), then tap Remove.

Move apps and widgets on the Home Screen on iPhone

You can change the layout of your Home Screen—move apps and widgets around or drag them to other Home Screen pages, temporarily hide Home Screen pages, change where new apps get downloaded, and more.

Tip: You can move all your apps and widgets related to a particular Focus (your Work Focus, for example) onto one Home Screen page, and make that page accessible during that Focus.

Move apps and widgets around on your iPhone

1. Touch and hold any app or widget on the Home Screen, then tap Edit Home Screen. The apps begin to jiggle.
2. Drag an app to one of the following locations:
   o Another location on the same page
   o Another Home Screen page
     Drag the app or widget to the right edge of the screen. You might need to wait a second for the new page to appear. The dots above the Dock show how many pages you have and which one you're viewing.
3. When you're finished, tap Done.

Reset the Home Screen and apps to their original layout

1. Go to Settings ⊛ > General > Transfer or Reset iPhone.
2. Tap Reset, tap Reset Home Screen Layout, then tap Reset Home Screen.
   Any folders you've created are removed, and apps you've downloaded are arranged alphabetically after apps that came with your iPhone.

Remove apps from iPhone

You can easily remove apps from your iPhone. If you change your mind, you can download the apps again later.

Remove apps

Do any of the following:

- Remove an app from the Home Screen: Touch and hold the app on the Home Screen, tap Remove App, then tap Remove from Home Screen to keep it in App Library, or tap Delete App to delete it from iPhone.
- Delete an app from App Library and Home Screen: Touch and hold the app in App Library, tap Delete App, then tap Delete.

If you change your mind, you can redownload apps you've removed.

In addition to removing third-party apps from the Home Screen, you can remove the following built-in Apple apps that came with your iPhone:

- Books
- Calculator
- Calendar
- Compass
- Contacts (Contact information remains available through Phone, Messages, Mail, FaceTime, and other apps. To remove a contact, you must restore Contacts.)
- FaceTime
- Files

- Find My (Removing this app doesn't turn off location sharing or Find My for your device or items—it just removes the ability to view locations in the Find My app on that device.)
- Home
- iTunes Store
- Mail
- Maps
- Measure
- Music
- News
- Notes
- Podcasts
- Reminders
- Shortcuts
- Stocks
- Tips
- Translate
- TV
- Voice Memos
- Watch
- Weather

Note: When you remove a built-in app from your Home Screen, you also remove any related user data and configuration files. Removing built-in apps from your Home Screen can affect other system functionality.

Use and customize Control Center on iPhone

Control Center on iPhone gives you instant access to useful controls—including airplane mode, Do Not Disturb, a flashlight, volume, screen brightness—and apps.

Open Control Center

- Swipe down from the top-right edge. To close Control Center, swipe up from the bottom.

Access more controls in Control Center

Many controls offer additional options. To see available options, touch and hold a control. For example, you can do the following in Control Center:

- Touch and hold the top-left group of controls, then tap to open the AirDrop options.

- Touch and hold 📷 to take a selfie, take a photo, or record a video.

Touch and hold to
see Camera options.

Add and organize controls

You can customize Control Center by adding more controls and shortcuts to many apps, such as Calculator, Notes, Voice Memos, and more.

1. Go to Settings ⚙ > Control Center.
2. To add or remove controls, tap ⊕ or ⊖ next to a control.
3. To rearrange controls, touch ☰ next to a control, then drag it to a new position.

Temporarily disconnect from a Wi-Fi network

In Control Center, tap 📶 ; to reconnect, tap it again.

To see the name of the connected Wi-Fi network, touch and hold 📶 .

Because Wi-Fi isn't turned off when you disconnect from a network, AirPlay and AirDrop still work, and iPhone joins known networks when you change locations or restart iPhone. To turn off Wi-Fi, go to Settings ⚙ > Wi-Fi. (To turn on Wi-Fi again in Control Center, tap 📶 .)

Temporarily disconnect from Bluetooth devices

In Control Center, tap ❊ ; to allow connections, tap the button again.

Because Bluetooth isn't turned off when you disconnect from devices, location accuracy and other services are still enabled. To turn off Bluetooth, go to Settings ⚙ > Bluetooth, then turn off Bluetooth. To turn on Bluetooth again in Control Center, tap ❊ .

Turn off access to Control Center in apps

Go to Settings ⚙ > Control Center, then turn off Access Within Apps.

Change or lock the screen orientation on iPhone

Many apps give you a different view when you rotate iPhone.

Lock or unlock the screen orientation

You can lock the screen orientation so that it doesn't change when you rotate iPhone.

Open Control Center, then tap 🔒.

When the screen orientation is locked, 🔒 appears in the status bar (on supported models).

Set up Focus, notifications, and Do Not Disturb

View and respond to notifications on iPhone

Notifications help you keep track of what's new—they let you know if you missed a call, if the date of an event moved, and more. You can customize your notification settings so you see only what's important to you.

Unless you have notifications silenced with a Focus, iPhone displays them as they arrive—they roll in from the bottom of the screen to minimize distraction. You can view them on the Lock Screen in an expanded list view, stacked view, or count view. Pinch the notifications on the Lock Screen to change the layout.

Note: While you're using an app, you might be asked how you want to receive notifications from it—immediately, not at all, or in a scheduled summary. You can change this setting later in Settings > Notifications.

Find your notifications in Notification Center

To see your notifications in Notification Center, do any of the following:

- **On the Lock Screen**: Swipe up from the middle of the screen.
- **On other screens**: Swipe down from the top center. Then you can scroll up to see older notifications, if there are any.

To close Notification Center, swipe up from the bottom with one finger.

Respond to notifications

When you have multiple notifications in Notification Center or on the Lock Screen, they're grouped by app, which makes them easier to view and manage. Notifications from some apps may also be grouped by organizing features within the app, such as by topic or thread. Grouped notifications appear as small stacks, with the most recent notification on top.

Do any of the following:

- To expand a group of notifications to see them individually: Tap the group. To close the group, tap Show Less.

- To view a notification and perform quick actions if the app offers them: Touch and hold the notification.
- To open a notification's app: Tap the notification.

Schedule a notification summary

You can reduce distractions in your day by scheduling your notifications to be delivered as a summary—you choose which notifications to include in the summary and what time you want to receive it.

The notification summary is personalized to you and intelligently ordered by priority, based on your current activity, with the most relevant notifications at the top. The summary is especially useful because it allows you to engage with notifications on your own time. You can take this even further by using Focus to filter notifications while you focus on an activity.

1. Go to Settings ⚙ > Notifications > Scheduled Summary, then turn on Scheduled Summary.
2. Select the apps to include in your summary.
3. Set a time for your summary. If you want to receive another summary, tap Add Summary.
4. Tap A to Z below Apps in Summary, then make sure the apps you want to include in your summary are turned on.

View, dismiss, clear, and mute notifications

When notifications appear on your iPhone, do any of the following:

- Handle a notification you receive while using another app: Tap to view it, then swipe up to dismiss it.
- **Clear notifications**: Swipe left on a notification or group of notifications, then tap Clear or Clear All.
- **Mute notifications for an app**: Swipe left on the notification or group of notifications, tap Options, then tap an option to mute the app's notifications for an hour or a day. This sends them directly to Notification Center and prevents them from appearing on the Lock Screen, playing a sound, lighting up the screen, or presenting a banner.
  To see and hear these notifications again, swipe left on the notification in Notification Center, tap Options, then tap Unmute.
- **Turn off notifications for an app or notification group**: Swipe left on a notification or group of notifications, tap Options, then tap Turn Off.
- **Change how an app displays notifications**: Swipe left on a notification, tap Options, then tap View Settings.

- **Clear all your notifications in Notification Center**: Go to Notification Center, tap ⊗, then tap Clear.
- **Silence all notifications**: Turn on Do Not Disturb.

When you haven't used an app for a while, you may see a suggestion that you turn off notifications for that app.

Show recent notifications on the Lock Screen

You can allow access to Notification Center on the Lock Screen.

1. Go to Settings > Face ID & Passcode.
2. Enter your passcode.

3. Scroll down and turn on Notification Center (below Allow Access When Locked).

Change notification settings on iPhone

In Settings ⚙ , choose which apps can send notifications, change the alert sound, set up location-based alerts, allow government alerts, and more.

Change notification settings

Most notification settings can be customized for each app. You can turn app notifications on or off, have notifications play a sound, choose how and where you want app notifications to appear when your device is unlocked, and more.

1. Go to Settings ⚙ > Notifications.
2. Choose how you want notifications displayed on the Lock Screen:
   - View just the number of notifications: Tap Count.
   - View the notifications grouped into stacks by app: Tap Stack.
   - View the notifications in a list: Tap List.
3. When notifications arrive, you can change the layout by pinching the notifications on the Lock Screen.
4. To schedule a notifications summary, tap Scheduled Summary, then turn on Scheduled Summary.
   Select the apps you want notifications for in your summary, set a time for delivery of your summary, then tap ‹ at the top left.
5. To choose when you want notification previews to appear, tap Show Previews, select an option—Always, When Unlocked, or Never—then tap ‹ at the top left.
   Previews can include things like text (from Messages and Mail) and invitation details (from Calendar). You can override this setting for individual apps.
6. Tap an app below Notification Style, then turn Allow Notifications on or off.
   If you turn on Allow Notifications, choose when you want the notifications delivered—immediately or in the scheduled notifications summary—and turn Time Sensitive Notifications on or off.
   For many apps, you can also set a notification banner style and turn sounds and badges on or off.
7. Tap Notification Grouping, then choose how you want the notifications grouped:
   - Automatic: The notifications from the app are grouped according to organizing criteria within the app, such as by topic or thread.
   - By App: All the notifications from the app are grouped together.
   - Off: Turn off grouping.

To turn off notifications selectively for apps, go to Settings > Notifications > Siri Suggestions, then turn off any app.

When you use Focus, it delays the delivery of notifications on iPhone to prevent interruptions. You can schedule a time to receive a summary of the notifications you missed.

Set up or turn off location-based alerts

Some apps use your location to send you relevant alerts based on where you are. For example, you might get a reminder to call someone when you get to a specific place or when you leave for your next location.

If you don't want to see these types of alerts, you can turn them off.

1. Go to Settings ⚙ > Privacy & Security > Location Services.
2. Turn on Location Services.
3. Tap an app (if any appear in the list), then choose whether you want to share your location while using that app.

Get government alerts

In some countries or regions, you can turn on alerts in the Government Alerts list. For example, on iPhone in the United States, you can receive National Alerts, and you can turn AMBER, Public Safety, and Emergency Alerts (which include both Severe and Extreme Imminent Threat alerts) on or off (they're on by default). On iPhone in Japan, you can receive Emergency Earthquake Alerts from the Japan Meteorological Agency.

1. Go to Settings ⚙ > Notifications.
2. Scroll down to the Government Alerts section, then turn on the ones you want.

Government alerts vary by carrier and iPhone model, and may not work under all conditions.

Set up a Focus on iPhone

Focus is a feature that helps you reduce distractions and set boundaries. When you want to concentrate on a specific activity, you can customize one of the provided Focus options—for example Work, Personal, or Sleep—or create a custom Focus. You can use Focus to temporarily silence all notifications, or allow only specific notifications—ones that apply to your task, for example—and let other people and apps know you're busy.

You can set up a Focus right on your Lock Screen, when you create a personalized Lock Screen. When a Focus is linked to your Lock Screen, you can you can turn it on by simply swiping to the corresponding Lock Screen.

Likewise, you can customize a Home Screen page that has only apps related to a Focus and make that page your Home Screen during that Focus. iPhone also suggests Home Screens with apps and widgets that are relevant to the Focus you're setting up.

Tip: To quickly silence all notifications, open Control Center, tap Focus, then turn on Do Not Disturb.

Set up a Focus

1. Go to Settings ⚙ > Focus, then tap a Focus—for example, Do Not Disturb, Personal, Sleep, or Work.
   For the Focus you select, you can set up the options described in the steps below, but you don't have to set up all of them.
2. Specify which apps and people can send you notifications during your Focus.
   After you specify which people and apps to allow notifications from, an Options link appears.
3. Tap Options, then do any of the following:

- Show silenced notifications on the Lock Screen or send them to Notification Center: Turn Show On Lock Screen on or off.
- Darken the Lock Screen during this Focus: Turn on Dim Lock Screen.
- Hide notification badges on Home Screen apps: Turn on Hide Notification Badges.

4. When you're finished selecting options, tap ‹ at the top of the screen.
5. To change the Lock Screen to use with this Focus, tap the Lock Screen preview below Customize Screens, select a Lock Screen, then tap Done at the top of the screen.
6. To choose a Home Screen page to use with this Focus, tap the Home Screen preview below Customize Screens, select a page, then tap Done.
   The Home Screen options that appear include the apps and widgets most relevant to the Focus you're setting up.
   To make changes to the Home Screen to customize it further for your Focus, adjust it in Settings > Focus.

After setting up your Focus, you can return to Settings > Focus at any time and change any of the options you chose above.

You can schedule a Focus to turn on automatically or turn it on or off in Control Center.

When you set up a Sleep Focus, you can also change your next bedtime and wake-up time, or adjust your sleep schedule by tapping Set Up Sleep in Health.

Add Focus filters

When you set up a Focus, you can add app filters that determine what information apps will show during the Focus. For example, you can choose which mail account or which calendar to use during the Focus.

1. Go to Settings > Focus, then tap the Focus you want to add filters to.
2. Scroll down to Focus filters, then tap Add Filter.
3. Tap an app, then select the information from that app you want to use during the Focus:
   - **Calendar**: Choose which calendars you want to show during the Focus.
   - **Mail**: Choose which mail accounts you want to use during the Focus.
   - **Messages**: Choose which message conversations you want to see during the Focus—for example, only conversations from people you've allowed notifications from during this Focus.
   - **Safari**: Choose which Tab Group you want to use during the Focus.
4. Tap Add to add the filter to the Focus.

Create a Custom Focus

If you want to concentrate on an activity that's different from any of the provided Focus options, you can create a Custom Focus.

1. Go to Settings ⚙ > Focus.
2. Tap ＋ at the top right, then tap Custom.
3. Enter a name for your Focus, then tap Return.
4. Choose a color and an icon to represent your Focus, then tap Next.
5. Tap Customize Focus, then set up the options for your custom Focus.

Keep your Focus settings up to date across all your Apple devices

You can use the same Focus settings on all your Apple devices where you're signed in with the same Apple ID.

Go to Settings ⚙ > Focus, then turn on Share Across Devices.

Allow or silence notifications for a Focus on iPhone

While you're setting up a Focus, you can select people and apps you want to receive notifications from by either silencing them or allowing them. For example, set up a Work Focus and allow only notifications from your coworkers and the apps you use for work.

Allow or silence notifications from specific people during a Focus

1. Choose a Focus—for example, Do Not Disturb, Personal, Sleep, or Work.
2. Tap People (or tap Choose People), then do one of the following:

   o Allow specific people: Tap Allow Notifications From, tap ✚ , then select from your contacts.
   You can also turn on options to allow calls from certain groups of people and allow repeated calls.

   o Silence specific people: Tap Silence Notifications From, tap ✚ , then select from your contacts.
   You can also turn on Allow Calls From Silenced People.

Note: Regardless of your Focus settings, you can allow calls from your emergency contacts to come through.

Allow or silence notifications from specific apps during a Focus

1. Choose a Focus—for example, Do Not Disturb, Personal, Sleep, or Work.
2. Tap Apps (or tap Choose Apps), then do one of the following:

   o **Allow specific apps**: Tap Allow Notifications From, tap ✚ , then select apps.

   o **Silence specific apps**: Tap Silence Notifications From, tap ✚ , then select apps.

You can also turn on Time Sensitive Notifications, which allows all apps to send time-sensitive notifications immediately.

Share your Focus status

When you're using a Focus, it limits the notifications you receive from people and apps. When someone outside your allowed notifications tries to contact you, your Focus status appears in Messages and other apps you give permission to, so they know you're busy.

When you give an app permission to share your Focus status, others can see that you have notifications silenced, but not the name of the Focus you have turned on. This information is shared only when you have a Focus turned on and after you give the app permission.

1. Go to Settings > Focus > Focus Status.
2. Turn on Share Focus Status, then select the Focus options you want to share.

Allow calls from emergency contacts when notifications are silenced

You can allow sounds and vibrations from emergency contacts to come through even when your iPhone or notifications are silenced.

1. Open Contacts ⊙.
2. Select a contact, then tap Edit.
3. Tap Ringtone or Text Tone, then turn on Emergency Bypass.
Or, set up your Medical ID and identify an emergency contact.

Turn on or schedule a Focus on iPhone

To use a Focus, you can turn it on directly in Control Center, or schedule it to turn on automatically.

Turn on a Focus in Control Center

1. Open Control Center, tap Focus, then tap the Focus you want to turn on (for example, Do Not Disturb).
   Note: If another Focus is already on, it turns off when you tap the new one.
2. To choose an ending point for the Focus, tap ⋯, select an option (such as "For 1 hour" or "Until I leave this location"), then tap ⋯ again.

When a Focus is on, its icon (for example, 🌙 for Do Not Disturb) appears in the status bar and on the Lock Screen, and your status is automatically displayed in the Messages app. People who try to send you a message will see that you've silenced notifications, but they can still notify you if something is urgent.

Note: You can also turn a Focus on or off by going to Settings ⚙ > Focus, tapping the Focus, then turning it on.

Schedule a Focus to turn on automatically

You can schedule a Focus to turn on at certain times, when you're at a particular location, or when you open a specific app.

1. Go to Settings ⚙ > Focus, then tap the Focus you want to schedule.
2. To have this Focus turn on automatically at a set time, location, or while using a certain app, tap Smart Activation, turn on Smart Activation, then tap ‹ at the top left.
3. Tap Add Schedule, then set the times, a location, or an app you want to activate this Focus.

Note: When you set up a Sleep Focus, it follows the sleep schedule you set in the Health app. To add or edit a sleep schedule, tap Open Sleep in Health.

Turn off a Focus

When you're finished using a Focus, you can quickly turn it off to allow notifications again. After you turn off a Focus, it still appears in Control Center and can be reused.

1. Do any of the following:
   o Touch and hold the Focus icon on the Lock Screen.
   o Open Control Center, then tap Focus.
2. Tap the Focus that's on to turn it off.

Turn a Focus on or off using Siri

You can use Siri to turn a Focus on or off.

Siri: Say something like: "Turn on the Work Focus," or "Turn off the Work Focus."

Delete a Focus

When you no longer need a Focus you set up, you can delete it.

1. Go to Settings ⚙ > Focus.
2. Tap the Focus, scroll to the bottom of the screen, then tap Delete Focus.

If you delete a provided Focus, you need to set it up again by going to Settings > Focus, then tapping +.

Stay focused while driving with iPhone

Turning on the Driving Focus helps you stay focused on the road. When you turn it on, text messages and other notifications are silenced or limited. You can have Siri read replies to you, so you don't have to look at your iPhone. Incoming calls are allowed only when iPhone is connected to CarPlay—a car Bluetooth system—or a hands-free accessory.

Set up the Driving Focus

You can set up the Driving Focus to turn on automatically when you're in a moving car. (You can also turn it on manually in Control Center.)

1. Go to Settings ⚙ > Focus, tap Driving, then turn on Driving.
2. Tap Focus Status (below Options), then turn on Share Focus Status.
3. Tap Auto-Reply, then choose who should receive an auto-reply when the Driving Focus is on:
    o No one
    o Recents
    o Favorites
    o All Contacts
4. You can edit your auto-reply message to customize it.

    Then tap ‹ at the top left.
5. Tap While Driving (below Turn On Automatically), then select when to activate Driving:
    o **Automatically**: When iPhone detects you might be driving.
    o **When Connected to Car Bluetooth**: When your iPhone is connected to a car's Bluetooth system.
    o **Manually**: When you turn it on in Control Center.
    o **Activate With CarPlay**: Automatically when iPhone is connected to CarPlay.

Get calls, messages, and notifications when you're a passenger

If you receive a Driving notification when you're in a car, but you're not driving (for example, when you're a passenger), you can dismiss the notification.

Tap I'm Not Driving.

When the Driving Focus is on and you're a passenger in a moving car, you can receive calls, messages, and notifications.

Apps

App Store

Get apps in the App Store on iPhone

In the App Store app ⚖, you can discover new apps, featured stories, tips and tricks, and in-app events.

Note: You need an internet connection and an Apple ID to use the App Store. The availability of the App Store and Apple Arcade varies by country or region.

Find apps

Tap any of the following:

- **Today**: Browse featured stories, apps, and in-app events.
- **Games**: Find your next game across dozens of categories including action, adventure, racing, puzzles, and more.
- **Apps**: Explore new releases, see the top charts, or browse by category.
- **Arcade**: Enjoy the curated collection of premium games from Apple Arcade (subscription required) without ads or in-app purchases.
- **Search**: Enter what you're looking for, then tap Search on the keyboard.

Siri: Say something like: "Search the App Store for cooking apps."

Get more info about an app

Tap an app to see the following information and more:

- Screenshots or previews
- In-app events
- Ratings and reviews
- Supported languages
- Game Center and Family Sharing support
- Compatibility with other Apple devices
- File size
- Privacy information

Buy and download an app

1. Tap the price. If the app is free, tap Get.

   If you see ⬇ instead of a price, you already purchased the app, and you can download it again for free.
2. If required, authenticate with Face ID or your passcode to complete your purchase.

You can find the app in the Recently Added category in App Library. While the app is downloading, a progress indicator appears on the app icon.

Get the App Store widget

See stories, collections, and in-app events right on your Home Screen.

Share or give an app

1. Tap the app to see its details.
2. Tap ⬆️, then choose a sharing option or tap Gift App (not available for all apps).

Redeem or send an Apple Gift Card

1. Tap 👤 or your profile picture at the top right.
2. Tap one of the following:
   o Redeem Gift Card or Code
   o Send Gift Card by Email

Play Games

Subscribe to Apple Arcade on iPhone

In the App Store app 🅰️, you can subscribe to Apple Arcade to enjoy unlimited access to a curated collection of games on iPhone, iPad, Mac, and Apple TV. (Not all Apple Arcade games are available on Mac and Apple TV.)

You can subscribe to Apple Arcade or to Apple One, which includes Apple Arcade and other services.

Note: Apple Arcade and Apple One aren't available in all countries or regions. The availability of Apple Arcade games across devices varies based on hardware and software compatibility. Some content may not be available in all areas.

Subscribe to Apple Arcade

1. In the App Store, tap Arcade, then tap the subscription button.
2. Review the free trial (if eligible) and subscription details, then follow the onscreen instructions.

Share Apple Arcade with family members

When you subscribe to Apple Arcade or Apple One, you can use Family Sharing to share Apple Arcade with up to five other family members. Your family group members don't need to do anything—Apple Arcade is available to them the first time they open the App Store app after your subscription begins.

If you join a family group that subscribes to Apple Arcade or Apple One, and you already subscribe, your subscription isn't renewed on your next billing date; instead, you use the group's subscription. If you join a family group that doesn't subscribe, the group uses your subscription.

Note: To stop sharing Apple Arcade with a family group, you can cancel the subscription, leave the family group, or (if you're the family group organizer), stop using Family Sharing.

Play Apple Arcade games on your Apple devices

If you subscribe to Apple Arcade, you can play and access your game progress on your compatible Apple devices where you're signed in with your Apple ID.

Change or cancel your Apple Arcade subscription

Go to Settings ⚙️ > [your name] > Subscriptions, tap Apple Arcade, then follow the onscreen instructions.

If you cancel your subscription, you can't play any Apple Arcade games, even if you downloaded them to your device. Delete the apps if you don't want them anymore.

You can resubscribe to play Apple Arcade games again and regain access to your gameplay data. If you wait too long, some of your gameplay data might not be supported after you resubscribe.

Get games from the App Store on iPhone

In the App Store app , you can find your next game across dozens of categories including action, adventure, racing, puzzles, and more.

Note: Game Center, Apple Arcade, and Apple One aren't available in all countries or regions. The availability of Apple Arcade games across devices varies based on hardware and software compatibility. Some content may not be available in all areas.

Find games

Tap any of the following:

- **Games**: Explore new releases, see the top charts, or browse by category.
- **Arcade**: Enjoy the curated collection of premium games from Apple Arcade (subscription required) without ads or in-app purchases.
- **Search**: Tap the search bar, enter what you're looking for, then tap Search on the keyboard.

Siri: Say something like: "Get the Minecraft app."

Get more info about a game

Tap a game to see the following information and more:

- Screenshots or previews
- In-app events
- Ratings and reviews
- Supported languages
- Game Center and game controller support
- Compatibility with other Apple devices
- File size
- Privacy information

Buy and download a game

1. Tap the price. If the game is free, tap Get.

   If you see instead of a price, you already purchased the game, and you can download it again for free.
2. If required, authenticate with Face ID or your passcode to complete your purchase.

Play with friends in Game Center on iPhone

In Game Center on iPhone, you can send friend requests, manage your public profile, earn achievements, and compete on leaderboards across devices.

Set up your Game Center profile

1. Go to Settings 🎮 > Game Center, then sign in with your Apple ID.
2. Do any of the following:
   o **Choose a nickname**: Tap Nickname, then enter a name or choose one of the suggestions. Your friends see your nickname when you play games together.
   o **Personalize your profile picture**: Tap Edit at the top, then create a new Memoji, use an existing Memoji, or customize how your initials appear.

Add friends

1. Go to Settings 🎮 > Game Center > [your profile] > Friends.
2. Tap Add Friends, then enter their phone number or Apple ID, or tap ⊕ to invite someone in your Contacts list.
3. Recipients can respond to friend requests in any of the following ways:
   o In Messages, tap the link.
   o In a supported game, tap the Game Center profile picture, tap Friends, then tap Friend Requests.
   o In the App Store, tap 👤 or your profile picture at the top right, tap Game Center, then tap Friend Requests.

In your list of friends, tap a friend to see games they recently played and their achievements.

Report a user or remove a friend

You can report a user for cheating, an inappropriate picture or nickname, or another problem. You can also remove someone from your Friends list.

1. Go to Settings 🎮 > Game Center > [your profile] > Friends.
2. Tap the friend you want to report or remove, tap ⋯, then choose Report User or Remove Friend.

Set Game Center restrictions

You can set restrictions for multiplayer games, adding friends, private messaging, and more.

1. Go to Settings 🎮 > Screen Time > Content & Privacy Restrictions, then turn on Content & Privacy Restrictions.
2. Tap Content Restrictions, scroll down to Game Center, then set restrictions.

Connect a game controller to iPhone

You can connect a game controller to your iPhone through Bluetooth or the Lightning connector. You can customize the buttons and even add a second controller to get help from a friend.

Pair a Bluetooth game controller

1. Follow the instructions that came with the controller to put it in discovery mode.
2. On iPhone, go to Settings 🎮 > Bluetooth, turn on Bluetooth, then tap the name of the device.

Connect a game controller through the Lightning connector

If you have a compatible game controller, you can connect it to iPhone using the Lightning connector. Follow the instructions that came with your controller.

Depending on your iPhone model and controller, you may need a Lightning to USB adapter (sold separately).

Customize the game controller buttons

After you pair or connect a compatible game controller, you can customize the buttons for supported games from Apple Arcade and the App Store.

1. Go to Settings ⦿ > General > Game Controller.
2. Tap the buttons you want to change.
3. To customize for a specific app, tap Add App.

Add a second game controller and get help from a friend

With Buddy Controller, iPhone combines two controllers to drive a single player in a game so a friend can help you get to the next level. Buddy Controller is compatible with any game that supports game controllers.

1. Connect two compatible game controllers to iPhone through Bluetooth or the Lightning connector.
2. Go to Settings ⦿ > General > Game Controller > Buddy Controller.
3. Choose the primary controller, then choose the secondary controller.

Use App Clips on iPhone

An App Clip is a small part of an app that lets you do a task quickly, like rent a bike, pay for parking, or order food. You can discover App Clips in Safari, Maps, and Messages, or in the real world through NFC tags, QR codes, and App Clip Codes—unique markers that take you to specific App Clips.

Get and use an App Clip

1. Get an App Clip from any of the following:
   o **App Clip Code or QR code**: Scan the code using the iPhone camera or Code Scanner in Control Center.
   o NFC-integrated App Clip Code or NFC tag: Hold iPhone near the NFC tag.
   o **Maps:** Tap the App Clip link on the information card (for supported locations).
   o **Safari or Messages**: Tap the App Clip link.
2. When the App Clip appears on the screen, tap Open or Play.

In supported App Clips, you can use Sign in with Apple, then make a payment using Apple Pay.

With some App Clips, you can tap the banner at the top of the screen to see the full app.

Find an App Clip you used on iPhone

Go to App Library, tap the search field at the top of the screen, then scroll down to the end of the alphabetical list.

Remove App Clips

- **Remove a specific App Clip**: Go to App Library, tap the search field at the top of the screen, enter the name of the App Clip, then touch and hold the app icon.

- **Remove all App Clips**: Go to Settings 🔘 > App Clips.

Manage App Store purchases, subscriptions, settings, and restrictions on iPhone

In the App Store app 🄰 , you can manage subscriptions and review and download purchases made by you or other family members. You can also set restrictions and customize your preferences for the App Store in Settings 🔘 .

Approve purchases with Family Sharing

With Family Sharing set up, the family organizer can review and approve purchases made by other family members under a certain age.

Find and download apps purchased by you or family members

1. Tap 🔘 or your profile picture at the top right, then tap Purchased.
2. If you set up Family Sharing, tap My Purchases or choose a family member to view their purchases.

Note: You can see purchases made by family members only if they choose to share their purchases. Purchases made with Family Sharing may not be accessible after the family member leaves the family group.

3. Find the app you want to download (if it's still available in the App Store), then tap ☁.

Change or cancel your App Store subscriptions

1. Tap 🔘 or your profile picture at the top right, then tap Subscriptions. You may need to sign in with your Apple ID.
2. Choose a subscription, then do any of the following:
   - Change or cancel an existing subscription.
   - Resubscribe to an expired subscription.
   - Share an eligible App Store subscription with other family members in your Family Sharing group.

Change your App Store settings

Go to Settings 🔘 > App Store, then do any of the following:

- Automatically download apps purchased on your other Apple devices: Below Automatic Downloads, turn on App Downloads.
- Automatically update apps: Turn on App Updates.
- **Allow app downloads to use cellular data**: Below Cellular Data, turn on Automatic Downloads. To choose whether you want to be asked for permission for downloads over 200 MB or all apps, tap App Downloads.
- Automatically play app preview videos: Turn on Video Autoplay.
- **Automatically remove unused apps**: Turn on Offload Unused Apps. You can reinstall an app at any time if it's still available in the App Store.

Set content restrictions and prevent in-app purchases

After you turn on content and privacy restrictions, do the following.

1. Go to Settings ⚙️ > Screen Time > Content & Privacy Restrictions > Content Restrictions.
2. Set restrictions such as the following:
   - **Apps**: Restrict apps by age ratings.
   - **App Clips**: Prevent App Clips from opening.

Install and manage fonts on iPhone

You can download fonts from the App Store app 🅐 , then use them in documents you create on iPhone.

1. After you download an app containing fonts from the App Store, open the app to install the fonts.
2. To manage installed fonts, go to Settings ⚙️ > General, then tap Fonts.

Books

Buy books and audiobooks in Apple Books on iPhone

In the Books app 📖 , you can find today's bestsellers, view top charts, and browse lists curated by Apple Books editors. After you select a book or audiobook, you can read or listen to it right in the app.

1. Open Books, then tap Book Store or Audiobooks to browse titles, or tap Search to look for a specific title, author, or genre.
2. Tap a book cover to see more details, read a sample, listen to a preview, or mark as Want to Read.
3. Tap Buy to purchase a title, or tap Get to download a free title.
   All purchases are made with the payment method associated with your Apple ID.

Note: You can allow books and audiobooks to be downloaded automatically over your cellular network when you aren't connected to Wi-Fi. Go to Settings ⚙️ > Books, tap Downloads, then choose Always Allow, Ask If Over 200 MB or Always Ask.

Read books in the Books app on iPhone

In the Books app 📖 , you can view the books you're currently reading, want to read, book collections, and more.

- **Reading Now**: Tap to access the books and audiobooks you're currently reading. Scroll down to see books and audiobooks you've added to your Want To Read collection and books you've sampled. You can also set daily reading goals and keep track of the books you finish throughout the year.

- **Library**: Shows all of the books, audiobooks, series, and PDFs you got from the Book Store or manually added to your library. You can tap Collections to see your books sorted into collections, such as Want to Read, My Samples, Audiobooks, and Finished.

Read a book

Tap Reading Now or Library, tap a book cover, then do any of the following:

- **Turn the page**: Tap the right margin or swipe right to left.
- **Go back to the previous page**: Tap the left margin or swipe left to right.
- **Go back to where you started reading**: Tap the rounded arrow in the top-left corner of the page; tap the rounded arrow again, but in the top-right corner, to go back to your current location.
- **Go to a specific page or location**: Tap ☰, tap Search Book, enter a word, phrase, or page number, then tap a result.
- **Use the table of contents**: Tap ☰, then tap Contents.
  Tip: To quickly move through a book, touch and hold Contents, then drag your finger left or right; release your finger to go directly to that location in the book.
- **Lock Screen orientation**: Tap ☰, then tap 🔄 to lock the screen in horizontal or vertical orientation.
- **Close a book**: Tap the page, then tap ✕ in the top-right corner, or swipe down from the top of the page.

Tap to go back to reading start page.

Tap to close book.

Chapter 32

Elizabeth was sitting by herself the next morning, and writing to Jane while Mrs. Collins and Maria were gone on business into the village, when she was startled by a ring at the door, the certain signal of a visitor. As she had heard no carriage, she thought it not unlikely to be Lady Catherine, and under that apprehension was putting away her half-finished letter that she might escape all impertinent questions, when the door opened, and, to her very great surprise, Mr. Darcy, and Mr. Darcy only, entered the room.

He seemed astonished too on finding her alone, and apologised for his intrusion by letting her know that he had understood all the ladies were to be within.

Tap to navigate, search, and change the book's display.

When you finish a book, personalized recommendations appear to help you discover your next read.

Change text and page appearance

Tap ☰ at the bottom of the page, tap Themes & Settings, then do any of the following:

- **Change the font size**: Tap the large A to increase the font size or tap the small A to decrease it.
- **Change the font**: Tap Options, tap Font, select a font option such as Georgia or Palatino, then tap Done.
- **Turn on vertical scrolling**: Tap ▤ to scroll continuously through a book.

    For PDFs, tap A A at the top of the screen, then turn on Vertical Scrolling.
- **Adjust the display brightness**: Tap ☀, then choose an option.
- **Change the page background color**: Tap a page theme such as Quiet or Bold.
- **Make the font bold**: Tap Options, then turn on Bold Text (green is on).
- **Customize spacing and justification**: Tap Options, turn on Customize (green is on), then drag the sliders left or right to adjust line spacing, character spacing, and word spacing. You can also turn Full Justification and Allow Multiple Columns off or on (green is on).

Note: You can choose on which side of the screen the Menu button ⚏ appears. Go to Settings ⚙ > Books, then choose Left or Right below Reading Menu Position.

Bookmark a page

When you close a book, your place is saved automatically—you don't need to add a bookmark. Bookmark pages you want to return to again.

Tap ⚏, then tap ⛉; tap it again to remove the bookmark.

To see all your bookmarks, tap ⚏, tap Bookmarks & Highlights, then tap Bookmarks.

Share a text selection or book link

You can send text selections using AirDrop, Mail, or Messages. If the book is from the Book Store, a link to the book is included with the selection. (Sharing may not be available in all countries or regions.)

1. Touch and hold a word, then move the grab points to adjust the selection.
2. Tap Share, then choose how to share the selection.

You can also share a link to view the book in the Book Store. Tap any page, tap ⚏, tap ⬆, then choose how to share the link.

Annotate books in the Books app on iPhone

In the Books app ▥ you can highlight and underline text, and add notes as you read.

Highlight or underline text

1. Touch and hold a word, then move the grab points to adjust the selection.
2. Tap Highlight.
   To change the highlight color or switch to underline, tap the text, tap Highlight, then tap an option.
   To remove a highlight or underline, tap the text, then tap Remove.

To see all of your highlights, tap ≡, tap Bookmarks & Highlights, then tap Highlights.

Add a note

1. Touch and hold a word, then move the grab points to adjust the selection.
2. Tap Add Note, enter text, then tap Done.
   The selected text is highlighted.
   To remove a note, tap the text, then tap Remove. Both the note and the highlight are removed.

To see all of your notes, tap ≡, tap Bookmarks & Highlights, then tap Highlights.

Access books on other Apple devices in the Books app on iPhone

You can access the books and audiobooks in the Books app 📖 on other devices such as your iPad, iPod touch, and Mac. You can also sync your reading position, highlights, notes, library collections, and more.

Access your books across iOS and iPadOS devices

To keep your Books content and information updated across your iPhone, iPad, and iPod touch, sign in with the same Apple ID on each device, then do the following:

- Sync Reading position, bookmarks, notes, and highlights: Go to Settings ⚙ > [your name] > iCloud > iCloud Drive, then turn on Sync this iPhone (green is on). Tap iCloud, then tap Show All and turn on Books (green is on).
- Sync Reading Now, Library, and collections: Go to Settings > Books, then below Syncing, turn on Reading Now and iCloud Drive (green is on).
- Automatically download purchases made on other devices: Go to Settings > Books, then turn on Purchases from Other Devices (green is on).

Access your books on your Mac

To see your books, audiobooks, and PDFs on your Mac, do one of the following:

- **macOS 10.15–12.5**: Choose Apple menu > System Preferences, then click Apple ID. Click iCloud in the sidebar, then select iCloud Drive. Click Options, then select Books.
- **macOS 10.14 or earlier**: Choose Apple menu > System Preferences, then click iCloud. Select iCloud Drive, click Options, then select Books.

To see your collections, bookmarks, notes, and highlights on your Mac, choose Books > Preferences, click General, then select "Sync collections, bookmarks, and highlights across devices."

Listen to audiobooks in Books on iPhone

Use the Books app 📖 to listen to audiobooks on your iPhone.

Play an audiobook

91

Tap Reading Now or Library, tap the audiobook cover, then tap the play button.

While the audiobook is playing, do any of the following:

- **Skip forward or back**: Tap or touch and hold the rounded arrows next to the pause button. Or, use external controls such as headphones or car controls.

  Note: To change the number of seconds to skip forward or back, go to Settings 🔘 > Books, scroll down to Audiobooks, then tap Skip Forward or Skip Back.
- **Go to a specific time**: Drag the slider below the audiobook cover left or right.
- **Adjust the volume**: Drag the slider below the pause button left or right.
- **Speed it up, or slow it down**: Tap the playback speed, 1x, in the lower-left corner to choose a different speed.
- **Set a sleep timer**: Tap 🌙, then choose a duration.
- **Play on a different device**: Tap 📡, then choose an available device such as HomePod, Apple TV, or Bluetooth speakers.
- **Go to a chapter**: Tap ☰, then tap a chapter.
  Note: Some audiobooks refer to chapters as tracks, or don't define chapters.
- **Switch to the audiobook mini-player**: Tap ▔ or swipe down anywhere on the screen; tap the mini-player at the bottom of the screen to go back to full screen.
- Close the audiobook player: Tap ▔, touch and hold the mini-player, then tap Close Audio Player.

If a Wi-Fi connection to the internet isn't available, audiobooks play over your carrier's cellular network, which may result in additional fees.

Find supplemental PDFs

Some audiobooks come with supplemental PDFs.

To find the PDFs, play the audiobook, tap 🔘, then tap View Included PDF.

Set reading goals in Books on iPhone

The Books app 📖 helps you keep track of how many minutes you read every day, and how many books and audiobooks you finish each year. You can customize your goals to spend more time reading, set new reading streaks, and share your achievements with friends.

Change your daily reading goal

You can adjust your daily reading goal depending on how many minutes you want to read per day. If you don't customize your daily reading goal, it's set to five minutes per day.

1. Tap Reading Now, then swipe down to Reading Goals.
2. Tap Today's Reading, then tap Adjust Goal.
3. Slide the counter up or down to set the minutes per day that you want to read, then tap Done.

When you reach your daily reading goal, you receive a notification from Books; tap it to get more details about your achievement, or send your achievement to friends.

To make sure you receive a notification when you reach your daily reading goal, go to Settings > Notifications > Books, then turn on Allow Notifications.

Note: To count PDFs toward your reading goal, go to Settings > Books, then turn on Include PDFs.

Change your yearly reading goal

After you finish reading a book or audiobook in Books, the Books Read This Year collection appears below Reading Goals. The default yearly reading goal is three books per year, but you can increase or decrease your goal depending on how many books you want to finish.

1. Tap Reading Now, then swipe down to Books Read This Year.
2. Tap a placeholder square, or a book cover, then tap Adjust Goal.
3. Slide the counter up or down to set the books per year that you want to read, then tap Done.

When you reach your yearly reading goal, you receive a notification from Books; tap it to get more details about your achievement, or send your achievement to friends.

See your reading streaks and records

Books lets you know how many days in a row you reach your daily reading goal and notifies you when you set a record.

To view your current reading streak and record, tap Reading Now, then swipe down to Reading Goals.

Turn on coaching

You can turn on coaching to receive encouragement and nudges to help you reach your reading goals.

1. Tap Reading Now, then tap your account icon in the top-right corner.
2. Tap Notifications, then turn on Coaching.

Turn off reading goals notifications

You can stop receiving notifications when you achieve a reading goal or set a reading streak.

1. Tap Reading Now, then tap your account in the top-right corner.
2. Tap Notifications, then turn off Goal Completion.

Turn off reading goals

Go to Settings > Books, then turn off Reading Goals.

When Reading Goals is turned off, the reading indicators in Reading Now are hidden and you don't receive reading notifications.

Clear reading data

To clear your reading data, such as time spent reading and reading streaks, go to Settings > Books, then tap Clear Reading Goals Data.

Organize books in the Books app on iPhone

In the Books app 📖 , the books and audiobooks you purchase are saved in your library and automatically sorted into collections, such as Audiobooks, Want to Read, and Finished.

Create a collection and add books to it

You can create your own collections to personalize your library.

1. Tap Library, tap Collections, then tap New Collection.
2. Name the collection, for example, Beach Reads or Book Club, then tap Done.

To add a book in your library or the Book Store to a collection, tap ••• below the book cover, tap Add to Collection, then tap the collection.

You can add the same book to multiple collections.

Sort books in your library or a collection

Choose how the books in your library are sorted and appear.

1. Tap Library, then scroll down and tap the word that appears next to Sort or Sort By at the top of the screen.
2. Choose Recent, Title, Author, or Manually.
   If you choose Manually, touch and hold a book cover, then drag it to the position you want.

Tip: Tap ≔ to view books by title or cover.

Remove books, audiobooks, and PDFs

You can remove books, audiobooks, and PDFs from Reading Now and your library collections, or hide them on your iPhone.

1. Tap Library, then tap Edit.
2. Tap the items you want to remove.
3. Tap 🗑 and select an option.

To unhide books and audiobooks that you have hidden, tap Reading Now, tap your account icon, then tap Manage Hidden Purchases.

Read PDF documents in Books on iPhone

In the Books app 📖 , you can open and save PDFs that you receive in Mail, Messages, and other apps.

Open PDFs in Books

Tap the PDF attachment to open it, tap ⬆️, then tap Books.

Share or print a PDF document

Open the PDF document, tap ⬆️, then choose a share option such as AirDrop, Mail, or Messages, or tap Print.

Mark up a PDF

Open the PDF and tap Ⓐ to use the dra

Calculator

In the Calculator app ⚏ , you can perform basic arithmetic calculations with the standard calculator. Or use the scientific calculator for exponential, logarithmic, and trigonometric functions.

Siri: Say something like: "What's 74 times 9?" or "What's 18 percent of 225?"

Use the scientific calculator

Rotate iPhone to landscape orientation.

Copy, delete, or clear numbers

- **Copy a calculation result**: Touch and hold the calculation result in the display, tap Copy, then paste the result somewhere else, such as a note or message.
- **Delete the last digit**: If you make a mistake when you enter a number, swipe left or right on the display at the top.
- **Clear the display**: Tap the Clear (C) key to delete the last entry, or tap the All Clear (AC) key to delete all entries.

Calendar

Create and edit events in Calendar on iPhone

Use the Calendar app 7 to create and edit events, appointments, and meetings.

— View list of events.

Change calendars or accounts.

— View invitations.

Siri: Say something like:

- "Set up a meeting with Gordon at 9"
- "Do I have a meeting at 10?"

- "Where is my 3:30 meeting?"

Add an event

1. In Day view, tap + at the top of the screen.
2. Enter the title of the event.
3. Tap Location or Video Call, then enter a physical location or tap FaceTime to enter a video link for a remote event.
   You can also copy a FaceTime link you created or received and paste it in the Location field.
4. Enter the start and end times for the event, the travel time, invitees, attachments, and so on. (Swipe up, if necessary, to enter all the meeting information.)
5. Tap Add.

Add an alert

You can set an alert to be reminded of an event beforehand.

1. Tap the event, then tap Edit near the top right.
2. In the event details, tap Alert.
3. Choose when you want to be reminded.
   For example, "At time of event," "5 minutes before," or another choice.

Note: If you add the address of the event's location, Calendar uses Apple Maps to look up locations, traffic conditions, and transit options to tell you when it's time to leave.

Add an attachment

You can add an attachment to a calendar event to share with invitees.

1. Tap the event, then tap Edit near the top right.
2. In the event details, tap Add attachment.
3. Locate the file you want to attach.
   To find the file, you can enter its name in the search field, scroll, tap folders to open them, tap Browse to look in other locations (such as iCloud Drive), and so on.
4. Tap Done.

To remove the attachment, tap the event, tap Edit near the top right, swipe left over the attachment, then tap Remove.

Find events in other apps

Siri can suggest events found in Mail, Messages, and Safari—such as flight reservations and hotel bookings—so you can add them easily in Calendar.

1. Go to Settings ⚙ > Calendar > Siri & Search.

2. Turn on Show Siri Suggestions in App to allow Siri to suggest events found in other apps.

To allow Siri to make suggestions in other apps based on how you use Calendar, turn on Learn from this App.

Copy and paste an event

You can copy an event and paste it to another date.

1. Touch and hold the event, then tap Copy.
2. On another date, touch and hold the time where you want to paste the event.
   When you release, the New Event screen appears and the copied event appears below Title with the date and time where you want to paste the event.

   Tip: You can also tap ┬ at the top of the screen after copying an event.
3. Tap the copied event below Title.
4. Tap Add.

Edit an event

You can change the time of an event and any of the other event details.

- **Change the time**: In Day view, touch and hold the event, then drag it to a new time, or adjust the grab points.
- **Change event details**: Tap the event, tap Edit near the top right, then in the event details, tap a setting to change it, or tap in a field to type new information.

Delete an event

In Day view, tap the event, then tap Delete Event at the bottom of the screen.

Send invitations in Calendar on iPhone

In the Calendar app ⁷ , you can send meeting and event invitations. iCloud, Microsoft Exchange, and some CalDAV servers also let you send meeting invitations. (Not all calendar servers support every feature.)

Before you begin

Before you can invite people to events you've scheduled, you need to make sure your calendar accounts are turned on.

- Go to Settings ⚙ > Calendar > Accounts, then select an account.
- Check if Calendar is turned on.

Invite others to an event

You can invite people to an event you've scheduled.

97

1. Tap the event, then tap Edit near the top of the screen.
2. Tap Invitees.
3. Enter the names or email addresses of people you want to invite, or tap ⊕ to select Contacts.
4. Tap Done.

If you don't want to be notified when someone declines a meeting, go to Settings ◉ > Calendar, then turn off Show Invitee Declines.

Note: With Microsoft Exchange and some other exchange servers, you can invite people to an event even if you're not the one who scheduled it.

Schedule an event without blocking your schedule

You can add an event to your calendar without having the timeframe appear as busy to others who send you invitations.

1. Tap the event, then tap Edit.
2. Tap Show As, then tap Free.

Quickly email attendees

You can email all attendees of an event—for example, to share event details.

1. Tap an event that has attendees.
2. Tap Invitees, then tap ✉.

Reply to invitations in Calendar on iPhone

In the Calendar app 7 , reply to meeting and event invitations you've received.

Reply to an event invitation

1. To respond to an event notification, tap it.
   Or, in Calendar, tap Inbox, then tap an invitation.
2. Tap your response—Accept, Maybe, or Decline.

To respond to an invitation you receive by email, tap the underlined text in the email, then tap Show in Calendar.

If you add comments to your response, your comments can be seen by the organizer but not by other attendees (comments may not be available for all calendars). To see events you declined, tap Calendars at the bottom of the screen, then turn on Show Declined Events.

Suggest a different meeting time

You can suggest a different time for a meeting invitation you've received.

1. Tap the meeting, then tap Propose New Time.
2. Tap the time, then enter a new one.

Depending on the capabilities of your calendar server, the organizer will receive either a counter-proposal or an email with your suggestion.

Change how you view events in Calendar on iPhone

In the Calendar app 7 , you can view one day, a week, a month, or a year at a time, or view a list of upcoming events. To change your view of Calendar, do any of the following:

- **Zoom in or out**: Tap a year, month, or day to zoom in or out on your calendar. In Week or Day view, pinch to zoom in or out.
- **View a weekly calendar**: In Day view, rotate iPhone sideways.
- **View a list of events**: In Month view, tap ☷ to see the day's events. (Tap ☷ again to return to Month view.)

Search for events in Calendar on iPhone

In the Calendar app 7 , you can search for events by title, invitees, location, and notes.

Tap 🔍, then, in the search field, enter the text you want to find.

Siri: Say something like: "What's on my calendar for Friday?"

Customize your calendar on iPhone

In the Calendar app 7 , you can choose which day of the week Calendar starts with, display week numbers, choose alternate calendars (for example, to display Chinese or Hebrew dates), override the automatic time zone, and more.

Go to Settings ⚙ > Calendar, then choose the settings and features you want.

Keep track of events in Calendar on iPhone

In the Calendar app 7 , you can customize the notifications that let you know about upcoming calendar events, invitations, and more. You can also make sure your events and other calendar information are kept up to date on all your devices.

Customize calendar notifications

1. Go to Settings ⚙ > Notifications > Calendar.
2. Turn on Allow Notifications.
3. Choose how and where you want the notifications to appear—for example, on the Lock Screen, in Notification Center, as banners at the top of the screen, with an alert sound, and so on.

Turn on customized notifications for specific calendar events

After customizing your calendar notifications, you can choose if you want these notifications to appear for various types of events.

1. Scroll down and tap Customize Notifications.
2. Turn the specific customized notifications on or off.

Keep your calendar up to date across your devices

You can use iCloud to keep your calendar information up to date on all your devices where you're signed in with the same Apple ID.

Go to Settings ⚙ > [your name] > iCloud, then turn on Calendars.

Note: If you don't see Calendars, tap Show All to see more options.

If you don't want to use iCloud for your calendar, you can sync your calendar information between your iPhone and your computer.

Set up multiple calendars on iPhone

In the Calendar app  on iPhone, you can set up multiple calendars to keep track of different kinds of events. You can keep track of all your events and appointments in one calendar, but additional calendars are easy to set up and a great way to stay organized.

Set up a calendar

1. Tap Calendars at the bottom of the screen, then tap Add Calendar.
2. Do one of the following:
   ○ **Create an iCloud calendar**: Tap Add Calendar, enter a name for the calendar, then choose a color for it.
   ○ **Subscribe to an external, read-only calendar**: Tap Add Subscription Calendar, enter the URL of the .ics file you want to subscribe to (and any other required server information), then click Subscribe.
   ○ **Add a Holiday calendar**: Tap Add Holiday Calendar, tap the holiday calendar you want to subscribe to, then tap Add.

You can also subscribe to an iCalendar (.ics) calendar by tapping a link to it.

Unsubscribe from a calendar

You can unsubscribe from a calendar you're subscribed to. When you unsubscribe, you can also report the calendar as junk.

1. Tap Calendars at the bottom of the screen.
2. Tap ⓘ next to the calendar you want to unsubscribe from.
3. Tap Unsubscribe, then Tap Unsubscribe or Unsubscribe and Report Junk.
   Note: When you tap Unsubscribe and Report Junk, the calendar is reported to Apple as a suspected junk subscription.

See multiple calendars at once

To view multiple calendars, tap Calendars at the bottom of the screen, then do any of the following:

- Select the calendars you want to view.
- Tap US Holidays to include national holidays with your events.
- Tap Birthdays to include birthdays from Contacts with your events.

Set a default calendar

You can set one of your calendars as the default calendar. When you add an event using Siri or other apps, it's added to your default calendar.

1. Go to Settings ⚙ > Calendar > Default Calendar.
2. Select the calendar you want to use as your default calendar.

Turn on calendar event alerts

You can turn on event notifications for calendars you create or subscribe to.

1. Tap Calendars at the bottom of the screen.
2. Tap ⓘ next to a calendar.
3. Go to Event Alerts below Notifications to turn event alerts on or off.
4. Tap Done.

Change a calendar's color

1. Tap Calendars at the bottom of the screen.
2. Tap ⓘ next to the calendar, then choose a color.
3. Tap Done.

For some calendar accounts, such as Google, the color is set by the server.

Set up iCloud, Google, Exchange, or Yahoo calendar accounts

1. Go to Settings ⚙ > Calendar > Accounts > Add Account.
2. Do any of the following:
    o Tap a mail service (iCloud, Microsoft Exchange, or Google, for example), then sign in.
    o Tap Other, tap Add CalDAV Account or Add Subscribed Calendar, then enter your server and account information.

Add a CalDAV account

1. Go to Settings ⚙ > Calendar > Accounts > Add Account > Other.
2. Tap Add CalDAV account.
3. Enter your server and account information.

Move an event to another calendar

Tap the event, tap Calendar, then select a calendar to move the event to.

Use the Holidays calendar on iPhone

In the Calendar app 7 , the Holidays calendar displays holidays based on the region set on your iPhone.

Note: The Holidays calendar is a subscription calendar. You can't add or delete holidays, because subscription calendars can be modified only by the calendar provider.

Show or hide holidays

1. Tap Calendars at the bottom of the screen.
2. Select or deselect US Holidays (or the holiday calendar for your country or region).

Change your primary holiday calendar to a different region

1. Go to Settings 🌐 > General > Language & Region, then tap Region.
2. Tap a region, then tap Change to [region].
3. In Calendar, tap Calendars at the bottom of the screen.
4. Deselect the Holidays calendar, then select it again.

Share iCloud calendars on iPhone

In the Calendar app 7 , you can share an iCloud calendar with other iCloud users. When you share a calendar, others can see it, and you can let them add or change events. You can also share a read-only version that anyone can view but not change.

Create an iCloud calendar

1. Tap Calendars at the bottom of the screen.
2. Tap Add Calendar.
3. Type a name for the new calendar, then tap Done.

Share an iCloud calendar

You can choose to share a calendar with one or more people in iCloud. Those you invite receive an invitation to join the calendar.

1. Tap Calendars at the bottom of the screen.
2. Tap ⓘ next to the iCloud calendar you want to share.
3. Tap Add Person, then enter a name or email address, or tap ⊕ to browse your contacts.
4. Tap Add.

Change a person's access to a shared calendar

After you invite a person to share your calendar, you can turn on or off their ability to edit the calendar, or stop sharing the calendar with that person.

1. Tap Calendars, tap ⓘ next to the shared calendar, then tap the person's name.
2. Do any of the following:
   o Turn on or off Allow Editing.
   o Tap Stop Sharing.

Turn off notifications for shared calendars

When someone modifies a calendar you're sharing, you're notified of the change. You can turn off notifications, if you don't want to receive them.

1. Go to Settings ⚙ > Notifications > Calendar > Customize Notifications.
2. Turn off Shared Calendar Changes.

Share a read-only calendar with anyone

1. Tap Calendars, then tap ⓘ next to the iCloud calendar you want to share.
2. Turn on Public Calendar, then tap Share Link to copy or send the URL for your calendar.
3. Choose a method for sending the URL—Messages, Mail, and so on.

Anyone you send the URL to can use it to subscribe to the calendar using a compatible app, such as Calendar for macOS.

Delete a calendar

1. Tap Calendars at the bottom of the screen.
2. Tap ⓘ next to the iCloud calendar you want to delete.
3. Tap Delete Calendar at the bottom of the list.

Camera

iPhone camera basics

Learn how to take photos with Camera 📷 on your iPhone. Choose from camera modes such as Photo, Video, Cinematic, Pano, and Portrait, and zoom in or out to frame your shot.

Open Camera

To open Camera, do any of the following:

- Tap Camera 📷 on the iPhone Home Screen.
- Swipe left on the iPhone Lock Screen.
- Touch and hold 📷 on the iPhone Lock Screen.
- Open Control Center, then tap 📷.
  Siri: Say something like: "Open Camera."

Note: For your security, a green dot appears in the top-right corner of the screen when Camera is in use.

Take a photo

Open Camera, then tap the Shutter button or press either volume button to take the shot.

Switch between camera modes

Photo is the standard mode that you see when you open Camera. Use Photo mode to take still photos and Live Photos. Swipe left or right on the camera screen to choose one of the following camera modes:

- **Video**: Record a video
- **Time-lapse**: Create a time-lapse video of motion over a period of time

- **Slo-mo**: Record a video with a slow-motion effect
- **Pano**: Capture a panoramic landscape or other scene
- **Portrait**: Apply a depth-of-field effect to your photos
- **Cinematic**: Apply a depth-of-field effect to your videos
- **Square**: Take photos with a square ratio.

    On iPhone 11 and later, tap ⌄, then tap 4:3 to choose between square, 4:3, or 16:9 aspect ratios.

Zoom in or out

- Toggle between 0.5x, 1x, 2x, 2.5x, and 3x to quickly zoom in or out (depending on your model). For a more precise zoom, touch and hold the zoom controls, then drag the slider right or left.

Use iPhone camera tools to set up your shot

Before taking a photo, you can use Camera 📷 tools to customize and improve your shot.

Adjust the camera's focus and exposure

Before you take a photo, the iPhone camera automatically sets the focus and exposure, and face detection balances the exposure across many faces. If you want to manually adjust the focus and exposure, do the following:

1. Open Camera.
2. Tap the screen to show the automatic focus area and exposure setting.
3. Tap where you want to move the focus area.
4. Next to the focus area, drag ☀ up or down to adjust the exposure.
   To lock your manual focus and exposure settings for upcoming shots, touch and hold the focus area until you see AE/AF Lock; tap the screen to unlock settings.

You can precisely set and lock the exposure for upcoming shots. Tap ⌄, tap ±, then move the slider to adjust the exposure. The exposure locks until the next time you open Camera. To save the exposure control so it's not reset when you open Camera, go to Settings ⚙ > Camera > Preserve Settings, then turn on Exposure Adjustment.

Turn the flash on or off

Your iPhone camera is set to automatically use the flash when needed. To manually control the flash before you take a photo, do the following:

- Tap ⚡ to turn the automatic flash on or off. Tap ⌄, then tap ⚡ below the frame to choose Auto, On, or Off.

Take a photo with a filter

Use a filter to give your photo a color effect.

1. Open Camera, choose Photo or Portrait mode, then do one of the following:
   - Tap ⌄, then tap ⊛.
2. Below the viewer, swipe the filters left or right to preview them; tap one to apply it.

You can remove or change a photo's filter in Photos.

Use the timer

You can set a timer on your iPhone camera to give yourself time to get in the shot.

To set a timer, open Camera, then do one of the following:

- Tap ⌃, tap 🕐, choose 3s or 10s, then tap the Shutter button to start the timer.

Use a grid to straighten your shot

To display a grid on the camera screen that can help you straighten and compose your shot, go to Settings ⚙ > Camera, then turn on Grid.

After you take a photo, you can use the editing tools in the Photos app to further align shots and adjust horizontal and vertical perspective.

Apply Photographic Styles with your iPhone Camera

On iPhone 14 models, you can apply a Photographic Style that customizes how Camera 📷 captures photos. Choose from the preset styles—Rich Contrast, Vibrant, Warm, or Cool—then customize them further by adjusting the tone and warmth values. Camera applies your choice every time you take a photo in Photo mode. You can change and adjust Photographic Styles right in Camera.

Choose a Photographic Style

Camera is automatically set to Standard—a balanced style that is true to life. To apply a different Photographic Style, do the following:

1. Open Camera, then tap ⌃.
2. Tap 🎞, then swipe left to preview the different styles:
    ○ **Rich Contrast**: Darker shadows, richer colors, and stronger contrast create a dramatic look.
    ○ **Vibrant**: Wonderfully bright and vivid colors create a brilliant yet natural look.
    ○ **Warm**: Golden undertones create a warmer look.
    ○ **Cool**: Blue undertones create a cooler look.
3. To customize a Photographic Style, tap the Tone and Warmth controls below the frame, then drag the slider left or right to adjust the value. Tap ↺ to reset the values.
4. Tap 🎞 to apply the Photographic Style.

To change or adjust a Photographic Style that you set, tap 🎞 at the top of the screen.

You can also change Photographic Styles in Settings: go to Settings ⚙ > Camera > Photographic Styles.

Take Live Photos with your iPhone camera

Use Camera 📷 to take Live Photos with your iPhone. A Live Photo captures what happens just before and after you take your photo, including the audio. You take a Live Photo just like you do a normal photo.

1. Open Camera.
2. Make sure Camera is set to Photo mode and that Live Photo is turned on.

   When Live Photo is on, the Live Photo button ◎ appears at the top of the camera screen. A slash through the Live Photo button means that the feature is off. Tap the button to turn Live Photo on or off.
3. Tap the Shutter button to take a Live Photo.
4. To play the Live Photo, tap the photo thumbnail at the bottom of the screen, then touch and hold the screen to play it.

Capture action shots with Burst mode on your iPhone camera

Use Burst mode with Camera 📷 to capture a moving subject, or when you want to take multiple high-speed photos so that you have a range of photos to choose from. You can take Burst photos with the rear and front-facing cameras.

1. Open Camera.
2. Do one of the following:
   ○ Swipe the Shutter button to the left.
3. Lift your finger to stop.
4. To select the photos you want to keep, tap the Burst thumbnail, then tap Select. Gray dots below the thumbnails mark the suggested photos to keep.
5. Tap the circle in the lower-right corner of each photo you want to save as an individual photo, then tap Done.

To delete the entire Burst, tap the thumbnail, then tap 🗑.

Tip: You can also press and hold the volume up button to take Burst shots. Go to Settings ⚙ > Camera, then turn on Use Volume Up for Burst (available on iPhone XS, iPhone XR, and later).

Take a selfie with your iPhone camera

Use Camera 📷 to take a selfie in Photo mode and Portrait mode (on iPhone X and later), or to record in Video mode.

To learn about camera modes, see Switch between camera modes.

1. Open Camera.
2. Tap 🔄 or 🔄 (depending on your model) to switch to the front-facing camera.
3. Hold your iPhone in front of you.
   Tip: Tap the arrows inside the frame to increase the field of view.
4. Tap the Shutter button or press either volume button to take the shot or start recording.

To take a selfie that captures the shot as you see it in the front-facing camera frame, rather than reversing it, go to Settings ⚙ > Camera, then turn on Mirror Front Camera.

Take panoramic photos with your iPhone camera

Use Camera 📷 to take a panoramic photo of your surroundings in Pano mode.

1. Choose Pano mode.
2. Tap the Shutter button.
3. Pan slowly in the direction of the arrow, keeping it on the center line.
4. To finish, tap the Shutter button again.

Tap the arrow to pan in the opposite direction. To pan vertically, rotate iPhone to landscape orientation. You can reverse the direction of a vertical pan, too.

Take macro photos and videos with your iPhone camera

Camera 📷 oniPhone 14 Pro and iPhone 14 Pro Max uses the Ultra Wide camera to capture macro photography—stunning close-ups in sharp focus. You can take macro photos and Live Photos, and shoot macro slow-motion and time-lapse videos.

Take a macro photo or video

1. Open Camera, then select Photo or Video mode.
2. Get close to the subject—as close as 2 centimeters. The camera will automatically switch to the Ultra Wide camera.
3. Tap the Shutter button to take a photo or the Record button to start and stop recording video.

Take a macro slow-motion or time-lapse video

1. Open Camera, then select Slo-mo or Time-lapse mode.
2. Tap .5x to switch to the Ultra Wide camera, then move close to the subject.
3. Tap the Record button to start and stop recording.

Control automatic macro switching

You can control when the camera automatically switches to the Ultra Wide camera for capturing macro photos and videos.

1. Go to Settings ⚙ > Camera, then turn on Macro Control.
2. Open Camera, then get close to your subject.

   When you get within macro distance of your subject, 🌷 appears on the screen.

3. Tap 🌷 to turn off automatic macro switching.
   Tip: If the photo or video becomes blurry, you can back up or tap .5x to switch to the Ultra Wide camera.
4. Tap 🌼 to turn automatic macro switching back on.

Automatic macro switching is re-enabled the next time you use Camera within macro distance. If you want to maintain your Macro Control setting between camera sessions, go to Settings > Camera > Preserve Settings and turn on Macro Control.

Take Portrait mode photos with your iPhone camera

With Camera 📷 on models that support Portrait mode, you can apply a depth-of-field effect that keeps your subject—people, pets, objects, and more—sharp while creating a beautifully blurred foreground and background. You can apply and adjust different lighting effects to your Portrait mode photos, and on iPhone X and later, you can even take a selfie in Portrait mode.

Take a photo in Portrait mode

You can apply studio-quality lighting effects to your Portrait mode photos.

1. Open Camera, then select Portrait mode.
2. Follow the tips onscreen to frame your subject in the yellow portrait box.
3. Drag ⬡ to choose a lighting effect:
   o **Natural Light**: The face is in sharp focus against a blurred background.
   o **Studio Light**: The face is brightly lit, and the photo has an overall clean look.
   o **Contour Light**: The face has dramatic shadows with highlights and lowlights.
   o **Stage Light**: The face is spotlit against a deep black background.
   o **Stage Light Mono**: The effect is similar to Stage Light, but the photo is in classic black and white.
   o **High-Key Light Mono**: Creates a grayscale subject on a white background (available on iPhone XS, iPhone XR, and later).
4. Tap the Shutter button to take the shot.

After you take a photo in Portrait mode, you can remove the Portrait mode effect if you don't like it. In the Photos app 🌸 , open the photo, tap Edit, then tap Portrait to turn the effect on or off.

Note: On iPhone 14 Pro and iPhone 14 Pro Max, Night mode turns on when you take a Portrait mode photo in low-light situations with the wide (1x) lens.

Adjust Depth Control in Portrait mode

On iPhone XS, iPhone XR, and later, use the Depth Control slider to adjust the level of background blur in your Portrait mode photos.

1. Open Camera, select Portrait mode, then frame your subject.
2. Tap 🔵 in the top-right corner of the screen.
   The Depth Control slider appears below the frame.
3. Drag the slider to the right or left to adjust the effect.
4. Tap the Shutter button to take the shot.

After you take a photo in Portrait mode, you can use the Depth Control slider in Photos to further adjust the background blur effect.

Adjust Portrait Lighting effects in Portrait mode

On iPhone XS, iPhone XR, and later, you can virtually adjust the position and intensity of each Portrait Lighting effect to sharpen eyes or brighten and smooth facial features.

1. Open Camera, select Portrait mode, then drag ⬡ to choose a lighting effect.
2. Tap ⬢ at the top of the screen.
   The Portrait Lighting slider appears below the frame.
3. Drag the slider to the right or left to adjust the effect.
4. Tap the Shutter button to take the shot.

After you take a photo in Portrait mode, you can use the Portrait Lighting slider in Photos to further adjust the lighting effect.

Take Night mode photos with your iPhone camera

On iPhone 14 models, Camera 📷 can use Night mode to capture more detail and brighten your shots in low-light situations. The length of the exposure in Night mode is determined automatically, but you can experiment with the manual controls.

Tip: Use a tripod for even more detailed Night mode photos.

Night mode is available on the following iPhone models and cameras:

- iPhone 14 Pro, iPhone 14 Pro Max: Ultra Wide (0.5x) camera, Wide (1x) camera, Telephoto (3x) camera, and front camera
- iPhone 14 models: Ultra Wide (0.5x) camera, Wide (1x) camera, and front camera

Night mode is also available in Portrait mode on iPhone 14 Pro and iPhone 14 Pro Max.

1. Open Camera.

   In low-light situations, Night mode turns on automatically. At the top of the screen, ⬤ turns yellow and a number appears next to it to indicate how many seconds the camera will take to expose the photo.

2. To experiment with Night mode, tap ⬤, then use the slider below the frame to choose between the Auto and Max timers. With Auto, the time is determined automatically; Max uses the longest time. The setting you choose is saved for your next Night mode shot.

3. Tap the Shutter button, then hold the camera still to take your shot.
   Crosshairs appear in the frame if your iPhone detects movement during capture—align the crosshairs to help you reduce motion and improve the shot.
   To stop taking a Night mode shot mid-capture, tap the Stop button below the slider.

You can take Night mode selfies and time-lapse videos with all iPhone 14 models. You can capture Portrait mode photos with Night mode on iPhone 14 Pro and iPhone 14 Pro Max.

Take Apple ProRAW photos with your iPhone camera

On iPhone 14 Pro and iPhone 14 Pro Max, you can use Camera 📷 to take photos in Apple ProRAW. Apple ProRAW combines the information of a standard RAW format along with iPhone image processing to offer additional creative control when you make adjustments to exposure, color, and white balance.

Apple ProRAW is available on all cameras, including the front camera. Apple ProRAW isn't supported in Portrait mode.

Set up Apple ProRAW

To set up Apple ProRAW, go to Settings ⚙ > Camera > Formats, then turn on Apple ProRAW.

Note: Apple ProRAW photos retain more information about the images, resulting in larger file sizes.

Take a photo with Apple ProRAW

1. Open Camera, then tap (RAW) to turn ProRAW on.
2. Take your shot.

   As you shoot, you can toggle between (RAW) and (RAW) to turn ProRAW on and off. To preserve your ProRAW setting, go to Settings > Camera > Preserve Settings, then turn on Apple ProRAW.

Change Apple ProRAW resolution

On iPhone 14 Pro and iPhone 14 Pro Max, you can capture ProRAW photos in 12 MP and 48 MP.

1. Go to Settings ⚙ > Camera > Formats.
2. Turn on Apple ProRAW (green is on), tap ProRAW Resolution, then choose 12 MP or 48 MP.

Adjust the shutter volume on your iPhone camera

You can adjust the sound of the shutter in Camera 📷, or mute it using the Ring/Silent switch on the side of your iPhone.

Adjust the shutter sound

When Camera is open, swipe down from the top-right corner of the screen to open Control Center, then drag 🔊 to adjust the sound.

Note: The shutter doesn't make a sound when Live Photos ⊚ is turned on.

Mute the shutter sound

Mute the shutter sound using the Ring/Silent switch on the side of your iPhone. (In some countries or regions, muting is disabled.)

Adjust HDR camera settings on iPhone

HDR (high dynamic range) in Camera 📷 helps you get great shots in high-contrast situations. iPhone takes several photos in rapid succession at different exposures and blends them together to bring more highlight and shadow detail to your photos.

By default, iPhone takes photos in HDR (for the rear camera and the front camera) when it's most effective. iPhone 14 models record video in HDR to capture true-to-life color and contrast.

Turn off automatic HDR

By default, iPhone automatically uses HDR when it's most effective.

Keep the non-HDR version of a photo

By default, the HDR version of a photo is saved in Photos.

Go to Settings ⚙ > Camera, then turn on Keep Normal Photo.

Turn HDR video off and on

OniPhone 14 models, iPhone records video in Dolby Vision HDR for true-to-life color and contrast. To turn off HDR video recording, go to Settings ⚙ > Camera > Record Video, then turn off HDR Video.

Record videos with your iPhone camera

Use Camera 📷 to record videos and QuickTake videos on your iPhone. Learn how to change modes to take Cinematic, slow-motion, and time-lapse videos.

Note: For your privacy, a green dot appears in the top-right corner of the screen when Camera is in use.

Record a video

1. Open Camera, then select Video mode.
2. Tap the Record button or press either volume button to start recording. While recording, you can do the following:
   o Press the white Shutter button to snap a still photo.
   o Pinch the screen to zoom in and out.
   o For a more precise zoom on models with Dual and Triple camera systems, touch and hold 1x, then drag the slider to the left.
3. Tap the Record button or press either volume button to stop recording.

By default, video records at 30 frames per second (fps). Depending on your model, you can choose other frame rates and video resolution settings in Settings ⚙ > Camera > Record Video. Faster frame rates and higher resolutions result in larger video files.

Use Action mode

On iPhone 14 models, Action mode provides improved stabilization while recording in Video mode. Tap 🏃 at the top of the screen to turn Action mode on and 🏃 to turn it off.

Note: Action mode works best in bright light. If you want to use Action mode in lower light, go to Settings ⚙ > Camera > Record Video, then turn on Action Mode Lower Light. Action mode has a maximum capture resolution of 2.8K.

Record a QuickTake video

You can record a QuickTake video. A QuickTake video is a video you record in Photo mode. While you record a QuickTake video, you can move the Record button into the lock position and keep taking still photos.

1. Open Camera in Photo mode, then touch and hold the Shutter button to start recording a QuickTake video.
2. Slide the Shutter button to the right and let go over the lock for hands-free recording.
   - Both the Record and Shutter buttons appear below the frame—tap the Shutter button to take a still photo while recording.
   - Swipe up to zoom in on your subject, or if you're recording hands-free, you can pinch out on the screen to zoom in.
3. Tap the Record button to stop recording.

Tip: Press and hold the volume up or volume down button to start recording a QuickTake video in Photo mode.

Tap the thumbnail to view the QuickTake video in the Photos app.

Record a slow-motion video

When you record a video in Slo-mo mode, your video records as normal and you see the slow-motion effect when you play it back. You can also edit your video so that the slow-motion action starts and stops at a specific time.

1. Open Camera, then select Slo-mo mode.

   On iPhone 14 models, you can tap 🔄 to record in Slo-mo mode with the front camera.
2. Tap the Record button or press either volume button to start recording.
   You can tap the Shutter button to take a still photo while recording.
3. Tap the Record button or press either volume button to stop recording.

To set a portion of the video to play in slow motion and the rest at regular speed, tap the video thumbnail, then tap Edit. Slide the vertical bars below the frame viewer to define the section you want to play back in slow motion.

Depending on your model, you can change the slow motion frame rate and resolution. To change slow-motion recording settings, go to Settings ⚙ > Camera > Record Slo-mo.

Tip: Use quick toggles to adjust the video resolution and frame rate while you record.

Record a time-lapse video

Capture footage at selected intervals to create a time-lapse video of an experience over a period of time—such as a setting sun or traffic flowing.

1. Open Camera, then select Time-lapse mode.
2. Set up your iPhone where you want to capture a scene in motion.
3. Tap the Record button to start recording; tap it again to stop recording.

Tip: Use a tripod to capture time-lapse videos with more detail and brightness when recording in low-light situations.

Record ProRes videos with your iPhone camera

On iPhone 14 Pro and iPhone 14 Pro Max, you can use Camera 📷 to record and edit videos in ProRes, which offers higher color fidelity and less compression.

ProRes is available on all cameras, including the front camera. ProRes isn't supported in Cinematic, Time-lapse, or Slo-Mo mode.

Note: ProRes videos result in larger file sizes. ProRes is available for recording up to 4K at 30 fps, except on 128GB iPhone models, where recording is only available at 1080p at 30 fps.

Set up ProRes

To set up ProRes, go to Settings ⚙ > Camera > Formats, then turn on Apple ProRes.

Record a video with ProRes

1. Open Camera, select Video mode, then tap ⬭ProRes to turn ProRes on.
2. Tap the Record button or press either volume button to start recording.
   While recording with the back camera, you can pinch to zoom in or out, tap .5x, 1x, 2x, and 3x (depending on your model) to toggle between lenses, or touch and hold the lens picker, then slide the dial for more precise zoom control.
3. Tap the Record button or press either volume button to stop recording.
4. Tap ⬭ProRes when you want to turn off ProRes.

Record video in Cinematic mode with your iPhone camera

Cinematic mode applies a depth-of-field effect that keeps the subject of your video sharp while creating a beautifully blurred foreground and background. iPhone automatically identifies the subject of the video and keeps it in focus throughout the recording; if a new subject is identified, iPhone automatically transitions the point of focus. You can also manually adjust the point of focus while you record, or change it later in the Photos app. Cinematic mode is available on all iPhone 14 models.

1. Open Camera, then select Cinematic mode.
   On iPhone 14 Pro and iPhone 14 Pro Max, you can tap 3 next to 1x before recording to zoom in.

   To adjust the depth-of-field effect, tap 𝒇, then drag the slider left or right before recording.
2. Tap the Record button or press either volume button to start recording.
   o A yellow frame on the screen indicates the person in focus; a gray frame indicates a person is detected, but not in focus. Tap the gray box to change the focus; tap again to lock the focus on that person.
   o If there isn't a person in the video, tap anywhere on the screen to set the focus point.
   o Touch and hold the screen to lock the focus at a single distance.
3. Tap the Record button or press either volume button to stop recording.

Tip: On iPhone 14 models, you can use quick toggles at the top of the screen to change the video resolution and frame rate.

After you record a video in Cinematic mode, you can remove or change the cinematic effect.

Change the camera's video recording settings on iPhone

By default, Camera 📷 records video at 30 frames per second (fps). Depending on your iPhone model, you can choose other frame rates and video resolution settings. Faster frame rates and higher resolutions result in larger video files.

You can also use quick toggles to easily change video resolution and frame rates right on the camera screen.

Use quick toggles to change video resolution and frame rate

In Video mode, use quick toggles at the top of the screen to change the video resolution and frame rates available on your iPhone.

Tap the quick toggles in the top-right corner to switch between HD or 4K recording and 24, 25, 30, or 60 fps in Video mode.

On iPhone 14 models, quick toggles are available in Cinematic mode to switch between HD or 4K and 24, 25, or 30 fps.

Adjust Auto FPS settings

iPhone can improve the video quality in low-light situations by automatically reducing the frame rate to 24 fps.

Go to Settings ⚙️ > Camera > Record Video, then do one of the following:

- Tap Auto FPS, then apply Auto FPS to only 30-fps video or to both 30- and 60-fps video.

Turn stereo recording on and off

iPhone uses multiple microphones to achieve stereo sound. To turn off stereo recording, go to Settings ⚙️ > Camera, then turn off Record Stereo Sound.

Turn HDR video off and on

On iPhone 14 models, iPhone records video in HDR and shares HDR videos with devices using iOS 13.4, iPadOS 13.4, macOS 10.15.4, or later; other devices receive an SDR version of the same video. To turn off HDR recording, go to Settings ⚙️ > Camera > Record Video, then turn off HDR Video.

Turn Lock Camera on and off

The Lock Camera setting prevents automatic switching between cameras while recording video.

Lock Camera is off by default. To turn on Lock Camera, go to Settings ⚙️ > Camera > Record Video, then turn on Lock Camera.

Turn Enhanced Stabilization off and on

The Enhanced Stabilization setting zooms in slightly to provide improved stabilization while recording in Video mode and Cinematic mode. Enhanced Stabilization is on by default. To turn Enhanced Stabilization off, go to Settings ⚙️ > Camera > Record Video, then turn off Enhanced Stabilization.

Save camera settings on iPhone

You can save the last camera mode, filter, lighting, depth, and Live Photo settings you used so they're not reset when you next open Camera 📷.

1. Go to Settings 🔘 > Camera > Preserve Settings.
2. Turn on any of the following:
   - **Camera Mode**: Save the last camera mode you used, such as Video or Pano.
   - **Creative Controls**: Save the last settings you used for the filter, lighting option, or depth control.
   - **Macro Control**: Preserve the Auto Macro setting rather than automatically using the Ultra Wide camera to capture macro photos and videos.
   - **Exposure Adjustment**: Save the exposure control setting.
   - **Night Mode**: Save the Night mode setting rather than reset to Auto.
   - **Portrait Zoom**: Save the Portrait mode zoom rather than reset to the default lens (on iPhone 14 Pro and iPhone 14 Pro Max).
   - **Action Mode**: Keep the Action Mode setting turned on rather than reset to off.
   - **Apple ProRAW**: Save the Apple ProRAW setting (on iPhone 14 Pro and iPhone 14 Pro Max).
   - **Apple ProRes**: Save the Apple ProRes setting (on iPhone 14 Pro and iPhone 14 Pro Max).
   - **Live Photo**: Save the Live Photo setting.

Change advanced camera settings on iPhone

Learn about advanced Camera 📷 features that let you capture photos faster, apply tailored and enhanced looks to your photos, and view content outside the camera frame.

Turn View Outside the Frame off and on

The camera preview displays content outside the frame to show you what can be captured by using another lens in the camera system with a wider field of view. To turn off this display, go to Settings 🔘 > Camera, then turn off View Outside the Frame.

Turn Prioritize Faster Shooting off and on

The Prioritize Faster Shooting setting modifies how images are processed—allowing you to capture more photos when you rapidly tap the Shutter button.

Prioritize Faster Shooting is on by default. To turn off Prioritize Faster Shooting, go to Settings 🔘 > Camera, then turn off Prioritize Faster Shooting.

Turn Lens Correction off and on

The Lens Correction setting adjusts photos taken with the front camera or Ultra Wide camera for more natural-looking results.

Lens Correction is on by default. To turn off Lens Correction, go to Settings 🔘 > Camera, then turn off Lens Correction.

Turn Scene Detection off and on

Scene Detection is on by default. To turn off Scene Detection, go to Settings ⚙ > Camera, then turn off Scene Detection.

View, share, and print photos on iPhone

All photos and videos you take with Camera 📷 are saved in Photos. With iCloud Photos turned on, all new photos and videos are automatically uploaded and available in Photos on all your devices that are set up with iCloud Photos (with iOS 8.1, iPadOS 13, or later).

Note: If Location Services is turned on in Settings ⚙ > Privacy & Security > Locations Services, photos and videos are tagged with location data that can be used by apps and photo-sharing websites.

View your photos

1. Open Camera, then tap the thumbnail image in the lower-left corner.
2. Swipe left or right to see the photos you've taken recently.
3. Tap the screen to show or hide the controls.
4. Tap All Photos to see all your photos and videos saved in Photos.

Share and print your photos

1. While viewing a photo, tap ⬆.
2. To share your photo, select an option such as AirDrop, Mail, or Messages.
3. To print your photo, swipe up to select Print from the list of actions.

Upload photos and keep them up to date across devices

Use iCloud Photos to upload photos and videos from your iPhone to iCloud and then access them on other devices where you're signed in with the same Apple ID. iCloud Photos is useful if you want to keep your photos up to date across multiple devices or save space on your iPhone.

To turn on iCloud Photos, go to Settings ⚙ > Photos.

Use Live Text with your iPhone camera

Camera 📷 can copy, share, look up, and translate text that appears within the camera frame. Camera also provides quick actions to easily call phone numbers, visit websites, convert currencies, and more, based on the text that appears in the frame.

1. Open Camera, then position iPhone so the text appears within the camera frame.
2. After the yellow frame appears around detected text, tap 🔲, then do any of the following:
   o **Copy Text**: Copy text to paste into another app such as Notes or Messages.
   o **Select All**: Select all the text within the frame.
   o **Look Up**: Show personalized web suggestions.
   o **Translate**: Translate text.
   o **Search the web**: Look up the selected text on the web.
   o **Share**: Share text using AirDrop, Messages, Mail, or other available options.

Note: You can also touch and hold the text, then use the grab points to select specific text and perform the actions above.

Tap a quick action at the bottom of the screen to do things like make a phone call, visit a website, start an email, convert currencies, and more.

3. Tap ⬚ to return to Camera.

To turn off Live Text on your iPhone camera, go to Settings ⊚ > Camera, then turn off Show Detected Text.

Scan a QR code with your iPhone camera

You can use Camera ⬚ or the Code Scanner to scan Quick Response (QR) codes for links to websites, apps, coupons, tickets, and more. The camera automatically detects and highlights a QR code.

Use the camera to read a QR code

1. Open Camera, then position iPhone so that the code appears on the screen.
2. Tap the notification that appears on the screen to go to the relevant website or app.

Open the Code Scanner from Control Center

1. Go to Settings ⊚ > Control Center, then tap ⊕ next to Code Scanner.
2. Open Control Center, tap the Code Scanner, then position iPhone so that the code appears on the screen.
3. To add more light, tap the flashlight to turn it on.

Clock

See the time in cities worldwide on iPhone

Use the Clock app ⬚ to see the local time in different time zones around the world.

Siri: Say something like: "What time is it?" or "What time is it in London?

1. Tap World Clock.
2. To manage your list of cities, tap Edit, then do any of the following:

   ○ **Add a city**: Tap ＋ , then choose a city.

   ○ Delete a city: Tap ⊖ .

   ○ **Reorder the cities**: Drag ≡ up or down.

Set an alarm on iPhone

In the Clock app ⬚, you can set alarms for any time of day and have them repeat on one or more days of the week.

Siri: Say something like: "Set an alarm for 7 a.m."

Note: You can also set up a wake up alarm as part of a full sleep schedule (including bedtimes, wake up times, and more) in the Health app. If you don't want to set up a sleep schedule, you can set a regular alarm in Clock for the time you want to wake up.

Set a regular alarm

You can set regular alarms for any time, including one for the time you want to wake up. A regular alarm is unrelated to any sleep schedule.

1. Tap Alarm, then tap ╋ .
2. Set the time, then choose any of the following options:
    ○ **Repeat**: Choose the days of the week.
    ○ **Label**: Give the alarm a name, like "Water the plants."
    ○ **Sound**: Choose a vibration, song, or ringtone.
    ○ **Snooze**: Give yourself a few more minutes of sleep.
3. Tap Save.

To change the alarm, tap Edit at the top left, then tap the alarm time.

Turn off a regular alarm

Tap the button next to the alarm time.

Remove a regular alarm

To remove a regular alarm in the Clock app, tap Edit at the top left, tap the Delete button ⊖, then tap Delete.

Change the next wake up alarm

The wake up alarm in the Clock app shows the next wake up time in your sleep schedule (if you've set up a sleep schedule in the Health app). Although you don't set the wake up alarm in Clock, you can make changes to it in Clock after you've set up a sleep schedule.

1. Tap Alarm, then tap Change.
2. Adjust your sleep and wake times.

    Drag ⏰ to change your wake up time, 🛏 to change your bedtime, or the semicircle between the icons to shift both times simultaneously.
3. Scroll down to Alarm Options, then change any of the following:
    ○ **Alarm**: Tap to turn the alarm off or on.
    ○ **Sounds & Haptics**: Tap to choose a vibration or ringtone.
    ○ **Alarm volume**: Drag the slider.
    ○ **Snooze**: Turn on to give yourself a few more minutes of sleep.

To make changes to your sleep schedule that extend beyond your next wake up alarm, tap Edit Sleep Schedule in Health.

Turn off the next wake up alarm

You can turn off the next wake up alarm in your sleep schedule, or you can turn off all wake up alarms for a sleep schedule.

1. Tap Alarm, then tap Change.
2. Scroll down to Alarm Options, then turn off Alarm.
3. Tap Done, then choose one of the following:

o   Change Next Alarm Only
o   Change This Schedule

Remove the wake up alarm

You can remove the wake up alarm by deleting or turning off your sleep schedules.

Do one of the following:

- Tap Change, tap Edit Sleep Schedule in Health, then turn off Sleep Schedule.
- Go to the Health app, then delete a sleep schedule or turn off all sleep schedules.

Use the timer or stopwatch on iPhone

In the Clock app ⏰, you can use the timer to count down from a specified time. You can also use the stopwatch to measure the duration of an event.

Siri: Say something like: "Set the timer for 3 minutes" or "Stop the timer."

Track time with the stopwatch

1. Tap Stopwatch.
   To switch between the digital and analog faces, swipe the stopwatch.
2. Tap Start.
   The timing continues even if you open another app or if iPhone goes to sleep.
3. To record a lap or split, tap Lap.
4. Tap Stop to record the final time.
5. Tap Reset to clear the stopwatch.

Set the timer

1. Tap Timer.
2. Set the duration of time and a sound to play when the timer ends.
   Tip: If you want to fall asleep while playing audio or video, you can set the timer to stop the playback. Tap When Timer Ends, then tap Stop Playing at the bottom.
3. Tap Start.

The timer continues even if you open another app or if iPhone goes to sleep.

Compass

Use the compass on iPhone

The Compass app 🧭 shows you the direction iPhone is pointing, your current location, and elevation.

Note: Your coordinates and elevation may not be available in certain countries or regions.

See your bearings, coordinates, and elevation

Your bearings, coordinates, and elevation are shown at the bottom of the screen.

1. For accurate bearings, hold iPhone flat to align the crosshairs at the center of the compass.

2. To lock your current direction, tap the compass dial.
   A red band appears when you're off course.

To open your location in Maps, tap the coordinates at the bottom of the screen.

Allow Compass to access your location

If Compass doesn't see your location, make sure you've turned on Location Services.

1. Go to Settings ⚙ > Privacy & Security > Location Services, then turn on Location Services.
2. Tap Compass, then tap While Using the App.

Important: The accuracy of the compass can be affected by magnetic or environmental interference; even the magnets in the iPhone EarPods can cause a deviation. Use the digital compass only for basic navigation assistance. Don't rely on it to determine precise location, proximity, distance, or direction.

Contacts

Add and use contact information on iPhone

In the Contacts app 📇 , you can view and edit your contacts lists from personal, business, and other accounts. You can also create contacts and set up a contact card with your own information.

Siri: Say something like:

- "What's my brother's work address?"
- "Sarah Milos is my sister"
- "Send a message to my sister"

Create a contact

Tap +.

Siri also suggests new contacts based on your use of other apps, such as email you receive in Mail and invitations you receive in Calendar. (To turn this feature off, go to Settings ⚙ > Contacts > Siri & Search, then turn off Show Siri Suggestions for Contacts.)

Based on how you use Contacts, Siri also provides contact information suggestions in other apps. (To turn this feature off, go to Settings ⚙ > Contacts > Siri & Search, then turn off Learn from this App.)

Find a contact

Tap the search field at the top of the contacts list, then enter a name, address, phone number, or other contact information.

You can also search your contacts using Search.

Share a contact

Tap a contact, tap Share Contact, then choose a method for sending the contact information.

Sharing the contact sends all of the info from the contact's card.

Quickly reach a contact

To start a message, make a phone call or a FaceTime call, compose an email, or send money with Apple Pay, tap a button below the contact's name.

To change the default phone number or email address for a contact method, touch and hold the button for that method below the contact's name, then tap a selection in the list.

Delete a contact

1. Go to the contact's card, then tap Edit.
2. Scroll down, then tap Delete Contact.

Edit contacts on iPhone

In the Contacts app , assign a photo to a contact, change a label, add a birthday, and more.

1. Tap a contact, then tap Edit.
2. Do any of the following:
   - **Assign a photo to a contact**: Tap Add Photo. You can take a photo or add one from the Photos app.
   - **Add a pronunciation**: Tap Edit, scroll down and tap "add field," select a pronunciation name field, then type how to say your contact's name. Siri will then use this pronunciation when speaking their name.
   - **Change a label**: Tap the label, then select one in the list, or tap Add Custom Label to create one of your own.
   - Add a birthday, social profile, related name, and more: Tap next to the item.
   - Allow calls or texts from a contact to override Do Not Disturb: Tap Ringtone or Text Tone, then turn on Emergency Bypass.
   - **Add notes**: Tap the Notes field.
   - **Add a prefix, phonetic name, and more**: Tap "add field," then select an item in the list.
   - Delete contact information: Tap next to a field.
3. When you're finished, tap Done.

On models with Dual SIM, when you call or text a contact, iPhone uses the same line you used for your previous communication with this contact by default. To choose a preferred line for phone calls and SMS/MMS message conversations, select the contact, tap default (below the contact's name), then choose a line.

To change how your contacts are sorted and displayed, go to Settings ⚙ > Contacts.

Add your contact info on iPhone

In the Contacts app ⊙, add your information to your contact card. iPhone uses your Apple ID to create your contact card, called My Card, but you may need to provide your contact information (such as name and address) to complete it.

Complete My Card

Tap My Card at the top of your contacts list, then tap Edit. Contacts suggests addresses and phone numbers to help you set up My Card.

If there is no My Card, tap ＋, then enter your information. Next, go to Settings ⚙ > Contacts > My Info, then tap your name in the contacts list.

Edit My Card

Tap My Card at the top of your contacts list, then tap Edit.

You can also teach Siri how to pronounce your name.

Create or edit your Medical ID

Tap My Card at the top of your contacts list, tap Edit, scroll down, then tap Create Medical ID or Edit Medical ID.

Use other contact accounts on iPhone

You can include contacts from other accounts in the Contacts app ⊙.

Use your iCloud contacts

Go to Settings ⚙ > [your name] > iCloud, then turn on Contacts.

Use your Google contacts

1. Go to Settings ⚙ > Contacts > Accounts, then tap Google.
2. Sign in to your account, then turn on Contacts.

Add contacts from another account

1. Go to Settings ⚙ > Contacts > Accounts, then tap Add Account
2. Choose an account, sign in to it, then turn on Contacts.

Access a Microsoft Exchange Global Address List

1. Go to Settings ⚙ > Contacts > Accounts, then tap Exchange.
2. Sign in to your Exchange account, then turn on Contacts.

Set up an LDAP or CardDAV account to access business or school directories

1. Go to Settings ⚙ > Contacts > Accounts > Add Account, then tap Other.
2. Tap Add LDAP Account or Add CardDAV Account, then enter the account information.

Keep contacts up to date across devices

To keep your contact information up to date across all your devices where you're signed in with the same Apple ID, you can use iCloud.

Go to Settings > [your name] > iCloud, then turn on Contacts.

Alternatively, you can sync the information between iPhone and your Mac or Windows PC to keep the information up to date across iPhone and your computer.

If you use iCloud for Contacts, your contacts are kept up to date automatically, and no options appear for syncing them with your computer.

Import contacts from a SIM card (GSM)

Go to Settings ⚙ > Contacts > Import SIM Contacts.

Import contacts from a vCard

Tap a .vcf attachment in an email or message.

Add a contact from a directory

1. Tap Groups, then tap the GAL, CardDAV, or LDAP directory you want to search.
2. Tap Done, then enter your search.
3. Tap the person's name to save their info to your contacts.

Show or hide a group

Tap Groups, then select the groups you want to see.

This button appears only if you have more than one source of contacts.

Use Contacts from the Phone app on iPhone

In the Phone app on iPhone, you can call contacts and add recent callers to the Contacts app 📇.

Add a Favorite

You can add VIP contacts to your Favorites list for quick dialing.

Select a contact, scroll down, then tap Add to Favorites.

Calls from these contacts bypass Do Not Disturb.

Save the number you just dialed

1. In the Phone app 📞, tap Keypad, enter a number, then tap Add Number.
2. Tap Create New Contact, or Add to Existing Contact, then select a contact.

Add a recent caller to Contacts

1. In the Phone app 📞, tap Recents, then tap ⓘ next to the number.
2. Tap Create New Contact, or Add to Existing Contact, then select a contact.

Automate dialing an extension or passcode

If the number you're calling requires dialing an extension, iPhone can enter it for you. When editing a contact's phone number, tap + ✕ # , then do any of the following:

- Tap Pause to enter a two-second pause (a two-second pause is represented as a comma in the phone number).
- Tap Wait to stop dialing until you tap Dial again (wait-to-dial is represented as a semicolon in the phone number).

Get rid of duplicate contacts on iPhone

In the Contacts app 　, link contact cards for the same person in different accounts so they appear only once in your All Contacts list. When you have contacts from multiple sources, you might have multiple entries for the same person in Contacts. To keep redundant contacts from appearing in your All Contacts list, contacts from different sources with the same name are linked and displayed as a single unified contact.

Resolve duplicate contacts

If you have more than one contact card with the same first and last name, you can merge the duplicate contacts.

1. Below My Card, tap Duplicates Found.
2. Tap individual contacts to review and merge them, or tap Merge All to merge all duplicate contacts.

Link contacts manually

If two entries for the same person aren't linked automatically, you can unify them manually.

1. Tap one of the contacts, tap Edit, then tap Link Contacts.
2. Choose the other contact entry to link to, then tap Link.

When you link contacts with different first or last names, the names on the individual cards don't change, but only one name appears on the unified card. To choose which name appears on the unified card, tap one of the linked cards, tap the contact's name on that card, then tap Use This Name For Unified Card.

Note: When you link contacts, those contacts aren't merged. If you change or add information in a unified contact, the changes are copied to each source account where that information already exists.

FaceTime

Set up FaceTime on iPhone

You can use the FaceTime app 　 to stay connected with friends and family, whether they're using an iPhone, iPad, iPod touch, or a Mac. With Spatial Audio in FaceTime, people on the call sound like they're in the room with you, talking from their positions on the screen. Spatial Audio works with AirPods (3rd generation and later), AirPods Pro (all generations), and AirPods Max (sold separately).

With SharePlay, you can watch movies and TV shows together, or listen to music together, during a FaceTime call. You can also share your screen and show apps, webpages, and more during the conversation—collaborate on a document, show a photo album, plan your next group vacation, or get feedback on something you're working on—all while seeing and hearing the reactions of others on the call.

You can use the front camera to talk face to face, or switch to the rear camera to share what you see around you.To capture a moment of your conversation, take a FaceTime Live Photo.

Note: Not all features and content are available in all countries or regions.

1. Go to Settings ⚙ > FaceTime, enter your Apple ID and password, then tap Sign In.
   Note: If you don't have an Apple ID.
2. Make sure FaceTime is turned on, then do any of the following:
   - View TV shows and movies together, listen to music together, or share your screen in calls: Tap SharePlay, then turn on SharePlay.
   - Highlight the speaker in calls: Turn on Speaking.
   - **Display live captions in your calls**: Turn on Live Captions (beta). (Let everyone on your calls know their speech is being transcribed on-device.)
     Note: Live Captions is currently in beta.
   - Take Live Photos in FaceTime calls: Turn on FaceTime Live Photos.
   - Establish natural eye contact in FaceTime calls: Turn on Eye Contact.

Make and receive FaceTime calls on iPhone

With an internet connection and an Apple ID, you can make and receive calls in the FaceTime app ▢ .

Note: You must set up FaceTime before you can make and receive calls.

You can also make FaceTime calls over a cellular data connection, which may incur additional charges. To turn this feature off, go to Settings > Cellular, then turn off FaceTime.

Turn off your mic.

Turn off your camera.

Drag your image to any corner.

Add stickers and other fun effects.

Switch to the rear camera.

Take a Live Photo.

Make a FaceTime call

125

Siri: Say something like: "Make a FaceTime call."

1. In FaceTime, tap New FaceTime near the top of the screen.

2. Type the name or number you want to call in the entry field at the top, then tap  to make a video call or ✆ to make an audio call (not available in all countries or regions). Alternatively, you can tap ⊕ to open Contacts and add people from there; or tap a suggested contact in your call history to quickly make a call.

Tip: To see more during a FaceTime video call, rotate iPhone to use landscape orientation.

Receive a FaceTime call

When a FaceTime call comes in, do any of the following:

- Take the call: Drag the slider or tap Accept.
- Decline the call: Tap Decline.
- Set a reminder to call back: Tap Remind Me.
- Send a text message to the caller: Tap Message.

Set up a reminder to return the call later.

Send the caller a text message.

If you're on another call when a FaceTime call comes in, instead of Accept, you see the End & Accept option, which terminates the previous call and connects you to the incoming call.

Tip: You can have Siri announce incoming calls, which you can accept or decline using your voice.

Start a FaceTime call from a Messages conversation

In a Messages conversation, you can start a FaceTime call with the person you're chatting with.

1. Tap  at the top right of the Messages conversation.
2. Do any of the following:
    o Tap FaceTime Audio.
    o Tap FaceTime Video.

Leave a message

If no one answers your FaceTime call, do one of the following:

- Tap Leave a Message.

- Tap Cancel.
- Tap Call Back.

Call again

In your call history, tap the name or number of the person (or group) you want to call again.

Delete a call from your call history

In FaceTime, swipe left over the call in your call history, then tap Delete.

Create a link to a FaceTime call on iPhone

In the FaceTime app ▣ on iPhone, you can create a link to a FaceTime call and send the link to a friend or a group (using Mail or Messages), which they can use to join or start a call.

1. Tap Create Link near the top of the screen.
2. Choose an option for sending the link (Mail, Messages, and so on).

In Calendar, you can schedule a remote video meeting by inserting FaceTime as the location of the meeting.

Note: You can invite anyone to join you in a FaceTime call, even people who don't have an Apple device. They can join you in one-on-one and Group FaceTime calls from their browser— no login is necessary. (They need the latest version of either Chrome or Edge. Sending video requires H.264 video encoding support.)

Take a Live Photo in FaceTime on iPhone

When you're on a video call in the FaceTime app ▣ , you can take a FaceTime Live Photo to capture a moment of your conversation (not available in all countries or regions). The camera captures what happens just before and after you take the photo, including the audio, so you can see and hear it later just the way it happened.

To take a FaceTime Live Photo, first make sure FaceTime Live Photos is turned on in Settings ⚙ > FaceTime, then do one of the following:

- On a call with one other person: Tap ◯ .
- On a Group FaceTime call: Tap the tile of the person you want to photograph, tap ⬉ , then tap ◯ .

You both receive a notification that the photo was taken, and the Live Photo is saved in your Photos app.

Turn on Live Captions in a FaceTime call on iPhone

While you're on a video call in the FaceTime app ▣ , you can turn on Live Captions (beta) to see the conversation transcribed on the screen. If you're having difficulty hearing the conversation, Live Captions can make it easier to follow along.

127

The accuracy of Live Captions may vary and shouldn't be relied upon in high-risk situations. Live Captions uses additional battery.

Note: Live Captions is currently in beta.

1. During a FaceTime video call, tap the screen to show the FaceTime controls (if they aren't visible).
2. Tap ⓘ at the top of the controls, turn on Live Captions, then tap Done.

A Live Captions window appears, showing the automatically transcribed dialogue of the call near the top of the screen and who's speaking.

To stop showing the conversation on the screen, tap the screen, tap ⓘ at the top of the FaceTime controls, then turn off Live Captions.

Use other apps during a FaceTime call on iPhone

While you're on a call using the FaceTime app 📷, you can use other apps—for example, to look up information or perform a calculation.

Go to the Home Screen, then tap an app icon to open the app.

To return to the FaceTime screen, tap the green bar (or the FaceTime icon) at the top of the screen.

You can also share your screen with the other people in your FaceTime call while using another app.

Make a Group FaceTime call on iPhone

In the FaceTime app 📷, you can have up to 32 participants in a Group FaceTime call (not available in all countries or regions).

Start a Group FaceTime call

1. In FaceTime, tap New FaceTime near the top of the screen.
2. Type the names or numbers of the people you want to call in the entry field at the top.

   You can also tap ⊕ to open Contacts and add people from there. Or tap suggested contacts in your call history.
3. Tap 🎥 to make a video call or tap 📞 to make a FaceTime audio call.

Each participant appears in a tile on the screen. When a participant speaks (verbally or by using sign language) or you tap the tile, that tile becomes more prominent. Tiles that can't fit on the screen appear in a row at the bottom. To find a participant you don't see, swipe through the row. (The participant's initials may appear in the tile if an image isn't available.)

To prevent the tile of the person speaking or signing from becoming larger during a Group FaceTime call, go to Settings ⚙ > FaceTime, then turn off Speaking below Automatic Prominence.

Note: Sign language detection requires a supported model for the presenter. In addition, both the presenter and participants need iOS 14, iPadOS 14, macOS 11, or later.

Start a Group FaceTime call from a group Messages conversation

In a group Messages conversation, you can start a Group FaceTime call with all the people you're chatting with in Messages.

1. Tap ⬜️◀ at the top right of the Messages conversation.
2. Do any of the following:
    o Tap FaceTime Audio.
    o Tap FaceTime Video.

Add another person to a call

Any participant can add another person at any time during a FaceTime call.

1. During a FaceTime call, tap the screen to show the FaceTime controls (if they aren't visible), tap ⓘ at the top of the controls, then tap Add People.
2. Type the name, Apple ID, or phone number of the person you want to add in the entry field at the top.

    Or tap ⊕ to add someone from Contacts.
3. Tap Add People.

Join a Group FaceTime call

When someone invites you to join a Group FaceTime call, you receive a notification of the incoming call—you can either join or decline.

Leave a Group FaceTime call

To leave a group call at any time, tap Leave.

The call remains active if two or more participants remain.

View participants in a grid layout in FaceTime on iPhone

During a call with four or more people in the FaceTime app 📷, you can view participants in same-size tiles, arranged in a grid. The speaker's tile highlights automatically, so it's easy to know who's talking. (Depending on your iPhone model, some tiles may appear blurred.)

In a FaceTime call, tap the Grid button at the bottom left of the screen (if the button isn't visible, tap the screen).

To turn the Grid off, tap it again.

Use SharePlay to watch and listen together in FaceTime on iPhone

With SharePlay in the FaceTime app 📷, you can stream TV shows, movies, and music in sync with friends and family while on a FaceTime call together. Enjoy a real-time connection with others on the call—with synced playback and shared controls, you see and hear the same moments at the same time. With smart volume, media audio is adjusted dynamically, so you can continue to chat while watching or listening.

SharePlay can also be used in other apps during a FaceTime call. To see which apps can be used for SharePlay during a call, tap ⬜ , then scroll through the apps below Apps for SharePlay.

Note: Some apps that support SharePlay require a subscription. To watch a movie or TV show together, every participant needs to have access to the content on their own device, through either a subscription or purchase, on a device that meets the minimum system requirements. SharePlay may not support the sharing of some movies or TV shows across different countries or regions. FaceTime, some FaceTime features, and other Apple services may not be available in all countries or regions.

Watch video together while on a FaceTime call

You can watch movies and TV shows during a FaceTime call with your friends and family.

1. Start a FaceTime call.
2. Go to the Home Screen, then open a video streaming app that supports SharePlay (for example, the Apple TV app).

Select a show or movie you want to watch, tap the Play button, then select Play for Everyone (if it appears) to begin watching with everyone on the call. (Others on the call may have to tap Join SharePlay to see the video.)

For everyone on the call who has access to the content, the video starts playing at the same time. People who don't have access are asked to get access (through a subscription, a transaction, or a free trial, if available).

Each person watching the content can use the playback controls to play, pause, rewind, or fast-forward. (Settings like closed captioning and volume are controlled separately by each person.)

You can use Picture in Picture to keep watching the video while using another app—order food, check your email, or jump into the Messages app and discuss the video by text when you want no interruptions to the sound of the movie or TV show.

Invite friends to watch video together from a supported app during a FaceTime call

On an iPhone that meets the minimum system requirements, you can start a FaceTime call in the Apple TV app (or other supported video app) while you're browsing or watching video content, and share the item in sync with others using SharePlay. Everyone on the call needs to have access to the content on their own device (for example, through a subscription or purchase).

1. In the Apple TV app (or other supported video app), find a show or movie you want to share, then tap the item to see its details.
2. Tap ⬆, then tap SharePlay.
3. In the To field, enter the contacts you want to share with, then tap FaceTime.
4. When the FaceTime call connects, tap Start or Play to begin using SharePlay.
   To begin viewing, recipients tap Open.

Note: If the content requires a subscription, people who aren't subscribers can subscribe before watching.

After the video starts playing, you can stream it to Apple TV.

Send what you're watching in SharePlay to Apple TV

If you've already started watching a video together on iPhone, you can send it to Apple TV to enjoy on the big screen.

On iPhone, do one of the following:

- In the streaming app, tap ⬆️, then choose Apple TV as the playback destination.
- Open Control Center, tap ⬆️, then choose Apple TV as the playback destination.

The video plays in sync on Apple TV, and you can keep the conversation going on your iPhone.

Listen to music together while on a FaceTime call

You can get together and listen to an album or favorite playlist with others on a FaceTime call. Anyone on the call who has access to the music (for example, through a subscription, a transaction, or a free trial) on a device that meets the minimum system requirements can listen along, see what's next, add songs to a shared queue, and more.

1. Start a Group FaceTime call.
2. Go to the Home Screen, then open a music streaming app that supports SharePlay (for example, the Music app 🎵).
3. Select the music you want to listen to, then tap the Play button to begin listening to the music together. (Others on the call may have to tap Join SharePlay to hear the music.)

For everyone on the call who has access to the content, the music starts playing at the same time. People who don't have access are asked to get access (through a subscription, a transaction, or a free trial, if available).

Each person can use the music controls to pause, rewind, fast-forward, scrub to a different part of the song, or go to the next track. And anyone on the call can add songs to the shared queue.

Invite friends to listen to music together from a supported app during a FaceTime call

On an iPhone that meets the minimum system requirements, you can start a FaceTime call in the Music app (or other supported music app) and use SharePlay to share the music in sync with others on the call. Each person can use the music controls to pause, rewind, fast-forward, or scrub to a different part of the song. And anyone using SharePlay can add songs to the shared queue. The people you want to share with must have access to the music (for example, through a subscription).

1. Open the Apple Music app 🎵 (or other supported music app), then tap the music you want to share.
2. Do one of the following:
    - Tap ⋯ next to the music, then tap SharePlay.
    - Tap ⋯ at the top right, tap 📤, then tap SharePlay.
3. In the To field, enter the contacts you want to share with, then tap FaceTime.
4. When the FaceTime call connects, tap Start.

To begin listening, recipients tap the song title at the top of the FaceTime controls, then tap Open. The music starts playing at the same time for everyone on the call who has access to the content.

Note: People who don't have access to the content you share are asked to get access.

With SharePlay, you can also share your screen to show apps, webpages, and more during the conversation.

SharePlay also lets you work out with others using Apple Fitness+.

Share your screen in a FaceTime call on iPhone

In the FaceTime app 🎥 on a device that meets the minimum system requirements, you can share your screen in a FaceTime call, to bring apps, webpages, and more into the conversation. You can get feedback on something you're working on, collaborate on a document with others, show off a photo album, or plan your next vacation together, all while seeing and hearing the reactions of others on the call.

Start sharing your screen

1. During a Group FaceTime call, tap the screen to show the controls (if they aren't visible), tap 📲, then tap Share My Screen.
2. Do one of the following:
   - **Start sharing your screen**: Tap an app below Apps for SharePlay.
   - **Show an app or document**: Go to the Home Screen, then open an app you want to share in the call.

     A countdown from 3 to 1 appears on 📲, then your screen appears in the FaceTime conversation for everyone to see.

To stop sharing your screen, tap 📲.

Hand off a FaceTime call to another device

During a call in the FaceTime app 🎥, you can move the call to another device where you're signed in with the same Apple ID.

Note: Your selected contact information for the call, shown in Settings ⚙ > FaceTime (below You Can Be Reached At), must match the selected contact information in Settings > FaceTime for the device you want to hand off to.

1. Make sure your other device is turned on, then tap the screen that's showing the call. A notification of the call appears on the other device, along with the suggestion "Move call to this [device]."
2. Tap the notification to switch the call, or tap 📱 at the top left of the screen, then tap Switch.

   A preview of the call appears, showing your camera, microphone, and audio settings.
3. Make sure the camera, microphone, and audio settings are the ones you want, then tap Switch.

The call moves to the new device. On the original device, a banner appears confirming that the call was continued elsewhere, along with Switch , which you can tap if you want to bring the call back.

Change FaceTime video settings on iPhone

During a call in the FaceTime app 📹, you can turn Portrait mode on or off, switch between cameras, or turn your camera on or off.

Blur the background with Portrait mode

You can turn on Portrait mode, which automatically blurs the background and puts the visual focus on you, the same way Portrait mode does in the Camera app.

1. When you're on a FaceTime call, tap your tile.
2. Tap 🔘 in your tile.
   To turn Portrait mode off, tap the button again.

Turn Portrait mode off or on.

You can also turn on Portrait mode in Control Center. Open Control Center, then tap Video Effects.

Switch to the rear camera

When you're on a FaceTime call, tap your tile, then tap 🔄.

To switch back to the front camera, tap 🔄 again.

Note: While you're using the rear camera, you can enlarge the image by tapping 1x. Tapping it again returns the image to normal size.

Turn off your camera

When you're on a FaceTime call, tap the screen to make the controls appear, then tap 📹. (Tap it again to turn the camera back on.)

Change FaceTime audio settings on iPhone

Spatial Audio in the FaceTime app ⬜ makes it sound like your friends are in the room with you. Their voices are spread out and sound like they're coming from the direction in which each person is positioned on the screen.

Note: Spatial Audio works with AirPods (2nd generation and later), AirPods Pro, and AirPods Max (sold separately).

Filter out background sounds

When you want your voice to be heard clearly in a FaceTime call and other sounds filtered out, you can turn on Voice Isolation mode. Voice Isolation mode prioritizes your voice in a FaceTime call and blocks out the ambient noise.

During a FaceTime call, open Control Center, tap Mic Mode, then select Voice Isolation.

Include the sounds around you

When you want your voice and all the sounds around you to be heard in a FaceTime call, you can turn on Wide Spectrum mode.

During a FaceTime call, open Control Center, tap Mic Mode, then select Wide Spectrum.

Turn off the sound

When you're on a FaceTime call, tap the screen to show the FaceTime controls (if they aren't visible), then tap 🎤 to turn the sound off.

To turn the sound back on, tap the button again.

When your sound is turned off, your mic detects whether you're speaking, and you're notified that your mic is muted and that you can tap 🎤 to unmute it.

Add camera effects in FaceTime calls on iPhone

On video calls using the FaceTime app ⬜, you can become your favorite Memoji or Memoji character (on an iPhone with Face ID). You can use a built-in filter to change your appearance and add stickers, labels, and shapes. You can take screenshots in FaceTime that include the special camera effects you add to a call.

Become a Memoji

In Messages on an iPhone with Face ID, you can create a Memoji character to use in your FaceTime calls. iPhone captures your movements, facial expressions, and voice, and conveys them through your character. (Your character imitates you even when you stick out your tongue!)

1. During a FaceTime call, tap ✩. (If you don't see ✩, tap the screen.)
2. Tap 😀, then choose a Memoji (swipe through the characters at the bottom, then tap one).
   The other caller hears what you say, but sees your Memoji doing the talking.

Use a filter to change your appearance

1. During a FaceTime video call, tap your tile, then tap ⊛.
2. Tap 🔵 to open the filters.
3. Choose your appearance by tapping a filter at the bottom (swipe left or right to preview them).

Add a text label

1. During a call, tap the screen, then tap ⊛.
2. Tap **Aa**, then tap a text label.
   To see more label options, swipe up from the top of the text window.
3. While the label is selected, type the text you want to appear in the label, then tap away from it.
4. Drag the label where you want to place it.
   To delete the label, tap it, then tap ⊗.

Add stickers

1. During a call, tap your tile, tap ⊛, then do any of the following:
   ○ Tap 😊 to add a Memoji sticker or 🫥 to add an Emoji sticker.
   ○ Tap **Aa**, swipe up, then tap 😀.
2. Tap a sticker to add it to the call.
   To see more options, swipe left or swipe up.
3. Drag the sticker to place it where you want.
   To delete the sticker, tap it, then tap ⊗.

Add shapes

1. During a call, tap your tile, then tap ⊛.
2. Tap 〰️, then tap a shape to add it to the call.
   To see more options, swipe up from the top of the shapes window.
3. Drag the shape where you want to place it.
   To delete the shape, tap it, then tap ⊗.

Leave a FaceTime call or switch to Messages on iPhone

You can leave a call in the FaceTime app 📷 at any time, or switch your conversation to Messages.

Leave a FaceTime call

Tap the screen to show the FaceTime controls (if they aren't visible), then tap ⊗.

Switch to a Messages conversation

To jump to a Messages thread that includes everyone on the call, tap the screen to show the FaceTime controls (if they aren't visible), tap ⓘ at the top of the controls, then tap Message or ◯ .

Block unwanted callers in FaceTime on iPhone

In the FaceTime app 🔲 , you can block FaceTime calls from unwanted callers.

1. In your FaceTime call history, tap ⓘ next to the name, phone number, or email address of the contact you want to block.
2. Scroll down, tap Block this Caller, then tap Block Contact.
3. Select the contact you want to block.

To unblock a contact, tap ⓘ next to the contact's name, phone number, or email address in your call log, scroll down, then tap Unblock this Caller.

Files

Connect servers or external devices with Files on iPhone

You can use the Files app 📁 to access files stored on file servers, other cloud storage providers like Box and Dropbox, and external devices, such as USB drives and SD cards, after you connect them to your iPhone.

Connect to a computer or file server

1. Tap ••• at the top of the Browse screen.

    If you don't see ••• , tap Browse again.
2. Tap Connect to Server.
3. Enter a local hostname or a network address, then tap Connect.
    Tip: After you connect to a computer or file server, it appears in the Recent Servers list on the Connect to Server screen. To connect to a recent server, tap its name.
4. Select how you want to connect:
    o   **Guest**: You can connect as a Guest user if the shared computer permits guest access.
    o   **Registered User:** If you select Registered User, enter your user name and password.
5. Tap Next, then select the server volume or shared folder in the Browse screen (under Shared).

To disconnect from the file server, tap ⏏ next to the server in the Browse screen.

Add a cloud storage service

1. Download the app from the App Store, then open the app and follow the onscreen instructions.

2. Open Files, then tap Browse at the bottom of the screen.
3. Tap More Locations (below Locations), then turn on the service.
4. To view your contents, tap Browse at the bottom of the screen, then tap the name of the storage service below Locations. If you don't see Locations, tap Browse again at the bottom of the screen.

View and modify files and folders in Files on iPhone

In the Files app , view and modify your documents, images, and other files.

Browse and open files and folders

1. Tap Browse at the bottom of the screen, then tap an item on the Browse screen.
   If you don't see the Browse screen, tap Browse again.
   To view recently opened files, tap Recents at the bottom of the screen.
2. To open a file, location, or folder, tap it.

Note: If you haven't installed the app that created a file, a preview of the file opens in Quick Look.

Modify and rearrange documents

When viewing a file in a supported document format, you can modify and rearrange the document's contents using the Files app.

1. Open a document, then tap the page number in the top left.

2. Tap , then choose any of the following
   o **Rotate Left**: Rotate the highlighted page left.
   o **Rotate Right**: Rotate the highlighted page right.
   o **Insert Blank Page**: Insert a blank page after the highlighted page.
   o **Insert from File**: Insert pages from a file after the highlighted page.
   o **Scan Pages**: Insert pages from a scanned document after the highlighted page.
   o **Delete**: Delete the highlighted page.
3. To rearrange a document, touch and hold a highlighted page and drag it to a new location.

   To mark up a document, tap Ⓐ.

Note: Not all document formats are supported by the Files app.

Find a specific file or folder

Enter a filename, folder name, or document type in the search field.

When you search, you have these options:

- **Focus the scope of your search**: Below the search field, tap Recents or the name of the location or tag.
- Hide the keyboard and see more results on the screen: Tap Search.
- **Start a new search**: Tap ⊗ in the search field.
- Open a result: Tap it.

Change to list view or icon view

From an open location or folder, drag down from the center of the screen, then tap ⦂☰.

Change how files and folders are sorted

1. From an open location or folder, drag down from the center of the screen.
2. Tap "Sorted by," then choose an option: Name, Date, Size, Kind, or Tags.

Rearrange the Browse screen

Tap ••• at the top of the Browse screen, tap Edit, then do any of the following:

- Hide a location: Turn the location off.

- Delete a tag and remove it from all items: Tap ⊖ next to the tag.

- Remove an item from the Favorites list: Tap ⊖ next to the item.

- **Change the order of an item**: Touch and hold ☰, then drag it to a new position.

Organize files and folders in Files on iPhone

In the Files app ▥, organize documents, images, and other files in folders.

Create a folder

1. Open a location or an existing folder.

2. Drag down from the center of the screen, tap •••, then tap New Folder.
   Note: If you don't see New Folder, you can't create a folder in that location.

Rename, compress, and make other changes to a file or a folder

Touch and hold the file or folder, then choose an option: Copy, Duplicate, Move, Delete, Rename, or Compress.

To modify multiple files or folders at the same time, tap Select, tap your selections, then tap an option at the bottom of the screen.

Note: Some options may not be available, depending on the item you select; for example, you can't delete or move an app library (a folder labeled with the app name).

Tag a file or folder

1. Touch and hold the file or folder, tap Tags, then tap one or more tags.
2. Tap Done.

To find tagged items, tap Browse, then tap an item below Tags.

To remove a tag, tap it again.

Mark a folder as a favorite

Touch and hold the folder, then tap Favorite.

To find Favorites, tap Browse.

Send files from Files on iPhone

You can send a copy of any file in the Files app [icon] to others. If you have a document you want to send that isn't digitized, you can scan it with Files first.

Send a file

1. Touch and hold the file, then tap Share.
    Tip: To send a smaller version of the file, tap Compress before you tap Share. Then touch and hold the compressed version of the file (identified as a zip file), and tap Share.
2. Choose an option for sending (for example, AirDrop, Messages, or Mail), then tap Send.

Scan a document

Tap [icon] at the top of the Browse screen, then tap Scan Documents.

Tip: If the files or folders you want to share are stored in iCloud Drive, you can invite others to view or edit their contents—you don't need to send them copies.

Set up iCloud Drive on iPhone

Use the Files app [icon] to store files and folders in iCloud Drive. You can access them from all your devices where you're signed in with the same Apple ID. Any changes you make appear on all your devices set up with iCloud Drive.

iCloud Drive is built into the Files app on devices with iOS 11, iPadOS 13, or later. You can also use iCloud Drive on Mac computers (OS X 10.10 or later) and PCs (iCloud for Windows 7 or later). Storage limits depend on your iCloud storage plan.

Turn on iCloud Drive

Go to Settings [icon] > [your name] > iCloud, then turn on iCloud Drive.

Choose which apps use iCloud Drive

Go to Settings [icon] > [your name] > iCloud, then turn each of the apps listed under iCloud Drive on or off.

Browse iCloud Drive

1. Tap Browse at the bottom of the screen.
2. Under Locations, tap iCloud Drive.
    If you don't see Locations, tap Browse again. If you don't see iCloud Drive under Locations, tap Locations.
3. To open a folder, tap it.

Share files and folders in iCloud Drive on iPhone

After you set up iCloud Drive, you can use the Files app [icon] to share folders and individual files with friends and colleagues. When you make changes to a shared folder or file, others see your changes automatically. If you allow people to make edits, their changes appear automatically as well.

Files and folders shared in iCloud Drive have these important characteristics:

- If you collaborate on a folder, all items added to that folder by you or other participants are automatically shared.
- The link to a shared file includes its name. If the name or content is confidential, be sure to ask recipients not to forward the link to anyone else.
- If you move a shared file to another folder or location, the link no longer works, and people lose access to the item.
- Depending on the app, users might need to reopen a file or tap the original link to see the latest changes.

Share a folder or file

If you own a folder or file in iCloud Drive, you can invite others to view or collaborate on its contents.

You can share a folder and file so that only people you invite can open it, or anyone with the link can open it.

You can allow the contents of a folder or file to be changed, or you can restrict access so that the contents can only be viewed.

When you share a folder, only the people you invite can access the files in the shared folder by default. To invite more people to access the files, you must change the settings of the shared folder to add more participants. You can't select an individual file within the shared folder and add participants to it.

1. Touch and hold the folder or file.
2. Tap Share ⬆️, then choose if you want to collaborate or send a copy of the folder or file.
3. Do one of the following:
   - **Allow only invitees to view and edit the contents**: Tap Share Options, tap "Only people you invite," tap "Can make changes," then choose a method—such as Messages or Mail—for sending people a link to the folder or file.
   - **Allow only invitees to view the contents**: Tap Share Options, tap "Only people you invite," tap "View only," then choose a method for sending the link.
   - **Allow anyone with the link to view and edit the contents**: Tap Share Options, tap "Anyone with the link," tap "Can make changes," then choose a method for sending the link.
   - **Allow anyone with the link to view the contents**: Tap Share Options, tap "Anyone with the link," tap "View only," then choose a method for sending the link.
   - **Allow anyone to invite more people**: Tap Share Options, then tap "Anyone can add people."
4. Choose how you want to send your invitation, then tap Send.

Invite more people to collaborate on a folder or file

If you already shared a folder or file and its access is set to "Only people you invite," you can share it with more people.

1. Touch and hold the folder or file.
2. Tap Manage Shared Folder or Manage Shared File.
3. Tap Add People and choose a method for sending the link.
4. Enter any other requested information, then send or post the invitation.

Share a folder or file with more people using a link

If you set the access to a shared folder or file to "Anyone with the link," anyone with the link can share it with others.

1. Touch and hold the folder or file.
2. Tap Manage Shared Folder or Manage Shared File, then tap Copy Link.
3. Choose a method for sending the link, enter any other requested information, then send or post the invitation.

Change access and permission settings for everyone

If you're the owner of a shared folder or file, you can change its access at any time. However, everyone you shared the link with is affected.

1. Touch and hold the folder or file.
2. Tap Manage Shared Folder or Manage Shared File, then tap Share Options.
3. Change either or both of the options.
   - **Access option**: When you change the access option from "Anyone with the link" to "Only people you invite," the original link no longer works for anyone, and only people who receive a new invitation from you can open the folder or file.
   - **Permission option**: When you change the permission option, everyone who has the file open when you change the permission sees an alert. New settings take effect when the alert is dismissed.

Change access and permission settings for one person

If you're the owner of a shared folder or file and its access is set to "Only people you invite," you can change the permission for one person without affecting the permission of others. You can also remove the person's access.

1. Touch and hold the folder or file.
2. Tap Manage Shared Folder or Manage Shared File.
3. Tap the person's name, then select an option.

Stop sharing a folder or file

If you're the owner of a shared folder or file, you can stop sharing it.

1. Touch and hold the folder or file.
2. Tap Manage Shared Folder or Manage Shared File.
3. Tap Stop Sharing.

Anyone who has a file open when you stop sharing it sees an alert. The item closes when the alert is dismissed, the file is removed from the person's iCloud Drive, and the link no longer works. If you later share the item again and set the access to "Anyone with the link," the original link works. If the access is set to "Only people you invite," the original link works again only for people you reinvite to share the item.

Find My

Share your location in Find My on iPhone

Before you can use the Find My app ⊙ to share your location with friends, you need to set up location sharing.

Note: If you set up location sharing and others still can't see your location, make sure Location Services is on in Settings ⚙ > Privacy & Security > Location Services > Find My.

Set up location sharing

1. In the Find My app, tap Me at the bottom of the screen, then turn on Share My Location. The device sharing your location appears next to From.
2. If your iPhone isn't currently sharing your location, you can tap Use This iPhone as My Location.

Note: To share your location from another device, open Find My on the device and change your location to that device. If you share your location from an iPhone that's paired with Apple Watch (GPS + Cellular models), your location is shared from your Apple Watch when you're out of range of your iPhone and Apple Watch is on your wrist.

You can also change your location sharing settings in Settings ⚙ > [your name] > Find My.

Set a label for your location

You can set a label for your current location to make it more meaningful (like Home or Work). When you tap Me, you see the label in addition to your location.

1. Tap Me at the bottom of the screen, then tap Location.
2. Select a label.
    To add a new label, tap Add Custom Label, enter a name, then tap Done.

Share your location with a friend

1. Tap ╋, then choose Share My Location.

2. In the To field, type the name of a friend you want to share your location with (or tap ⊕ and select a contact).
3. Tap Send and choose how long you want to share your location.

You can also notify a friend or family member when your location changes.

142

Stop sharing your location

You can stop sharing your location with a specific friend or hide your location from everyone.

- **Stop sharing with a friend**: Tap People at the bottom of the screen, then tap the name of the person you don't want to share your location with. Tap Stop Sharing My Location, then tap Stop Sharing Location.
- **Hide your location from everyone**: Tap Me at the bottom of the screen, then turn off Share My Location.

Respond to a location sharing request

1. Tap People at the bottom of the screen.
2. Tap Share below the name of the friend who sent the request and choose how long you want to share your location.
   If you don't want to share your location, tap Cancel.

Stop receiving new location sharing requests

Tap Me at the bottom of the screen, then turn off Allow Friend Requests.

Add or remove a friend in Find My on iPhone

In the Find My app , once you share your location with a friend, you can ask to see their location on a map.

Ask to see a friend's location

1. Tap People at the bottom of the screen, then tap the name of the person whose location you want to see.
   If you don't see a person in the list, make sure you're sharing your location with them.
2. Tap Ask To Follow Location.

After your friend receives and accepts your request, you can see their location.

Note: If you see your friend's name in the People list but can't see their location on the map, ask them to make sure they're sharing their location and that Location Services is on in Settings > Privacy & Security > Location Services > Find My.

Remove a friend

When you remove a friend, that person is removed from your People list and you are removed from theirs.

1. Tap People at the bottom of the screen, then tap the name of the person you want to remove.
2. Tap Remove [name], then tap Remove.

Locate a friend in Find My on iPhone

When a friend shares their location with you, you can use the Find My app to locate them on a map.

Note: If you want to see how far away your friends are from you, make sure you turn on Precise Location for the Find My app.

Tap a person to see contact information, get directions, and more.

See the location of a friend

Tap People at the bottom of the screen, then tap the name of the person you want to locate.

- If your friend can be located: They appear on a map so you can see where they are.
- If your friend can't be located: You see "No location found" below their name.
- If you aren't following your friend: You see "Can see your location" below their name. You can ask to see a friend's location.

You can also use Siri to locate a friend who has shared their location with you.

Siri: Say something like: "Where's Gordon?"

Contact a friend

1. Tap People at the bottom of the screen, then tap the name of the person you want to contact.
2. Tap Contact and choose how you want to contact your friend.

Get directions to a friend

You can get directions to a friend's current location in the Maps app  .

1. Tap People at the bottom of the screen, then tap the name of the person you want to get directions to.
2. Tap Directions to open Maps.

Set a label for a friend's location

You can set a label for a friend's current location to make it more meaningful (like Home or Work). The label appears below your friend's name when they're at that location.

1. Tap People at the bottom of the screen, then tap the name of the person you want to set a location label for.
2. Tap Edit Location Name, then select a label.
   To add a new label, tap Add Custom Label, enter a name, then tap Done.

Mark favorite friends

Favorite friends appear at the top of the People list and are marked by a star.

1. Tap People at the bottom of the screen, then find the person you want to mark as a favorite.
2. Do one of the following:
   o Tap the name of the person, then tap Add [name] to Favorites.
   o Swipe left across the person's name, then tap the star.

To remove a friend from your Favorites, swipe left and tap the star, or tap the friend, then tap Remove [name] from Favorites.

Get notified when a friend's location changes in Find My on iPhone

Use the Find My app to get a notification when your friend's location changes. You can get notified when a friend arrives at a location, leaves a location, or is not at a location.

Important: In order to receive a notification when your friend's location changes, make sure you allow notifications for the Find My app.

Get notified when your friend arrives at or leaves a location

1. Tap People at the bottom of the screen, then tap the name of the person you want to be notified about.
2. Below Notifications, tap Add, then tap Notify Me.
3. Choose whether you want to be notified when a friend arrives at or leaves a location.
4. Choose a location, or tap New Location to create a new location and set a location radius.
   With a larger radius, you're notified when your friend is near the location instead of right at the location.
5. Choose whether you want to be notified only once or every time.
6. Tap Add, then tap OK.
   Your friend gets an alert after you set the notification.

If you set a recurring notification, your friend must approve it before it's set. They get an alert asking for approval when they arrive at or leave the location you chose for the first time.

Get notified when your friend isn't at a location

You can receive a notification if your friend or family member isn't at a specific location during a set schedule. For example, you can be notified if your child isn't at school during school hours.

1. Tap People at the bottom of the screen, then tap the name of the person you want to be notified about.
2. Below Notifications, tap Add, then tap Notify Me.
3. Below When, tap [your friend's name] Is Not At.
4. Choose a location, or tap New Location to create a new location and set a location radius.
   With a larger radius, you're notified when your friend is near the location instead of right at the location.
5. Select when you want to be notified.
   o Time: Select a start and end time.
   o Days: Select the days of the week.

6. Tap Add, then tap OK.
   Your friend must approve the notification before it's set. They get an alert asking for approval on the time and day the notifications start.

Change or turn off a notification you set

1. Tap People at the bottom of the screen, then tap the name of the person whose notification you want to change or turn off.
   This could be a notification you receive about a friend, or a notification your friend receives about you.
2. Below Notifications, tap the notification.
3. Do either of the following:
   ○ Change a notification: Change any details, then tap Done.
   ○ Turn off a notification: Tap Delete Notification, then tap Delete Notification again.

You can create up to 25 Notify Me notifications.

Note: You can only create recurring notifications for friends who have two-factor authentication turned on.

Notify a friend when your location changes in Find My on iPhone

Use the Find My app to let a friend know when your location changes.

You can also get a notification when your friend's location changes.

Notify a friend when your location changes

1. Tap People at the bottom of the screen, then tap the name of the person you want to notify.
2. Below Notifications, tap Add, then tap Notify [your friend's name].
3. Choose whether you want to notify your friend when you arrive at or leave a location.
4. Choose a location, or tap New Location to create a new location and set a location radius.
   With a larger radius, your friend is notified when you're near the location instead of right at the location.
5. Choose whether you want your friend to be notified only once or every time.
6. Tap Add.

You can stop notifying friends when your location changes at any time.

See all notifications about you

1. Tap Me at the bottom of the screen.
   Below Notifications About You, you see a list of people who are notified when your location changes.
   If you don't see the Notifications About You section, you aren't notifying any friends when your location changes.
2. Select a name to see more details.

Turn off notifications about you

You can turn off any location notification about you. This includes notifications you set and notifications your friends create.

1. Tap Me at the bottom of the screen.
   Below Notifications About You, you see a list of people who are notified when your location changes.
   If you don't see the Notifications About You section, you aren't notifying any friends when your location changes.
2. Select a name, then tap a notification.
3. Tap Delete Notification, then tap Delete Notification again.

Find Devices

Add your iPhone to Find My

Before you can use the Find My app ⊙ to locate a lost iPhone, you need to connect the device to your Apple ID.

When you add your iPhone to Find My, you can also get notified if you leave it behind.

Add your iPhone

1. On your iPhone, go to Settings ⚙ > [your name] > Find My.
   If you're asked to sign in, enter your Apple ID. If you don't have one, tap "Don't have an Apple ID or forgot it?" then follow the instructions.
2. Tap Find My iPhone, then turn on Find My iPhone.
3. You can also turn on or off either of the following:
   - **Find My network**: If your device is offline (not connected to Wi-Fi or cellular), Find My can locate it using the Find My network.
     On a supported iPhone, turning on the Find My network allows you to locate your iPhone for up to 24 hours after it's turned off, or up to 5 hours when it's in power reserve mode.
   - **Send Last Location**: If your device's battery charge level becomes critically low, its location is sent to Apple automatically.

Your iPhone also includes a feature called Activation Lock that prevents anyone else from activating and using your device, even if it's completely erased.

Add a family member's device

You can see your family members' devices in Find My if you set up Family Sharing first. Their devices appear below yours in the Devices list.

You can't add friends' devices to Find My. Friends who lose a device can go to icloud.com/find and sign in with their Apple ID.

Add your iPhone Wallet with MagSafe to Find My on iPhone

If your iPhone Wallet with MagSafe has Find My support, you can connect it to your Apple ID so you can see its last known location in the Find My app 🔵. You can allow someone who finds it to see your contact information to help them return it to you.

When you add your iPhone Wallet with MagSafe to Find My, you can get notified if it detaches from your iPhone.

Note: iPhone Wallet with MagSafe and Find My support can be used with compatible iPhone models.

Add iPhone Wallet with MagSafe when you first attach it to your iPhone

1. Go to the Home Screen on your iPhone.
2. Attach your iPhone Wallet with MagSafe and Find My support to your iPhone.
3. Tap Continue on your iPhone screen, then follow the onscreen instructions.

Add iPhone Wallet with MagSafe later

If you decide not to add your iPhone Wallet with MagSafe and Find My support when you first attach it to your iPhone, you can add it later from the Find My app.

1. Attach your iPhone Wallet with MagSafe and Find My support to your iPhone.
2. In Find My, tap ╋, choose Add MagSafe Accessory, then follow the onscreen instructions.

If the iPhone Wallet with MagSafe and Find My support is associated with someone else's Apple ID, they need to remove it before you can add it.

Set separation alerts in case you leave a device behind in Find My on iPhone

In the Find My app 🔵, you can turn on separation alerts for a device so you don't accidentally leave it behind. You can also set Trusted Locations, which are locations where you can leave your device without receiving an alert.

If you have an iPhone Wallet with MagSafe and Find My support, you can get an alert if it detaches from your iPhone.

Important: In order to receive separation alerts, make sure you allow notifications for the Find My app.

Set up alerts for your iPhone, iPad, iPod touch, Mac, or AirPods

You can set up separation alerts for your iPhone, iPad, or iPod touch with iOS 15, iPadOS 15, or later; Mac with Apple silicon and macOS 12 or later; or AirPods with the Find My network turned on.

You can only set up a separation alert from the device sharing your location. You receive an alert every time the device sharing your location separates from the device you set an alert for.

1. Tap Devices at the bottom of the screen, then tap the name of the device you want to set up an alert for.
2. Below Notifications, tap Notify When Left Behind.
3. Turn on Notify When Left Behind, then follow the onscreen instructions.

4. If you want to add a Trusted Location, you can choose a suggested location, or tap New Location, select a location on the map, then tap Done.
5. Tap Done.

Get notified when your iPhone Wallet with MagSafe detaches from your iPhone

You can get an alert one minute after your iPhone Wallet with MagSafe and Find My support separates from your iPhone. Then you can use the Find My app to see its last known location on a map.

1. Tap Devices at the bottom of the screen, then tap the name of your iPhone Wallet with MagSafe.
2. Below Notifications, tap Notify When Detached.
3. Turn off or on Notify When Detached, then tap Done.

Locate a device in Find My on iPhone

Use the Find My app to locate and play a sound on a missing iPhone, iPad, iPod touch, Mac, Apple Watch, AirPods, or Beats headphones. In order to locate a device, you must turn on Find My [device] before it's lost.

Note: If you want to see how far away your devices are from you, make sure you turn on Precise Location for the Find My app.

If you lose your iPhone and don't have access to the Find My app, you can locate or play a sound on your device using Find My iPhone on iCloud.com.

About locating a device

- You can use Find My on your iPhone to see the location of your device on a map and play a sound on it to help you find it. If the device is online, you see the location of the device. If the device is offline, you see the location of the device the last time it went online or connected to the Find My network.
- For AirPods and supported Beats headphones, you can locate them when they're nearby your device and connected to Bluetooth. For supported AirPods, you can also see their location via the Find My network for up to 24 hours after they last connected to your device, even if they're not nearby.
- For iPhone Wallet with MagSafe and Find My support, you can see its location when it's attached to your iPhone and its last known location if it detaches from your iPhone.

See the location of your device on a map

You can see your device's current or last known location in the Find My app.

Tap Devices at the bottom of the screen, then tap the name of the device you want to locate.

- If the device can be located: It appears on the map so you can see where it is.
- If the device can't be located: You see "No location found" below the device's name. Below Notifications, turn on Notify When Found. You receive a notification when it's located.
  Important: Make sure you allow notifications for the Find My app.

Play a sound on your device

1. Tap Devices at the bottom of the screen, then tap the name of the device you want to play a sound on.
2. Tap Play Sound.
    - **If the device is online**: A sound starts after a short delay and gradually increases in volume, then plays for about two minutes. If applicable, a Find My [device] alert appears on the screen.
    A confirmation email is also sent to your Apple ID email address.
    - **If the device is offline**: You see Sound Pending. The sound plays the next time the device connects to a Wi-Fi or cellular network. For AirPods and Beats headphones, you receive a notification the next time your device is in range of your iPhone or iPad.

If your AirPods are separated, you have additional options to play a sound.

Stop playing a sound on a device

If you find your device and want to turn off the sound before it stops automatically, do one of the following:

- **iPhone, iPad, or iPod touch**: Press the power button or a volume button, or flip the Ring/Silent switch. If the device is locked, you can also unlock it, or swipe to dismiss the Find My [device] alert. If the device is unlocked, you can also tap OK in the Find My [device] alert.
- **Apple Watch**: Tap Dismiss in the Find My Watch alert, or press the Digital Crown or side button.
- **Mac**: Click OK in the Find My Mac alert.
- AirPods or Beats headphones: Tap Stop in Find My.

Get directions to a device

You can get turn-by-turn directions to your device if you see its location on the map.

1. Tap Devices at the bottom of the screen, then tap the name of the device you want to get directions to.
2. Tap Directions to open the Maps app .

If you're near your supported AirPods, you can tap Find for additional directions.

Locate or play a sound on a friend's device

If your friend loses a device, they can locate it or play a sound on it by going to icloud.com/find and signing in with their Apple ID and password.

If you set up Family Sharing, you can use Find My to locate a family member's missing device.

You can also use Siri to help locate a device.

Siri: Say something like: "Play a sound on my iPhone" or "Where's my iPad?"

Mark a device as lost in Find My on iPhone

Use the Find My app to mark a missing iPhone, iPad, iPod touch, Apple Watch, Mac, supported AirPods, or iPhone Wallet with MagSafe as lost. In order to mark a device as lost, you must turn on Find My [device] before it's lost.

What happens when you mark a device as lost?

- A confirmation email is sent to your Apple ID email address.
- You can create a message for the device that says it's lost and how to contact you.
- For an iPhone, iPad, iPod touch, Mac, or Apple Watch, your device doesn't display alerts or make noise when you receive messages or notifications, or if any alarms go off. Your device can still receive phone calls and FaceTime calls.
- For applicable devices, payment cards and other services are suspended.

Mark a device as lost

If your device is lost or stolen, you can turn on Lost Mode (for your iPhone, iPad, iPod touch, Apple Watch, supported AirPods, or iPhone Wallet with MagSafe), or lock your Mac.

1. Tap Devices at the bottom of the screen, then tap the name of the lost device.
2. Below Mark As Lost, tap Activate.
3. Follow the onscreen instructions, keeping the following in mind:
   - **Passcode**: If your iPhone, iPad, iPod touch, or Apple Watch doesn't have a passcode, you're asked to create one now. For a Mac, you must create a numerical passcode, even if you already have a password set up on your Mac. This passcode is distinct from your password and is only used when you mark your device as lost.
   - **Contact information**: For iPhone, iPad, iPod touch, Mac, or Apple Watch, the contact information and message appear on the device's Lock Screen. For AirPods or iPhone Wallet with MagSafe, the information appears when someone tries to connect with your device.
4. Tap Activate (for an iPhone, iPad, iPod touch, Apple Watch, AirPods, or iPhone Wallet with MagSafe) or Lock (for a Mac).

When the device has been marked as lost, you see Activated below the Mark As Lost section. If the device isn't connected to a network when you mark it as lost, you see Pending until the device goes online again.

Change the information for a lost device

After you mark your iPhone, iPad, iPod touch, Apple Watch, or iPhone Wallet with MagSafe as lost, you can adjust the information in the Lost Mode message.

1. Tap Devices at the bottom of the screen, then tap the name of the lost device.
2. Below Mark As Lost, tap Pending or Activated.
3. Update the information, then tap Done.

Turn off Lost Mode for an iPhone, iPad, iPod touch, Apple Watch, AirPods, or iPhone Wallet with MagSafe

When you find your lost device, you can turn off Lost Mode.

1. In Find My, tap Devices at the bottom of the screen, then tap the name of the device.
2. Tap Pending or Activated below Mark As Lost, tap Turn Off Mark As Lost, then tap Turn Off.

For iPhone, iPad, iPod touch, or Apple Watch, you can also turn off Lost Mode by entering your passcode on the device. For iPhone Wallet with MagSafe, you can turn off Lost Mode by attaching the wallet to your iPhone.

Unlock a Mac

When you find your lost Mac, enter the numeric passcode on the Mac to unlock it (the one you set up when you marked your Mac as lost).

If you forget your passcode, you can recover it using Find My iPhone on iCloud.com.

If you lose your iPhone, you can turn on Lost Mode using Find My iPhone on iCloud.com.

Erase a device in Find My on iPhone

Use the Find My app to erase an iPhone, iPad, iPod touch, Apple Watch, or Mac. In order to remotely erase a device, you must turn on Find My [device] before it's lost.

What happens when you erase a device in Find My?

- A confirmation email is sent to your Apple ID email address.
- When you erase a device remotely using Find My, Activation Lock remains on to protect it. Your Apple ID and password are required to reactivate it.
- If you erase a device that had iOS 15, iPadOS 15, or later installed, you can use Find My to locate or play a sound on the device. Otherwise, you won't be able to locate or play a sound on it. You may still be able to locate your Mac or Apple Watch if it's near a previously used Wi-Fi network.

Erase a device

1. Tap Devices at the bottom of the screen, then tap the name of the device you want to erase.
2. Tap Erase This Device, then tap Continue.
   If the device is a Mac, enter a passcode to lock it (you need to use the passcode to unlock it).
3. If the device is lost and you're asked to enter a phone number or message, you may want to indicate that the device is lost or how to contact you. The number and message appear on the device's Lock Screen.
4. Tap Erase.
5. Enter your Apple ID password, then tap Erase again.

If your device is offline, you see Erase Pending. The remote erase begins the next time it connects to a Wi-Fi or cellular network.

Cancel an erase

If you erase an offline device and find it before it comes online again, you can cancel the erase request.

1. Tap Devices at the bottom of the screen, then tap the name of the device whose erase you want to cancel.
2. Tap Cancel Erase, then enter your Apple ID password.

If you lose your iPhone, you can erase it using Find My iPhone on iCloud.com.

Remove a device from Find My on iPhone

You can use the Find My app ⊙ to remove a device from your Devices list or turn off Activation Lock on a device you already sold or gave away. When you remove Activation Lock, someone else can activate the device and connect it to their Apple ID.

If you still have the device, you can turn off Activation Lock and remove the device from your account by turning off the Find My [device] setting on the device.

Remove a device from your Devices list

If you're not planning on using a device, you can remove it from your Devices list. The device must be offline in order for you to remove it.

The device appears in your Devices list the next time it comes online if it still has Activation Lock turned on (for an iPhone, iPad, iPod touch, Mac, or Apple Watch), or is paired with your iOS or iPadOS device (for AirPods or Beats headphones).

1. Do one of the following:
   o For an iPhone, iPad, iPod touch, Mac, or Apple Watch: Turn off the device.
   o For AirPods: Put AirPods in their case and close the lid or turn the AirPods off.
   o For Beats headphones: Turn off the headphones.
2. In Find My, tap Devices at the bottom of the screen, then tap the name of the offline device.
3. Tap Remove This Device, then tap Remove.

Remove an iPhone Wallet with MagSafe

You can remove an iPhone Wallet with MagSafe and Find My support from your Devices list if you don't want it to appear in the Find My app. Removing it from Find My allows someone else to connect it to their Apple ID.

1. In Find My, tap Devices at the bottom of the screen, then tap the name of your iPhone Wallet with MagSafe.
2. Tap Remove This Device, then follow the onscreen instructions.

Turn off Activation Lock on a device you have

Before you sell, give away, or trade in a device, you should remove Activation Lock so the device is no longer associated with your Apple ID.

Find Items

Add an AirTag in Find My on iPhone

You can register an AirTag to your Apple ID using your iPhone. When you attach it to an everyday item, like a keychain or a backpack, you can use the Find My app ⊙ to locate it if it's lost or misplaced.

You can also get notified if you leave your AirTag behind.

You can also add supported third-party products to Find My.

Add an AirTag

1. Go to the Home Screen on your iPhone.
2. Remove the battery tab from the AirTag (if applicable), then hold it near your iPhone.

3. Tap Connect on the screen of your iPhone.
4. Choose a name from the list or choose Custom Name to type a name and select an emoji, then tap Continue.
5. Tap Continue to register the item to your Apple ID, then tap Finish.

You can also register an AirTag in the Find My app. Tap ╬, then choose Add AirTag.

If the item is registered to someone else's Apple ID, they need to remove it before you can add it.

Change the name or emoji of an AirTag

1. Tap Items at the bottom of the screen, then tap the AirTag whose name or emoji you want to change.
2. Tap Rename Item.
3. Choose a name from the list or choose Custom Name to type a name and select an emoji.
4. Tap Done.

View more details about an AirTag

When you register an AirTag to your Apple ID, you can view more details about it in the Find My app.

1. Tap Items at the bottom of the screen, then tap the AirTag you want to see more details about.
2. Tap the name of the AirTag to see the serial number and the firmware version.

If the battery level is low, a message appears below the location of the AirTag. You can also see a low battery indicator next to the name of the AirTag in the Items list.

Add or update a third-party item in Find My on iPhone

You can use certain third-party products with the Find My app . You can register these products to your Apple ID using your iPhone, and then use Find My to locate them if they're lost or misplaced.

You can also get notified if you leave your item behind.

You can also add an AirTag to Find My.

Add a third-party item

1. Follow the manufacturer's instructions to make the item discoverable.

2. In the Find My app, tap ╬, then choose Add Other Item.
3. Tap Connect, type a name and select an emoji, then tap Continue.
4. Tap Continue to register the item to your Apple ID, then tap Finish.

If you have trouble adding an item, contact the manufacturer to see if Find My is supported.

If the item is registered to someone else's Apple ID, they need to remove it before you can add it.

Change an item's name or emoji

1. Tap Items at the bottom of the screen, then tap the item whose name or emoji you want to change.
2. Tap Rename Item.
3. Choose a name from the list or choose Custom Name to type a name and select an emoji.
4. Tap Done.

Keep your item up to date

Keep your item up to date so you can use all the features in Find My.

1. Tap Items at the bottom of the screen, then tap the item you want to update.
2. Tap Update Available, then follow the onscreen instructions.
   Note: If you don't see Update Available, your item is up to date.
   While the item is updating, you can't use Find My features.

View details about an item

When you register an item to your Apple ID, you can use Find My to see more details about it, like the serial number or model. You can also see if a third-party app is available from the manufacturer.

1. Tap Items at the bottom of the screen, then tap the item you want more details about.
2. Do either of the following:
   o **View details**: Tap Show Details.
   o **Get or open third-party app**: If an app is available, you see the app icon. Tap Get or ⬇ to download the app. If you've already downloaded it, tap Open to open it on your iPhone.

Set separation alerts in case you leave an AirTag or item behind in Find My on iPhone

In the Find My app ⊙ , you can turn on separation alerts for an AirTag or other item so you don't accidentally leave it behind. You receive an alert every time the device sharing your location separates from the item.

You can also set Trusted Locations, which are locations where you can leave an item without receiving an alert.

Important: In order to receive separation alerts, make sure you allow notifications for the Find My app.

1. Tap Items at the bottom of the screen, then tap the name of the item you want to set an alert for.
2. Below Notifications, tap Notify When Left Behind.
3. Turn on Notify When Left Behind.
4. If you want to add a Trusted Location, you can choose a suggested location, or tap New Location, select a location on the map, then tap Done.
5. Tap Done.

Locate an AirTag or other item in Find My on iPhone

You can use the Find My app ⊙ to locate a missing AirTag or third-party item that you've registered to your Apple ID.

See the location of an item

Tap Items at the bottom of the screen, then tap the item you want to locate.

- If the item can be located: It appears on the map so you can see where it is. The location and timestamp appear below the item's name. The item's location is updated when it connects to the Find My network.
- If the item can't be located: You see where and when it was last located. Below Notifications, turn on Notify When Found. You receive a notification once it's located again.

Important: Make sure you allow notifications for the Find My app.

Play a sound

If the item is nearby, you can play a sound on it to help you find it.

Note: If you can't play a sound on an item, you won't see the Play Sound button.

1. Tap Items at the bottom of the screen, then tap the item you want to play a sound on.
2. Tap Play Sound.
   To stop playing the sound before it ends automatically, tap Stop Sound.

Get directions to an item

You can get directions to an item's current or last known location in the Maps app 🧭 .

1. Tap Items at the bottom of the screen, then tap the item you want to get directions to.
2. Tap Directions to open Maps.

Find the precise location of an AirTag

If you have a supported iPhone and are near your AirTag, you can find its precise location.

1. Tap Items at the bottom of the screen, then tap the nearby AirTag.
2. Tap Find.
3. Do any of the following:
   - **Move closer to the AirTag**: Start moving around to locate the AirTag and follow the onscreen instructions. You may see an arrow pointing in the direction of the AirTag, an approximate distance telling you how far away it is, and a note if it's located on a different floor.
   - **Play a sound**: Tap 🔊 to play a sound on the AirTag.
4. When you locate the AirTag, tap ⊗ .

Mark an AirTag or other item as lost in Find My on iPhone

If you lose an AirTag or third-party item registered to your Apple ID, you can use the Find My app ⊙ to mark it as lost.

What happens when you mark an item as lost?

- You can add a message saying that the item is lost and include your phone number or email address.
- If someone else finds your item, they can use a supported device to see a website with the Lost Mode message.

Turn on Lost Mode for an item

To mark an item as lost, you need to turn on Lost Mode.

1. Tap Items at the bottom of the screen, then tap the name of the lost item.
2. Below Lost Mode, tap Enable.
3. Follow the onscreen instructions to enter a phone number where you can be reached.
   To enter an email address instead, tap "Use an email address."
   Important: Make sure you allow notifications for the Find My app.
4. Tap Activate.

Change the contact information in the Lost Mode message

1. Tap Items at the bottom of the screen, then tap the name of the lost item.
2. Below Lost Mode, tap Enabled.
3. Edit the phone number or email address, then tap Save.

Turn off Lost Mode for an item

When you find your lost item, turn off Lost Mode.

1. Tap Items at the bottom of the screen, then tap the name of the item.
2. Below Lost Mode, tap Enabled.
3. Tap Turn Off Lost Mode, then tap Turn Off.

Remove an AirTag or other item from Find My on iPhone

You can use the Find My app 	to remove an AirTag or third-party item from your Apple ID so someone else can register it.

Learn how to register an AirTag or third-party item.

1. Tap Items at the bottom of the screen, then tap the item you want to remove.
2. Bring the item near your iPhone.
   If the item is not near your device, you can still remove it from your account. However, the item must be reset before anyone can register it to their Apple ID.
3. Tap Remove Item, then follow the onscreen instructions.

Note: Follow the manufacturer's instructions to reset an item.

Adjust map settings in Find My on iPhone

You can change the map view or distance units that appear In the Find My app 	.

Change the map view

The button at the top right of a map indicates if the current map is for exploring 	or viewing from a satellite 	. To choose a different map, do the following:

1. Tap the button at the top right.
2. Choose another map type.

    You can also tap to further customize the map.

3. Tap ✕ .

You can also tap 2D or 3D at the top right to change the view (not available in all locations).

Tip: If you don't see 2D or 3D, zoom in. You can also swipe up with two fingers to see the 3D view.

Change distance units

You can change the default distance units in Settings ⊚ .

Fitness

Track daily activity in Fitness on iPhone

You can use the Fitness app ⊚ to track your daily activity, set a move goal, see your progress, and see your movement trends over time—even if you don't have an Apple Watch.

Get started

The first time you open Fitness on your iPhone, you're asked to provide basic health information about yourself. You can always go back and make updates too.

1. Tap your profile picture or initials at the top right.
2. Tap Health Details.
3. To make a change, tap a field.
4. When you're finished, tap Done.

Change your move goal

If you ever find your move goal either too challenging or not challenging enough, you can change it any time.

1. Tap Summary, then tap the Activity area.
2. Scroll down, then tap Change Move Goal.
3. Tap ⊖ or ⊕ to adjust the goal.
4. When you're finished, tap Change Move Goal.

Every Monday, you're notified about the previous week's achievements, and you can adjust your goals for the upcoming week. Goals are suggested based on your performance in the previous week.

Check your progress

Open the Fitness app at any time to see how you're doing.

When you carry your iPhone with you, motion sensors track your steps, distance, and flights climbed to estimate active calories burned. Any workouts you complete in compatible third-party apps also contribute to the progress shown on your Move ring.

Note: You can add a Fitness widget that lets you track your daily activity directly from your Home Screen or Lock Screen.

An overlapping ring means you exceeded your goal. Tap the Activity area to see a summary, including total steps, your workouts, and more.

See your activity history, trends, and awards

In the Fitness app ⊚ on iPhone, you can see your activity history, trends, and awards to keep track of your progress.

See your activity history

1. Tap Summary, then tap the Activity area.
2. Tap ▦ , then tap a date.

See your trends

The Trends area shows your daily trend data for active calories, walking distance, walking pace, and running pace. Your last 90 days of activity are compared to the last 365.

Note: It takes 180 days of activity to start your trends.

To see how ou're trending, follow these steps:

1. Tap Summary.
2. In the Trends area, tap Show More.
3. To see the history of a specific trend, tap it.

If the trend arrow for a particular metric points up, then you're maintaining or improving your fitness levels. If an arrow points down, your 90-day average for that metric has started to decline. To help motivate you to turn the trend around, you receive coaching—for example, "Walk an extra quarter mile a day."

See your awards

You can earn awards for personal records, streaks, and major milestones using the Fitness app on iPhone. You can view all your awards, including awards you're making progress toward.

1. Tap Summary.
2. In the Awards area, tap Show More.
3. To see an award, tap it.

Connect a third-party workout app to Fitness on iPhone

You can connect a compatible third-party workout app to the Fitness app ⊚ on iPhone to help you meet your fitness goals. Any workouts you complete in these apps contribute to the progress toward closing your Move ring.

1. Tap Summary, then tap the Activity area.
2. Scroll down to Workout Apps.
3. Choose an app, then, if you want, download it from the App Store.

Customize notifications for Fitness on iPhone

The Fitness app ◎ on iPhone can help you reach your daily activity goals. You can set up notifications to keep you up to date about your progress throughout the day, and even get coaching tips to help you stay on track.

Turn on activity notifications

1. Go to Settings ◉ > Notifications > Fitness, then turn on Allow Notifications.
2. Tap Fitness Notification Settings, then customize how you want to receive notifications.

Turn off activity notifications

1. Go to Settings ◉ > Notifications > Fitness.
2. Tap Fitness Notification Settings, then turn off Daily Coaching.

Share your activity in Fitness on iPhone

In the Fitness app ◎, keep your fitness routine on track by sharing your activity with your family and friends—you can even share with a trainer or coach. You can get notifications when your friends meet their goals, finish workouts, and earn achievements.

Add or remove a friend

1. Tap Sharing.
2. Tap ⊕ , then tap ┼ .
3. Enter the names or phone numbers of friends you want to share your activity with.

   You can also tap ⊕ to select a name from your contacts.
4. Tap Send.

To remove a friend, tap a friend you're sharing with, then tap Remove Friend.

After a friend accepts your invitation, you can see their activity and they can see yours. If a friend hasn't accepted an invitation, tap their name in the Invited area of the Sharing screen, then tap Invite Again.

Check your friends' progress

Tap Sharing, then tap a friend to see their stats for the day.

Send a message to a friend

1. Tap Sharing, then tap a friend.
2. Tap ◯ to send a message in the Messages app ◻ .

Change your friend settings

You can easily adjust friend settings.

1. Tap Sharing, then tap a friend.
2. Scroll down, then do any of the following:
   - Tap Mute Notifications to stop receiving notifications about a friend's activity progress.

- Tap Hide My Activity to stop sharing your activity progress with a friend.
- Tap Remove Friend to remove the friend from the list of people you share your activity progress with.

Health

Fill out your Health Details in Health on iPhone

To personalize the Health app ♥, add your name, date of birth, sex, and other basic information into Health Details. To help first responders and others in case you have a medical emergency, create a Medical ID that contains information about medical conditions, medications, allergies, emergency contacts, and more. To better manage your health with the help of the Health app, periodically review the Health Checklist.

Fill out the Health Details screen

When you first open Health, you're asked to provide basic health information about yourself. If you don't supply all of the requested information, you can add it later on the Health Details screen.

1. Tap your profile picture or initials at the top right.
   If you don't see your profile picture or initials, tap Summary or Browse at the bottom of the screen, then scroll to the top of the screen.
2. Tap Health Details, then tap Edit.
3. To make a change, tap a field.
4. When you're finished, tap Done.

Create a Medical ID

First responders and others can view critical medical information about you in your Medical ID, even while your iPhone is locked.

Review your Health Checklist

1. Tap your profile picture or initials at the top right.
   If you don't see your profile picture or initials, tap Summary or Browse at the bottom of the screen, then scroll to the top of the screen.
2. Tap Health Checklist.
3. To turn on or learn more about an item in the list, tap it.
4. When you're finished, tap Done.

View and share health data

View your data in Health on iPhone

In the Health app ♥, you can view your health and fitness information in one place. For example, you can check whether your symptoms are improving over time, and see how well you're meeting goals for activity, sleep, mindfulness, and more.

View your health trends

To help you keep track of your health data over time, Health can alert you to significant changes in types of data like resting heart rate, number of steps, and amount of sleep. Trend lines show you how much these metrics have changed and for how long.

1. Tap Summary at the bottom left, then scroll down to Trends to view any recent trends.
2. If Health has detected trends, you can do the following:
   - View more data about a trend: Tap its graph.
   - **View more trends**: Tap View Health Trends.

To receive notifications about your health trends, tap View Health Trends on the Summary screen, tap "Manage notifications," then turn on Trends.

View your highlights

Tap Summary at the bottom left, then scroll down to see highlights of your recent health and fitness data.

To see more details about a highlight, tap 〉.

Add or remove a health category from Favorites on the Summary screen

1. Tap Summary at the bottom left.
2. Tap Edit for the Favorites section.
3. Tap a category to turn it on or off, then tap Done.

View trends, highlights, and details for a specific health category

Tap Browse at the bottom right to display the Health Categories screen, then do one of the following:

- Tap a category. (To see all categories, scroll up and down.)
- Tap the search field, then type the name of a category (such as Mobility) or a specific type of data (such as Walking Speed).

Depending on the data type, you may be able to do the following:

- View details about any of the data: Tap 〉.
- See weekly, monthly, and yearly views of the data: Tap the tabs at the top of the screen.
- **Manually enter data**: Tap Add Data in the top-right corner of the screen.
- **Add a data type to Favorites on the Summary screen**: Turn on Add to Favorites. (You may need to scroll down.)
- **View which apps and devices are allowed to share the data**: Below Options, tap Data Sources & Access. (You may need to scroll down.)
- **Delete data**: Tap Show All Data below Options, swipe left on a data record, then tap Delete. To delete all data, tap Edit, then tap Delete All.
- **Change the measurement unit**: Tap Unit below Options, then select a unit.

Learn more about health and fitness

The bottom of the Summary screen provides introductory articles, app suggestions, and other information. Tap an item to learn more.

When you view the details in many health categories, recommended apps are shown in addition to your data.

Share your data in Health on iPhone

You can share health data stored in the Health app ♥ —such as health alerts and trends—with friends, family, and others caring for you.

Share health data with a loved one

People you share health data with can also view the health notifications you receive, including high heart rate and irregular rhythm notifications. You can also share notifications for significant trends, such as a steep decline in activity.

To share with somebody, you need to include them in your contacts, and they need an iPhone with iOS 15 or later.

1. Tap Sharing at the bottom of the screen.
2. Do one of the following:
    ○ Set up sharing for the first time: Tap Share with Someone.
    ○ **Share with an additional contact**: Tap "Add another person," then tap Next.
3. Use the search field to find someone in your contacts list.
4. To select someone, tap their contact information.
5. Tap See Suggested Topics or Set Up Manually.
6. Choose topics to share.
7. Scroll down to see all topics on a screen, then tap Next to see the next screen.
8. Tap Share, then tap Done.

Your invitation appears as a notification on your contact's iPhone and on their Sharing screen in Health, where they can accept or decline your invitation.

You receive a notification when your invitation is accepted.

Share health data with your doctor

You can share health data (such as heart rate, exercise minutes, hours of sleep, lab results, and heart health notifications) with your doctors. Doctors view the data in a dashboard in their health records systems (U.S. only; on systems that support Health app data Share with Provider).

1. Tap Sharing at the bottom of the screen.
2. Do one of the following:
    ○ Set up sharing for the first time: Tap "Share with your doctor."
    ○ **Share with an additional provider**: Tap "Share with another doctor."
3. Tap Next, then select one of the suggested providers, or use Search to find your provider.
4. If Connect to Account appears, tap it, enter the user name and password you use for the patient web portal for that account, then follow the onscreen instructions.
    In addition to sharing your health data, connecting to your account also causes your health records for that account to download to Health.
5. Choose topics to share with your doctor.
6. Scroll down to see all topics on a screen, then tap Next to see the next screen.
7. Tap Share, then tap Done.

Review or change the data you're sharing with others

1. Tap Sharing at the bottom of the screen.
2. Tap the name of a person or a healthcare provider.
3. Scroll down, then tap View Shared Data.
4. Make any changes, then tap Done.

Stop sharing data with a contact or a provider

1. Tap Sharing at the bottom of the screen.
2. Tap the name of a person or a healthcare provider.
3. Tap Stop Sharing or Remove Account.

Note: If you start sharing data with someone, simply removing them from Contacts doesn't stop the information from being shared.

Share health and fitness data with apps and devices

You can give other apps permission to share health and fitness data with Health. For example, if you install a workout app, its exercise data can appear in Health. The workout app can also read and make use of data (such as your heart rate and weight) shared by other devices and apps. If you didn't give an app permission to share data with Health when you set up the app, you can give permission later. You can also remove permission from an app.

1. Tap your profile picture or initials at the top right.
   If you don't see your profile picture or initials, tap Summary or Browse at the bottom of the screen, then scroll to the top of the screen.
2. Below Privacy, tap Apps or Devices.
   The screen lists the items that requested access to Health data.
3. To change the access for an item, tap it, then turn on or off permission to write data to—or read data from—Health.

Share your health and fitness data in XML format

You can export all of your health and fitness data from Health in XML format, which is a common format for sharing data between apps.

1. Tap your profile picture or initials at the top right.
   If you don't see your profile picture or initials, tap Summary or Browse at the bottom of the screen, then scroll to the top of the screen.
2. Tap Export All Health Data, then choose a method for sharing your data.

View data shared by others in Health on iPhone

You can receive notifications about a loved one's health, and you can view data about their activity, mobility, heart rate, and health trends in the Health app .

Accept an invitation to view another person's health data

For a loved one to send you an invitation to view their health data, and for you to receive it, each of you must have your own iPhone with iOS 15 or later.

1. After the invitation arrives, do one of the following:
   o Tap the invitation, such as on the Lock Screen or in Notification Center.
   o In Health, tap Sharing at the bottom of the screen, then tap View in the invitation at the top of the screen.
2. Tap Accept, then tap Done.

View shared data and quickly respond to it

1. Tap Sharing at the bottom of the screen.
2. Tap the contact card listed below Sharing With You.

3. You can do any of the following:
   - **Quickly respond**: Tap Message, Call, or FaceTime.
   - **See more detail**: Tap an item on the screen.
     If the detail includes chart data, you can start a conversation about it by tapping Message. The chart is included in your message.

Ask another person to share their health data with you

You can ask someone to share their health data with you. They control which data they share and when to stop sharing.

Note: For you to ask someone to share their health data with you, each of you must have your own iPhone with iOS 16 or later.

1. Tap Sharing at the bottom of the screen.
2. Tap Ask Someone to Share, then choose an option.
3. Let your invitee know that you need to be included in their contacts to share with you, and that if they need assistance, sharing instructions are available in Share health data with a loved one.

Get health records from your providers

Download health records on iPhone

The Health app ♥ offers secure access to information about your vaccinations, allergies, conditions, medications, and more (not available in all countries or regions).

You can use a QR code or a link from a healthcare provider or authority to download a verifiable COVID-19 vaccination or test result record, and you can set up automatic downloads for a range of health records from supporting healthcare organizations.

Note: When iPhone is locked with a passcode or Face ID, all of the health data in the Health app—other than what you add to your Medical ID—is encrypted.

Use a QR code or a link to download a verifiable COVID-19 vaccination or test result record

You can securely download verifiable COVID-19 vaccination and test result records and store them in the Health app. You can also add verifiable COVID-19 vaccination records to the Wallet app.

1. If your healthcare provider or authority makes a QR code or a link available to you, do one of the following:
   - Use your iPhone camera to scan the QR code.
   - Tap the link.
2. Do one of the following:
   - Add a vaccination record to Wallet and Health: Tap Add to Wallet & Health, then tap Done.
   - Add a test result to Health: Tap Add to Health, then tap Done.

To view a verifiable COVID-19 vaccination or test result record in Health, tap Browse at the bottom right of the screen, scroll down, then tap Immunizations (for a vaccination) or Lab Results (for a test result).

You can also view and present a vaccination record as a vaccination card in Wallet on your iPhone. If you have an Apple Watch paired with your iPhone, the vaccination card is also added to and accessible from your Apple Watch (watchOS 8 or later).

Note: If you set up automatic health record downloads from a healthcare provider that supports verifiable health records and Health Records on iPhone, and you receive a COVID-19 vaccination or test from the provider, the record is automatically downloaded to Health.

Set up automatic health record downloads from your healthcare provider

Supporting healthcare organizations can securely and automatically download records of your allergies, medical conditions, medications, labs, vaccinations, and more to Health.

1. Tap your profile picture or initials at the top right.
   If you don't see your profile picture or initials, tap Summary or Browse at the bottom of the screen, then scroll to the top of the screen.
2. Tap Health Records, then do one of the following:
   ○ Set up your first download: Tap Get Started.
   ○ Set up downloads for additional accounts: Tap Add Account.
3. A list of nearby organizations appears. If your organization doesn't appear in the list, enter the name of a clinic, hospital, or other place where you obtain health records. Or enter the name of a city, state, or province to find organizations near there.
4. Tap the name of your organization.
5. Tap Connect to Account (below Available to Connect) to go to the sign-in screen for your patient portal.
6. Enter the user name and password you use for the patient web portal of that organization, then follow the onscreen instructions.

After you set up downloads from an organization, you automatically receive new records in Health as they become available.

Note: Your healthcare organization might not appear in this feature. Organizations are added frequently.

Add a previously downloaded vaccination record to Wallet

You may have a verifiable COVID-19 vaccination record in Health that doesn't appear in Wallet if you did either of the following:

- You set up health record downloads from a healthcare provider that supports verifiable health records and Health Records on iPhone, and you received your COVID-19 vaccination from the provider.
- You used a QR code or a link to obtain a verifiable COVID-19 vaccination record using a version of iOS earlier than iOS 15.1.

To add this information as a vaccination card in Wallet, do the following:

1. Tap Summary in Health (at the bottom left of the screen).
2. Tap Add to Wallet (in an alert near the top of the screen).

View health records in Health on iPhone

After you set up health record downloads from a healthcare provider, your records are securely and automatically downloaded to iPhone, where they're available for viewing in the Health app ♥.

View your health records

Tap Browse at the bottom right to display the Health Categories screen, then do one of the following:

- Tap the search field, then enter the name of a health record category (such as clinical vitals) or a type of data (such as blood pressure).
- Scroll down, then tap a category (such as Allergies or Clinical Vitals) below Health Records.
- Scroll down, then tap the name of a specific organization.

To see more details, tap any section where you see ›.

Note: If you don't see health records that you expect from a healthcare provider, ensure that you're signed in to your account with the provider. Tap Browse, scroll to your list of accounts, tap the name of your provider, then sign in if you're asked.

Pin important lab results

You can pin results so that they appear at the top of the Lab Results screen for quick access.

1. Tap Browse at the bottom right, scroll down, then tap Lab Results.
2. Do any of the following:
   - Swipe right on a result, then tap 📌.
   - Touch and hold a result, then tap Pin this Lab.

Share your health records with other apps

Third-party apps can request access to your health records. Before you grant access, be sure that you trust the app with your records.

1. To grant access, choose which categories to share—such as allergies, medications, or immunizations—when asked.
2. Choose whether to grant access to your current and future health records or to only your current records.
   If you choose to share only your current records, you're asked to grant access whenever new records are downloaded to your iPhone.

To stop sharing health records with the app, turn off its permission to read data from Health.

Delete an organization and its records from iPhone

1. Tap your profile picture or initials at the top right, then tap Health Records.
   If you don't see your profile picture or initials, tap Summary or Browse at the bottom of the screen, then scroll to the top of the page.
2. Tap the name of an organization, then tap Remove Account.

Monitor your walking steadiness in Health on iPhone

When you carry your iPhone in a pocket or holster near your waist, the Health app 🤍 uses custom algorithms that assess your balance, strength, and gait. You can receive a notification if your steadiness becomes low or stays low, and you can automatically share the notification with someone close to you. Health can also show you exercises to help improve your walking steadiness. (iPhone 8 and later.)

Receive notifications when your steadiness is low or very low

1. Tap your profile picture or initials at the top right.
   If you don't see your profile picture or initials, tap Summary or Browse at the bottom of the screen, then scroll to the top of the screen.
2. Tap Health Checklist.
3. Tap Set Up for Walking Steadiness Notifications, then following the onscreen instructions.

To review your notifications, tap Browse at the bottom right, tap Mobility, scroll down, then tap Walking Steadiness Notifications.

View your walking steadiness data

1. Tap Browse at the bottom right, then tap Mobility.
2. Tap Walking Steadiness (you may need to scroll down).
3. To learn about the three steadiness levels (OK, Low, and Very Low), tap ⓘ.

Learn how to improve your walking steadiness

1. Tap Browse at the bottom right, then tap Mobility.
2. Scroll down, then tap Exercises that May Improve Walking Steadiness

Track your menstrual cycle

Log menstrual cycle information in Health on iPhone

In the Health app 🤍, you can log menstrual cycle information to get period and fertile window predictions.

Set up cycle tracking

1. Tap Browse at the bottom right, then tap Cycle Tracking.
2. Tap Get Started, then follow the onscreen instructions.
   To help improve predictions for your period and fertile windows, enter the requested information.

Log your cycle information

You can log the days of a period and track information like symptoms, spotting, basal body temperature, and more.

1. Tap Browse at the bottom right, then tap Cycle Tracking.
2. Do any of the following:
   - **Log a period day**: Tap a day in the timeline at the top of the screen. Or tap Add Period at the top right, then select days from the monthly calendar.

- Log the flow level for a day: Swipe the timeline to select a day, tap Period (below Menstruation), then choose an option.
- Log symptoms, spotting, or other information: Swipe the timeline to select a day, tap a category (below Other Data), supply the information, then tap Done.
- Add data logging categories: Tap Options, then choose from the categories below Cycle Log.

Note: You can use Apple Watch (sold separately) to help log your cycle information.

Edit your log

Your logged information appears in the timeline at the top of the screen, where a solid red circle ● represents a day you logged a period and a purple dot · represents a day you logged with additional information. Data for the day selected in the timeline appears in the Cycle Log (below the timeline). To change your logged information, do the following:

1. Swipe the timeline to select a day.
2. Tap a category of data (such as Menstruation or Symptoms), make your changes, then tap Done.

To unmark a period day, tap its solid red circle in the timeline.

Manage cycle factors

When you enter information about pregnancy, lactation, and contraceptive use, that information is used to help manage your cycle predictions.

1. Tap Browse at the bottom right, then tap Cycle Tracking.
2. Scroll down, tap Factors, then do any of the following:
   - Add a factor: Tap Add Factor, select a factor, tap Started if you need to change the start date, then tap Add.
   - Change the end date for a current factor: Tap the factor, tap Ended, select a date, then tap Done.
   - Delete a current factor: Tap the factor, then tap Delete Factor.
   - Set up factors: Select any factor that currently applies to you, then tap Done.

The information you add about yourself in Health is yours to use and share. You can decide what information is stored in Health as well as who can access your data. When your iPhone is locked with a passcode or Face ID, all of your health and fitness data in Health, other than your Medical ID, is encrypted. Any health data synced to iCloud is encrypted both in transit and on Apple servers. And if you have a recent version of iOS (and watchOS, if you're using Apple Watch for cycle tracking) with default two-factor authentication and a passcode, your health and activity data is stored in a way that Apple can't read it. This means that when you use the Cycle Tracking feature and two-factor authentication, your health data synced to iCloud is encrypted end-to-end, and Apple does not have the key to decrypt the data and therefore cannot read it.

View menstrual cycle predictions and history in Health on iPhone

When you log your menstrual cycle in the Health app 💜, you can check the date for your next period or fertile window, receive notifications about when your next period or fertile window is approaching, view details about your cycle history, and more.

Note: Health can also use data from Apple Watch to improve the predictions for your period and fertile windows.

View your cycle timeline

Tap Browse at the bottom right, then tap Cycle Tracking.

At the top of the screen, a timeline shows the following icons.

Icon	Description
	A predicted period day.
	A predicted day of your fertile window.
	A day you likely ovulated (requires Apple Watch Series 8 to be paired with your iPhone; Apple Watch sold separately).
	A day you logged a period.
	A day you added information (for example, noting a headache or cramping).

To select different days, swipe the timeline.

Check the dates for your predicted next period and for your reported last period

1. Tap Browse at the bottom right, then tap Cycle Tracking.
2. Scroll to Predictions to see when your next period is likely to start.
   If you don't see the estimate, tap Show All next to Predictions.
3. Scroll to Summary to see the date of your last period and your typical cycle length.

Change cycle tracking notifications, cycle prediction displays, and other options

You can turn off period, fertility, and cycle deviation notifications, hide period and fertility predictions, and more. You can turn these on again at any time.

1. Tap Browse at the bottom right, then tap Cycle Tracking.
2. Scroll down, tap Options, then turn options on or off.

View your cycle history

1. Tap Browse at the bottom right, then tap Cycle Tracking.
2. To see a summary of your last three cycles, scroll down to Your Cycles.
3. To see summaries of all previous cycles, tap Cycle History.

   To send or a save a PDF of your cycle history, tap Export PDF, tap ⬆️, then choose an option.
4. To see details about a cycle, tap it.
   To change any details for the cycle, tap Edit.

To send or a save a PDF of the cycle details, tap Export PDF, tap ⬆, then choose an option.

If you receive a Cycle Deviation notification

You can receive a notification if your logged cycle history shows a possible cycle deviation. Irregular periods, infrequent periods, prolonged periods, and persistent spotting are common cycle deviations that may indicate an underlying condition, or may be due to other factors.

When you receive a notification, do the following to review your logged cycle history:

1. In Health, tap Summary at the bottom of the screen.
2. Tap Review Cycle History in the Possible Cycle Deviation notification.
3. Follow the onscreen instructions to confirm, add, or edit the data in your cycle history.

If a cycle deviation is detected, a screen suggests what to do next.

The information you add about yourself in Health is yours to use and share. You can decide what information is stored in Health as well as who can access your data. When your iPhone is locked with a passcode or Face ID, all of your health and fitness data in Health, other than your Medical ID, is encrypted. Any health data synced to iCloud is encrypted both in transit and on Apple servers. And if you have a recent version of iOS (and watchOS, if you're using Apple Watch for cycle tracking) with default two-factor authentication and a passcode, your health and activity data is stored in a way that Apple can't read it. This means that when you use the Cycle Tracking feature and two-factor authentication, your health data synced to iCloud is encrypted end-to-end, and Apple does not have the key to decrypt the data and therefore cannot read it.

Manage your medications

Track your medications in Health on iPhone

In the Health app 💙, you can track and manage the medications, vitamins, and supplements you take.

Note: Some features are not available in all countries or regions. The Medications feature is not a substitute for professional medical judgment. Additional information is available on the labels of your medications. Consult your healthcare provider prior to making any decisions related to your health.

Add and schedule a new medication

1. Tap Browse at the bottom right, then tap Medications.
2. Tap Add a Medication (to start your list) or Add Medication (to add to your list).
3. To identify the medication, do one of the following:
   - **Type the name**: Tap the text field, enter the name, then tap Add.
     In the U.S. only, suggestions appear as you begin typing. You can select a suggestion, or finish typing the name, then tap Add.
   - **Use the camera**: (U.S. only) Tap 📷 next to the text field, then follow the onscreen instructions.
     If a match isn't found, tap Search by Name, then type the name (as described above).

4. Follow the onscreen instructions to optionally create a custom visual of the medication and to optionally set a schedule.

When you set a schedule, you receive notifications from Health reminding you to log the medication.

Change the schedule for a medication or update other information

1. Tap Browse at the bottom right, then tap Medications.
2. Do any of the following:
   - **Change the schedule for a medication**: Tap its name in the list of your medications, scroll down to Schedule, tap Edit (for Schedule), then tap a field to change it.
   - **Change the icon, nickname, or notes for a medication**: Tap its name in the list of your medications, scroll down to Details, tap Edit (for Details), tap Edit or either of the text fields, then make your changes.
   - **Reorder your list**: Tap Edit above the list of your medications, touch and hold ≡ for a medication, then drag it to a new position.
   - **Archive a medication**: Swipe left on its name in the list of your medications, then tap Archive.
   - **Make an archived medication reappear in your list of medications**: Tap Edit above the list of your medications, then tap ⊕ next to the medication name (in the list of Archived Medications). Any schedule you previously set is not preserved.
   - Change how you receive notifications about taking medications.

Log when you take a medication

You can log a medication, scheduled or unscheduled, at any time.

1. Tap Browse at the bottom right, then tap Medications.
2. Select a day at the top of the screen.
3. Do one of the following:
   - **Log whether you took a scheduled medication**: Tap the name of a medication in the list below Log, then below the medication, tap Taken or Skipped.
   - **Log an unscheduled medication**: Tap As Needed Medications in the list below Log, then below the medication, tap Taken.

Tip: When you receive a notification to log a scheduled medication, press and hold the notification, then choose an option.

To review your history of taking the medication, tap Browse at the bottom right, tap Medications, then tap the medication (in the list of your medications).

Share your medication list

1. Do one of the following:
   - Share your list—or just specific medications—with a loved one who has an iPhone with iOS 15 or later.

Tip: If you add a new medication after you start sharing, add it to your shared list.

   - Share your list as a PDF: Tap Browse at the bottom right, tap Medications, scroll down, tap Export PDF, tap ⬆, then choose an option.

Learn more about your medications in Health on iPhone (U.S. only)

You can learn more about the medications you add to your medications list in the Health app ♥.

Learn about a medication

You can learn more about what a medication is used for, how it works, potential side effects, and how to pronounce it.

1. Tap Browse at the bottom right, then tap Medications.
2. Tap the medication (in the list of your medications), then scroll down.

Learn about interactions between your medications

1. Tap Browse at the bottom right, then tap Medications.
2. Tap Drug Interactions.
3. To learn whether interaction factors like alcohol might interact with your medications, tap Edit (in the Interaction Factors area), select the factors that apply, then tap Done.
4. To learn more about an interaction, tap it.

Prioritize your sleep

Set up a schedule for a Sleep Focus in Health on iPhone

You can use the Health app ♥ to help meet your sleep goals by scheduling regular times for going to bed and waking up. You can create multiple schedules—for example, one for weekdays and another for weekends.

For the sleep schedules you set, a Sleep Focus helps reduce distractions before and during bedtime. For example, it can filter out notifications and phone calls, and it can signal to others that you're not available. You can also schedule a wind down period to begin from 15 minutes to 3 hours before your bedtime. Your Sleep Focus begins at the start of your wind down time.

To help you wake up on time, you can select an alarm sound, a vibration, and a snooze option. Or you can choose to have no alarm at all.

Set up a Sleep Focus

1. Go to Settings ⚙ > Focus, then tap Sleep.

   If you don't see Sleep as an option, tap ✛ at the top right, tap Sleep, then tap Customize Focus.
2. Customize your focus.
   For example, you can allow interruptions from people important to you, customize the Lock Screen and Home Screen, and customize how apps and your iPhone behave when a Sleep Focus is on.

Note: If you set up Wind Down Shortcuts in iOS 15, they automatically appear in iOS 16 as Shortcuts on your Sleep Focus Home Screen.

Set up your first recurring sleep schedule

When you set up a Sleep Focus, you can set your next bed and wake up times. This schedule repeats only once. To set up a recurring sleep schedule, do the following:

1. In the Health app, tap Browse at the bottom right, then tap Sleep.
2. Scroll down to Your Schedule, then tap Sleep Schedule.
3. Tap Set Your First Schedule, then select your options:
   - Set the days for your schedule: Tap a day at the top of the screen to add or remove it from your schedule. The schedule applies only to days shown with solid-color circles.
   - Adjust your bedtime and wake up schedule: Drag 🛏 to change your bedtime, ⏰ to change your wake up time, or the semicircle between the icons to shift both times simultaneously.
   - Set the alarm options: Turn Alarm on or off.
     When Alarm is turned on, you can choose a sound, its volume, a vibration, and the snooze option.
4. Tap Add.

Add, modify, or delete sleep schedules

After setting up your first sleep schedule, you can do the following:

- **Set up additional schedules**: For example, if you have a weekday schedule, you can add a weekend schedule.
- **Change schedules**: You can adjust the bedtimes, wake up times, and alarm options for an entire sleep schedule or for only your next schedule.
- **Turn off alarms**: You can turn off alarms for all sleep schedules, for a particular schedule, or for only your next scheduled wake up time.
- Remove a schedule.

Turn off alarms and delete sleep schedules in Health on iPhone

In the Health app ♥, you can turn off your scheduled alarms and turn off or delete your sleep schedules.

Turn off all sleep schedules and alarms

After you create one or more sleep schedules, you can turn them all off at once. When all sleep schedules are turned off, scheduled alarms are also turned off.

1. Tap Browse at the bottom right, then tap Sleep.
2. Scroll down to Your Schedule.
3. Tap Full Schedule & Options, then turn off Sleep Schedule (at the top of the screen).

You can turn them all on again later.

Delete a sleep schedule and its alarm

1. Tap Browse at the bottom right, then tap Sleep.
2. Scroll down to Your Schedule, then tap Full Schedule & Options.
3. Tap Edit for the schedule you want to remove.
4. Tap Delete Schedule (at the bottom of the screen).
5. Tap Done.

Permanently turn off the alarm for a sleep schedule

1. Tap Browse at the bottom right, then tap Sleep.
2. Scroll down to Your Schedule, then tap Full Schedule & Options.
3. Tap Edit for the sleep schedule you want to change.
4. Turn off Alarm.
   You can turn it back on again later.
5. Tap Done.

The rest of your sleep schedule remains in effect.

Turn off only your next scheduled alarm

1. Tap Browse at the bottom right, then tap Sleep.
2. Scroll down to Your Schedule, then tap Edit (below Next).
3. Turn off Alarm.
4. Tap Done.

After your next wake up time, your normal alarm resumes.

Note: You can also use the Clock app 🕐 to change your next sleep schedule alarm.

Add or change sleep schedules in Health on iPhone

After you set up your first sleep schedule in the Health app 💗, you can set additional schedules—for example, you can create separate schedules for weekdays and the weekend. You can also modify any schedule—for example, you can change its wake up time.

Add or change a sleep schedule

1. Tap Browse at the bottom right, then tap Sleep.
2. Scroll down to Your Schedule, then tap Full Schedule & Options.
3. Do one of the following:
   - **Add a sleep schedule**: Tap Add Another Schedule.
   - **Change a sleep schedule**: Tap Edit for the schedule you want to change.
4. Do any of the following:
   - **Set the days for your schedule**: Tap a day at the top of the screen to add or remove it from your schedule. The schedule applies only to days shown with solid-color circles.
   - **Adjust your bedtime and wake up schedule**: Drag 🛏 to change your bedtime, ((⏰)) to change your wake up time, or the semicircle between the icons to shift both times simultaneously.
   - **Set the alarm options**: Turn Alarm on or off.
     When Alarm is turned on, you can choose a sound, its volume, a vibration, and the snooze option.

175

Note: You can't select a song for a sleep schedule alarm. However, you can select a song for an alarm with the Clock app ⊙.

5. When you're finished, tap Add or Done.
   When you tap Done, the changes apply to every day in the schedule.

Change only your next schedule

You can make a temporary change to a sleep schedule.

1. Tap Browse at the bottom right, then tap Sleep.
2. Scroll down to Your Schedule, then tap Edit (below Next).
3. Drag 🛏 to change your bedtime, ⏰ to change your wake up time, or the semicircle between the icons to shift both times simultaneously.
4. Choose alarm options.
   When Alarm is turned on, you can choose a sound, its volume, a vibration, and the snooze option.
5. Tap Done.

Note: You can also use the Clock app ⊙ to change your next sleep schedule alarm.

After your next wake up time, your normal schedule resumes.

Turn your Sleep Focus on or off on iPhone

Quickly turn your Sleep Focus on or off

Open Control Center, then tap Sleep.

Your Sleep Focus turns on or off again at your next scheduled bedtime or wake up time.

Turn off your Sleep Focus for all sleep schedules

1. In the Health app ♥, tap Browse at the bottom right, then tap Sleep.
2. Scroll down to Your Schedule, then tap Full Schedule & Options.
3. Turn off Use Schedule for Sleep Focus.

When this setting is off, your sleep schedules remain in effect, but your Sleep Focus doesn't automatically turn on. You can turn this setting on again at any time.

Change your wind down period, sleep goal, and more in Health on iPhone

You can change Sleep options in the Health app ♥.

1. Tap Browse at the bottom right, then tap Sleep.
2. Scroll down to Your Schedule, then tap Full Schedule & Options.
3. Scroll down to Additional Details, then make your changes:
   o **Wind down period**: Tap Wind Down, then select how many minutes or hours to give yourself to wind down before your scheduled bedtime. Your Sleep Focus turns on at the beginning of the wind down period.
   o **Sleep goal**: Tap Sleep goal, then select a time. Any new schedules you set up reflect your new goal.

- **Track time in bed with iPhone**: When you turn this on, iPhone automatically tracks your time in bed by analyzing when you pick up and use your iPhone. You can view this data in your sleep history in Health. Alternatively, you can turn off this setting and use a sleep tracker or monitor to help determine the amount of time you're in bed, or open the Sleep category in Health, then tap Add Data to manually add the data.
- **Sleep notifications**: Turn Sleep Reminders or Sleep Results on or off.
  Note: Sleep Results notifications require data from Apple Watch or other sleep tracking apps and hardware.

View your sleep history in Health on iPhone

Sleep data in the Health app ♥ provides insight into your sleep habits.

To obtain sleep data, you can use a sleep tracker or monitor, set up a sleep schedule and let iPhone estimate your time in bed, or open the Sleep category, then tap Add Data to manually add the data.

1. Tap Browse at the bottom right, then tap Sleep.
2. Do any of the following:
   - **View sleep data by week or month**: Tap a tab at the top of the screen.
   - Change the time span displayed in the graph: Swipe the graph left or right.
   - **View the details for a day**: Tap the column for the day.
   - **Manually add sleep data**: Tap Add Data in the top-right corner of the screen.
   - **Get cumulative sleep data**: Tap Show More Sleep Data.

Use headphone hearing safeguards

Use headphone audio level features on iPhone

If you listen to loud headphone audio for long enough to affect your hearing, iPhone automatically sends you a notification that you should turn down the volume. After you receive a notification, the next time you plug in your headphones or connect them using Bluetooth, your volume is automatically set to a lower level. You can turn the volume up again if you choose.

Note: Depending on your country or region, Headphone Notifications may be turned on by default, and in some countries or regions, you may not be able to turn it off. If allowed in your

country or region, you can turn Headphone Notifications on or off in Settings ⚙ > Sounds & Haptics > Headphone Safety.

You can find headphone notifications on the Summary screen of the Health app ♥.

Tip: To review the details of a headphone notification, tap Browse at the bottom right of Health, tap Hearing, then tap Headphone Notifications.

In addition, you can use the Settings app ⚙ to set a maximum decibel level that keeps your headphone audio at a comfortable level.

Reduce loud headphone sounds in Settings

1. Go to Settings 🔘, then tap Sounds & Haptics.
2. Tap Headphone Safety.
3. Turn on Reduce Loud Sounds, then drag the slider.
   iPhone analyzes your headphone audio and reduces any sound above the level you set.

Note: If you set up Screen Time for family members, you can prevent them from changing the Reduce Loud Sounds level. Go to Settings > Screen Time > Content & Privacy Restrictions > Reduce Loud Sounds, then select Don't Allow.

Improve the accuracy of audio measurements for third-party Bluetooth headphones

Classify your Bluetooth devices as headphones, speakers, or other devices.

1. Go to Settings 🔘 > Bluetooth, then tap ⓘ next to the name of the device.
2. Tap Device Type, then choose a classification.

Headphone audio measurements are most accurate when using Apple or Beats headphones. Audio played through other headphones can be estimated based on the volume of your iPhone.

Check your headphone levels on iPhone

While using headphones with iPhone, you can check whether the audio level is OK by viewing the Hearing control in Control Center. In the Health app 🩷, you can review the history of your headphone listening habits.

Check your headphone level while you listen

1. Go to Settings 🔘 > Control Center, then add Hearing.
2. Connect your headphones, then play audio.
3. Open Control Center, then tap 👂.
   The audio level (in decibels) of your headphones is displayed on the Headphone Level meter.

Note: You can also tap Live Listen (below the Headphone Level meter) to turn Live Listen on or off. See Use iPhone as a remote microphone with Live Listen. Typically, headphone level monitoring and Live Listen aren't used at the same time. The Headphone Level monitor is intended for listening to audio playback. Live Listen is intended for listening to external sounds with the iPhone microphone.

Check your headphone levels over time

1. In Health, tap Browse at the bottom right, then tap Hearing.
2. Tap Headphone Audio Levels, then do any of the following:
   - **View exposure levels over a time period:** Tap the tabs at the top of the screen. (All levels are measured in decibels.)
   - Learn about the sound level classifications: Tap ⓘ.
   - Change the time span displayed in the graph: Swipe the graph left or right.
   - **See details about a moment in time**: Touch and hold the graph, then drag to move the selection.
   - **View details about average exposure**: Tap Show All Filters, then tap Daily Average.

- View a line representing average exposure: Tap Exposure below the graph.
- **View the high and low range**: Tap Show All Filters, then tap Range.
- **Filter the data by headphones**: Tap Show All Filters, scroll to the bottom of the screen, then choose one of your headphones.
- **View highlights**: Scroll down; to see more, tap Show All.

Headphone audio measurements are most accurate when using Apple or Beats headphones. Audio played through other headphones can be estimated based on the volume of your iPhone.

Register as an organ donor in Health on iPhone (U.S. only)

In the Health app ♥, you can register to be an organ, eye, or tissue donor with Donate Life America. If you later change your decision, you can remove your registration. Your decision to donate is accessible to others in your Medical ID.

Learn about organ donation

1. Tap your profile picture or initials at the top right.
   If you don't see your profile picture or initials, tap Summary or Browse at the bottom of the screen, then scroll to the top of the screen.
2. Tap Organ Donation, then tap Learn More for an overview of organ donation and Donate Life America.

Register with Donate Life America

1. Tap your profile picture or initials at the top right.
   If you don't see your profile picture or initials, tap Summary or Browse at the bottom of the screen, then scroll to the top of the screen.
2. Tap Sign Up with Donate Life.

To later change your donor information or remove your registration, tap your profile picture or initials, tap Organ Donation, then tap Edit Donor Registration.

Back up your Health data on iPhone

If you sign in with your Apple ID, your health and fitness information in the Health app ♥ is stored automatically in iCloud. Your information is encrypted as it goes between iCloud and your device and while it's stored in iCloud.

In addition to using iCloud, or if you aren't using iCloud, you can back up your Health data by encrypting a computer backup.

Stop storing your Health data in iCloud

Go to Settings ⚙ > [your name] > iCloud > Show All, then turn off Health.

Home

Set up accessories with Home on iPhone

The first time you open the Home app ⬆, the setup assistant helps you create a home, where you can add accessories and define rooms. If you've already created a home when setting up a different accessory, you skip this step.

Add an accessory to Home

Before you add an accessory such as a light or camera, be sure that it's connected to a power source, is turned on, and is using your Wi-Fi network.

1. Tap Home at the bottom left, then tap Add Accessory.

   You can also tap ┼ at the top of the screen, then choose Add Accessory.
2. Follow the onscreen instructions.

You may need to scan a QR code or enter an 8-digit HomeKit setup code found on the accessory itself (or its box or documentation). A supported smart TV displays a QR code for you to scan. You can assign the accessory to a room, and give it a name, and then use this name when controlling the accessory with Siri. You can also add suggested automations during set up.

When you set up Apple TV in tvOS and assign it to a room, it automatically appears in that room in the Home app on iPhone.

Show accessories in a room

You can show individual rooms, scenes assigned to them, and a room's accessories organized by category.

In Room View, do one of the following.

- Tap > next to a room's name.
- Tap ⋯, then choose a room.

Change an accessory's room assignment

1. Touch and hold an accessory tile, tap Accessory Details, then swipe up or tap ⚙.
2. Tap Room, then choose a room.

Edit a room

You can change a room's name and wallpaper, remove the room, and more. When you remove the room, the accessories assigned to it move to Default Room.

1. On the Home tab, tap > next to a room, or tap ⋯, then choose a room.
2. Tap ⋯, then tap Room Settings.

Organize rooms into zones

You can group rooms together into a zone to easily control different areas of your home with Siri. For example, if you have a two-story home, you can assign the rooms on the first floor to a downstairs zone. Then you can say something to Siri like "Turn off the lights downstairs."

1. Tap > next to a room on the Home tab or tap ⋯, then choose a room.
2. Tap ⋯, then tap Room Settings.
3. Tap Zone, then tap an existing zone, or tap Create New to add the room to a new zone.

Control accessories with Home on iPhone

Use the Home app 🏠 and Control Center to control accessories in your home.

Control accessories in the Home app

On the Home tab, tap an accessory's icon on the left side of the tile—a light, for example—to quickly turn the accessory on or off. Tap the accessory's name on the right side of the tile to show the accessory's control.

The available controls depend on the type of accessory. For example, with some lightbulbs, there are controls for changing colors. With your smart TV, you can choose an input source.

Control accessories in Control Center

When you're home with your iPhone, you can see the relevant scenes and accessories for that moment in Control Center. For example, a coffee maker may appear in the morning and be replaced by your bedside lamp at night.

Open Control Center, then tap a button to turn an accessory on or off, or touch and hold the button until controls appear.

To quickly see all your scenes and accessories (except cameras), tap 🏠.

If you don't want accessories to appear in Control Center, go to Settings ⚙️ > Control Center, then turn off Show Home Controls.

View categories and home status

The Lights, Climate, Security, Speakers and TVs, and Water categories let you quickly access all the relevant accessories organized by room.

1. Open the Home app 🏠 to show the Home tab.
   Below your home's name, buttons show the status of accessories belonging to a category—for example, a Lights category that shows "3 on."
2. Tap one of the category buttons to show all accessories within that category, organized by room.
3. While viewing a category, tap the icon on the left side of an accessory tile to perform an action—turn a light or group of lights on or off, start playing music on a HomePod, or lock the front door.

Turn on Adaptive Lighting

Some lights let you adjust their color temperature, from cool blue to warm yellow. You can set supported lights to automatically adjust the color temperature throughout the day. Wake up to warm colors, stay alert and focused mid-day with cooler ones, and wind down at night by removing blue light. For a light that supports Adaptive Lighting, follow these steps.

1. Tap the right side of the light's tile to show the controls.
   You can also touch and hold the tile, then choose Accessory Details.

2. Tap .

Edit home accessories

To edit accessory settings, tap the right side of an accessory tile, swipe up or tap ⚙, then do any of the following:

- Rename an accessory: Tap ⓧ to delete the old name, then type a new one.
- Change an accessory's icon: Tap the icon next to the accessory's name, then select a new icon. If you don't get a choice of other icons, it means the icon can't be changed for this accessory.

Group accessories

You can control multiple accessories with the tap of a button by grouping them.

1. Tap the right side of an accessory tile, swipe up or tap ⚙, then tap Group with Other Accessories.
2. Tap the accessory you want to group with this accessory—another light in the room, for example.
3. In the Group Name field, type a name for the group.
4. Tap Done.
   Turn on Include in Favorites to include the group in Favorites on the Home tab.

Control your home using Siri on iPhone

In addition to using the Home app 🏠, you can use Siri to control your accessories and scenes. Here are some of the things you can say to Siri for the accessories you add and the scenes, rooms, or homes you set up:

- "Turn off the lights" or "Turn on the lights"
- "Set the temperature to 68 degrees"
- "Turn on the bedroom lights at 9 PM"
- "Did I lock the front door?"
- "Show me the entryway camera"
- "Turn down the kitchen lights"
- "Set my reading scene"
- "Turn off the lights in the Chicago house"

Set up HomePod in Home on iPhone

Use Home to send and receive Intercom messages

1. In the Home app, tap ⋯, then tap Home Settings.
2. Tap Intercom, then configure these settings:
   - When you can receive Intercom messages
   - Who is allowed to send or receive Intercom messages
   - Which HomePod speakers can use Intercom
3. **Note**: Any member of the Home can choose when they receive Intercom messages. Only a home owner or admin can choose who can send or receive Intercom messages and which HomePod speakers can use Intercom.
4. Tap Back, then tap Done.

5. Tap ⁘ , say something like "Who ate the last cookie?" then tap Done.
   Your Intercom message is sent to all the HomePod speakers in your home, and to the iOS, iPadOS, and watchOS devices of all members of your home who can send and receive Intercom messages.
   To send a message to a HomePod in a specific room or zone, say something like "Hey Siri, tell the office 'The movie is starting'" or "Hey Siri, announce upstairs 'I'm going to the store.'"

Use Home to add and edit HomePod alarms

In the Home app, tap the right side of a HomePod tile, swipe up, then do any of the following:

- **Add an alarm**: Tap New Alarm, create the alarm, then tap Done.
- **Edit an alarm**: Tap the alarm, change the time, then tap Done.
- **Turn alarms on or off**: Tap the switch next to an alarm.
- **Delete an alarm**: Tap the alarm, then tap Delete Alarm.

Change HomePod settings

1. In the Home app, tap the right side of a HomePod tile.
2. Swipe up or tap ⚙, then configure HomePod settings.
   You can assign HomePod to a different room, add an automation, create a stereo pair with two HomePod speakers in the same room, and more.

Add a Siri-enabled accessory

You can extend access to HomePod throughout your home by enabling Siri on compatible HomeKit accessories. If you enable "Hey Siri" on these accessories, you can control them with your voice, get help with everyday questions or tasks, and play your favorite music and podcasts.

Control your home remotely with iPhone

In the Home app 🏠 , you can control your accessories even when you're away from home. To do so, you need a home hub, a device such as Apple TV (4th generation or later), HomePod, or iPad (with iOS 10.3, iPadOS 13, or later).

Go to Settings ⚙ > [your name] > iCloud, tap Show All, then turn on Home.

You must be signed in with the same Apple ID on your home hub device and your iPhone.

If you have an Apple TV or HomePod, and you're signed in with the same Apple ID as your iPhone, it's set up automatically as a home hub. To set up iPad as a home hub, tap Settings > Home, then turn on Use this iPad as a Home Hub.

Note: iPad will not be supported as a home hub on the new Home architecture, which will be available as an update in the Home app. You can still use iPad as a home hub if you can't update to the new architecture, or choose not to.

Create and use scenes in Home on iPhone

In the Home app ⌂ , you can create scenes that allow you to control multiple accessories at once. For example, you might define a "Reading" scene that adjusts the lights, plays soft music on HomePod, closes the drapes, and adjusts the thermostat.

Create a scene

1. On the Home tab, tap ╈ , then tap Add Scene.
2. Tap Custom, enter a name for the scene (such as "Dinner Party" or "Watching TV"), then tap Add Accessories.
3. Select the accessories you want this scene to include, then tap Done.
    The first accessory you select determines the room the scene is assigned to. If you first select your bedroom lamp, for example, the scene is assigned to your bedroom.
4. Set each accessory to the state you want it in when you run the scene.
    For example, for a Reading scene, you could set the bedroom lights to 100 percent, choose a low volume for the HomePod, and set the thermostat to 68 degrees.
5. Test the scene and choose whether or not to show it on the Home tab (scenes appear on the Home tab by default), then tap Done.

Use scenes

Do one of the following:

*   **Run a scene**: Tap the scene on the Home tab.

    If you've decided not to show the scene on the Home tab, tap ⋯ , choose the room the scene is assigned to, then tap the scene.
*   **Edit a scene**: Touch and hold a scene, then tap Edit Scene.
    You can change the scene's name, test the scene, add or remove accessories, and more.

Use automations in Home on iPhone

In the Home app ⌂ , you can run automations based on the time of day, your location, the activation of a sensor, or the action of an accessory. You can use preconfigured automations included with the Home app, or create automations of your own.

Use a preconfigured automation

1. On the Home tab, touch and hold an accessory, tap Accessory Details, then swipe up or tap ⊗ .
2. Turn on an automation.

To disable an automation, return to the accessory's setting screen, then turn it off.

Create an automation

1. On the Home tab, tap ╈ .
2. Tap Add Automation, then choose one of the following automation triggers:
    *   **When arriving at or leaving a location**: Tap People Arrive or People Leave. Choose when the automation is activated by people arriving or leaving, the location, and the time the automation works.

- **At a time of day**: Tap A Time of Day Occurs, then choose when you want this automation to run.
  If you choose Sunset or Sunrise, times vary as the season changes.
  You can also set an automation to only occur after sunset, which is useful for turning on lights just when they're needed.
- **When an accessory changes**: Tap An Accessory is Controlled, select an accessory, tap Next, then follow the onscreen instructions.
  You might use this, for example, to run a scene when you unlock the front door.
- **A sensor detects something**: If you've added a sensor to Home, tap A Sensor Detects Something, select an accessory, tap Next, then follow the onscreen instructions.
  You might use this, for example, to turn on lights in a stairway when motion is detected nearby.

You can also tap the right side of an automation tile, tap ⚙, then add, enable, or disable automations.

Manage and edit automations

1. Tap the Automation tab at the bottom of the Home app screen.
2. Tap an automation, then do any of the following:
   - Enable or disable the automation
   - Choose when the automation happens
   - Add or remove accessories
   - Test the automation
   - Delete the automation

Add a Siri shortcut

To make your automation even more efficient, you can add a Siri Shortcut to it.

1. When choosing accessories to control with an automation, swipe up, then tap Convert To Shortcut.
2. Tap ⊕, then choose a shortcut.

Set up security cameras in Home on iPhone

You can use the Home app 🏠 to view video activity captured by your home's cameras. With any HomeKit-compatible camera, you can view video streams in the Home app, choose who can view those streams, and set up notifications when activity is detected.

If you have one or more HomeKit Secure Video cameras, you can additionally take advantage of these features:

- **Encrypted video**: Video captured by your cameras is privately analyzed and encrypted on your home hub device (HomePod, Apple TV, or iPad) and securely uploaded to iCloud so that only you and those you share it with can view it.
- **Record video**: If you subscribe to iCloud+, you can view the last 10 days of activity from one to an unlimited number of cameras. The 50 GB iCloud+ plan supports a single camera, the 200 GB iCloud+ plan supports up to five cameras, and the 2 TB iCloud+

plan supports an unlimited number of cameras.
Note: Video content doesn't count against your iCloud storage limit.
- **Activity Zones**: Create zones that focus your camera on the most important areas within its view.
- **Face recognition**: Receive notifications when people you've tagged in the Photos app are within the camera's view.

Use Face Recognition in Home on iPhone

With a HomeKit Secure Video camera or doorbell, you can use the Home app to receive notifications when people you've tagged in the Photos app are within the camera's view.

Set up Face Recognition

Face Recognition identifies people by the faces that appear in your photo library or pictures of recent visitors captured by your camera or doorbell.

If you're setting up a camera or doorbell for the first time, do the following:

1. Add the accessory to the Home app.
2. In the Recognize Familiar Faces card, turn on Face Recognition, then tap Continue.
3. Choose who can access your photo library:
   - **Never**: Only faces you've added from clips in the Home app are recognized.
   - **Only Me**: Only the notifications you receive have the names of people in your photo library.
   - **Everyone in this Home**: The notifications for everyone in your home have the names of people in your photo library.
4. Tap Continue, then finish setting up the camera or doorbell.

If you have an existing doorbell or camera and want to use it to identify visitors, tap it on the Home tab, tap , tap Face Recognition, then turn on Face Recognition. Tap your photo library, then choose who can access it.

Note: Notifications can appear on any of the devices associated with your Apple ID.

Identify recent visitors

You can use Face Recognition to help identify people that aren't in your photo library using a picture captured by your camera or doorbell.

1. With Face Recognition turned on, open the Home app .
2. On the Home tab, tap the camera or doorbell, then tap .
3. Tap Face Recognition, tap an unidentified person listed below Recent, then tap Add Name.
4. Add the person's name or their relationship to you—Mom or Mail Carrier, for example.
5. Choose whether to be notified when they're seen by your camera or doorbell.

Note: People with a face mask don't appear in this list.

Share faces with your household

You can allow the members of your household to see the names of visitors identified in your photo library.

1. With Face Recognition turned on, open the Home app , tap , then tap Home Settings.
2. Tap Cameras & Doorbells below Notifications, then tap Face Recognition.
3. Tap your photo library, then tap Everyone in this Home.

Unlock your door with a home key on iPhone

Some lock makers provide the ability to unlock your door with a home key in Apple Wallet on your compatible iPhone and Apple Watch (Series 4 and later). You add a home key to Apple Wallet with the Home app on your iPhone.

When you have a home key on your iPhone or Apple Watch, place your device near the lock to unlock it. You can use the Home app to share access with other people.

Set up a home key

1. Add a supported lock to the Home app.
2. Choose an unlocking option.
   o **Express Mode**: Unlock the door just by holding your iPhone or Apple Watch near the lock.
   o **Require Face ID or Passcode**: Hold your device near the lock, then use Face ID to unlock it.
3. Choose automations such as Lock After Door Closes and Lock When Leaving Home.

If the lock you add supports HomeKit, all residents of your household receive the home key automatically.

Set up an access code for a guest

In the Home app you can set up an access code for people who need temporary access to your home.

1. Open the Home app on your iPhone.
2. On the Home tab, touch and hold the lock, tap Accessory Details, tap , tap Manage Access, then tap Add Guest.
3. Give the guest a name—Dog Walker, for example—then turn on the locks you want them to have access to.
4. Tap Change Access Code, enter an access code, then tap Done.
5. Touch and hold the access code, tap Share, choose a sharing option, then share the access code with the guest.

You can return to this screen to change the access code, turn off access to some or all of the locks, or remove the guest.

Configure a router in Home on iPhone

You can use the Home app 🏠 to make your smart home more secure by allowing a compatible router to control which services your HomeKit accessories can communicate with on your home Wi-Fi network and on the internet. HomeKit-enabled routers require that you have a HomePod, Apple TV, or iPad set up as a home hub.

To configure the router's settings, follow these steps:

1. Set up the router with the manufacturer's app on an iOS device.
2. On the Home tab, tap ⋯.
3. Tap Home Settings, then tap Wi-Fi Network & Routers.
4. Turn on HomeKit Accessory Security, tap an accessory, then choose one of these settings:
   - **Restrict to Home**: The router only allows the accessory to connect to your home hub.
     This option may prevent firmware updates or other services.
   - **Automatic**: The router allows the accessory to connect to an automatically updated list of manufacturer-approved internet services and local devices.
   - **No Restriction**: The router allows the accessory to connect to any internet service or local device.
     This provides the lowest level of security.

Allow others to control accessories in your home

In the Home app 🏠, you can invite other people to control your smart accessories. You and the people you invite need to be using iCloud and have iOS 11.2.5, iPadOS 13, or later. You also need to be at your home or have a home hub set up in your home.

Invite others to control accessories

1. On the Home tab, tap ⋯, tap Home Settings, then tap Invite People.
2. Tap ⊕ to choose people with an Apple ID from your contacts list, or enter their Apple ID email addresses in the To field.
3. Tap Send Invite.
4. Ask the invitee to do one of the following:
   - **In the notification**: (iOS or iPadOS device) Tap Accept.
   - **In the Home app**: (iOS or iPadOS device) Tap ⋯, tap Home Settings, then tap their name.
   - **On Apple TV**: Tap Show Me on Apple TV, then turn on one or more Apple TVs.

Allow others to access your AirPlay 2-enabled speakers and TVs

1. On the Home tab, tap ⋯.
2. Tap Home Settings > Allow Speaker & TV Access, then choose an option.

You can allow everyone, anyone on the same network, or only people you've invited to share the home. You can also require a password that allows speaker access.

Add more homes with iPhone

In the Home app 🏠 , you can add more than one physical space—a home and a small office, for example.

1. Tap ✛ , then tap Add New Home.
2. Name the home, choose its wallpaper, then tap Save.
3. To switch to another home, tap ⊙ , then tap the home you want.

iTunes Store

Get music, movies, and TV shows in the iTunes Store on iPhone

Use the iTunes Store app ⭐ to add music, movies, and TV shows to iPhone.

Note: You need an internet connection to use the iTunes Store. The availability of the iTunes Store and its features varies by country or region.

Find music, movies, and TV shows

1. In the iTunes Store, tap any of the following:
   - **Music, Movies, or TV Shows**: Browse by category. To refine your browsing, tap Genres at the top of the screen.
   - **Charts**: See what's popular on iTunes.
   - **Search**: Enter what you're looking for, then tap Search on the keyboard.
   - **More**: Browse recommendations based on what you bought from iTunes.
2. Tap an item to see more information about it. You can preview songs, watch trailers for movies and TV shows, or tap ⬆ to do any of the following:
   - **Share a link to the item**: Choose a sharing option.
   - Give the item as a gift: Tap Gift.
   - **Add the item to your wish list**: Tap Add to Wish List.

   To view your wish list, tap ☰, then tap Wish List.

Buy and download content

1. To buy an item, tap the price. If the item is free, tap Get.

   If you see ⬇ instead of a price, you already purchased the item, and you can download it again without a charge.
2. If required, authenticate your Apple ID with Face ID or your passcode to complete the purchase.
3. To see the progress of a download, tap More, then tap Downloads.

Redeem or send an App Store & iTunes Gift Card

1. Tap Music, then scroll to the bottom.
2. Tap Redeem or Send Gift.

Get ringtones, text tones, and alert tones in the iTunes Store on iPhone

In the iTunes Store app ⭐, you can purchase ringtones, text tones, and other alert tones for clock alarms and more.

Buy new tones

1. In the iTunes Store, tap More, then tap Tones.
2. Browse by category or tap Search to find a specific song or artist.
3. Tap a tone to see more information or play a preview.
4. To buy a tone, tap the price.

Redownload tones purchased with your Apple ID

If you bought tones on another device, you can download them again.

1. Go to Settings ⚙ > Sounds & Haptics or Sounds (on other iPhone models).
2. Below Sounds and Vibration Patterns, tap any sound.
3. Tap Download All Purchased Tones. You might not see this option if you already downloaded all the tones that you purchased or if you haven't purchased any tones.

Manage your iTunes Store purchases and settings on iPhone

In the iTunes Store app ⭐, you can review and download music, movies, and TV shows purchased by you or other family members. You can also customize your preferences for the iTunes Store in Settings.

Approve purchases with Family Sharing

With Family Sharing set up, the family organizer can review and approve purchases made by other family members under a certain age.

View and download music, movies, or TV shows purchased by you or family members

1. In the iTunes Store, tap More, then tap Purchased.
2. If you set up Family Sharing, choose a family member to view their purchases.
   Note: You can see purchases made by family members only if they choose to share their purchases.
3. Tap Music, Movies, or TV Shows.
4. Find the item you want to download, then tap ☁.

View your entire iTunes Store purchase history

To see a chronological list of the apps, songs, movies, TV shows, books, and other items purchased with your Apple ID, view your iTunes Store purchase history.

In your purchase history, you can do any of the following:

• View when an order was billed to your account.
• View the date of a purchase.
• Resend email receipts.
• Report a problem with purchased content.

Set content restrictions

After you turn on content and privacy restrictions, go to Settings ⚙ > Screen Time > Content & Privacy Restrictions > Content Restrictions, then set any of the available restrictions. You can block explicit content, turn off music videos, restrict content by age-appropriate ratings, and more.

Magnifier

Magnify objects around you with iPhone

In the Magnifier app 🔍, you can use your iPhone as a magnifying glass to zoom in on objects near you. You can also use your iPhone to detect people, objects, and scenes around you with Detection Mode and Image Descriptions.

Turn on Magnifier

Open the Magnifier app in any of the following ways:

- Tap 🔍. (If you don't see the Magnifier app icon on the Home Screen, go to App Library, then look in the Utilities folder.)
- Use accessibility shortcuts.
- Open Control Center, then tap ⊕🔍.

  (If you don't see ⊕🔍, add it to Control Center—go to Settings ⚙ > Control Center, then tap ⊕ next to Magnifier.)
- Tap the back of iPhone.

Adjust the image

1. To adjust the zoom, drag the slider left or right.
2. Swipe up to reveal more controls. If you don't see the controls you want, you can add more controls.
3. Use any of the following controls:
   - Adjust the brightness: Tap ☀.
   - Adjust the contrast: Tap ◐.
   - Apply color filters: Tap ⊛.
   - **Add more light**: Tap 🔦 to turn on the flashlight.
   - Lock the focus: Tap 🔒.
   - Switch to a different camera: Tap 📷 to switch to the front or rear camera.

On iPhone 14 Pro and iPhone 14 Pro Max, you can also choose Close-up when you need to see something very small on an object in front of you.

Freeze the frame

You can freeze one or more frames and review them.

Note: Freeze frames aren't saved to Photos.

1. Tap ⊚.

   When you're finished, tap ⊗.

2. To freeze more frames, tap 🗔, reposition the camera, then tap ⊕.
3. To review the freeze frames, tap View, then tap the frames you want to see.
4. To return to the live lens, tap End.

Create activities in Magnifier on iPhone

In the Magnifier app 🔍, you can save your preferred Magnifier controls, such as zoom level, brightness, contrast, or filters for recurring tasks and situations—like reading a menu at a restaurant, for example.

Create an activity

You can use any customized settings to create an activity.

1. Tap ⚙, then tap Save New Activity.
2. Enter a name for the activity, then tap Done.

If you make changes to the activity in the control panel, tap ⚙, then tap Update [activity name].

Edit an activity

You can edit any activity that you created.

1. Tap ⚙, tap Settings, then tap 🎚.
2. Tap an activity, then customize any of the settings.
3. When you're finished, tap Done.

Delete an activity

You can delete any activity that you created.

1. Tap ⚙, tap Settings, then tap 🎚.
2. Tap the activity you want to delete, then tap Delete Activity.

Change Magnifier settings on iPhone

In the Magnifier app 🔍, you can add controls to lock the focus, change the camera, and more. You can also reorder the controls and choose your favorite color filters.

Add and organize the controls you use most often

Tap ⚙, tap Settings, then do any of the following:

- Add or remove controls: Tap ⊕ or ⊖ next to a control.

- Reorder controls: Drag ☰ next to a control to move it up or down.

Choose your favorite color filters

If you have color blindness or other vision challenges, you can use color filters to help you differentiate between colors. To customize the filters shown in the Filters control, do the following:

1. Tap ⚙, tap Settings, then tap Filters (below Other Controls).
2. Choose your favorite filters.

   Filters with a checkmark are shown when you tap ⊛.

Detection Mode

Detect people around you using Magnifier on iPhone

You can use the Magnifier app 🔍 to detect people around you to help you maintain a physical or social distance from others. When iPhone detects people nearby, you're notified with sounds, speech, or haptic feedback. The feedback is more frequent when a person is closer to you.

Important: Don't use People Detection for navigation or in circumstances where you could be harmed or injured.

Customize the settings for People Detection

1. Tap ⚙, then tap Settings.
2. Tap People Detection to customize any of the following:
   o Units: Choose Meters or Feet.
   o Sound pitch distance: Tap − or + to adjust the distance. When people are detected within this distance, the pitch of the sound feedback increases.
   o Feedback: Turn on any combination of Sounds, Speech, and Haptics. If you turn on Speech, iPhone speaks the distance between you and another person.
3. When you're finished, tap Back, then tap Done.

Detect people near you

1. Turn on Magnifier, tap ⌞ ⌟, then tap 👥 .
2. Position iPhone so the rear camera can detect people around you.
   If you don't hear the sound or speech feedback, make sure silent mode is turned off. See Adjust the volume on iPhone.
3. When you're finished, tap End to return to the Magnifier screen.

Detect doors around you using Magnifier on iPhone

You can use the Magnifier app 🔍 to detect doors around you, help you understand how far you are from a door, how to open the door, and get a description of the door's attributes.

When doors are detected nearby, you're notified with sounds, speech, or haptic feedback. The feedback is more frequent when a door is closer to you.

Important: Don't use Door Detection for navigation or in circumstances where you could be harmed or injured.

193

Customize the settings for Door Detection

1. Tap ⚙, then tap Settings.
2. Tap Door Detection to customize any of the following:
   o **Units**: Choose Meters or Feet.
   o **Sound pitch distance**: Tap − or + to adjust the distance. When a door is detected within this distance, the pitch of the sound feedback increases.
   o **Feedback**: Turn on any combination of sounds, speech, and haptics. If you turn on Speech, iPhone speaks the distance between you and the door.
   o **Color**: Select a color to outline detected doors.
   o **Back tap**: When you double-tap the back of your iPhone, you can hear more information about doors around you.
   o **Door Attributes**: Turn on any combination of door attributes, such as the size of the detected door, how to open the door, and if the door is currently open.
   o **Door Decorations**: Turn on door decorations to get information about text and signs on or near the detected door, such as a sign for an accessible entrance or a restroom.
3. When you're finished, tap Back, then tap Done.

Detect doors near you

1. Turn on Magnifier, tap ⌐⌐, then tap ▮.
2. Position iPhone so the rear camera can detect doors around you.
   If you don't hear the sound or speech feedback, make sure silent mode is turned off.
3. When you're finished, tap End to return to the Magnifier screen

Get image descriptions of your surroundings in Magnifier on iPhone

On all models, you can use the Magnifier app 🔍 to scan your surroundings and get live image descriptions of the scenes and people detected in the camera view.

You're notified of live descriptions by text or speech feedback.

Customize settings for image descriptions

1. Tap ⚙, then tap Settings.
2. Tap Image Descriptions to customize feedback settings.
3. Turn on any combination of text and speech:
   o **Text**: Image descriptions appear in the camera view.
   o **Speech**: When you turn on Speech, iPhone speaks the description of the scenes and people detected in the camera view.
4. When you're finished, tap Back, then tap Done.

Take live image descriptions

1. Turn on Magnifier, then do one of the following:
   o On models with a LiDAR Scanner: Tap ⌐⌐, then tap 💬.
   o On other models: Tap 💬.

2. Position iPhone so the rear camera can take image descriptions around you. If you don't hear the speech feedback, make sure silent mode is turned off.
3. When you're finished, tap End to return to the Magnifier screen.

Set up shortcuts for Detection Mode

- **Accessibility shortcut**: Go to Settings ⚙ > Accessibility > Accessibility Shortcut, then select Detection Mode.
- **VoiceOver gesture**: By default, the four-finger triple-tap gesture turns Detection Mode on or off. To assign a different gesture, go to Settings > Accessibility > VoiceOver > Commands > Touch Gestures.
- **Tap the back of iPhone**: Go to Settings ⚙ > Accessibility > Touch > Back Tap, choose Double Tap or Triple Tap, then choose Detection Mode.

Mail

Add or remove email accounts

Add and remove email accounts on iPhone

In the Mail app ✉ on iPhone, you can add email accounts to send and receive emails, and remove email accounts you no longer need.

Add email accounts

The first time you open the Mail app on your iPhone, you may be asked to set up an email account—just follow the onscreen instructions.

To add additional email accounts, do the following:

1. Go to Settings ⚙ > Mail > Accounts > Add Account.
2. Do one of the following:
   - Tap an email service—for example, iCloud or Microsoft Exchange—then enter your email account information.
   - Tap Other, tap Add Mail Account, then enter your email account information.

Remove email accounts

1. Go to Settings ⚙ > Mail > Accounts.
2. Tap the email account you want to remove, then do one of the following:
   - **If you're removing an iCloud email account**: Tap iCloud, tap iCloud Mail, then turn off "Use on this iPhone."
   - If you're removing another email account: Turn off Mail.

Note: To remove the email account from all apps on your iPhone, tap Delete Account.

Set up a custom email domain with iCloud Mail on iPhone

When you subscribe to iCloud+, you can add up to five custom email domains and create email addresses for those domains on your iPhone (iOS 15.4 or later). Then, you can send and receive mail in the Mail app ⊠ on your iPhone, iPad, iPod touch, and Mac, in your Mail account on iCloud.com, and in the email app on a Windows computer.

You need to have a primary iCloud Mail address before you can add a custom email domain on iPhone.

Note: Make sure you're signed in with the same Apple ID on each device. If you have devices where you're not signed in with your Apple ID or that have the Mail feature turned off, you won't be able to see your custom email domains and mail on those devices.

Purchase a custom email domain

You can purchase a custom email domain in iCloud Mail, then create custom email addresses.

1. Go to Settings ⚙ > [your name] > iCloud > iCloud Mail, then make sure "Use on this iPhone" is turned on.
2. Tap Custom Email Domain.
   Follow the onscreen instructions, or tap Buy a New Domain.
3. Follow the onscreen instructions to finish setting up your domain.

Add a custom email domain you already own to iCloud Mail

You can add a custom email domain you already own to iCloud Mail. If you already have email addresses at that domain, you can configure them during setup. If you don't, you can create email addresses after you add the domain to iCloud Mail.

1. Go to Settings ⚙ > [your name] > iCloud > iCloud Mail, then make sure "Use on this iPhone" is turned on.
2. Tap Custom Email Domain.
   Follow the onscreen instructions, or tap Add a Domain You Own.
3. Follow the onscreen instructions to finish setting up your domain.
4. After you set up your domain, follow the onscreen instructions to log in to the registrar you purchased the domain from, then tap Connect to verify your domain. This usually takes a few minutes, but could take up to 24 hours.
   Some registrars require you to change DNS records to set up your domain.

Import existing email messages

After you or a member of your Family Sharing group sets up a custom email domain for iCloud Mail, you can use iCloud.com to import existing email messages from your previous email provider (not available for all email providers).

Create and delete email addresses

After you add a custom email domain, you can easily create and delete email addresses for that domain.

1. Go to Settings ⚙ > [your name] > iCloud > iCloud Mail, then make sure "Use on this iPhone" is turned on.
2. Tap Custom Email Domain, then tap the domain you want to make changes to.

3. Tap Manage Email Addresses, then do one of the following:
   - **Add a new email address**: Tap Create Email Address, enter the new address, then tap Continue.
   - **Delete an email address**: Swipe left on an email address, tap Delete, then tap Remove.

Remove a custom email domain

If you no longer want to use a custom email domain, you can remove it using your iPhone. When you remove a custom email domain, you can't send or receive email for any addresses at that domain in Mail.

1. Go to Settings ⚙ > [your name] > iCloud > iCloud Mail.
2. Tap Custom Email Domain, then tap Edit next to Your Domains.
3. Tap ➖, then tap Delete.
4. If you're moving your domain to a new provider, make sure to do the following:
   - Go to your domain registrar to update the domain records to your new email provider and remove iCloud-related records.
   - Set up any email addresses you want to continue using with your new provider.

Note: When you remove a custom email domain, you can still send and receive email from your primary @icloud.com address.

Allow all incoming messages to your domain

You can use your iCloud Mail email address as a catch-all address. This allows you to receive all messages sent to your custom email domain, even if the exact address they were sent to hasn't already been created.

1. Go to Settings ⚙ > [your name] > iCloud > iCloud Mail.
2. Tap Custom Email Domain, then tap your custom domain.
3. Turn on Allow All Incoming Messages.

Note: You must be the domain owner to use this feature. Any addresses that have been previously created for other members of the domain aren't eligible for this feature.

Check your email in Mail on iPhone

In the Mail app ✉, you can read emails, add contacts, and preview some of the contents of an email without opening it.

Change mailboxes or accounts.

Delete, move, or mark multiple messages.

Compose a message.

Filter messages.

Read an email

In the inbox, tap the email you want to read.

Use Remind Me to come back to emails later

If you don't have time to handle an email right away, you can set a time and date to receive a reminder and bring a message back to the top of your inbox.

Tap ↰, tap Remind Me, then choose when to be reminded.

Preview an email and a list of options

If you want to see what an email is about but not open it completely, you can preview it. In the inbox, touch and hold an email to preview its contents and see a list of options for replying, filing it, and more.

Show a longer preview for every email

In your inbox, Mail displays two lines of text for each email by default. You can choose to see more lines of text without opening the email.

Go to Settings ⚙ > Mail > Preview, then choose up to five lines.

Show the whole conversation

Go to Settings ⚙ > Mail, then turn on Organize by Thread (below Threading).

Tip: You can also change other settings in Settings > Mail—such as Collapse Read Messages or Most Recent Message on Top.

Show To and Cc labels in your Inbox

Go to Settings ⚙ > Mail, then turn on Show To/Cc Labels (below Message List).

You can also view the To/Cc mailbox, which gathers all mail addressed to you. To show or hide it, tap ＜ in the upper-left corner of the Mail app, tap Edit, then select "To or Cc."

Add someone to your contacts or make them a VIP

In an email, tap a person's name or email address, then do one of the following:

- **Add to your contacts**: Tap Create New Contact or Add to Existing Contact. You can add a phone number, other email addresses, and more.
- Add to your VIP list: Tap Add to VIP.

Write and send email

Send email in Mail on iPhone

In the Mail app ✉, you can write and edit email from any of your email accounts.

Write an email message

1. Tap ✐.
2. Tap in the email, then type your message.
   Tip: With the onscreen keyboard, try sliding your finger from one letter to the next to type, lifting your finger only after each word.
3. To change the formatting, tap ⟨ above the keyboard, then tap Aa.
   You can change the font style and color of text, use a bold or italic style, add a bulleted or numbered list, and more.
4. Tap ⬆ to send your email.
   Note: If you forget to add an attachment or recipient that you mention in your message, you may get a reminder to add them before sending.

Add recipients

1. Tap the To field, then type the names of recipients.
   As you type, Mail automatically suggests people from your Contacts, along with email addresses for people who have more than one email address.

   You can also tap ⊕ to open Contacts and add recipients from there.
2. If you want to send a copy to other people, tap the Cc/Bcc field, then do any of the following:
   - Tap the Cc field, then enter the names of people you're sending a copy to.
   - Tap the Bcc field, then enter the names of people you don't want other recipients to see.

Tip: After you enter recipients, you can reorder their names in the address fields, or drag them from one address field to another—for example, to the Bcc field if you decide you don't want their names to appear.

Use Camera to capture an email address

You can use Live Text to scan an email address printed on a business card, poster, and more using the Mail app on iPhone. This allows you to quickly begin emails without entering an address manually.

1. Tap the To field, then tap Scan Email Address ⌧.

2. Position iPhone so the email address appears within the camera frame.
3. After the yellow frame appears around detected text, tap "insert."

Tip: You can use the same Live Text feature to capture an email address from a photo.

Schedule an email with Send Later

Touch and hold ⬆, then choose when you want to send the email.

To see more options, tap Send Later.

Automatically send a copy to yourself

Go to Settings ⚙ > Mail, then turn on Always Bcc Myself (below Composing).

Send an email from a different account

If you have more than one email account, you can specify which account to send email from.

1. In your email draft, tap the Cc/Bcc, From field.
2. Tap the From field, then choose an account.

Recall email with Undo send in Mail on iPhone

With the Mail app ✉, you can change your mind and unsend an email. You can also set a delay for all emails to give yourself a little more time to unsend them.

Undo a sent email

You have ten seconds to change your mind after you send an email.

Tap "Undo send" at the bottom of the screen to pull back the email.

Delay sending emails

You can give yourself a little more time to change your mind and unsend emails by setting a delay.

Go to Settings ⚙ > Mail, tap Undo Send Delay, then choose a length of time to delay outgoing email messages.

Reply to and forward emails in Mail on iPhone

With the Mail app ✉, you can reply to or forward emails.

Reply to an email

1. Tap in the email, tap ↩, then do one of the following:
   ○ Reply to just the sender: Tap Reply.
   ○ Reply to the sender and the other recipients: Tap Reply All.
2. Type your response.

Tip: With the onscreen keyboard, try sliding your finger from one letter to the next to type, lifting your finger only after each word.

Quote some text when you reply to an email

When you reply to an email, you can include text from the sender to clarify what you're responding to.

1. In the sender's email, touch and hold the first word of the text, then drag to the last word.

2. Tap ↰, tap Reply, then type your message.

To turn off the indentation of quoted text, go to Settings ⚙ > Mail > Increase Quote Level (below Composing), then turn off Increase Quote Level.

Forward an email

You can send an email forward to new recipients.

1. Tap in the email, tap ↰, then tap Forward.
2. Enter the email addresses of the new recipients.
3. Tap in the email, then type your response. The forwarded message appears below.

Follow up on emails

If you send a message and don't receive a response for several days, the email automatically moves back to the top of your inbox to help you remember to follow up.

Go to Settings ⚙ > Mail, then turn Follow Up Suggestions on or off.

Save a draft in Mail on iPhone

In the Mail app ✉, you can save a draft to finish later, or look at existing emails while you're writing a new one.

Save a draft for later

If you're writing an email and want to finish it later, tap Cancel, then tap Save Draft. To resume work on an email you saved as a draft, touch and hold ✐, then select a draft.

You can also swipe down on the title bar of an email you're writing to save it for later. When you're ready to return to your email, tap its title at the bottom of the screen.

If you have a Mac with OS X 10.10 or later, you can also hand off unfinished emails between your iPhone and your Mac.

Show draft emails from all your accounts

If you have more than one email account, you can show draft emails from all your accounts.

1. Tap ‹ in the upper-left corner to view your mailboxes.
2. Tap Edit at the top of the list.
3. Tap Add Mailbox, then turn on the All Drafts mailbox.

Work with attachments

Add email attachments in Mail on iPhone

In the Mail app ✉, you can attach photos, videos, and documents to an email. You can also scan a paper document and send it as a PDF attachment, or draw directly in an email and send the drawing as an attachment. Depending on the file size, the attachment might appear inline with the text in the email or as 📄 at the end of the email.

Attach a photo, video, or document to an email

You can attach and send documents, videos, and photos in your emails for recipients to easily download and save.

1. Tap in the email where you want to insert the attachment, then tap ‹ above the keyboard.
2. Do one of the following:

    ○ **Attach a document**: Tap 📄 above the keyboard, then locate the document in Files.
      In Files, tap Browse or Recent at the bottom of the screen, then tap a file, location, or folder to open it.

    ○ **Attach a saved photo or video**: Tap 🖼 above the keyboard, then choose a photo or video.

    ○ **Take a new photo or video and attach it to the email**: Tap 📷 above the keyboard, then take a new photo or video.Tap Use Photo or Use Video to insert it into your email, or tap Retake if you want to reshoot it.

Note: If your file exceeds the maximum size allowed by your email account, follow the onscreen instructions to send it using Mail Drop.

Scan and attach a document to an email

You can scan a paper document and send it as a PDF.

1. Tap in the email where you want to insert the scanned document, then tap ‹ above the keyboard.
2. Tap 📑 above the keyboard.
3. Position iPhone so that the document page appears on the screen—iPhone automatically captures the page.

   To capture the page manually, tap ◯ or press a volume button. To turn the flash on or off, tap ⚡.
4. Tap Retake or Keep Scan, scan additional pages, then tap Save when you're done.
5. To make changes to the saved scan, tap it, then do any of the following:

    ○ Crop the image: Tap ⊐.

    ○ Apply a filter: Tap ⬤.

    ○ Rotate the image: Tap ↻.

    ○ Delete the scan: Tap 🗑.

Create and attach a drawing to your email

202

You can draw in an email to demonstrate ideas that are hard to put into words. Your drawing is added to the email as an attachment for recipients to view and download.

1. Tap in the email where you want to insert a drawing, then tap ❮ above the keyboard.
2. Tap Ⓐ to show the Markup toolbar.
3. Choose a drawing tool and color, then write or draw with your finger.
4. When you're finished, tap Done, then tap Insert Drawing.

To resume work on a drawing, tap the drawing in the email, then tap Ⓐ.

Download email attachments in Mail on iPhone

In the Mail app 📧, you can download attachments that are sent to you in email or easily search for emails with attachments in your mailboxes.

Download an attachment sent to you

Touch and hold the attachment, then choose Save Image or Save to Files.

If you choose Save Image, you can find it later in the Photos app. If you choose Save to Files, you can find it later in the Files app.

Tip: To open the attachment with another app, tap Share ⬆️, then choose the app.

Find emails with attachments

If you're having trouble finding an attachment someone sent you, you can filter your emails to show only those with attachments.

1. In a mailbox, tap ☰ to turn on filtering.
2. Tap "Filtered by," then turn on Only Mail with Attachments.

Tip: You can also show emails with attachments from all accounts in one mailbox. To set up the attachment mailbox, tap ❮ at the top left, tap Edit, then select Attachments. The attachments mailbox appears in the mailboxes list with your other mailboxes.

Annotate email attachments on iPhone

In the Mail app 📧, you can give feedback on a draft, decorate a photo, and more. You can also draw and write on a photo, video, or PDF attachment, then save it or send it back.

1. In the email, tap the attachment, then tap Ⓐ.
2. Using the drawing tools, draw with your finger.
3. When you're finished, tap Done, then choose to save, send, or discard your edited attachment.

Set email notifications on iPhone

In the Mail app ✉, you can change your Mail notification settings and choose which mailboxes and email threads to receive notifications from.

Mute email notifications

To reduce interruptions from busy email threads, you can mute notifications from messages in a conversation.

1. Open an email in the conversation.
2. Tap ↰, then tap Mute.

To specify what you want done with emails you muted, go to Settings ⚙ > Mail > Muted Thread Action, then select an option.

Receive notifications about replies to an email or thread

You can set up mail notifications that let you know when you receive emails in favorite mailboxes or from your VIPs.

- **When reading an email**: Tap ↰, then tap Notify Me.
- **When writing an email**: Tap the Subject field, tap 🔔 in the Subject field, then tap Notify Me.

To change how notifications appear, go to Settings ⚙ > Notifications > Mail, then turn on Allow Notifications.

Change your Mail notification settings

1. Go to Settings ⚙ > Mail > Notifications, then make sure that Allow Notifications is on.
2. Tap Customize Notifications, then tap the email account you want to make changes to.
3. Select the settings you want, like Alerts or Badges. When you turn on Alerts, you have the option to customize your sounds by changing the alert tone or ringtone.

You can set times when you want to allow notifications from the Mail app.

Search for email in Mail on iPhone

In the Mail app ✉, you can search for emails using different criteria.

Search for text in an email

1. From a mailbox, swipe down to reveal the search field, tap it, then type the text you're looking for.
2. Choose between searching all mailboxes or the current mailbox above the results list.
3. Tap search, then tap an email in the results list to read it.

Mail searches the address fields, the subject, the email body, documents, and links. The most relevant emails appear in Top Hits above the search suggestions as you type.

Search by timeframe

1. Tap the search field of a mailbox list.

2. Enter a timeframe, like "September," then tap an option below Dates to see all emails from that timeframe.
To narrow the search, tap the search field again, then enter a keyword, like "meeting."

Search by email attributes

1. In an inbox, tap the search field.
Before you begin typing, you may see suggested recent searches, recent documents, and links listed.
2. Enter your search criteria, then tap one of the listed items, or do any of the following:
   ○ **Find all flagged emails**: Enter "flag" in the search field, scroll down, then tap Flagged Messages below Other.
   ○ **Find all unread emails**: Enter "unread" in the search field, scroll down, then tap Unread Messages below Other.
   ○ **Find all emails with attachments**: Enter "attachment" in the search field, scroll down, then tap Messages with Attachments below Other.

Organize email in mailboxes on iPhone

In the Mail app , you can manage your email in mailboxes.

Manage an email with a swipe

While viewing an email list, you can use a simple swipe to move individual emails to the Trash, mark them as read, and more. Do any of the following:

- To reveal a list of actions, slowly drag an email to the left until the menu appears, then tap an item.
- To quickly use the rightmost action, swipe all the way to the left.
- Swipe right to reveal one other action.

To choose the actions you want to appear in the menus, go to Settings > Mail > Swipe Options (below Message List).

Organize your mail with mailboxes

You can choose which mailboxes to view, reorder your mailboxes, create new ones, or rename or delete mailboxes. (Some mailboxes can't be changed.)

To organize your mailboxes, tap ‹ in the upper-left corner, tap Edit, then do any of the following:

- **View mailboxes**: Select the checkboxes next to the mailboxes you want to include in the mailboxes list.
- **Reorder mailboxes**: Touch and hold ☰ next to a mailbox until it lifts up, then drag it to the new position.
- **Create a new mailbox**: Tap New Mailbox in the lower-right corner, then follow the onscreen instructions.
- **Rename a mailbox**: Tap the mailbox, then tap the title. Delete the name, then enter a new name.
- **Delete a mailbox**: Tap the mailbox, then tap Delete Mailbox.

Move or mark multiple emails

1. While viewing a list of emails, tap Edit.
2. Select the emails you want to move or mark by tapping their checkboxes.
   Tip: To select multiple emails quickly, swipe down through the checkboxes.
3. Tap Mark, Move, or Trash at the bottom of the screen.

View emails from one account at a time

If you use multiple email accounts with the Mail app, you can use the mailboxes list to view emails from one account at a time.

Tap ❮ in the upper-left corner, then tap a mailbox below the email account you want to access.

Each mailbox listed below a particular email account only displays emails from that email account. For example, to view only emails sent from your iCloud account, tap iCloud, then tap Sent.

Move an email to junk

To move an email to the Junk folder, open it, tap ↰, then tap Move to Junk.

Flag and filter email

Flag emails in Mail on iPhone

In the Mail app ✉, you can flag your emails, create flagged mailboxes, and flag emails from VIPs.

Flag an email

You can flag an email to make it easier to find later. An email you flag remains in your Inbox, but also appears in the Flagged mailbox.

1. Open the email, tap ↰, then tap Flag.
2. To choose a color for the flag, tap a colored dot.

   To change or remove a flag, open the email, tap ↰, then select another color, or tap ⚑.

Note: Flags you add to an email appear on that email in Mail on all your Apple devices where you're signed in with the same Apple ID.

Create a Flagged mailbox

You can add a Flagged mailbox so all your flagged emails are easily accessible in one location.

1. Tap ❮ in the upper-left corner.
2. Tap Edit, then select Flagged.

Flag emails from your VIPs

Add important people to your VIP list, so their emails appear with a VIP flag and in the VIP mailbox.

1. While viewing an email, tap the name or email address of a person in the email.
2. Tap Add to VIP.

Block email from specified senders

To block a sender, tap their email address, then select Block this Contact.

Filter emails in Mail on iPhone

In the Mail app ✉, you can use filters to temporarily show only certain messages—the ones that meet all the criteria you select in the filter list. For example, if you select Unread and Only Mail with Attachments, you see only unread emails that have attachments.

1. Tap ⊜ in the bottom-left corner of a mailbox list.
2. Tap "Filtered by," then select or turn on the criteria for emails you want to view.

To turn off all filters, tap ⊜. To turn off a specific filter, tap "Filtered by," then deselect it.

Privacy and Security

Use Hide My Email in Mail on iPhone

When you subscribe to iCloud+, Hide My Email lets you send and receive email messages that forward to your real email account, to keep your real email address private. With iOS 15.2 or later, you can generate unique email addresses on demand in the Mail app ✉.

Send an email with Hide My Email

1. Tap ✐.
2. Add a recipient and subject for your email.
   Note: You can only send a message using Hide My Email to one recipient at a time.
3. Tap the From field, tap it again, then tap Hide My Email. A new, unique email address appears in the From field.

Tip: When the recipient replies to an email you sent with Hide My Email, their reply forwards to your real email address.

Reply to an email using Hide My Email

When you receive an email sent to one of your unique, random addresses, you can reply using the same address. This allows you to continue the conversation and keep your real email address private. To reply, do the following:

1. Tap ↩, then tap Reply.
2. Type your response.
   You can tap the From field to view the email address the recipient sees.

Manage the addresses generated by Hide My Email

You can create, deactivate, reactivate, and manage the random addresses you create with Hide My Email.

Use Mail Privacy Protection on iPhone

In the Mail app ✉, turn on Mail Privacy Protection to make it harder for senders to learn about your Mail activity. Mail Privacy Protection hides your IP address so senders can't link it to your other online activity or determine your exact location. It also prevents senders from seeing if you've opened the email they sent you.

1. Go to Settings ⚙ > Mail > Privacy Protection.
2. Turn on Protect Mail Activity.
   Note: When you subscribe to iCloud+, you can also use Hide My Email to generate unique, random email addresses that forward to your personal email account, so you don't have to share your personal email address when filling out forms on the web or signing up for newsletters.

Change email settings in Mail on iPhone

In the Mail app ✉, you can customize your email signature and mark addresses outside specific domains.

Customize your email signature

You can customize the email signature that appears automatically at the bottom of every email you send.

1. Go to Settings ⚙ > Mail, then tap Signature (below Composing).
2. Tap the text field, then edit your signature.
   You can only use text in your Mail signatures.

Tip: If you have more than one email account, tap Per Account to set a different signature for each account.

Mark addresses outside certain domains

When you're addressing an email to a recipient who's not in your organization's domain, you can have the recipient's name appear in red to alert you.

1. Go to Settings ⚙ > Mail > Mark Addresses (below Composing).
2. Enter the domains that are in your organization—ones that you don't want marked in red.
   You can enter multiple domains separated by commas (for example, "apple.com, example.org").

The names of recipients in domains outside your organization appear in red, whether you send them an email or receive one from them.

Delete and recover emails in Mail on iPhone

In the Mail app ✉, you can delete or archive emails you no longer need. If you change your mind, you can recover deleted emails.

Delete emails

There are multiple ways to delete emails. Do any of the following:

- While viewing an email: Tap ↩, then tap 🗑.
- **While viewing the email list**: Swipe an email left, then choose Trash from the menu. To delete the email in a single gesture, swipe it all the way to the left.
- **Delete multiple emails at once**: While viewing a list of emails, tap Edit, select the emails you want to delete, then tap Trash. To select multiple emails quickly, swipe down through the checkboxes.

To turn the deletion confirmation on or off, go to Settings 🔘 > Mail, then turn Ask Before Deleting on or off (below Messages).

Recover a deleted email

1. Tap ‹ in the upper-left corner, then tap an account's Trash mailbox.
2. Tap the email you want to recover, then tap ↩.
3. Tap Move Message, then choose another mailbox.

Archive instead of delete

Instead of deleting emails, you can archive them in the Archive mailbox.

1. Go to Settings 🔘 > Mail, then tap Accounts.
2. Do one of the following:
   - **If you're using an iCloud email account**: Tap iCloud, tap iCloud again, tap iCloud Mail, then tap iCloud Mail Settings.
   - **If you're using another email account**: Tap your email provider, then tap your email account.
3. Tap Advanced, then change the destination mailbox for discarded emails to the Archive mailbox.

When this option is turned on, to delete an email instead of archiving it, touch and hold 🗄, then tap Trash Message.

Decide how long to keep deleted emails

With some email clients, you can set how long deleted emails stay in the Trash mailbox.

1. Go to Settings 🔘 > Mail, then tap Accounts.
2. Do one of the following:
   - If you're using an iCloud email account: Tap iCloud, tap iCloud again, tap iCloud Mail, then tap iCloud Mail Settings.
   - If you're using another email account: Tap your email provider, then tap your email account.
3. Tap Advanced, then tap Remove.
4. Select a time interval.

Note: Some email services might override your selection; for example, iCloud doesn't keep deleted emails longer than 30 days, even if you select Never.

Add a Mail widget to your iPhone Home Screen

Widgets show you current information from your favorite apps at a glance. On iPhone, you can add a Mail widget and customize which mailbox it shows on your Home Screen. Choose between displaying recent unread emails, new emails from your VIPs, or any other mailbox.

Print an email or attachment in Mail on iPhone

In the Mail app ⊠, you can print an email or an attachment.

Print an email

In the email, tap ⤺, then tap Print.

Print an attachment or picture

Tap an attachment to view it, tap Share ⬆, then choose Print.

Maps

View maps on iPhone

In the Maps app 📍, you can find your location on a map and zoom in and out to see the detail you need.

On supported models and in select cities, Maps provides enhanced detail for elevation, roads, trees, buildings, landmarks, and more.

Allow Maps to use your precise location

To find your location and provide accurate directions, iPhone must be connected to the internet, and Precise Location must be on.

- **If Maps displays a message that Location Services is off**: Tap the message, tap Turn On in Settings, then turn on Location Services.
- **If Maps displays a message that Precise Location is off**: Tap the message, tap Turn On in Settings, tap Location, then turn on Precise Location.

Cellular data rates may apply.

Note: To obtain useful location-related information in Maps, leave Significant Locations turned on in Settings ⚙ > Privacy & Security > Location Services > System Services.

Show your current location

Tap ◹.

Your position is marked in the middle of the map. The top of the map is north. To show your heading instead of north at the top, tap ◹. To resume showing north, tap ⬆ or ◉.

Choose the right map

The button at the top right of a map indicates if the current map is for exploring 📖, driving 🚗, riding transit 🚆, or viewing from a satellite 🌐. To choose a different map, do the following:

1. Tap the button at the top right.
2. Choose another map type, then tap ✕.

View a 3D map

On a 2D map, do one of the following:

- Drag two fingers up.
- On the Satellite map, tap 3D near the top right.
- Tap 3D near the top right.

On a 3D map, you can do the following:

- **Adjust the angle**: Drag two fingers up or down.
- See buildings and other small features in 3D: Zoom in.
- **Return to a 2D map**: Tap 2D near the top right.

Move, zoom, or rotate a map or 3D globe

- Move around in a map: Drag the map.
- **Zoom in or out**: Double-tap (leaving your finger on the screen after the second tap), then drag up to zoom in or drag down to zoom out. Or, pinch open or closed on the map. On a 2D map, a scale appears in the upper left while you zoom. To change the unit of distance, go to Settings ⚙ > Maps, then select In Miles or In Kilometers.
- **Rotate the map**: Touch and hold the map with two fingers, then rotate your fingers.

  To show north at the top of the screen after you rotate the map, tap ⊙.
- **View the earth with an interactive 3D globe**: Zoom out until the map changes to a globe. Drag the globe to rotate it, or zoom in or out to explore details for mountain ranges, deserts, oceans, and more.

Add a name to Maps, or report an issue with Maps

1. Tap your picture or initials next to the search field, then tap Reports.
   If neither your picture nor initials appears, tap Cancel next to the search field, or tap the search field, then tap Cancel.
2. Choose one of the options, then provide your information.

Apple is committed to keeping personal information about your location safe and private. To learn more, go to Settings ⚙ > Maps, then tap About Apple Maps and Privacy.

Search for places in Maps on iPhone

You can use the Maps app 🗺 to search for addresses, landmarks, services, and more.

Search for a place

Siri: Say something like: "Show me the Golden Gate Bridge."

Or you can tap the search field (at the top of the search card), then begin typing.

You can search in different ways. For example:

- Intersection ("8th and Market")
- Area ("Greenwich Village")
- Landmark ("Guggenheim")
- Zip code ("60622")
- Business ("movies," "restaurants San Francisco CA," "Apple Inc New York")

If you get a list of results, scroll the list to see more. To learn about a place or get directions to it, tap a search result.

Display, lengthen, or shorten the search card

If you see a different kind of card instead of the search card, tap ✕ at the top right of the card.

To show more or less information on the search card, drag the bottom of the search card down or up.

Quickly find or delete recent searches

To get a list of recent search results, scroll down in the search card to Recents.

To delete an item from the list, swipe the item left. Or tap More directly above the list, then do one of the following:

- **Delete a group**: Tap Clear above the group.
- **Delete a single item**: Swipe the item left.

Find nearby attractions, restaurants, and services in Maps on iPhone

You can use the Maps app to find nearby attractions, services, and more.

Find a nearby attraction, restaurant, or other service

Siri: Say something like: "Find a gas station" or "Find coffee near me."

- Tap a category like Grocery Stores or Restaurants in the Find Nearby section of the search card.
- Enter something like "playgrounds" or "parks" in the search field, then tap the Search Nearby result.

To change the nearby area, drag the map.

Depending on what you look for, you may be able to apply more search criteria, tap a suggestion to get additional information, and more.

Note: Nearby suggestions aren't available in all countries or regions.

Find your way around an airport or shopping mall

1. Do one of the following:
   - **Before you get there**: Search for the airport or mall in Maps (tap Indoor Map if it appears in the search result). Or drag the map to show it, zoom in, then tap Look Inside.

   - **When you're at the airport or mall**: Open Maps, tap ◁ , then tap Look Inside.

2. To find nearby services, tap a category (like Food, Restrooms, or Gates) on the place card, then scroll down to see all results.
To get more information about a result, tap it.
3. To get a map of a different floor, tap the button showing the floor level (zoom in if the button doesn't appear).

Note: Indoor maps are available for select airports and shopping malls.

Get information about places in Maps on iPhone

You can find street addresses and other information about places that appear in the Maps app ⬛.

Get information about a place

Tap the place (for example, a city or landmark on a map, a spot that you marked with a pin, or a search result in Maps), then do any of the following:

- **Get a route to the location**: Tap the directions button.
- **View more information**: Scroll down in the place card.
  The information might include the street address, a phone number, a webpage link, customer reviews, and more. Many restaurants and other businesses offer App Clips that allow you to order or make a reservation by tapping buttons on their place cards.
- Close the place card: Tap ✕.

Note: If you install an app that has a table booking extension, it can also help you make reservations at restaurants. If you want to stop sending the names of restaurants that you view to the extension, go to Settings ⚙ > Maps > Restaurant Booking, then turn off the app extension.

Save information about a place

You can save a place as one of your favorites, in one of your My Guides, and as one of your contacts.

Tap a place on a map or a search result in Maps, tap ••• (to the right of the directions button on the place card), then choose an option.

Mark places in Maps on iPhone

You can mark places in the Maps app ⬛ with pins to help you find those places later.

Tip: To quickly mark your location so you can find your way back later, touch and hold the Maps icon on the Home Screen, then choose Mark My Location.

Mark an unlabeled location

Touch and hold the map until a pin marker appears, then do any of the following:

- **Refine the location**: Tap Move, then drag the map.

213

- **Save the location to your favorites**: Tap ••• (next to the directions button on the place card), then Tap Add to Favorites. (You can give the location a name in your Favorites.)
- **Save the location to a guide you created**: Tap •••, tap Guides, choose a guide, enter a name for the location, then tap Save.
- Close the place card: Tap ✕.

Delete a pin marker

1. Tap the marker.
2. Scroll down in the place card, then tap Remove.

You can also touch and hold the marker, then tap Remove Pin.

Share places in Maps on iPhone

In the Maps app 🧭 , you can share places with others. For example, you can send a message or email to show people where to meet you.

Tip: To quickly share your current location, touch and hold Maps on the Home Screen, then tap Send My Location.

1. Tap a place on the map or a search result in Maps.
2. Tap ••• (to the right of the directions button on the place card).
3. Tap Share, then choose an option.

You can also touch and hold the place, then tap Share Location.

Rate places in Maps on iPhone

In the Maps app 🧭 , you can provide ratings and photos of places you visit to help others.

Note: Apple Ratings and Photos is not available in all countries or regions.

Provide ratings and photos for a place

1. Tap a place on the map or a search result in Maps.
2. Depending on the location, either scroll down the place card or tap Rate (near the top of the place card), then do any of the following:
   - **Provide ratings**: Tap 👍 or 👎 for the available categories.
   - **Submit photos**: Tap Add Your Photos, then follow the onscreen instructions. Before you tap Add to submit your photos, you can credit yourself for the photos you contribute, using either your name or a nickname. Tap Photo Credit, then turn on Show Credit and if desired, enter a nickname for yourself. (The photo credit option you choose applies to all photos you previously submitted and continue to submit.)

Note: If neither ratings categories or the Rate button appear on the place card, you can't rate the location or add a photo.

To upload your ratings and photos to Apple, you must have an Apple ID.

View or edit your ratings and photos

You can view and change your ratings, add and remove photos, add or remove your photo credit, and provide a nickname for your photo credit.

1. Tap your picture or initials at the top right of the search card, then tap Ratings & Photos. If neither your picture nor initials appears, tap Cancel next to the search field, or tap the search field, then tap Cancel.
2. Select one of your rated places.
3. To edit your ratings, tap Rate, make your changes, then tap Done.
4. To edit your photos, tap the Your Photos album, then do any of the following:
   - Submit another photo: Tap Add.
   - **Remove a photo**: Select the photo, tap ⬤, then tap Delete Your Photo.
   - **Change your photo credit**: Select the photo, tap ⬤, then tap Change Photo Credit. The photo credit option you choose applies to all photos you previously submitted and continue to submit.

   -

Your ratings and photos appear on all devices where you're signed in with the same Apple ID.

You may receive suggestions in Maps to submit a rating or photo if you recently visited or took a photo of a point of interest. These suggestions use on-device processing and cannot be read by Apple. If you wish to stop receiving these suggestions, go to Settings ⚙ > Maps, then turn off Show Ratings and Photos Suggestions.

Save favorite places in Maps on iPhone

In the Maps app 🗺, you can save places—such as your home, your work, and where you go for coffee—to your favorites list. You can quickly find your favorites on the search card.

Tip: To make Home and Work automatically appear as favorites, add your work and home addresses to My Card in Contacts.

Add a place to your favorites

1. In the row of Favorites on the search card, tap ＋.

   If ＋ doesn't appear, swipe the Favorites row left.
2. Do one of the following:
   - Choose a suggestion below the search field.
   - Enter a place or address in the search field, then choose a search result.

You can also tap a place on a map or a search result in Maps, tap ••• (to the right of the directions button on the place card), then tap Add to Favorites.

Quickly find your favorites

A row of Favorites appears near the top of the search card.

To see more, swipe the row left, or tap More above the row.

Edit a favorite

1. On the search card, tap More above the row of favorites.
2. Tap (i) next to the favorite.
3. Depending on the location, you may be able to make the following changes:
    - **Rename the favorite**: Tap the title, then enter a new name.
    - **Change the address**: Tap the address, then tap Open Contact Card.
    - Delete the location from your favorites list: Tap Remove Favorite.
    - **Change the label**: Tap a label type.
    - **Tell someone your ETA**: Tap Add Person, then choose one or more suggested contacts, or search for a contact. Whenever you start turn-by-turn navigation to this location, the person automatically receives a notification about your estimated time of arrival (ETA).
4. Tap Done.

Refine your home or work location

If Maps isn't precisely locating your home or work place, you can help improve directions to and from your home or work by correcting the location.

1. On the search card, tap More above the row of favorites, then tap (i) next to Home or Work.
2. Tap Refine Location on Map, drag the map to move the marker over the correct location, then tap Done.

Delete a place from your favorites

On the search card, tap More above the row of favorites, then swipe the item left.

Explore new places with Guides in Maps on iPhone

Editorially curated Guides from trusted brands and partners are available in the Maps app to help you discover great places around the world to eat, shop, and explore. Guides are automatically updated when new places are added, so you always have the latest recommendations.

Explore cities of the world with Guides

Scroll down in the search card, then tap Explore Guides.

You can browse by interest, publisher, city, and more. For example, to browse Guides for locations worldwide, tap at the top of the screen.

View, share, and save a Guide

To open a Guide, tap its cover. To view its contents, scroll down.

You can also do the following:

- **Save the Guide**: Scroll to the top of the Guide, then tap .
  It's saved in your collection of My Guides.

- **Share the Guide**: Scroll to the top of the Guide, tap , then choose an option.

- **Add a destination to My Guides**: Tap + , then select one of your guides.

- Explore related media: In select Guides, tap links to find relevant music, books, and more.
- Close the Guide: Tap ⊗.

Tip: Look for App Clips buttons that allow you to do things like reserve a table directly from a Guide.

Guides are available for many cities worldwide, with more places coming.

Organize places in My Guides in Maps on iPhone

In the Maps app 🗺, you can organize places into your own guides for easy reference. For example, you can add destinations for an upcoming vacation into a guide named Summer Road Trip. You can quickly get to your guides from the search card, and you can share your guides with others.

Create a guide

Scroll down in the search card, tap New Guide, enter a name, then tap Create.

Add a place to My Guides

1. Tap a place on a map or a search result in Maps.
2. Tap ••• (to the right of the directions button on the place card).
3. Tap Guides, then choose one of your guides.

You can also add editorially curated Guides to My Guides.

Share a guide

1. Tap your picture or initials at the top right of the search card, then tap Guides.
   If neither your picture nor initials appears, tap Cancel next to the search field, or tap the search field, then tap Cancel.
2. Choose a guide.
3. Tap ⬆ at the bottom of the guide card, then choose an option.

Edit a guide that you created

For any guide that you create, you can supply a cover image, change the title, and add or remove places.

1. Tap your picture or initials at the top right of the search card, then tap Guides.
   If neither your picture nor initials appears, tap Cancel next to the search field, or tap the search field, then tap Cancel.
2. Choose a guide that you created.
3. Tap Edit at the bottom of the guide card.
4. Make your changes, then tap ✕ at the top right of the guide card.

Get traffic and weather info in Maps on iPhone

Find out about traffic conditions

1. With a map showing, tap the button at the top right, choose Driving or Satellite, then tap ✕.

   Orange indicates slowdowns, and red indicates stop-and-go traffic.
2. To get an incident report, tap an incident marker.

   Markers indicate incidents such as hazards ⚠, road closures ⊖, road construction ⬦, accidents ⬦, and more.

You can also report traffic incidents.

Note: Traffic features and information are not available in all countries or regions.

Find out about the weather and the air quality

Zoom in on a map until the weather icon appears in the lower-right corner; the icon shows the current conditions for that area. In some regions, the air quality index (AQI) also appears in the lower-right corner.

To get the hourly forecast, touch and hold the weather icon. Tap the hourly forecast to get a multiday forecast in the Weather app.

If you don't want to get the weather information or the air quality index in Maps, go to Settings ⚙ > Maps, then turn off Weather Conditions or Air Quality Index.

Delete significant locations on iPhone

The Maps app 🧭 keeps track of the places you recently visited, as well as when and how often you visited them. Maps uses this information to provide you with personalized services like predictive traffic routing. You can delete this information.

Note: Significant locations are end-to-end encrypted and cannot be read by Apple.

1. Go to Settings ⚙ > Privacy & Security > Location Services > System Services, then tap Significant Locations.
2. Tap Clear History. This action clears all your significant locations on any devices that are signed in with the same Apple ID.

Quickly find your Maps settings on iPhone

In the Maps app 🧭, you can quickly find your settings for preferences, guides, favorites, and more.

Tap your picture or initials at the top right of the search card, then choose an option.

(If neither your picture nor initials appears next to the search field, tap Cancel next to the field, or tap the search field, then tap Cancel.)

To find more Maps settings, choose Preferences, scroll down, then tap Maps Settings at the bottom of the screen.

Get Directions

Use Siri, Maps, and the Maps widget to get directions on iPhone

You can get travel directions in the Maps app 🧭 in several ways.

Important: To get directions, iPhone must be connected to the internet, and Precise Location must be turned on. Cellular data rates may apply.

Use Siri to get directions

Without opening Maps or even looking at your iPhone, you can get directions by speaking to Siri.

Siri: Say something like:

- "Get directions to the nearest coffee shop"
- "Find a charging station"
- "Give me directions home"

Tip: To use "home" or "work" when using Siri or searching in Maps, add your home and work addresses to My Card in Contacts.

Get directions in Maps

1. Do one of the following:
     o Tap a destination (for example, a landmark on a map or a spot that you marked with a pin).
     o Touch and hold anywhere on the map.
     o Tap the search field, begin typing, then tap a result.
2. Tap the directions button on the place card.
   After you tap the directions button, you can choose a different mode of travel, a different starting point, and other options.
3. Tap Go for the route you want.

After you tap Go, you can share your ETA, get an overview of your route or a list of directions, add stops to your driving directions, and more.

Use the Maps widget

To quickly get directions to a likely destination and track your ETA during navigation, add the Maps widget to your Home Screen.

Get directions with other devices

You can also gets directions using these devices:

- **Your car**: After you connect your iPhone to CarPlay, you can use CarPlay to get driving directions, estimate your arrival time, and more.
- **Your Mac**: You can plan a route on your Mac, then follow the driving, walking, transit, or cycling directions on your iPhone.
- **Your Apple Watch**: You can use Apple Watch to get driving, walking, transit, and cycling directions, which you can follow on the watch face and your iPhone.

Choose your default mode of travel

Maps defaults to your preferred way to travel when providing directions. To change your preference, do the following:

1. Tap your picture or initials at the top right of the search card, then tap Preferences.
   If neither your picture nor initials appears, tap Cancel next to the search field, or tap the search field, then tap Cancel.
2. Tap Driving, Walking, Transit, or Cycling.

Select other route options in Maps on iPhone

With a route showing in the Maps app , you can select various options before you tap Go.

Drag to reverse the starting point and destination.

Switch travel mode.

View the directions in a list.

Choose an alternate route.

Change the starting point or destination

- Reverse the starting point and destination: In the Directions list, touch and hold ≡ for the starting location, then drag it below the destination.
- Choose a different starting point or destination: In the Directions list, tap either the start or destination, then use the search field or a recent search result to find and select a different location.

Switch to a different mode of travel

Tap the travel mode button (below the Directions list), then tap 🚗, 🚶, 🚇, 🚴, or 🧍 (ridesharing not available in all countries or regions).

Add a stop to your driving directions

You can add up to 14 stops along your route.

1. Do one of the following:
   - Tap Add Stop (below Directions), use the search field or a recent search result to find and select a place to stop, then tap Add (in the list of search results) or Add Stop (in the place card for a search result).
   - Zoom in and move the map, tap a place (for example, a landmark or business), then tap Add Stop in the place card. Or touch and hold a spot to mark it with a pin, then tap Add Stop in the place card.
2. Your selected stop appears as the final destination in the Directions list.

3. Touch and hold ≡ for the stop, then drag it ahead of your final destination. To delete the stop, swipe it left.

View a route's directions in a list

1. Tap the route's estimated travel time on the route card so that the route appears at the top of the card.
2. Tap the estimated travel time again.
3. To share the directions, scroll to the bottom of the card, then tap Share.
4. When you're finished, tap Done.

Depending on the mode of travel, you may have other route options, such as choosing an arrival time when driving, avoiding heavy traffic when cycling or walking, or choosing which transit method you prefer.

Share your ETA in Maps on iPhone

You can share your estimated time of arrival (ETA) while following driving, walking, and cycling directions in the Maps app .

Share your estimated time of arrival (ETA)

Siri: Say something like: "Share my ETA."_

Or without using Siri, you can do the following:

1. Tap the route card at the bottom of the screen, then tap Share ETA.
2. Choose one or more suggested contacts, or tap Open Contacts to find a contact.

You can also add a location to your Favorites, then choose a contact to automatically receive your ETA whenever you start turn-by-turn navigation to that location.

To stop sending ETA information, tap Sharing at the bottom of the screen, then tap a name.

People using devices with iOS 13.1, iPadOS 13.1, or later receive a Maps notification with your ETA, and they can track your progress in Maps. People using devices with earlier versions receive the notification through iMessage. People using other mobile devices receive an SMS message.

Note: Standard carrier data and text rates may apply.

To turn off Share ETA, go to Settings > Maps.

Find stops along your route in Maps on iPhone

While following driving or cycling directions in the Maps app , you can find places to stop along your route.

Add a stop while following a driving route

1. Tap the route card at the bottom of the screen.
2. Tap Add Stop, then use the search field or a recent search result to find and select a place to stop.

3. Tap Add (in the list of search results) or Add Stop (in the place card for a search result). Your directions are rerouted to take you to the stop next.
4. While on your route, you can do the following:
    o **Remove the stop**: Tap the route card at the bottom of the screen, then tap ⊖ next to the stop.
    o **Pause directions when you stop**: Tap Pause Route; when you get back on the road, tap Resume Route.

You can plan a multistop route before you start your trip.

Find a place to stop while following a cycling route

1. Tap the route card at the bottom of the screen.
2. Tap Add a Stop, then tap a category.
3. Tap Go for one of the nearby suggestions.
4. To get directions again to your original destination, tap Resume Route at the top of the screen.

View a route overview or a list of turns in Maps on iPhone

While following driving, walking, and cycling directions in the Maps app 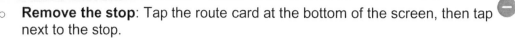, you can get an overview of your route and a list of upcoming turns.

Get an overview of your route

Tap ↱. To return to turn-by-turn directions, tap ⋏.

View a list of upcoming turns

Tap the banner at the top of the screen. Scroll down to see more directions. When finished, tap ⌃.

Change settings for spoken directions in Maps on iPhone

Turn spoken directions on or off

On the map, tap the audio button (for example, 🔊), then choose an option.

Button	Description
🔊	All directions are spoken.
🔊⚠	Only driving alerts are spoken.
🔇	No directions are spoken.

Change the volume for spoken directions

Press the volume buttons on the side of iPhone.

Change other settings for spoken directions

Go to Settings > Maps > Spoken Directions, then turn on or off the following options:

- **Directions Pause Spoken Audio**: Turn on this setting to pause spoken audio (like podcasts and audio books) when you receive spoken directions.
- **Directions Wake Device**: Turn on this setting to wake the iPhone display when you receive spoken directions while following driving or cycling directions.
- **Directions on Radio**: On supported cars, turn on this setting to hear spoken directions when you're listening to the radio.

Turn-by-turn spoken directions require iPhone to be connected to the internet, and Precise Location must be turned on. Cellular data rates may apply.

Note: Turn-by-turn spoken directions are not available in all countries or regions.

Set up electric vehicle routing in Maps on iPhone

The Maps app can help you plan trips that include stops for charging your electric vehicle (EV).

Note: Available on select vehicles. Refer to the owner's guide for your vehicle for compatibility information.

When you get driving directions, Maps can track your vehicle's charge. By analyzing elevation changes along the route and other factors, Maps identifies appropriate charging stations along the way. If you drive until your charge gets too low, you're offered a route to the nearest compatible charging station.

Set up EV routing through CarPlay

For a compatible vehicle that doesn't require an app from its manufacturer, use CarPlay to set up EV routing in Maps.

1. Connect your iPhone to CarPlay.
2. In Maps on iPhone, get driving directions, tap Connect (above the list of routes), then follow the onscreen instructions.

Set up EV routing using a vehicle manufacturer's app

For a compatible vehicle that requires an app from its manufacturer, use the app to set up EV routing in Maps.

1. In the App Store, search for the manufacturer of your vehicle.
2. Download the app that supports EV routing for your vehicle.
3. Open the app, then follow its setup instructions.
4. In Maps, tap your picture or initials at the top right of the search card.
   If neither your picture nor initials appears, tap Cancel next to the search field, or tap the search field, then tap Cancel.
5. Tap Vehicles, tap Connect Your Electric Vehicles, then follow the onscreen instructions.

Choose a different vehicle when you get directions

If you drive multiple vehicles, you can change which vehicle Maps provides routing instructions for.

1. Get driving directions.
2. Before you tap Go, scroll down in the route card.
3. Choose another electric vehicle, or if you're driving a vehicle that doesn't have an EV routing app on your iPhone, tap Different Car.

Get driving directions in Maps on iPhone

In the Maps app 📍, you can get detailed driving directions to your destination.

When you drive in select cities, you see enhanced details for crosswalks, bike lanes, buildings, and a street-level perspective that helps you find the right lane as you approach complex interchanges.

Note: Turn-by-turn spoken directions are not available in all countries or regions.

Get directions for driving

1. Do one of the following:
   o Say something like "Hey Siri, give me driving directions home.
   o Tap your destination (such as a search result in Maps or a landmark on a map), or touch and hold anywhere on the map, then tap the directions button.
2. When a suggested route appears, you can do any of the following:
   o Switch to driving directions: If driving isn't your default mode of travel or if you're viewing a transit map, tap the travel mode button (below the Directions list), then tap 🚗.
   o Choose a future departure or arrival time: Tap Now (below the Directions list), select a time or date for departure or arrival, then tap Done. The estimated travel time may change based on predicted traffic.
   o Add stops along your route: You can add up to 14 stops on the way to your destination.
   o Avoid tolls or highways: Tap Avoid (below the Directions list), choose your options, the tap Apply.
   o View a route's directions in a list: On the route card, tap the route's estimated travel time so that the route appears at the top of the card, then tap the estimated travel time again. To share the directions, scroll to the bottom of the card, then tap Share.
   o Choose other route options: You can reverse the starting point and destination, select a different starting point or destination, and more.
3. Tap Go for the route you want.

As you travel along your route, Maps speaks turn-by-turn directions to your destination.

While following the route, you can share your ETA, find a place to stop, turn off spoken directions, and view a route overview or a list of turns.

When Driving Focus is turned on, or if iPhone locks automatically, Maps remains onscreen and continues to speak directions. Even if you open another app, you continue to receive turn-by-turn directions. (To return to Maps from another app, tap the directions banner at the top of the screen or the navigation indicator `9:41` in the status bar.)

End driving directions before you arrive

Siri: Say something like: "Hey Siri, stop navigating."

Or without using Siri, you can tap the card at the bottom of the screen, then tap End Route.

Show or hide the compass or the speed limit

Go to Settings ⚙ > Maps, tap Driving (below Directions), then turn Compass or Speed Limit on or off.

Get directions to your parked car in Maps on iPhone

When you disconnect iPhone from your car's CarPlay or Bluetooth system and exit your vehicle, a parked car marker is dropped in the Maps app 🅿️ so you can easily find the way back to your car.

Find your parked car

Choose Parked Car below Siri Suggestions on the search card.

If you don't find your parked car in Maps

Make sure your iPhone is paired to CarPlay or Bluetooth in your car, then make sure of the following settings:

- Location Services is turned on in Settings ⚙ > Privacy & Security.
- Significant Locations is turned on in Settings > Privacy & Security > Location Services > System Services.
- Show Parked Location is turned on in Settings > Maps.

Note: Your parked car isn't marked at a location where you frequently park, like at home or work.

Don't show your parked location

Do one of the following:

- Remove the Parked Car marker for your car's current location: Touch and hold the marker, then tap Remove Car.

- Never show your parked location: Go to Settings ⚙ > Maps, then turn off Show Parked Location.

Report traffic incidents in Maps on iPhone

In select regions and countries, you can report accidents, hazards, speed checks, and road work, and you can report when they're cleared (features vary by region and country).

Apple evaluates incoming incident reports. When there's a high level of confidence in the reports, incident markers—such as for hazards ⚠ and accidents ◈ —are displayed in the Maps app 📍 for other users too.

Note: Speed checks, where supported, are not displayed with incident markers. Instead, notifications for speed checks appear when you follow turn-by-turn driving directions.

Report traffic incidents

Siri: Say something like:

- "Report an accident"
- "There's something on the road"
- "There's a speed check here"

Or without using Siri, you can do the following:

- When following turn-by-turn driving directions: Tap the route card at the bottom of the screen, tap Report an Incident, then choose an option.
- When not following directions: Tap your picture or initials next to the search field, then tap Reports, tap Report an Incident, then choose an option.
  If neither your picture nor initials appears, tap Cancel next to the search field, or tap the search field, then tap Cancel.

Report on the status of a hazard or accident

A map may display hazard ⚠ and accident ◈ markers. When you're near the incidents in select countries or regions, you can report whether they cleared.

Siri: Say something like: "The hazard is gone" or "Clear the accident."

Or without using Siri, you can do the following:

1. Tap the incident marker.
2. Tap Cleared or Still Here.

Apple evaluates incoming incident reports. When there's a high level of confidence in reports that an incident has been cleared, its marker is removed from Maps.

Note: You can't clear reports of speed checks.

Get cycling directions in Maps on iPhone

In the Maps app 📍 , you can get detailed cycling directions. Maps offers routes on bike paths, bike lanes, and bike-friendly roads (when available). You can preview the elevation for your ride, check how busy a road is, and choose a route that best avoids hills.

As you travel along your route, Maps speaks cycling-specific directions for turns and maneuvers. With a handlebar mount for iPhone, you can glance at the directions on the iPhone screen. Or with Apple Watch, you can glance at them on your wrist. (Handlebar mount and Apple Watch sold separately.)

Note: Cycling directions are available in select areas. Features vary by country and region.

Get directions for cycling

1. Do one of the following:
   - Say something like "Hey Siri, give me cycling directions home."
   - Tap your destination (such as a search result in Maps or a landmark on a map), or touch and hold anywhere on the map, then tap the directions button.
2. When a suggested route appears, you can do the following:
   - Switch to cycling directions: If cycling isn't your default mode of travel or if you're viewing a transit map, tap the travel mode button (below the Directions list), then tap 🚲 to see a suggested cycling route.
   - Avoid hills or busy roads: Tap Avoid (below the Directions list), choose your options, the tap Apply.
   - Choose other route options: You can reverse the starting point and destination, select a different starting point or destination, and more.
3. Tap Go for the route you want.
   As you travel along your route, Maps speaks turn-by-turn directions to your destination.

While following the route, you can share your ETA, find a place to stop, turn off spoken directions, and view a route overview or a list of turns.

End cycling directions before you arrive

Siri: Say something like: "Hey Siri, stop navigating."

Or without using Siri, you can tap the card at the bottom of the screen, then tap End Route.

Get walking directions in Maps on iPhone

In the Maps app 🗺️ , you can get detailed walking directions to your destination. You can preview the elevation for your walk and choose a route that best avoids hills, stairs, and busy roads.

As you walk along your route, Maps speaks walking-specific directions for turns and maneuvers like walking up stairs.

On supported models and in select areas, you can view immersive walking instructions that use the iPhone camera and augmented reality to show you where to turn.

Note: Turn-by-turn spoken directions are not available in all countries or regions.

Get directions for walking

1. Do one of the following:
   - Say something like "Hey Siri, give me walking directions home."
   - Tap your destination (such as a search result in Maps or a landmark on a map), or touch and hold anywhere on the map, then tap the directions button.
2. When a suggested route appears, you can do the following:
   - Switch to walking directions: If walking isn't your default mode of travel or if you're viewing a transit map, tap the travel mode button (below the Directions list), then tap 🚶 to see a suggested walking route.
   - Avoid hills, busy roads, or stairs: Tap Avoid (below the Directions list), choose your options, the tap Apply.

- Choose other route options: You can reverse the starting point and destination, select a different starting point or destination, and more.
3. Tap Go for the route you want.
4. To view directions in augmented reality, tap ⚓, then follow the onscreen instructions. To return to the map, tap ✕.
   Note: To automatically return to the augmented reality screen whenever you raise iPhone after tapping ⚓, go to Settings ⚙ > Maps > Walking, then turn on Raise to View.

While following the route, you can share your ETA, turn off spoken directions, and view a route overview or a list of turns.

To improve the accuracy of your position and heading while walking, iPhone uses the camera and the motion sensors. This feature may increase battery usage. To turn this feature off, go to Settings ⚙ > Maps > Walking (below Directions), then turn off Enhanced.

End walking directions before you arrive

Siri: Say something like: "Hey Siri, stop navigating."

Or without using Siri, you can tap the card at the bottom of the screen, then tap End Route.

Get transit directions in Maps on iPhone

In the Maps app 🗺, you can get detailed transit directions to your destination, including departure times, connection information, and fare amounts. You can also add transit cards, see low balances, and replenish your card while using Maps to get directions.

Note: Public transportation information is not available in all countries or regions.

Find a transit route
1. Do one of the following:
   - Say something like "Hey Siri, give me transit directions to the Ferry Building."
     Note: Siri transit directions aren't available in all countries or regions.
   - Tap your destination (such as a search result in Maps or a landmark on a map), or touch and hold anywhere on the map, then tap the directions button.
2. When a suggested route appears, you can do any of the following:
   - **Switch to transit directions**: If transit isn't your default mode of travel, tap the travel mode button (below the Directions list), then tap 🚆 to see a suggested transit route.
   - **Choose a future departure or arrival time**: Tap Now (below the Directions list), select a time or date for departure or arrival, then tap Done.
   - **Select which transit method you prefer**: Tap Prefer (below the Directions list), then select your preferences.
   - **Switch from transit card to cash fares**: In some countries and regions, fares are listed for the suggested routes. To view cash fares (where available), tap Transit Card Fares (below the Directions list), then tap Cash Fares.

- o **Choose other route options**: You can reverse the starting point and destination, select a different starting point or destination, and more.
3. Tap Go for the route you want.
   To get upcoming directions during your trip, scroll down in the route card.

Quickly find nearby transit departures in Favorites

You can get one-tap access to the departure times for stops and stations near you.

- **Add Nearby Transit to Favorites**: In the row of Favorites on the search card, tap ➕, tap Nearby Transit, then tap Done. (If ➕ doesn't appear, swipe the Favorites row left.)
- **View upcoming departures**: Tap Transit in the row of Favorites on the search card. To see stop details and additional departure times, tap any row on the Nearby Transit card.
- **Choose a line to appear at the top of the Nearby Transit list**: Tap Transit in the row of Favorites on the search card, touch and hold a line, then tap Pin. (To remove the pin, touch and hold the line again, then tap Remove Pin.)

Add a transit station or stop to Favorites

You can get one-tap access to the departure times for and directions to your favorite stop or station.

1. Do one of the following:
   - o Use Siri or search to find a transit station or stop.
   - o View a transit map, zoom in or move the map until you see the transit stop or station, then tap the transit stop or station.
2. Tap ••• (to the right of the directions button on the place card), then Tap Add to Favorites.

See the major transit lines

1. With a map showing, tap the button at the top right.
2. Select Transit, then tap ✕.

Pay for transit with your iPhone

With many transit agencies, you can use your iPhone to pay for your fare.

- **Use Apple Pay**: With Apple Cash, credit, and debit cards stored in the Wallet app 🗔, you can make contactless transit payments with agencies that support Apple Pay.
- **Use transit cards**: With participating transit systems, you can pay for your fare when you store your transit cards in Wallet.

When you get directions for select transit systems in Maps, you may also get a message that you can use Apple Pay to pay for transit or do the following—without opening the Wallet app or leaving Maps:

- **Add a transit card**: When you get an invitation for a transit system that supports iPhone payments, tap Learn More, then tap Add Transit Card (or similar).
- **Add money to your transit card**: When you get a message (for example, that the fare exceeds your balance), tap Reload Transit Card (or similar).

Delete recent directions in Maps on iPhone

You can delete directions that you recently viewed in the Maps app 🧭 .

Scroll down in the search card to Recents, then do one of the following:

- Swipe a recent route left.
- Tap More directly above the list, then swipe a recent route left, or to delete a group of routes, tap Clear above the group.

Use Maps on your Mac to get directions for iPhone

Before a big trip or a day of cycling, you can plan your route on your Mac, and then share the details to your iPhone. The larger screen on your Mac can help you look around and see what's ahead, and for some locations you can get an interactive 3D view. You must be signed in with the same Apple ID on both your Mac and your iPhone.

1. In Maps on your Mac, create a route for your trip.
2. Choose File > Share > Send to [your device].

You can also use Handoff to send directions from iPhone to Mac.

Take Tours

Look around streets in Maps on iPhone

You can view cities in the Maps app 🧭 in interactive 3D that lets you pan 360 degrees and move through the streets.

1. In select cities, tap 👓 near the bottom of a map.
2. To change the view, do any of the following:
   - **Pan**: Drag a finger left or right.
   - **Move forward**: Tap the scene.
   - **Zoom in or out**: Pinch open or closed.
   - Switch to or from full-screen view: Tap ⤢ or ⤡ .
   - **View another point of interest**: Switch from full-screen view, then tap elsewhere on the map.
   - **Hide labels in full-screen view**: Tap the place card at the bottom of the screen, then tap 👁 .
3. When finished, tap Done.

Take Flyover tours in Maps on iPhone

In the Maps app 🧭 , you can fly over many of the world's major landmarks and cities. Flyover landmarks are identified by the Flyover button on their place cards.

View a city or landmark from above

1. Use the button at the top right to select any map except Transit.

230

2. Tap the name of a city or the name of a landmark.
3. Tap Flyover on the place card.

   For some landmarks, if Flyover doesn't appear on the place card, tap • • •, then tap Flyover.
4. Do any of the following:
   - **Change viewing direction**: Point or tilt iPhone in the direction you want to view.
   - **Move around:** Drag a finger in any direction. To rotate perspective, touch and hold the screen with one finger, then continue holding it in place while you drag another finger around it.
   - **Watch an aerial 3D tour**: Tap Start Tour or Start City Tour in the card at the bottom of the screen. (If the card doesn't appear, tap anywhere on the screen.)
5. To return to the map, tap ✕ (tap anywhere on the screen if ✕ doesn't appear).

Book rides in Maps on iPhone

In the Maps app 🧭, you can request a ride with a compatible ridesharing app (not available in all countries or regions). If you don't have one installed, Maps shows you apps that are available from the App Store.

Find your destination, tap Directions, then tap 🧍 (at the bottom right).

To estimate wait times and fares with ride sharing apps, Maps may share your location with these apps. To stop sharing your location with a ride sharing app, go to Settings ⚙ > Maps > Ride Booking, then turn off the app.

Measure

Measure dimensions with iPhone

Use the Measure app 📐 and your iPhone camera to measure nearby objects. iPhone automatically detects the dimensions of rectangular objects, or you can manually set the start and end points of a measurement.

For best results, use Measure on well-defined objects located 0.5 to 3 meters (2 to 10 feet) from iPhone.

Note: Measurements are approximate.

Start a measurement

1. Open Measure 📐, then use the iPhone camera to slowly scan nearby objects.
2. Position iPhone so that the object you want to measure appears on the screen.

Note: For your privacy, when you use Measure to take measurements, a green dot appears at the top of the screen to indicate your camera is in use.

Take an automatic rectangle measurement

1. When iPhone detects the edges of a rectangular object, a white box frames the object; tap the white box or ⊕ to see the dimensions.
2. To take a photo of your measurement, tap ○.

Take a manual measurement

1. Align the dot at the center of the screen with the point where you want to start measuring, then tap ⊕.
2. Slowly pan iPhone to the end point, then tap ⊕ to see the measured length.
3. To take a photo of your measurement, tap ○.
4. Take another measurement, or tap Clear to start over.

Use edge guides

You can easily measure the height and straight edges of furniture, countertops, and other objects using guide lines that appear automatically.

- Position the dot at the center of the screen along the straight edge of an object until a guide appears.
- Tap ⊕ where you want to begin measuring.
- Slowly pan along the guide, then tap ⊕ at the endpoint to see the measured length.
- To take a photo of your measurement, tap ○.

Use Ruler view

You can see more detail in your measurements with Ruler view.

1. After measuring the distance between two points, move iPhone closer to the measurement line until it transforms into a ruler, showing incremental inches and feet.
2. To take a photo of your measurement, tap ○.

View and save measurements on iPhone

In the Measure app ▦ you can save a list of all the measurements you take in a single session, complete with screenshots, so you can easily share and access them whenever you need them.

1. Tap ☰ to see a list of your recent measurements.
   Swipe up from the top of the list to see more measurements.
2. To save the measurements, tap Copy, open another app (for example, Notes), tap in a document, then tap Paste.

Measure a person's height with iPhone

You can use the Measure app ▦ to instantly measure a person's height from the floor to the top of their head, hair, or hat. (You can even measure the seated height of a person in a chair.)

1. Position iPhone so that the person you want to measure appears on the screen from head to toe.
   After a moment, a line appears at the top of the person's head (or hair, or hat), with the height measurement showing just below the line.
2. To take a photo of the measurement, tap ◯.
3. To save the photo, tap the screenshot in the lower-left corner, tap Done, then choose Save to Photos or Save to Files.
   You can easily access and share the height measurement image from Photos or Files on iPhone whenever you want.

To take the measurement again, turn iPhone away for a moment to reset the height.

Use iPhone as a level

Use your iPhone to determine whether an object near you is level, straight, or flat (measurements are approximate).

1. Open Measure.
2. Tap Level, then hold iPhone against an object, such as a picture frame.
   - **Make an object level**: Rotate the object and iPhone until you see green.
   - **Match the slope**: Tap the screen to capture the slope of the first object. Hold iPhone against another object and rotate them until the screen turns green.
     To reset the level, tap the screen again.

Messages

Set up Messages on iPhone

In the Messages app 💬, you can send text messages in two different ways:

- Over Wi-Fi or cellular service, using iMessage with others who also use iMessage on an iPhone, iPad, iPod touch, or Mac. iMessage texts appear in blue bubbles.
- Through your cellular service as SMS/MMS messages. SMS/MMS messages appear in green bubbles.

Texts you send and receive using iMessage don't count against your SMS/MMS allowances in your cellular messaging plan, but cellular data rates may apply.

iMessage texts can include photos, videos, and other content. You can see when other people are typing, and send read receipts to let them know when you've read their messages. You can also undo and edit sent messages. For security, messages sent using iMessage are encrypted before they're sent.

SMS messages are short text messages, while MMS messages may include text, graphics, audio, video, and other media.

Sign in to iMessage

Signing in to iMessage keeps your messages up to date and available wherever you're signed in, and it backs up all the messages that you send and receive on iPhone. When you communicate with others using iMessage, you can use more apps and features, like collaboration, read receipts, undo send, audio messages, Memoji, Animoji, and more.

1. Go to Settings 🔘 > Messages, then turn on iMessage.
2. To select the phone numbers and email addresses you want to use with iMessage, go to Settings > Messages > Send & Receive, then choose from the available options below "You can receive iMessages to and reply from."

You can see all the messages you send and receive on all your Apple devices where you're signed in with the same Apple ID and have iMessage turned on.

Use Messages in iCloud

When you turn on Messages in iCloud, every message you send and receive on your iPhone is saved in iCloud. And, when you sign in with the same Apple ID on a new device that also has Messages in iCloud turned on, all your conversations show up there automatically.

Go to Settings 🔘 > [your name] > iCloud, then turn on Messages (if it's not already turned on).

After you turn on Messages in iCloud, any messages or attachments you delete from iPhone are also deleted from your other Apple devices (iOS 11.4, iPadOS 13, macOS 10.13.5, or later) where Messages in iCloud is turned on.

Note: Messages in iCloud uses iCloud storage.

Share your name and photo

In Messages, you can share your name and photo when you send or receive a message from someone new. Your photo can be a Memoji or custom image. When you open Messages for the first time, follow the instructions on your iPhone to choose your name and photo.

To change your name, photo, or sharing options, open Messages, tap ⋯ , tap Edit Name and Photo, then do any of the following:

- **Change your profile image**: Tap Edit below the circle, then choose an option.
- **Change your name**: Tap the text fields where your name appears.
- **Turn sharing on or off**: Tap the button next to Name and Photo Sharing.
- **Change who can see your profile**: Tap an option below Share Automatically (Name and Photo Sharing must be turned on).

Your Messages name and photo can also be used for your Apple ID and My Card in Contacts.

Send and receive messages on iPhone

Use the Messages app 💬 to send and receive texts, photos, videos, and audio messages.

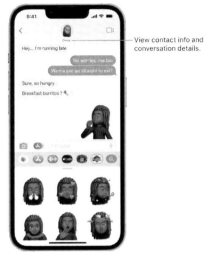
View contact info and conversation details.

Tip: Send a message from whichever device is closest to you, then use Handoff to continue the conversation elsewhere.

Send a message

You can send a text message to one or more people to start a conversation.

1. Tap ⌐ at the top of the screen to start a new message, or tap an existing message.

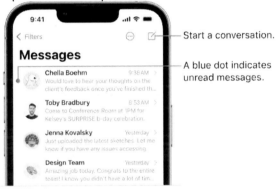
Start a conversation.

A blue dot indicates unread messages.

2. Enter the phone number, contact name, or Apple ID of each recipient. Or, tap ⊕, then choose contacts.

If you set up Dual SIM on a compatible model and want to send an SMS/MMS message from a different line, tap the line shown, then choose the other line.

3. Tap the text field, type your message, then tap ⬆ to send.
   - A blue send button indicates the message will be sent with iMessage; a green send button indicates the message will be sent with SMS/MMS, or your cellular service.
   - An alert ⓘ appears if a message can't be sent. Tap the alert to try sending the message again.

Tip: Rather than typing every letter of your message, tap 🎙 to dictate text.

To view conversation details, tap the name or phone number at the top of the screen. You can tap the contact to edit the contact card, share your location, view attachments, leave a group conversation, and more.

To return to the Messages list from a conversation, tap ❮ or swipe from the left edge.

Continue a conversation

When someone sends you a message for the first time, a conversation opens. If you've interacted with that person in Messages before, their message is added to the end of the earlier conversation.

1. In the Messages list, tap the conversation that you want to participate in.
   To look for contacts and content in conversations, tap the search field above the Messages lists. (You may need to swipe down to reveal the search field.) The search field also opens suggested contacts, links, photos, and more.
2. Tap the text field, then type your message. To replace text with emoji, tap 😃 or 🌐, then tap each highlighted word.
3. Tap ⬆ to send your message.

To let your recipients know when you read their messages, go to Settings > Messages, then turn on Send Read Receipts.

Tip: To see what time a message was sent or received, drag the message bubble to the left.

Reply to a specific message in a conversation

You can respond to a specific message inline in group or individual conversations to improve clarity and help keep the conversation organized.

1. In a conversation, touch and hold a message, then tap Reply ↰.
2. Write your response, then tap ⬆.

Tip: You can quickly reply to messages with a Tapback expression (for example, a thumbs-up or a heart). Double-tap the message bubble that you want to respond to, then select a Tapback.

People can respond inline as long as they're using an iPhone, iPad, iPod touch, or Mac and have iMessage turned on.

Use Siri to send and receive messages

Siri can read your incoming messages out loud to you, and you can speak a reply for Siri to send._

Siri: Say something like:

- "Send a message to Eliza saying how about tomorrow"
- "Read my last message from Bob"
- "Reply that's great news"

You can set up Siri to automatically send a message after it has been read back to you. If you want to skip the confirmation step when sending messages, go to Settings ⚙ > Siri & Search > Automatically Send Messages.

Send a message to a business

Some businesses allow you to communicate with them directly to ask questions, resolve issues, get advice on what to buy, make purchases with Apple Pay, and more.

1. Search for the business you want to communicate with using Maps, Safari, Search, or Siri.
2. Start a conversation by tapping a messaging link in the search results—the appearance of the link varies, and might look like a button, a text link, or the company logo.

You can send a message to some businesses from their website or app.

Note: Messages sent to participating businesses appear in dark gray to distinguish them from messages sent using iMessage (in blue) and SMS/MMS messages (in green).

Send a recorded audio message

Instead of writing a text message, you can quickly record an audio message that can be played right in the Messages conversation.

Audio recording is an iMessage app. In a Messages conversation, tap to show the app icons below the text field, tap , then do one of the following:

- **To record and review before sending**: Tap . Tap to review, then tap to send the recording or to cancel.
- To record a message and send it immediately: Hold .

Note: Your audio message disappears from your conversation two minutes after you send it, unless you tap Keep. Recipients can still play your recording. To always keep audio messages, go to Settings > Messages > Expire (below Audio Messages), then tap Never.

To make an audio or video call instead of sending a message, you can switch to FaceTime . In a Messages conversation, tap .

Listen or reply to a recorded audio message

1. Raise iPhone to your ear to play incoming audio messages.
2. Raise it again to reply.

To turn this feature on or off, go to Settings > Messages, then turn off Raise to Listen.

Forward text messages to other devices

When you send a message to someone who uses a phone other than an iPhone, your message is sent as an SMS message. You can set up your iPhone so that when you send or receive an SMS message, it appears on your other devices.

1. Go to Settings > Messages.
2. Tap Text Message Forwarding, then turn on any devices you want to include.
3. If you're not using two-factor authentication, a six-digit activation code appears on your other device; enter this code on your iPhone, then tap Allow.

Unsend and edit messages on iPhone

In the Messages app ⬜ , you can unsend or edit recent messages, giving you the opportunity to fix a typo or pull back a message that you accidentally sent to the wrong person. Your recipient sees that you unsent a message and your edit history.

Note: To unsend or edit text messages, you must be using iMessage with iOS 16 or later. If your recipients have devices with earlier versions of iOS, they receive follow-up messages with the preface "Edited to" and your new message in quotation marks. SMS messages can't be unsent or edited.

Unsend a message

You can undo a recently sent message for up to two minutes after sending it.

Touch and hold the message bubble, then tap Undo Send.

A note confirming that you unsent the message appears in both conversation transcripts: yours and your recipient's.

If the person you're messaging is using a device with iOS 16 or later, unsending removes the message from their device.

If the person you're messaging is using a device with iOS 15.6 or earlier, iPadOS 15.6 or earlier, macOS 12 or earlier, or is using SMS, the original message remains in the conversation. When you unsend a message, you're notified that the recipient may still see the original message in the message transcript.

Edit a sent message

You can edit a recently sent message up to five times within 15 minutes of sending it.

1. In Messages, select a conversation with the message you want to edit.
2. Touch and hold the message bubble, then tap Edit.
3. Make any changes, then tap ✅ to resend with edits or ✕ to revert.

Note: The message is marked as Edited in the conversation transcript.

If the person you're messaging is using a device with iOS 16 or later, the message bubble is updated to reflect your edits on their device, and both of you can tap Edited to see previous versions of your message.

If the person you're messaging is using a device with iOS 15.6 or earlier, iPadOS 15.6 or earlier, macOS 12 or earlier, or is using SMS, they receive a new message with your updated text.

Keep track of conversations in Messages on iPhone

In the Messages app ⬜ , you can mark messages as unread or pin and unpin conversations to prioritize messages in the Messages list.

Mark messages as unread

You can mark conversations as unread so you can return to them later when you have time to respond.

In the Messages list, swipe right on a conversation to mark it as unread. Or drag right and tap 💬 .

To see a list of your unread messages, you must first turn on Filtering. Go to Settings > Messages, scroll down to Message Filtering, then turn on Filter Unknown Senders.

Tip: You can also mark several messages as unread at once. Tap ⊙, tap Select Messages, select the conversations you want to mark as unread, then tap Unread in the bottom-left corner.

Pin a conversation

You can pin specific conversations to the top of the Messages list so the people you contact most always come first in the list.

Do any of the following:

- Swipe right on a conversation, then tap 📌.
- Touch and hold a conversation, then drag it to the top of the list.

Unpin a conversation

You can unpin specific conversations at the top of the Messages list.

Do any of the following:

- Touch and hold a conversation, then drag the message to the bottom of the list.

- Touch and hold a conversation, then tap 📌.

Have a group conversation in Messages on iPhone

Use the Messages app 💬 to send a group text message. In a group conversation, you can call people's attention to specific messages and even collaborate on projects.

Send a new message to a group

You can send a message to multiple people to start a group conversation.

1. Tap ✍️ at the top of the screen to start a new conversation.
2. Enter the phone number, contact name, or Apple ID of each recipient, or tap ⊕, then choose contacts.
   Note: If one or more of your recipients isn't using iMessage, messages appear in green bubbles instead of blue ones.
3. Tap the text field, type your message, then tap ⬆️.

Add someone to an existing group conversation

If you have at least three people in a group conversation, you can add additional contacts (as long as everyone in the group is using an iPhone, iPad, iPod touch, or Mac and has turned on iMessage). Otherwise, you need to start a new group conversation.

1. Tap the group message you want to add someone to.
2. Tap the group name at the top of the conversation.
3. Tap Add Contact to add a new person to the conversation.

Tip: To remove someone from a group conversation, swipe left on their name, then tap Remove.

Leave a group conversation

You can leave a group message (as long as everyone in the group has an iPhone, iPad, iPod touch, or Mac and has turned on iMessage).

1. Tap the group message you want to leave.
2. Tap the group name at the top of the conversation.
3. Scroll down and tap Leave this Conversation.

Regardless of how many people are in your group conversation, you can also mute the conversation so you don't get notifications.

Mention people in a group conversation

You can mention someone by name in a group message to call their attention to a specific message, and they'll get a notification (as long as everyone in the group has an iPhone, iPad, iPod touch, or Mac and has turned on iMessage). Depending on their settings, they'll be notified even if they have the conversation muted.

1. In a conversation, begin typing a contact's name in the text field.
2. Tap the contact's name when it appears.
   You can also mention a contact in Messages by typing @ followed by the contact's name.

To set your own notification preferences for when you're mentioned in Messages, go to Settings

 > Messages > Notify Me.

Change the name and image of a group conversation

You can name a group conversation and choose an image to represent it (as long as everyone in the group has an iPhone, iPad, iPod touch, or Mac and has turned on iMessage).

1. Tap the name or number at the top of the conversation.
2. Tap Change Name and Photo, then choose an option.

Add photos and videos to messages on iPhone

In the Messages app , you can send messages with photos and videos. You can also edit the photos and videos before you send them and share, save, or print attachments.

To send SMS/MMS attachments on models with Dual SIM, you need to set up Dual SIM.

Note: Your carrier may set size limits for attachments; iPhone may compress photo and video attachments when necessary.

Send a photo or video

1. In Messages, do any of the following while writing a message:
   o **Take a photo within Messages**: Tap , frame the shot in the viewfinder, then tap .
   o **Take a video within Messages**: Tap , choose Video mode, then tap .
   o **Choose an existing photo or video**: Tap to see recent shots, then swipe up to search or browse through all photos and albums.
2. Tap to send your message or to cancel.

If you receive multiple photos or videos at the same time, they're automatically grouped into a collage (two to three items) or a stack (four or more). You can swipe through a stack to view, reply, or interact with each photo or video individually.

To save a photo or video, tap 🖫 next to the photo or stack.

Note: You can turn communication safety on or off on a family member's device. When you turn on this setting, the Messages app can detect nudity in photos on your child's device before the photos are sent or received, and provides resources to help your child handle the situation (not available in all countries or regions). Apple doesn't get access to the photos as a result of this feature.

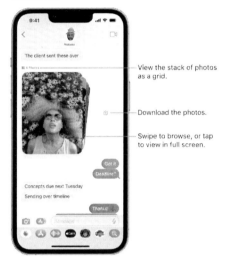

View the stack of photos as a grid.

Download the photos.

Swipe to browse, or tap to view in full screen.

Mark up or edit a photo

You can mark up or edit a photo before you send it in a Messages conversation.

1. Tap 🌸 below the text field, then choose a photo.
2. Tap the photo in the message bubble, then do any of the following:
   o Tap Markup, use the Markup tools to draw on the photo, then tap Save.
   o Tap Edit, then use the photo editing tools to edit the photo.
3. Tap Done, add a message (optional), then tap ⬆ to send the photo, or tap ⊗ to remove the photo from the message bubble.

Add camera effects to a photo or video

When you take a photo or video in a Messages conversation, you can add camera effects to it—such as filters, stickers, labels, and shapes.

1. In a Messages conversation, tap 📷, then choose Photo or Video mode.
2. Tap ✩, then do any of the following:
   o Tap 😊, then choose a Memoji.
   o Tap ⬤, then choose a filter to apply to your picture.
   o Tap Aa to add a text label, or 〰 to add a shape.

- Tap ⬡ to add a Memoji sticker, or ⬡ to add an Emoji sticker.
3. Tap ⊗ to close the effect window.
4. Tap ◯ to take a photo or ⬤ to record video.
5. Tap Done to add the photo or video to the message bubble, where you can add a message, or tap ⬆ to send the photo or video directly.

Work with attachments

In a conversation, you can do any of the following with attachments:

- **Save an attachment**: Tap ⬇ to the right of the message bubble containing the attachment.

- **Share, copy, save, or print an attachment**: Tap the attachment, then tap ⬆ and choose an option.

- **Save or copy an attachment**: Touch and hold the attachment, then tap Save or Copy.

- **Forward a message or attachment**: Touch and hold a message or attachment, tap More, select additional items if desired, then tap ⤳ .

- **Delete an attachment**: Touch and hold a message or attachment, tap More, select additional items if desired, then tap 🗑 .

Note: Attachments you send over iMessage (such as photos or videos) may be uploaded to Apple and encrypted so that no one but the sender and receiver can access them. To improve performance, your device may automatically upload attachments to Apple while you're composing an iMessage. If your message isn't sent, the attachments are deleted from the server after several days.

Send and receive content in Messages on iPhone

When someone shares links, images, and other content with you in the Messages app ⬡ , you can find that content in a Shared with You section in supported apps. This allows you to view the content at a time that's convenient for you. Apps that support Shared with You include Books, Files, Keynote, Music, News, Notes, Numbers, Pages, Photos, Podcasts, Reminders, Safari, and TV.

Share content with others

To share photos and videos in the Messages app, paste a link into your message, or tap ✳ to add photos and videos, then tap ⬆ .

To share content from another app (for example Podcasts, News, or Music), select the content you want to share, tap ⬆ , then choose Messages.

See what others have shared with you

When someone shares content such as a link to a news story or TV show, you can find that content in several places: in the Messages conversation, in a Shared with You section in the

Details view of your Messages conversation, and in the Shared with You section of the corresponding app. Here are a few ways to find what's been Shared with You in other apps:

- **Photos**: Tap For You, then scroll to the Shared with You section.
- **Safari**: Tap the address field, then scroll up to Shared with You.
- **News**: Tap Following, then tap Shared with You.
- **Music**: Tap Listen Now, then scroll to the Shared with You section.
- **Podcasts**: Tap Listen Now, then scroll to the Shared with You section.
- **Apple TV**: Tap Watch Now, then scroll to the Shared with You section.

You can also find a Shared with You section in Books, Files, Keynote, Notes, Numbers, Pages, Photos, Reminders, and other supported apps.

Content that's been shared with you previously has a label indicating who shared it. To continue the conversation without leaving the app you're in, tap the label below the content and reply in Messages.

Note: Content only appears in Shared with You if the person who sent it is in your contacts.

Pin shared content

If someone shares content that's especially interesting, you can quickly pin it in Messages, and it will be elevated in the Shared with You section of supported apps, Messages search, and the Details view of the conversation.

In Messages, touch and hold a link, then tap 📌.

Note: Photos can be saved to your library, but not pinned.

Control what shared content appears in apps

You can adjust your settings to hide an app's Shared with You section.

1. Go to Settings > Messages > Shared with You.
2. Turn off Automatic Sharing, or turn off Shared with You for a specific app.

Enjoy content together live using SharePlay on iPhone

In the Messages app ⬜, you can get together with friends to watch the latest episode of your favorite show or listen to a new song in real time using SharePlay. On an iPhone that meets the minimum system requirements, you can start a Messages conversation right from a supported app like Apple TV 📺 and Music 🎵. Shared playback controls keep everyone in sync.

For everyone who has access to the content, the video starts playing at the same time. People who don't have access are asked to get access (through a subscription, a transaction, or a free trial, if available).

1. In a supported app, find a show, movie, song, album, or other content you want to share, then tap the item to see its details.
2. Do one of the following:
   - Tap 📤, then tap SharePlay.
   - Tap ••• at the top right, tap 📤, then tap SharePlay.
   - Tap ••• next to the content, then tap SharePlay.

3. In the To field, enter the contacts or conversation you want to share with, then tap Messages.
4. Tap Start or Play to begin using SharePlay.

To begin viewing or listening, recipients tap the content's title at the top of the Messages conversation, then tap Open.

Note: If the shared content requires a subscription, the service may ask those who don't have access to subscribe, make a transaction, or sign up for a free trial, if available.

When you select content to share and tap the Play button, you can also select Play for Everyone (if it appears) to begin it for everyone in the conversation. (Others on the thread may have to tap Join SharePlay to see the video.)

Each person in the conversation can use the playback controls to play, pause, rewind, or fast-forward for everyone, but settings like closed-captioning and volume are controlled separately by each person.

Use Messages when you want no interruptions to the sound of the movie, show, song, or podcast, or switch to FaceTime when you want to see and hear other people as you chat.

Tip: Use Picture in Picture to keep watching a video while using another app—to order food or check your email.

Collaborate on projects with Messages on iPhone

You can send an invitation to collaborate on a project in the Messages app , and everyone in the conversation is added to the document, spreadsheet, or other shared file.

Note: To start collaborating on a project with Messages, you and your recipients must be using iMessage with iOS 16 or later, and you must first save the content somewhere it can be accessed by others, such as iCloud Drive. For iPhone apps, you may need to turn on iCloud to use the collaboration features: go to Settings > [your name] > iCloud > Show All (below Apps Using iCloud).

Invite people to collaborate

You can invite people to collaborate on a project from another app, and then discuss your content in Messages. Share files from apps like Notes, Reminders, Safari, Keynote, Pages, Numbers, and more, as long as you first turn on their collaboration features in iCloud settings and save the content somewhere it can be accessed by others, such as iCloud Drive.

Choose Collaborate.

Change access and permissions.

The process for inviting someone to collaborate depends on the app. Here's one way you might start a collaboration in a supported app:

1. Select the file you want to share, then tap Collaborate or ⬆️.
2. Make sure Collaborate (rather than Send Copy) is selected, then tap Messages.
3. Select the group or individual you want to collaborate with. If you don't see your collaborator listed, tap the Messages icon.
4. A Messages conversation opens with the invitation ready to send. Add a note (optional), then tap ⬆️.

After you invite collaborators in Messages, you can work on the project in the other app and return to the Messages conversation by tapping the Collaborate button in that app.

Note: Your collaborators may need to accept your invitation or join the shared item before they can interact with it or see any updates.

Collaborate on a project in Messages

After you share your project, you see activity updates at the top of the Messages conversation whenever someone makes an edit.

Everyone in the group can access the shared document.

See who made changes.

Open the document in the other app.

To return to the project, open the conversation that has a project you've started collaborating on, then do any of the following:

- Tap the file in your conversation to open it.
- If you see an update at the top of the conversation, tap Show.
- Tap the name of your collaborator or group at the top of the screen, scroll to Collaboration, then tap the shared project.

When you make any changes or edits to the project, your collaborators get updates in the conversation.

Note: If you add a new person to a group message conversation, you have to grant them access to the projects you're collaborating on. If they've been added to the group conversation recently, you can tap a notification at the top of screen to add them. Or invite them to collaborate.

Manage the collaboration and group

The group of people in the Messages collaboration and the group collaborating on the file may not match. For example, you may invite people to collaborate on the file outside of Messages. Or you may have two different groups in Messages, each with its own collaboration conversation.

If you share a project with two or more people in a Messages conversation, you can add or remove collaborators. Tap the group icon at the top of the conversation to open conversation details, tap the button showing the participants in the conversation, then do any of the following:

- **Add new collaborators**: Scroll to the bottom of the list and tap ➕ , then add contacts. If you started collaborating with just one other person, you must start a new conversation to add people to the collaboration.
  Note: You must add new collaborators to any files shared in the conversation before they joined. As you add collaborators, a notification appears at the top of the conversation. Tap Show in the notification to grant access to each file.
- **Remove collaborators from the conversation**: Swipe left on the name of the person you want to remove, then tap Remove.

Important: The apps where the collaboration happens usually control access to the project. Check collaborator access in the app itself to remove viewing or editing privileges completely.

Stop collaborating on a project in Messages

The apps where the collaboration happens usually control access to the project. For example, if you're collaborating on a document in the Pages app, the Pages settings take precedence over the Messages settings. You can, however, unsend or delete the invitation from the conversation just as you would any other message.

Important: Deleting an invitation removes the conversation from the collaboration, it does not remove participants from the file. Check collaborator access in the app to remove viewing or editing privileges completely.

Animate messages on iPhone

In the Messages app ⬭, you can animate a single message with a bubble effect or fill the entire message screen with a full-screen effect (for example, balloons or confetti). You can even send a personal message with invisible ink that remains blurred until the recipient swipes to reveal it.

You need iMessage to send and receive message effects.

Send a handwritten message or doodle

Use your finger to write a message or draw a doodle. Recipients see what you wrote or drew, re-created before their eyes.

1. In a conversation, rotate iPhone to landscape orientation.
2. Tap ⟳ on the keyboard.
3. Write a message with your finger or choose a saved message at the bottom, then tap Done.
4. Tap ⬆ to send your message or ⊗ to cancel.

Scroll to write a longer message.

Choose a saved message. Touch and hold to delete a saved message.

Return to the keyboard.

After you create and send a handwritten message, the message is saved at the bottom of the handwriting screen. To use the saved messages again, tap it. To delete the saved message, touch and hold it until the messages jiggle, then tap ⊗.

Animate the message bubble

Use effects to animate the message bubble: you can send a message with Slam or Loud so that it appears to pop out, or use Gentle so it arrives softly. You can also use Invisible Ink to hide the message before it's read.

1. In a new or existing conversation, type a message or insert a photo or Memoji.

2. Touch and hold ⬆, then tap the gray dots to preview different bubble effects.

3. Tap ⬆ to send the message or ✕ to cancel the effect and return to your message.

Animate effects over the full screen

You can send messages with full-screen effects—such as lively lasers, a moving spotlight, or echoing bubbles—that play when your recipient gets your message.

1. In a new or existing conversation, type a message or insert a photo or Memoji.

2. Touch and hold ⬆, then tap Screen.
3. Swipe left to preview different screen effects.

4. Tap ⬆ to send the message or ✕ to cancel the effect and return to your message.

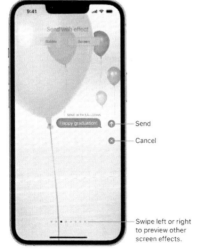

Messages automatically uses the following screen effects for specific text strings:

- Balloons for "Happy birthday"
- Confetti for "Congratulations"
- Fireworks for "Happy New Year"

Use iMessage apps in Messages on iPhone

In the Messages app 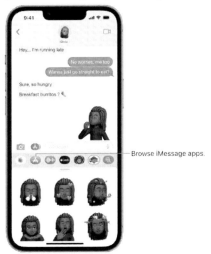, you can decorate a conversation with stickers, play a game, share songs, and more—all through iMessage apps—without leaving Messages. You can expand your message options by downloading more iMessage apps from the App Store.

Browse iMessage apps.

Browse and download iMessage apps

1. In a Messages conversation, tap ⒶⒶ to show the app icons below the text field.
2. Tap Ⓐ to open the App Store for iMessage.
3. Tap an app to see more details and reviews, then tap the price to purchase an app or tap Get to download a free app.
   All purchases are made with the payment method associated with your Apple ID.

Use an iMessage app

1. In a Messages conversation, tap ⒶⒶ to show the app icons below the text field.
2. Tap an iMessage app, then choose an item to add it to a message bubble.
3. Add a comment (optional), then tap ⬆ to send your message or ✕ to cancel.

Decorate with stickers

If you've downloaded a sticker app from the App Store, you can enhance your photos and videos with stickers in Messages.

1. In a Messages conversation, tap a sticker app below the text field.
2. Touch and hold a sticker, then drag it on top of a message in the conversation. Before you release it, you can do any of the following:
   o **Adjust the angle**: Rotate a second finger around the finger dragging the sticker.

- Adjust the size: Move a second finger closer to or away from the finger dragging the sticker.
3. You can also place the sticker on top of another sticker, or on a photo.

To see text that's covered by a sticker, double-tap the sticker.

To see more information about the sticker, touch and hold the sticker, then tap Sticker Details. You can do the following:

- See who sent the sticker.
- View the iMessage app that sent the sticker.
- Delete the sticker—swipe left, then tap Delete.

Manage iMessage apps

1. In a Messages conversation, swipe right on the app icons below the text field, then tap ●●● .
2. Tap Edit, then do any of the following with your iMessage apps:
   - Reorder apps: Drag ☰ .
   - Add an app to your Favorites: Tap ⊕ .
   - Remove an app from your Favorites: Tap ⊖ .
   - Hide an app: Turn the app off.
   - Delete an app: Swipe left on the app, then tap Remove from Favorites. Swipe left on the app again, then tap Delete.

Use Memoji in Messages on iPhone

Use the Messages app to express yourself with Memoji and personalized Memoji sticker packs that match your personality and mood. On models with a TrueDepth camera, you can send animated Memoji messages that record your voice and mirror your facial expressions.

Create your own Memoji

You can design your own personalized Memoji—choose skin tone, headwear, glasses, and more. You can create multiple Memoji for different moods.

1. In a conversation, tap 😀, then tap + .
2. Tap each feature and choose the options you want. As you add features to your Memoji, your character comes to life.
3. Tap Done to add the Memoji to your collection.

To edit, duplicate, or delete a Memoji, tap 😀, tap the Memoji, then tap ●●● .

Send Memoji and Memoji stickers

Messages automatically generates sticker packs based on your Memoji and Memoji characters. You can use stickers to express a range of emotions in new ways.

1. In a conversation, tap 😀.
2. Tap a Memoji in the top row to view the stickers in the sticker pack.
3. To send a sticker do one of the following:

- Tap the sticker to add it to the message bubble. Add a comment if you want, then tap ⬆ to send.
- Touch and hold a sticker, then drag it on top of a message in the conversation. The sticker is sent automatically when you add it to the message.

Send animated Memoji or Memoji recordings

You can send Memoji messages that use your voice and mirror your facial expressions.

1. In a conversation, tap 😀, then choose a Memoji.
2. Tap ⬤ to record your facial expressions and voice. Tap the red square to stop recording.
   Tap Replay to review your message.
3. Tap ⬆ to send your message or 🗑 to cancel.

You can also take a picture or video of yourself as a Memoji, decorate it with stickers, then send it. Or you can become a Memoji in a FaceTime conversation.

Send a Digital Touch effect in Messages on iPhone

In an iMessage conversation in the Messages app 💬, you can use Digital Touch to send animated sketches, taps, kisses, heartbeats, and more. You can even add a Digital Touch effect to a photo or video.

Send a sketch

1. Tap ⬤ in the app drawer.
2. Tap the color dot to choose a color, then draw with one finger.
   You can change the color, then start drawing again.
3. Tap ⬆ to send your message, or tap ✖ to delete it.

Express your feelings

1. Tap ⬤ in the app drawer.
2. Send one of the following animations using gestures on the canvas. Your feelings are sent automatically when you finish the gesture:
   - **Tap**: Tap with one finger to create a burst of color. You can change the color, then tap again.
   - **Fireball**: Touch and hold with one finger.
   - **Kiss**: Tap with two fingers.
   - **Heartbeat**: Touch and hold with two fingers.
   - **Heartbreak**: Touch and hold with two fingers until you see a heartbeat, then drag down to break the heart.

Note: If you have Apple Watch or another sensor that records heartbeat data, Messages may use the recorded data when you send a Digital Touch heartbeat.

Add a Digital Touch effect to a photo or video

1. Tap ⬤ in the app drawer.

2. Tap .
3. Tap ⚪ to take a photo or ⚫ to record a video.
4. Add a Digital Touch effect, such as a sketch or kiss.
5. Tap ⬆ to send your message, or tap ✖ to delete it.

Send, receive, and request money in Messages on iPhone (U.S. only)

You can use Apple Cash to send, receive, and request money quickly and easily in the Messages app 💬 and Wallet app ▢ . There's no additional app to download, and you can use the cards you already have in Apple Pay.

When you receive money in Messages, it's added to your Apple Cash card in Wallet.

— Tap to preset this amount.

Send or receive a payment in Messages

1. In an iMessage conversation, tap ⬤Cash, then enter the amount.
   Tip: If there's an underlined monetary amount in a message, tap it to preset the payment.
2. Tap Pay, then add a comment (optional).
3. To complete the payment, tap ⬆ , then authenticate the payment with Face ID or your passcode. If you don't have sufficient funds in Apple Cash, you can pay the balance using your debit card in Wallet.

You can cancel a payment that hasn't been accepted. Tap the payment bubble, then tap Cancel Payment.

Request a payment

You can also do the following:

1. In an iMessage conversation, tap ⬤Cash .
2. Enter the amount, then tap Request.

Change message notifications on iPhone

In Settings ⚙, you can set up and manage message notifications for the Messages app 💬 and filter unknown senders.

Manage notifications for messages

1. Go to Settings ⚙ > Notifications > Messages.
2. Choose options, including the following:
   - Turn Allow Notifications and immediate delivery for Time Sensitive Notifications on or off.
   - Set the position, locations, style, and sounds for alerts.
   - Choose when message previews should appear on the Lock Screen, and how they should be grouped.
   - Set how many times to repeat an alert (from Never to 10 Times) below Customize Notifications.

Set a Focus and schedule a summary of your notifications

Focus is a feature that helps you concentrate on a task by minimizing distractions. When you need to focus, or step away from your iPhone, Focus can temporarily silence all notifications— or allow only specific notifications (for example, ones that match your task).

When you turn on a Focus, Messages lets apps and people know you're busy. If something is urgent, people can choose to notify you anyway.

You can also schedule a summary of your notifications to arrive each day at a specific time. This helps you to reduce interruptions throughout the day, and then quickly catch up at a time more convenient for you.

Set the alert sound for messages

1. Go to Settings ⚙ > Sounds & Haptics.
2. Tap Text Tone, then do one of the following:
   - Tap Vibration, then choose an option.
   - Tap a sound below Alert Tones.
   - Tap Tone Store to download an alert sound from the iTunes Store.

Assign a different ringtone to a contact

1. Open Contacts, then select a contact.
2. Tap Edit, then tap Text Tone.
3. Choose an option below Alert Tones.

To allow alerts for messages sent by this contact even when Do Not Disturb is on, turn on Emergency Bypass.

Mute notifications for a conversation

1. In the Messages list, touch and hold a conversation.
2. Tap Hide Alerts.

Block, filter, and report messages on iPhone

In the Messages app 💬, you can block unwanted messages, filter messages from unknown senders, and report spam or junk messages.

253

Block messages from a specific person or number

1. In a Messages conversation, tap the name or number at the top of the conversation.
2. Tap the ⊖ info button, scroll down, then tap Block this Caller.

To view and manage your list of blocked contacts and phone numbers, go to Settings ⊚ > Messages > Blocked Contacts.

Filter messages from unknown senders

With iMessage, you can filter messages from unknown senders, and you won't get notifications from them.

Go to Settings ⊚ > Messages, scroll down to Message Filtering, then turn on Filter Unknown Senders.

When this setting is on, you can only see messages from people who aren't in your contacts when you go to Filters > Unknown Senders.

Note: You can't open any links in a message from an unknown sender until you add the sender to your contacts or reply to the message.

Report spam or junk messages

When you use iMessage, you can report spam messages to Apple. Depending on your carrier and country or region, you can also report spam you receive with SMS and MMS.

In the list of messages, press and hold the spam message, then tap Report Junk. Or, if you've opened the message and the person isn't saved in your contacts, scroll to the bottom of the message, tap Report Junk, then tap Delete and Report Junk.

The sender's information and the message are sent to Apple, and the message is permanently deleted from your device.

Note: Reporting junk or spam doesn't prevent the sender from sending messages, but you can block the number to stop receiving them.

If you don't see the option to report spam or junk messages you receive with SMS or MMS, contact your carrier.

Delete messages on iPhone

In the Messages app ◯, you can delete messages and entire conversations from your device.

With Messages in iCloud, anything you delete from iPhone is also deleted from your other Apple devices where Messages in iCloud is turned on.

Note: Deleting messages changes only your own Messages conversations, not those of your recipients. To retract a message you sent accidentally, use undo send instead.

Delete a message

1. Touch and hold a message bubble, then tap More.
2. Select the message bubbles you want to delete, then tap 🗑.

Delete a conversation

In the Messages list, swipe left on the conversation, then tap 🗑.

Recover deleted messages in a conversation

You can restore messages you deleted for up to 30 days.

1. At the top of the Messages conversation, tap ‹, then do one of the following:
   o Tap Edit, then tap Show Recently Deleted.
   o Tap Filters, then tap Recently Deleted.
2. Select the conversations whose messages you want to restore, then tap Recover.
3. Tap Recover Messages.

Note: Any message that you delete from a conversation using Undo Send is permanently deleted.

Music

Get music on iPhone

Use the Music app 🎵 to enjoy music stored on iPhone as well as music streamed over the internet. With an optional Apple Music subscription, you can listen to millions of songs ad-free, stream and download files encoded using lossless compression, listen to thousands of Dolby Atmos tracks, be notified when a favorite artist releases new music, and discover music together with friends. With an Apple Music Voice subscription, you can use Siri to stream any song, album, playlist, or radio station in the Apple Music catalog.

Get music to play on iPhone in the following ways:

- **Become an Apple Music subscriber**: With a subscription and a Wi-Fi or cellular connection, stream as much music as you like from the Apple Music catalog and your music library. You can download songs, albums, and playlists, and share music with friends.
- **Become an Apple Music Voice subscriber**: With a subscription and a Wi-Fi or cellular connection, stream as much music as you like from the Apple Music catalog and play the purchased music you've added to your music library.
- **Participate in Family Sharing**: Purchase an Apple Music family subscription, and everyone in your Family Sharing group can enjoy Apple Music.
- Purchase music from the iTunes Store.
- **Sync music with Music** (macOS 10.15 or later) or iTunes (macOS 10.14 or earlier and Windows PCs) on your computer.
- **Listen to Apple Music radio**: Apple Music radio offers three worldwide radio stations broadcasting live on Apple Music—Apple Music 1, Apple Music Hits, and Apple Music Country. Apple Music radio is available on Apple and Android devices as well as popular web browsers at music.apple.com.

Note: Services and features aren't available in all countries or regions, and features may vary by region. Additional charges may apply when using a cellular connection.

View albums, playlists, and more in Music on iPhone

In the Music app 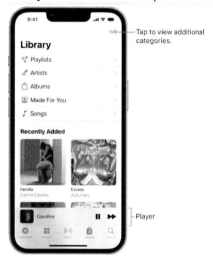, the library includes music you added or downloaded from Apple Music, music and videos you synced to iPhone, TV shows and movies you added from Apple Music, and your iTunes Store purchases.

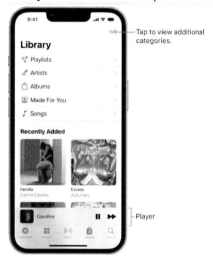

Browse and play your music

1. In the Music app, tap Library, then tap a category, such as Albums or Songs; tap Downloaded to view only music stored on iPhone.
2. Scroll to browse or swipe down the page and type in the search field to filter your results and find what you're looking for.
3. Tap an item, then tap Play, or tap Shuffle to shuffle an album or playlist.
   You can also touch and hold the album art, then tap Play.

To change the list of categories, tap Edit, then select categories you'd like to add, such as Genres and Compilations. Tap any existing categories to remove them.

Sort your music

1. Tap Library, then tap Playlists, Albums, Songs, TV & Movies, or Music Videos.
2. Tap Sort, then choose a sorting method, such as title, artist, recently added, or recently played.

Play music shared on a nearby computer

If a computer on your network shares music through Home Sharing, you can stream its music to your iPhone.

1. On your iPhone, go to Settings ⚙ > Music, tap Sign In below Home Sharing, then sign in with your Apple ID.
2. Open the Music app 🎵, go to Library > Home Sharing, then choose a shared library.

Remove Apple Music songs from iPhone

Go to Settings ⚙ > Music, then turn off Sync Library.

The songs are removed from iPhone but remain in iCloud. Music you purchased or synced also remains.

Play music on iPhone

Use Now Playing in the Music app 🎵 to show lyrics and play, pause, skip, shuffle, and repeat songs. You can also use Now Playing to view album art.

Control playback

Tap the player near the bottom of the screen to show the Now Playing screen, where you can use these controls:

Control	Description
▶	Play the current song.
❙❙	Pause playback.
▶▶	Skip to the next song. Touch and hold to fast-forward through the current song.
◀◀	Return to the song's beginning. Tap again to play the previous song in an album or playlist. Touch and hold to rewind through the current song.
↻	Open the queue, then tap to repeat an album or playlist. Double-tap to repeat a single song.
⤬	Open the queue, then tap to play your songs in random order. Tap again to turn off shuffle.
—	Hide the Now Playing Screen button.
•••	Tap for more options.
💬	Show time-synced lyrics (lyrics not available for all songs).
◎	Stream music to Bluetooth or AirPlay-enabled devices.
☰	Show the Queue.

Adjust the volume, see song details, and more

The Now Playing screen contains additional options for controlling and accessing music.

- **Adjust volume**: Drag the volume slider.
  You can also use the volume buttons on the side of iPhone.
- **Navigate to the artist, album, or playlist**: Tap the artist name below the song title, then choose to go to the artist, album, or playlist.

- Scrub to any point in a song: Drag the playhead.

See time-synced lyrics

Time-synced lyrics appear for many songs in Apple Music.

Tap the player to open Now Playing, then tap 💬. Lyrics scroll in time with the music.

To hide lyrics, tap 💬.

Tip: Tap a specific lyric—the first line of the chorus, for example—to go to that part of the song.

To see all of a song's lyrics, tap •••, then tap View Full Lyrics.

Note: You need an Apple Music subscription to view lyrics.

Share lyrics

You can share up to 150 characters of a song's lyrics if time-synced lyrics are available.

1. Tap the player to open Now Playing.
2. Tap •••, then tap Share Lyrics.
   You can also touch and hold a lyrics line to open the sharing screen.
3. Tap the first and last lyrics you want to share, then choose a sharing option.

Note: You need an Apple Music subscription to share lyrics.

Report a concern

To report a concern about time-synced lyrics, touch and hold a lyrics line, then tap Report a Concern at the bottom of the screen.

Get audio controls from the Lock Screen or when using another app

Open Control Center, then tap the audio card.

Stream music to Bluetooth or AirPlay-enabled devices

1. Tap the player to open Now Playing.
2. Tap 🔘, then choose a device.

Note: You can play the same music on multiple AirPlay 2-enabled devices, such as two or more HomePod speakers. You can also pair two sets of AirPods to one iPhone and enjoy the same song or movie along with a friend.

Queue up your music on iPhone

Use the queue in the Music app 🎵 to see a list of upcoming songs, add songs and videos to the queue, and see what you've recently played.

Note: Not all features are available in the Apple Music Voice Plan.

Use the queue

1. Tap the player to open Now Playing.
2. Tap ☰, then tap a song to play it and the songs that follow.
   To reorder the list, drag ☰.

3. Tap ⸬☰ again to hide the queue.

By default, if you're an Apple Music subscriber, Autoplay adds music similar to what you last played to the end of the queue. To turn off Autoplay, tap ∞.

Note: When you turn off Autoplay on a device that uses your Apple ID—your iPhone, for example—Autoplay is turned off on all other devices that use the same Apple ID.

Add music and videos to the queue

When browsing or playing music, touch and hold a song, album, playlist, or video, then choose an option.

- Add music right after the currently playing item: Tap Play Next.
- Add music to the end of the queue: Tap Play Last.

Tip: If you're using HomePod to stream music and your friends are on the same Wi-Fi network, they can add and reorder items in the queue.

See what you've recently played

1. Tap the player to open Now Playing.
2. Tap ⸬☰, then swipe down to see your playing history.

To play a song in the history, tap it. To remove your playing history, tap Clear.

Listen to broadcast radio on iPhone

You can play thousands of broadcast radio stations on iPhone.

- **Ask Siri**: Activate Siri, then say something like, "Play Wild 94.9" or "Tune in to ESPN Radio."
- **Search for a station**: Tap Search, enter the station in the search field, then tap a result to play the station.
  You can search for stations by name, call sign, frequency, and nickname.
- **Choose a station in the Radio tab**: Tap Radio, swipe up, then choose a station below the Local Broadcasters or International Broadcasters heading.

Note: You don't need a subscription to Apple Music to listen to broadcast radio. Broadcast radio isn't available in all countries or regions and not all stations are available in all countries or regions.

Apple Music

Subscribe to Apple Music on iPhone

Apple Music is an ad-free streaming music service that lets you listen to millions of songs and your music library. As a subscriber, you can listen any time—online or off—and create your own playlists, stream and download lossless and Dolby Atmos music, get personalized recommendations, receive notifications when a favorite artist releases new music, see music your friends are listening to, watch exclusive video content, and more.

You can subscribe to Apple Music or to Apple One, which includes Apple Music and other services.

Alternatively, you can subscribe to Apple Music Voice and use Siri to stream any song, album, playlist, or radio station in the Apple Music catalog.

Note: Apple Music, Apple Music Voice, Apple One, lossless, and Dolby Atmos aren't available in all countries or regions.

Subscribe to Apple Music

You can subscribe to Apple Music when you first open the Music app 🎵; to subscribe later, go to Settings 🔘 > Music, then tap the subscription button.

New subscribers can start a trial and cancel at any time. If you end your Apple Music subscription, you can no longer stream Apple Music songs or play Apple Music songs you downloaded.

Qualified students can purchase a student subscription at a discounted price.

Share Apple Music with family members

When you subscribe to Apple Music, Apple One Family, or Apple One Premier, you can use Family Sharing to share Apple Music with up to five other family members. Your family group doesn't need to do anything—Apple Music is available to them the first time they open the Music app after your subscription begins.

If you join a family group that subscribes to Apple Music, Apple One Family, or Apple One Premier, and you already subscribe, your subscription isn't renewed on your next billing date; instead, you use the group's subscription. If you join a family group that doesn't subscribe, the group uses your subscription.

Note: To stop sharing Apple Music with a family group, you can cancel the subscription, leave a Family Sharing group, or remove a member from a Family Sharing group.

Listen to music shared with you

When a friend shares music with you with the Message app, you can easily find it in Shared with You in Apple Music. (Music must be turned on in Settings 🔘 > Messages > Shared with You, and your friend must be in your contacts list in Contacts.)

1. Open the Music app 🎵, then tap Listen Now.
2. Swipe up to Shared with You, then do any of the following:
   o Tap a song to listen to it.
   o Tap the name of the person, people, or group that shared the song to reply to them using the Messages app.
   o Touch and hold the song to take other actions—for example, add it to your library, create a station, reply to the sender, or remove it.

Change or cancel your Apple Music subscription

You can change your subscription plan or cancel your subscription.

1. Tap Listen Now, then tap 👤 or your profile picture.
2. Tap Manage Subscription, then follow the onscreen instructions.

If you're not a subscriber, you can use Music to listen to music synced to iPhone from a Mac or a Windows PC, play and download previous iTunes Store purchases, and listen to Apple Music radio for free.

Listen to lossless music on iPhone

In the Music app 🎵, Apple Music subscribers can access millions of tracks encoded using lossless audio compression.

Lossless compression is a form of compression that preserves all of the original data. Apple has developed its own lossless audio compression technology called Apple Lossless Audio Codec (ALAC). The entire Apple Music catalog is encoded using ALAC in resolutions ranging from 16-bit/44.1 kHz (CD Quality) up to 24-bit/192 kHz.

Note: Lossless music isn't available in the Apple Music Voice Plan.

What you need to know about lossless in Apple Music

- Streaming lossless audio over a cellular or Wi-Fi network consumes significantly more data. And downloading lossless audio uses significantly more space on your device. Higher resolutions use more data than lower ones.
- AirPods, AirPods Pro, AirPods Max, and Beats wireless headphones use Apple AAC Bluetooth Codec to ensure excellent audio quality. However, Bluetooth connections aren't lossless.
- To get a lossless version of music that you already downloaded from Apple Music, just delete the music and redownload it from the Apple Music catalog.
- To listen to songs at sample rates higher than 48 kHz on iPhone, you need an external digital-to-analog converter.

Note: Apple Music and lossless aren't available in all countries or regions.

Turn on Lossless Audio and choose audio quality settings

You can choose audio quality settings for cellular streaming, Wi-Fi streaming, and downloads.

1. Go to Settings ⚙ > Music.
2. Tap Audio Quality, then tap Lossless Audio to turn it on or off.
3. Choose the audio quality for streaming and downloading audio.
   - Choose Lossless for a maximum resolution of 24-bit/48 kHz.
   - Choose Hi-Res Lossless for a maximum resolution of 24-bit/192 kHz.

The audio quality of streamed music depends on song availability, network conditions, and the capability of connected headphones or speakers.

Identify lossless music

If music is available in lossless, 〰 appears on album pages. When you turn on Lossless Audio in Settings ⚙ > Music > Audio Quality, the Lossless badge also appears in Now Playing.

To learn more about a song's lossless encoding, tap 〰 on an album page or in Now Playing.

Listen to Dolby Atmos music on iPhone

In the Music app ![music icon], Apple Music subscribers can listen to available tracks in Dolby Atmos. Dolby Atmos creates an immersive, three-dimensional audio experience on stereo headphones and speakers or receivers compatible with Dolby Atmos.

Note: Dolby Atmos music isn't available in the Apple Music Voice Plan.

Albums available in Dolby Atmos have the Dolby Atmos badge ![badge]. If a track is playing in Dolby Atmos, the badge also appears on the Now Playing screen.

Note: Apple Music and Dolby Atmos aren't available in all countries or regions.

Turn on Dolby Atmos

1. Go to Settings ![settings icon] > Music > Dolby Atmos.
2. Choose Automatic or Always On.
   - **Automatic**: Plays Dolby Atmos whenever iPhone is connected to compatible headphones such as AirPods (3rd generation), AirPods Pro, or AirPods Max, or to speakers or receivers compatible with Dolby Atmos.
   - **Always On**: Plays Dolby Atmos on any headphones or speakers. The Music app will attempt to play Dolby Atmos tracks on any headphones or speakers connected to iPhone.

Dolby Atmos will play on any headphones, but not all speakers will play Dolby Atmos as intended.

Control Spatial Audio and head tracking on iPhone

When you listen to supported music on your iPhone with AirPods (3rd generation), AirPods Pro, or AirPods Max, you can use Spatial Audio and head tracking to create an immersive theater-like environment with sound that surrounds you. Follow these steps to control Spatial Audio and head tracking in Control Center.

1. Wear your AirPods, then open Control Center.
2. Touch and hold the volume control, then tap Spatial Audio at the lower right.
3. Tap one of the following:
   - **Off**: Turns off both Spatial Audio and head tracking.
   - **Fixed**: Turns on Spatial Audio without head tracking.
   - **Head Tracked**: Turns on both Spatial Audio and head tracking. This setting allows the sound to follow the movement of your head.

The settings you choose are saved and applied automatically the next time you use that app. For example, if you tap Fixed while listening to a song in Apple Music, the Fixed setting is automatically used the next time you play a song in Apple Music.

Note: To disable head tracking for all apps on your iPhone, go to Settings > Accessibility > AirPods, tap your AirPods, then turn off Follow iPhone.

Download songs in Dolby Atmos

1. Go to Settings ![settings icon] > Music.
2. Turn on Download in Dolby Atmos.

Find new music with Apple Music on iPhone

In the Music app 🎵 , Apple Music subscribers can browse new and noteworthy music, music videos, playlists, and more.

Note: Browsing isn't available in the Apple Music Voice Plan.

Browse Apple Music

Tap Browse to find new music. Do any of the following:

- **Explore featured music**: Swipe through featured songs and videos at the top of the Browse screen.
- **Browse playlists created by music experts**: Tap one of the many playlists created by music experts.
- **Explore new music**: Swipe through the albums listed below New Music.
- **Play music that matches your mood**: Tap a mood, such as Feel Good, Romance, or Party, then tap a playlist.
- **See what's hot**: Tap a song below the Best New Songs heading. Swipe left to see more songs.
- **Listen to the top songs from around the world**: Tap one of the Daily Top 100 playlists. These playlists reflect the day's most popular songs in countries across the globe.
- **Listen to songs from upcoming albums**: Tap an album below Coming Soon, then tap an available song to play it.
- **Browse your favorite categories**: Tap Browse by Category, choose a category, then tap a featured playlist, song, album, artist, radio station, or music video to enjoy music handpicked by music experts.
- **Play the day's most popular songs**: Tap Charts, then tap a song, playlist, album, or music video to play it. Tap All Genres at the top of the screen to see the top songs and music videos in a genre you choose.
- **Watch music videos**: Tap Music Videos, then tap a featured music video or playlist of music videos.

Note: To see more music, swipe left on the album art. To see all the music in a section—New Music, for example—tap > next to the section's name.

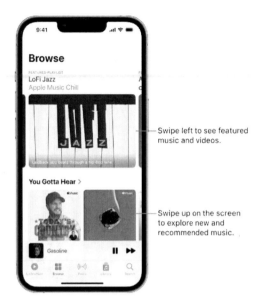

Swipe left to see featured music and videos.

Swipe up on the screen to explore new and recommended music.

Add music to iPhone and listen offline

In the Music app , Apple Music subscribers can add and download songs and videos from Apple Music. You can stream music you add to iPhone when you have an internet connection. To play music when you're not connected to the internet, you must first download it.

Note: You can't add and download music in the Apple Music Voice Plan.

Add music from Apple Music to your library

Do any of the following:

- Touch and hold a song, album, playlist, or video, then tap Add to Library.
- When viewing the contents of an album or playlist, tap ⊕ near the top of the screen to add the album or playlist, or tap °°°, then tap Add to Library to add individual songs.
- On the Now Playing screen, tap °°°, then tap Add to Library.

To delete music from the library, touch and hold the song, album, playlist, or music video, then tap Delete from Library.

Music you add to iPhone is also added to other devices if you're signed in to the iTunes Store and App Store using the same Apple ID and have Sync Library turned on (go to Settings > Music, then turn on Sync Library).

Add music to a playlist

1. Touch and hold an album, playlist, song, or music video.
2. Tap Add to a Playlist, then choose a playlist.

Download music from Apple Music to your iPhone

- **Download a song, album, or playlist**: Touch and hold music you've added to your library, then tap Download.

264

After you've added a playlist or album, you can also tap ↓ at the top of the screen.
Note: You must turn on Sync Library to download music from Apple Music to your library (go to Settings ⚙ > Music, then turn on Sync Library).

- **Always download music**: Go to Settings > Music, then turn on Automatic Downloads. Songs you add are automatically downloaded to iPhone.
- **See download progress**: On the Library screen, tap Downloaded Music, then tap Downloading.

Note: If the music you're downloading is available in Dolby Atmos, the Dolby button ◗◖ appears next to the item, and you can download it either in Dolby Atmos or in stereo. To download music in Dolby Atmos when available, go to Settings ⚙ > Music, then turn on Download in Dolby Atmos.

Manage storage space

- **Free up music storage**: If iPhone is low on storage space, you can automatically remove downloaded music that you haven't played in a while. Go to Settings ⚙ > Music > Optimize Storage.
- **Remove music and videos stored on iPhone**: Touch and hold a song, album, playlist, music video, TV show, or movie that you've downloaded. Tap Remove, then tap Remove Downloads.
  The item is removed from iPhone, but not from iCloud Music Library.
- **Remove all songs or certain artists from iPhone**: Go to Settings > Music > Downloaded Music, tap Edit, then tap ⊖ next to All Songs or the artists whose music you want to delete.

Choose cellular data options for Music

Go to Settings ⚙ > Music, turn on Cellular Data, then do any of the following:

- Turn Download over Cellular on or off.
- Tap Audio Quality, turn on Lossless Audio, then tap Cellular Streaming to choose a setting (None, High Efficiency, High Quality, Lossless, or High-Resolution Lossless). High Quality, Lossless, and High-Resolution Lossless use significantly more cellular data than High Efficiency, which may incur additional charges from your cellular carrier. Songs may also take longer to start playing.

See recommended music on iPhone

In the Music app 🎵, Apple Music subscribers can use Listen Now to discover and play your favorite albums, playlists, interviews, and personal mixes, based on your taste.

Note: Not all features are available in the Apple Music Voice Plan.

Select your favorite genres and artists

When you first tap Listen Now, you're asked to tell Apple Music about your preferences. Apple Music uses these preferences when recommending music.

1. Tap the genres you like (double-tap those you love, and touch and hold the genres you don't care for).
2. Tap Next, then do the same with the artists that appear.

To add a specific artist who isn't listed, tap Add an Artist, then enter the artist's name.

Play music

1. Tap Listen Now, then tap a playlist or album.
2. Tap Play, or tap Shuffle to shuffle the playlist or album.

You can also touch and hold a playlist or album, then tap Play.

Play songs from an artist's catalog

Go to an artist page, then tap ▶ next to the artist's name.

The Music app 🎵 plays songs from the artist's entire catalog, mixing hits and deep cuts.

Add favorite artists

Go to an artist page, then tap ☆ at the top of the screen.

When you mark an artist as a favorite, they appear under Favorite Artists in For You, and their music is recommended more often. You can also choose to receive notifications when they release new music.

Tell Apple Music what you love

Do any of the following:

• Touch and hold an album, playlist, or song, then tap Love or Suggest Less Like This.

• On the Now Playing screen, tap •••, then tap Love or Suggest Less Like This.

Telling Apple Music what you love and dislike improves future recommendations.

Rate music in your library

1. Go to Settings ⚙ > Music.
2. Turn on Show Star Ratings.
3. In Music, touch and hold a song in your library, tap Rate Song, then choose a rating from one to five stars.

Song ratings sync to all devices that use the same Apple ID.

This option appears only if you already have star ratings from a synced library on your device.

Tell Apple Music to ignore your listening habits

If you don't want your followers on Apple Music to see any of the music you play, follow these steps.

1. Go to Settings ⚙ > Music.
2. Turn off Use Listening History.

Turning off your listening history impacts new music recommendations and the contents of Replay playlists.

Listen to radio on iPhone

In the Music app 🎵, Apple Music subscribers can listen to Apple Music radio in the Radio tab. Apple Music radio features three world-class radio stations (Apple Music 1, Apple Music Hits, and Apple Music Country), the latest music from a variety of genres, and exclusive interviews. You can also listen to featured stations that have been created by music experts, and create your own custom stations from songs or artists you choose.

Listen to Apple Music radio

Tap Radio, then tap one of the currently playing Apple Music radio stations. No subscription is required to listen to Apple Music 1, Apple Music Hits, or Apple Music Country.

Note: Because Apple Music radio stations are live radio, you can't rewind or skip songs.

Listen to your favorite music genre

1. Tap Radio, then tap a genre listed below More to Explore.
2. Tap a featured station.

Create a station

You can create a radio station based on a particular artist or song. Chances are, if you like that artist or song, you'll like the music the station plays.

1. Touch and hold an artist or song.
2. Tap Create Station.

To create a station in Now Playing, tap ⋯, then tap Create Station.

Search for music on iPhone

Using Search in the Music app 🎵, you can quickly browse through music categories, see recent searches, and search Apple Music or your library.

Note: Not all features are available in the Apple Music Voice Plan.

1. Tap Search, then do any of the following:
   ○ Tap a category such as Pop or Fitness.
   ○ Tap the search field, then tap something you recently chose while searching—a song or artist, for example.
   ○ Tap the search field, tap Apple Music, then enter a song, artist, album, playlist, radio show or episode, station, video, category, curator, record label, or profile.
   ○ Tap the search field, tap Your Library, then enter a song, album, playlist, artist, video, compilation, or composer.
2. Tap a result to play it.

You can search for a song in Apple Music based on its lyrics. In the search field, enter a few of the words you remember to find a song.

Siri: Say something like: "Play the song with the lyrics" and then say a key phrase from the lyrics._

Create playlists on iPhone

In the Music app 🎵, you can organize music into playlists that you can share with your friends.

Note: You can't create playlists in the Apple Music Voice Plan.

Create playlists to organize your music

1. To create a new playlist, do any of the following:
   - Tap Library, tap Playlists, then tap New Playlist.
   - Touch and hold a song, album, or playlist; tap Add to a Playlist; then tap New Playlist.
   - On the Now Playing screen, tap ⋯, tap Add to a Playlist, then tap New Playlist.
2. To more easily identify the playlist later, enter a name and description.
3. To give your playlist cover art, tap 📷, then take a photo or choose an image from your photo library.
4. To add music to the playlist, tap Add Music, then tap Listen Now, Browse, Library, or the search field.
5. Choose or search for music, then tap ⊕ to add it to the playlist.

Tip: If you want to add songs to your library when you add them to a playlist, go to Settings ⚙ > Music, then turn on Add Playlist Songs.

Edit a playlist you created on iPhone

Tap the playlist, tap ⋯, tap Edit, then do any of the following:

- **Add more songs**: Tap Add Music, then choose music.
  You can also touch and hold an item (song, album, playlist, or music video), tap Add to a Playlist, then choose a playlist.
- **Delete a song**: Tap ⊖, then tap Delete. Deleting a song from a playlist doesn't delete it from your library.
- **Change the song order**: Drag ≡ next to a song.

Changes you make to your music library are updated across all your devices when Sync Library is turned on in Music settings. If you're not an Apple Music subscriber, the changes appear in your music library the next time you sync with your computer.

Sort a playlist

1. Tap a playlist, then tap ⋯ at the top right of the screen.
2. Tap Sort By, then choose an option—Playlist Order, Title, Artist, Album, or Release Date.

Delete a playlist

Touch and hold the playlist, then tap Delete from Library.

You can also tap the playlist, tap ⋯, then tap Delete from Library.

See what your friends are listening to

When you're an Apple Music subscriber, you can see music your friends are listening to by following them. You can also see the playlists they've shared. Likewise, your followers can see your shared playlists and the music you're listening to. You see this information on your profile screen in the Music app .

Note: Not all features are available in the Apple Music Voice Plan.

Create a profile

When you first open Music, you're asked to set up a profile and start following friends. If you skipped this step, you can set up a profile at any time.

1. Tap Listen Now, then tap .
2. Tap Start Sharing with Friends.
   Friends can now follow you.

View your profile

1. Tap Listen Now, then tap or your profile picture.
2. Tap View Profile at the top of the screen.

Follow your friends

There are several ways to follow people:

- Add friends when you set up your profile.
- After you set up your profile, swipe to the bottom of the profile screen, tap Follow More Friends, then tap Follow next to those you want to follow.
  You can follow friends who are in your contacts list and who use Apple Music.
- On the profile screen, touch and hold a profile picture, then tap Follow.
- Tap Search, enter a friend's name, tap it in the results, then tap Follow.
  Note: Your friends must have a profile for you to find them using search.

To see the people you're following and those who follow you, open the profile screen, then swipe up.

If a profile picture has a lock on it, you need to ask that person to follow them. After your request is accepted, you see the person's shared playlists and the music they're listening to.

Respond to follow requests

You can allow everyone to follow you, or just people you choose. You receive follow requests only if you choose who can follow you.

1. Tap Listen Now, then tap or your profile picture.
2. Tap View Profile.
3. Tap Edit, then tap People You Approve if you want to be followed only by people you choose.
4. Tap Follow Requests, then accept or decline the requests.

You may receive follow requests in other ways—as a link in an email or a text message, for example. To accept, tap the link.

Stop following and block followers

- **Stop following**: Touch and hold the profile picture of a person you follow, then tap Unfollow.
- **Block followers**: Touch and hold a profile picture, then choose Block.
  People you block won't see your music or be able to find your profile. They can still listen to your shared playlists if they've added them to their library.

Share music with followers

By default, your followers see the playlists you create, but you can choose not to share some playlists.

1. Tap Listen Now, then tap ⊖ or your profile picture.
2. Tap View Profile.
3. Tap Edit, then turn playlists on or off.
4. Drag ☰ to reorder them.

Your followers will see the playlists you create on your profile unless you turn off those playlists you don't want to share. You can turn off this option when you create a playlist or later, when you edit the playlist.

To share playlists with people who don't follow you, touch and hold a playlist, then tap Share Playlist.

Note: If you make changes to music you share—edit or stop sharing a playlist, for example—those changes are reflected on your followers' devices.

Hide music from your followers

1. Tap Listen Now, then tap ⊖ or your profile picture.
2. Tap View Profile.
3. Touch and hold the playlist or album (below Listening To).
4. Tap Hide from Profile.

The listening history for this item won't appear in your profile or be visible to the people who follow you. If you don't want your followers to see any of the music you listen to, tap Edit on the profile screen, then turn off Listening To at the bottom of the screen.

Note: It may take up to 10 minutes before music you hide is no longer visible to your followers.

See what others are listening to

Tap Listen Now, then do any of the following:

- **See what your friends are listening to**: Scroll down to Friends Are Listening To, then tap an item to play it.
- Listen to a mix of songs your friends are listening to: Swipe left on Made For You, then tap Friends Mix.
- **See what a follower or person you follow is listening to**: Tap ⊖ or your profile picture, then tap View Profile. Tap a person's profile picture to see shared playlists and music they're listening to. You also see their followers and the people they follow.

Share your profile

You can share your profile using email, Messages, or another app you choose.

1. Tap Listen Now, then tap ⊖ or your profile picture.

2. Tap View Profile.
3. Tap ⋯, tap Share Profile, then choose a sharing option.

You can also share the profile of anyone you follow, or who follows you.

Report a concern

If you have a concern about a follower, touch and hold their profile picture, then tap Report a Concern.

Use Siri to play music on iPhone

You can use Siri to control music playback in the Music app 🎵.

Activate Siri, then make your request. You can use Siri in a wide variety of ways:

- **Play Apple Music**: You can play any song, artist, album, playlist, or station. Say, for example, "Play 'Gasoline' by The Weeknd" or "Play Kehlani." Siri can also play popular songs from different genres or years. Say "Play the top songs from 1990." You can also play music on AirPlay 2-enabled devices in a specific room. Say something like "Play the latest album by Camila Cabello in the living room."
- **Let Apple Music be your personal DJ**: Say something like "Play my Chill Mix" or "Play something I like."
- **Add music from Apple Music to your library**: Say, for example, "Add 'Evergreen' by Omar Apollo to my library." Or while playing something, say "Add this to my library." (Apple Music subscription required. Not available with Apple Music Voice.)
- **Add a song or album to a playlist**: While playing a song, say something like "Add this song to my Workout playlist" or "Add this album to my Sunday Morning playlist."
- **Find out more about the current song**: Say "What's playing?", "Who sings this song?", or "Who is this song by?"
  Tip: You can also identify a song playing on or near iPhone by adding the Music Recognition control to Control Center. Go to Settings ⚙ > Control Center, then tap ⊕ next to Music Recognition. With a song playing, open Control Center, then tap 🎵.
- **Play songs based on their lyrics**: Say "Play the song with the lyrics" and then say a key phrase from the lyrics.

Listen to music with Apple Music Voice on iPhone

Apple offers the Apple Music Voice Plan, a subscription option for Apple Music designed around Siri. Using just your voice, you can access millions of songs, tens of thousands of playlists (including hundreds of mood and activity playlists), personalized mixes, genre stations, and Apple Music radio.

In addition to streaming music from Apple Music, you can play music you purchased from the iTunes Store and music you've synced to iPhone. You can also stream music with AirPlay, play music using Home Sharing, and search the Apple Music library and your music library.

Subscribe to Apple Music Voice

You can subscribe to Apple Music Voice when you first open the Music app 🎵.

As an Apple Music Voice subscriber, you can play music on all your devices that have Siri turned on, including HomePod mini, AirPods, or any other Apple device, and when using CarPlay.

Tip: If you want to preview Apple Music Voice for a few days, say "Hey Siri, start Apple Music Voice."

New subscribers can start a trial and cancel at any time. If you end your Apple Music Voice subscription, you can no longer stream Apple Music songs.

Play music with Apple Music Voice

To play music with Apple Music Voice, just say "Hey Siri," then make your request:

- "Play 'enough for you' by Olivia Rodrigo"
- "Play Apple Music Country"
- "Play cool jazz"
- "Play the dinner party playlist"
- "Play a playlist to help me relax"
- "Play more like this"

To see Siri suggestions created just for you, open the Music app 🎵, tap Listen Now, then swipe through the suggestions below Just Ask Siri. Say "Hey Siri," then speak the suggestion or tap to play it.

Play music you recently listened to

Open the Music app 🎵, tap Listen Now, then tap an item. Playlists and albums play in their original order.

Play purchased and synced music

You can play music you purchased from the iTunes Store as well as music you synced to your iPhone from a computer.

Open the Music app 🎵, tap Library, tap a category such as Playlists, Artists, or Albums, then tap an item.

To play music from a Home Sharing library, tap Library, tap Home Sharing, then tap a library.

Change the way music sounds on iPhone

Change the way music sounds on iPhone with EQ, volume limit settings, and Sound Check.

- Choose an equalization (EQ) setting: Go to Settings ⚙ > Music > EQ.
- **Normalize the volume level of your audio**: Go to Settings > Music, then turn on Sound Check.

News

Use News widgets on iPhone

You can easily see the day's top and trending stories from the News app ◼ , as well as stories about a topic of your choosing, just by tapping the Today or Topic widget.

Access stories from News widgets

In the Today or Topic widget, tap a story headline to open the story.

See news stories chosen just for you on iPhone

The Today feed in the News app ◼ presents top stories selected by Apple News editors, the best stories from the channels and topics you follow, and stories and issues from Apple News+. The Today feed also includes stories suggested by Siri, trending stories that are popular with other News readers, My Sports, and more. Depending on your location, the Today feed can also include Apple News Today audio briefings, and local news with your local weather conditions.

Note: Apple News Today audio briefings and local news aren't available in all countries or regions.

Access stories in the Today feed

- **Open a story**: Tap the story.
- **Read more stories within a group**: Tap the arrow at the bottom of the group.
- **Play a video**: Tap ⏵ in the thumbnail.
- **Get newer stories**: Pull down to refresh the Today feed with the latest stories.

Follow, unfollow, block, and unblock channels and topics

You can influence what appears in the Today feed by following and blocking channels and topics.

1. Do any of the following:
    ○ **Open a channel feed**: Touch and hold a story, tap the channel name, then tap Go to Channel. Or tap a story in the Today feed, then tap the channel name at the top of the story.
    ○ **Open a topic feed**: Tap the topic title—Movies or Travel, for example.
2. At the top of the feed, do any of the following:
    ○ **Follow**: Tap ⊕ .
    ○ **Unfollow**: Tap ⋯ , then tap Unfollow Channel or Unfollow Topic.
    ○ **Block**: Tap ⋯ , then tap Block Channel or Block Topic.
    ○ **Unblock**: Tap ⋯ , then tap Unblock Channel or Unblock Topic.

Note: When you browse Top Stories and other areas that feature stories curated by Apple News editors, placeholders may appear for stories from channels you blocked. To read a story from a blocked channel, tap Show Story Anyway.

Add, remove, and reorder favorites

You can mark channels and topics as favorites. Favorites appear in a group near the top of your Today feed.

Tap Following, tap Edit, then do any of the following.

- **Add a favorite**: Tap ⭐ next to a channel or topic to mark it as a favorite, then tap Done.

- **Remove a favorite**: Tap ⭐ next to a channel or topic you no longer want as a favorite, then tap Done.

- **Reorder favorites**: Touch and hold ☰, drag favorites to the order you prefer, then tap Done,

You can also swipe up to Favorites in the Today feed, tap ⋯, then tap Manage Favorites.

To remove your Favorites group from your Today feed, swipe up to Favorites, tap ⋯, then tap Block from Today. To unblock Favorites, tap Following, swipe up, tap Blocked Channels & Topics, tap ⊖ next to Favorites, then tap Unblock.

Stop suggesting specific channels and topic groups in the Today feed

Suggested channels and topic groups may appear in the Today feed, but you can stop these suggestions.

1. Tap Today.
2. Tap ⋯ in a channel or topic group, then tap Stop Suggesting.

The channel or topic isn't blocked, but News stops displaying the story group in Today.

Tell News what kind of stories you prefer

1. Tap Today.
2. Tap ⋯ below a headline, then tap Suggest More or Suggest Less.

Read stories in News on iPhone

You can read and share the stories in the News app 🗞 on iPhone.

Note: Apple News and Apple News+ aren't available in all countries or regions.

Read a story

Tap a story to read it. While viewing a story, you have these options:

- **Read the next story**: Tap → in the lower right of the screen or swipe left.

- **Read the previous story**: Tap ← in the lower right of the screen or swipe right.
- Return to the list of stories: Swipe from the left edge.
- **Tell News what stories you prefer**: When viewing a story that's not part of an Apple News+ issue, tap 👍 or 👎 at the bottom of the story. Your feedback is taken into account for future recommendations.

  If you're reading a story in an Apple News+ issue, tap ⋯, then tap Suggest More or Suggest Less.

- **Change the text size**: Tap AA, then tap the smaller or larger letter to change the text size in the story and all other stories in the channel. (Not available in all channels.)

- **Share a story**: Tap ⓘ, tap Share Story, then choose a sharing option, such as Messages or Mail.
- **Report a concern**: If you believe that a story you're viewing is mislabeled, inappropriate, offensive, or doesn't display properly, tap ⓘ, then tap Report a Concern.

In Apple News+ issues in PDF format, the Suggest More, Suggest Less, Save Story, and Report a Concern options aren't available.

Read stories shared with you

When a friend shares stories with you using the Messages app, you can easily find them in the Shared with You section in Apple News. (News must be turned on in Settings ⚙ > Messages > Shared with You, and your friend must be in your contacts list in Contacts.)

1. In the News app, tap Following.
2. Tap Shared with You, then do any of the following:
   - Tap a shared story to read it in News.
   - Tap the name of the person who shared a story to reply to them in the Messages app. You can also reply while reading the story—tap the name shown below the channel's logo.

Follow your favorite teams with My Sports on iPhone

In the News app 📰 , My Sports lets you follow your favorite sports, teams, leagues, and athletes; receive stories from top sports publications, local newspapers, and more; access scores, schedules, and standings for the top professional and college leagues; and watch highlights.

Get started with My Sports

1. Open the Today feed, then swipe up to My Sports.
2. Tap Get Started, then tap Turn On to allow syncing between Apple News and the Apple TV app.
   When you turn on My Sports syncing in the News app, teams you follow are also automatically followed in the Apple TV app, and vice versa. Turning on syncing is required to use My Sports.
3. On the Manage My Sports screen, tap ⊕ next to sports, teams, and leagues to follow them.
   Sports topics you've previously expressed interest in appear below Suggested.
   Sports topics such as Golf and Tennis appear below All Sports.
4. To search for a sports topic, tap the search field, enter a search term such as a team's name or location, tap ⊕ next to a result, then tap Done.

My Sports and My Sports syncing aren't available in all countries and regions.

View My Sports

The My Sports group in the Today feed provides the most important sports coverage at a glance.

To view it, tap Today, then swipe up. To view more comprehensive sports coverage, tap the My Sports heading.

You can also tap Following, then tap My Sports.

Browse all available sports

1. Tap the My Sports heading in the Today feed, then tap All Sports at the top of the screen.
2. Tap a sport or league to go to its feed.
3. To follow that sport or league, tap ⊕ at the top of the screen.

Manage sports topics

You can follow and unfollow sports topics after you've set up My Sports.

Tap My Sports, then tap Manage in the Following section, where you can do any of the following:

*   **Follow topics**: Tap ⊕ next to each topic you want to follow, then tap Done.
*   **Unfollow topics**: Tap ⊖ next to topics you want to unfollow, tap Unfollow, then tap Done.
*   **Reorder topics**: Touch and hold ☰, drag topics to the order you prefer, then tap Done.
    This changes the order topics appear in the My Sports group and My Sports feed.

You can also manage My Sports by tapping ⋯, then tapping Manage My Sports.

Show schedules and scores, highlights, and more

My Sports offers schedules and scores for your favorite teams, video highlights, and stories related to your favorite teams.

Scroll up to My Sports in Today, then do any of the following:

*   **Show schedules and scores**: Tap Scores & Schedule, then tap the Schedule or Scores tab.
*   **Watch a live game**: Tap Scores & Schedule, tap the Schedule tap, then tap Open in Apple TV next to a game. If the game is available in your area and you have the proper entitlements, you can watch it in the Apple TV app or in a supported app.
    Supported sports apps may require a separate subscription. Not all games are available in all areas.
*   **View highlights**: Swipe up to the Highlights section, then tap ▶ in the thumbnail. Tap > to see more highlights.
    Note: Highlights are available only for select leagues.
*   Read sports stories related to topics you follow: Swipe up to For You, then tap a story.

Remove the My Sports group from Today

1. In Today, swipe up to My Sports, then tap ⋯.
2. Tap Block from Today.

To remove My Sports from Following, go to Settings ⚙, tap News, then turn off Sync My Sports.

Listen to Apple News Today on iPhone

In the News app 📰 , you can listen to Apple News Today, an audio briefing of the day's top stories hosted by Apple News editors. With an Apple News+ subscription, you can also listen to audio versions of select Apple News+ stories.

Note: Apple News, Apple News+, and the audio feature aren't available in all countries or regions.

Play Apple News Today

1. Tap 🎧, then tap an episode of Apple News Today.
    Apple News Today briefings also appear in the Today feed below Listen Now.
2. For more audio controls, tap the mini player at the bottom to open the full-screen player.
3. To return to the mini player, swipe down to minimize the full-screen player.

    To close the full-screen player, tap ⋯, then tap Close Audio Player. To close the mini player, touch and hold the player, then tap Close Audio Player.

If you're not an Apple News+ subscriber, a preview of an Apple News+ audio story plays when the briefing concludes.

Apple News+

Subscribe to Apple News+ on iPhone

In the News app 📰 , Apple News+ lets you enjoy hundreds of magazines, popular newspapers, and content from premium digital publishers directly on your iPhone.

You can subscribe to Apple News+ or to Apple One Premier, which includes Apple News+ and other Apple services.

As a subscriber, you have access to current and available back issues of publications, and you can download content for offline reading and share stories and issues with others.

As a non-subscriber, you can browse, but not read, a collection of story headlines and publications personalized just for you, view the entire Apple News+ catalog, and browse issues by category—Entertainment and Food, for example. To read stories and issues, and to listen to Apple News+ audio stories, start a free trial or subscribe.

Note: Apple News, Apple News+, Apple One, and the audio feature aren't available in all countries or regions.

Subscribe to Apple News+

Tap the subscription button shown in a magazine or story in News, then follow the onscreen instructions.

You may be asked to sign in with your Apple ID.

Share Apple News+ with family members

When you subscribe to Apple News+ or Apple One Premier, you can use Family Sharing to share Apple News+ with up to five other family members. Your family group members don't need to do anything—Apple News+ is available to them the first time they open the News app after your subscription begins.

If you join a family group that subscribes to Apple News+ or Apple One Premier, and you already subscribe, your subscription isn't renewed on your next billing date; instead, you use the group's subscription. If you join a family group that doesn't subscribe, the group uses your subscription.

Cancel or change your Apple News+ subscription

Tap Following, swipe up, tap Subscriptions below Manage, then do one of the following:

- **Apple News+ only**: Tap Cancel Subscription, then follow the onscreen instructions.
- **Apple News+ and individual channels**: Select Apple News+, tap Cancel Subscription, then follow the onscreen instructions.

Browse and read Apple News+ stories and issues on iPhone

To get the most out of Apple News+, follow your favorite publications, and browse through current and back issues.

Note: Apple News and Apple News+ aren't available in all countries or regions.

Follow and unfollow publications

You follow an Apple News+ publication by following its channel. Do any of the following:

- Tap Today or News+ at the bottom of the screen, tap a story or issue from an Apple News+ publication, tap the publication's name at the top of the screen, then tap ⊕.
- Tap Search, enter the publication's name in the search field, then tap ⊕.
- Tap News+, swipe left on the categories near the top of the screen, tap Newspapers or Catalog, then tap Follow below the publication's cover.

To unfollow a publication, tap Following, swipe left, then tap Unfollow.

Browse Apple News+ issues and stories

Stories and issues from Apple News+ appear in the Today feed and channel feeds. Stories (but not issues) can also be found in topic feeds and search results. To access entire issues, tap the News+ tab at the bottom of the screen, where you can do any of the following:

- **View all available publications**: Near the top of the screen, swipe the options left, then tap Catalog.
- **View a specific content category**: Swipe left on the options near the top of the screen, tap Catalog, tap Featured, then tap a category such as Business, Entertainment, or Sports.
- **View new and recent issues**: Tap My Magazines. By default, new issues appear near the top of the screen. The issue you've most recently read appears first. If you've recently downloaded an issue, it appears next. To choose a different sorting option, tap ⊙, then tap Sort by Name or Sort by Date.

Note: If you block an Apple News+ publication, its issues are removed from My Magazines.

To open a story or issue, do any of the following:

- Tap an issue cover in News+ or the Today feed.
- Tap Search, enter the name of the Apple News+ channel in the search field, tap the channel, then tap the issue.
- Follow a link to a story or issue that someone shared with you.

Access back issues

Do any of the following:

- Tap News+, tap My Magazines, tap ··· below the issue cover (or touch and hold the cover), then tap Browse Back Catalog.
- Tap a channel you follow, or search for a channel, then tap it. Below Recent Issues, swipe to the issue you want to read, then tap to open it. Tap Issues near the top of the screen to browse all available issues.

Read Apple News+ issues

Open the issue, where you can do any of the following:

- **View the table of contents**: Tap the cover thumbnail at the bottom left of the screen.
- **Navigate to a story**: In an issue in Apple News Format, tap the story link in the table of contents. In a PDF issue, tap the thumbnail of the page you want to view.
- **Page through an issue**: Swipe left or tap → to go to the next story, or swipe right or tap ← to go to the previous story.
- **Change the text size**: In stories in Apple News Format, tap AA, then tap the smaller or larger letter to change the text size in the story and all other stories in the channel. In PDF issues, pinch to zoom.

If you sign out in Settings ⊚ > [your name] > Media & Purchases, you can only access free stories—you must sign back in to access stories and download issues that require an Apple News+ subscription.

Download Apple News+ issues on iPhone

With the News app 🗞 and an Apple News+ subscription, you can download issues to read later.

Note: Apple News and Apple News+ aren't available in all countries or regions.

Download an Apple News+ issue

1. Do any of the following:
   - Tap Today, then swipe down to My Magazines.
   - Tap News+, then tap My Magazines. You can also tap Catalog near the top of the screen, then tap a stack of magazines.
   - Tap Following, then tap a magazine channel you follow.

- Tap Search, enter the magazine channel name in the search field, then tap the channel.
2. When you find the issue you want, tap ⋯ below the issue cover (or touch and hold the cover), then tap Download Issue.

   To download multiple issues, tap My Magazines, tap ⓧ, tap Select, tap the issues you want to download, then tap ☁.

When you subscribe to Apple News+, the most recent issues of magazines you follow are automatically downloaded when iPhone is plugged into power, has sufficient storage space, and is connected to Wi-Fi. If you don't want to download issues automatically, go to Settings ⚙ > News, then turn off Download Issues. You can download issues only if you're an Apple News+ subscriber.

Read a downloaded issue

1. Tap the News+ tab.
2. Tap Downloaded near the top of the screen, then tap an issue.

Manually remove an Apple News+ issue

Under most conditions, automatically downloaded issues are removed from iPhone after 30 days, but you can remove them sooner.

Tap the News+ tab, then do any of the following:

1. Tap Downloaded near the top of the screen, tap ⋯ below the issue cover (or touch and hold the cover), tap Remove, then tap Remove Download.
   The issue is removed from the Downloaded tab, but its cover remains in My Magazines so you can easily access the issue again.
2. Tap My Magazines near the top of the screen, tap ⋯ below the issue cover (or touch and hold the cover), tap Remove, then tap Remove from My Magazines.
   The issue's cover and content are removed from iPhone and from any other devices where you're signed in with the same Apple ID and News is turned on in iCloud preferences or settings.

To remove multiple issues, tap My Magazines or Downloaded near the top of the screen, tap ⓧ, tap Select, tap the issues you want to remove, then tap 🗑.

To remove all downloaded issues, tap Following > History, tap Clear, then tap Clear All.

When storage on iPhone is limited, issues may be automatically removed sooner than 30 days.

Listen to audio stories on iPhone

If you subscribe to Apple News+, you can listen to audio versions of select stories in the News app 📰.

Note: Apple News, Apple News+, and the audio feature aren't available in all countries or regions.

Browse audio stories

Tap 🎧 to show Apple News+ audio stories and Apple News Today. If you're a subscriber, you have access to the following:

- **Editors' Picks**: Features audio stories chosen by the Apple News editors as well as the latest episodes of Apple News Today and Apple News In Conversation.
- **Up Next:** Stories you're currently listening to or have added to the Up Next queue.
- **For You**: Stories recommended to you based on your interests.
- **Story groups**: Dynamic collections of stories curated by the Apple News editors, based on a topic or theme, such as space exploration or stories to accompany your commute.
- **More to Explore**: Links to all audio stories, Apple News Today episodes, recently played stories, and story categories such as Arts & Entertainment, News & Politics, and Sports.

To learn more about a story before listening to it, tap See Details.

If you're not an Apple News+ subscriber, you can hear previews of audio stories in Editors' Picks, Audio Stories For You, and in story groups. You can also listen to full episodes of Apple News Today and Apple News In Conversation.

Play audio stories

1. Tap 🎧, then tap a story.
2. For more playback controls, tap the mini player at the bottom to open the full-screen player.
3. To return to the mini player, swipe down to minimize the full-screen player.

   To close the full-screen player, tap ⋯, then tap Close Audio Player. To close the mini player, touch and hold the player, then tap Close Audio Player.

Audio stories can also appear in a feed. To listen to the story, tap Play Now (Apple News+ subscription required). You can also tap the story to read it, then tap Play Now at the top of the story. If you're not a subscriber, you can listen to a preview of the story.

Use any of the following controls:

Control	Description
▶	Play
❚❚	Pause
▶❙	Next story
↺15	Jump back 15 seconds
1×	Choose a faster or slower playback speed
◉	Stream audio to other devices

•••	Choose more actions such as place a story next or last in the queue, read a story, or share it

Add stories to Up Next

Do one of the following:

- In the Audio tab or a news feed, tap •••, then choose Play Next or Play Last.
- At the top of a story, touch and hold Play Now, then choose Play Next or Play Last. To continue listening from your most recent reading or listening position, tap Play Next from Here or Play Last from Here.

To reorder stories in the queue, tap See All, touch and hold ☰, then drag stories to the order you prefer.

Note: By default, if you're an Apple News+ subscriber, audio stories in your queue are automatically downloaded when iPhone is plugged into power, has sufficient storage space, and is connected to Wi-Fi. If you don't want them to download automatically, go to Settings ⚙ > News, then turn off Download Audio.

Read, share, and remove audio stories

Do any of the following:

- Read, share, and more: Tap •••, then choose an option.
- Remove stories from the Up Next queue or For You: Touch and hold the story, then select Remove.

Note: Some of these options are also available when you swipe a story left or right.

When listening to a story, open the full-screen player, then tap ••• to see a list of similar options.

Search for stories in News on iPhone

The News app 📰 keeps track of a wide variety of channels, topics, and stories, which makes it easy to find content that interests you.

Search for channels, topics, or stories

1. Tap Search, then tap the search field.
2. Enter any of the following:
   - The name of a channel, such as CNN or Washington Post
   - A topic, such as fashion, business, or politics
   - An event, such as an upcoming meteor shower

In the results list, tap ⊕ to follow the channel or topic.

Save stories in News on iPhone

In the News app ⬛ , you can save stories to read later, online or offline.

Save a story

When reading a story, tap ⬛ to save it.

To read a saved story, tap Following, tap Saved Stories, then tap the story. To delete a saved story, swipe the story left.

Check and edit your reading history

Tap Following, tap History, then do any of the following:

- Read a story: Tap the story.
- Delete a story: Swipe the story left.
- Remove your reading history: Tap Clear, then tap Clear History.
- Remove the information used to create recommendations: Tap Clear, then tap Clear Recommendations.
- Clear everything: Tap Clear, then tap Clear All.
  Your News history, recommendation information, saved stories, and downloaded issues and audio stories are removed from all your devices where you're signed in with the same Apple ID.

Note: Story titles remain in Saved Stories, but you must be online to read the stories.

If you clear recommendations, and Show in App is on in Settings ⬛ > News > Siri & Search, recommendations based on your Safari and app usage and your reading habits in News are cleared. To prevent News from suggesting stories based on your Safari and app usage, turn off Show in App.

When you clear your history, the identifier used by Apple News to report statistics to news publishers is also reset. You can reset the identifier at any time by going to Settings > News, then turning on Reset Identifier.

How to subscribe to individual channels on iPhone

In the News app ⬛ , in addition to subscribing to Apple News+, you can subscribe to individual publications from select publishers. There are three ways to access these subscriptions in News:

- **Subscribe within News**: You can purchase a subscription directly in News. In a channel that offers subscriptions, tap the subscription button.
- **Access an existing subscription purchased from a publisher's app**: If you've downloaded a publisher's app from the App Store, and subscriptions you've bought as in-app purchases are also available in News, you're automatically granted access in News.
- **Access an existing subscription purchased from a publisher**: If you've purchased a subscription directly from a publisher's website or from the publisher's app on a non-Apple device, the publisher may allow you to sign in to your account in News to access your subscription there.

To sign in, tap a story that requires a subscription to read, then tap Already a Subscriber? Enter the user name and password for your existing subscription.

When you subscribe to a channel, you automatically follow it, and stories from the channel appear in the Today feed.

To cancel a subscription, tap the Following tab, swipe up, tap Subscriptions below the Manage heading, select the subscription, then tap Cancel Subscription.

Notes

Add or remove accounts in Notes on iPhone

In the Notes app, you can keep your notes from multiple accounts in one place. Store your notes in iCloud and keep them up to date on all your devices. Add other internet accounts—for example, Google, Yahoo, or Microsoft Exchange. You can also have an On My iPhone account for notes you keep only on this device.

Note: All Notes features described in this guide are available when you use iCloud and the On My iPhone account. Some features aren't available when using other accounts.

Keep your notes up to date on all your devices with iCloud

Go to Settings > [your name] > iCloud, then turn on Notes.

Your iCloud notes—and any changes you make to them—appear on your iPhone, iPad, iPod touch, and Mac where you're signed in with your Apple ID.

Add other accounts

1. Go to Settings > Notes > Accounts > Add Account.
2. Do one of the following:
    o Tap a service—for example, Google, Yahoo, or Microsoft Exchange—then enter your account information.
    o Tap Other, tap Add Mail Account, enter your email account information, then turn on Notes for that account.

Set up an On My iPhone account

Notes in this account appear only on your iPhone. Your notes in iCloud and other accounts aren't affected.

Go to Settings > Notes, then turn on "On My iPhone" Account.

Create and format notes on iPhone

Use the Notes app to jot down quick thoughts or organize detailed information with checklists, images, web links, scanned documents, handwritten notes, and sketches.

Create and format a new note

1. Tap, then enter your text.
    The first line of the note becomes the note's title.

2. To change the formatting, tap Aa.

   You can apply a heading style, bold or italic font, a bulleted or numbered list, and more.

3. To save the note, tap Done.

Tip: To choose a default style for the first line in all new notes, go to Settings ⚙ > Notes > New Notes Start With.

Add a checklist

In a note, tap ⊘⎯, then do any of the following:

- **Add items to the list**: Enter text, then tap return to enter the next item.
- Increase or decrease the indentation: Swipe right or left on the item.
- Mark an item as completed: Tap the empty circle next to the item to add a checkmark.
- **Reorder an item**: Touch and hold the empty circle or checkmark next to the item, then drag the item to a new position in the list.
- **Manage items in the list**: Tap the list to see the menu, tap ⟩, tap Checklist, then tap Check All, Uncheck All, Delete Checked, or Move Checked to Bottom.

To automatically sort checked items to the bottom in all your notes, go to Settings ⚙ > Notes > Sort Checked Items, then tap Automatically.

Add or edit a table

In a note, tap ⊞, then do any of the following:

- **Enter text**: Tap a cell, then enter your text. To start another line of text in the cell, touch and hold the Shift key and tap next.
- **Move to the next cell**: Tap next. When you reach the last cell, tap next to start a new row.
- **Format a row or column**: Tap a row or column selection handle, then choose a style, such as bold, italic, underline, or strikethrough.
- **Add or delete a row or column**: Tap a row or column selection handle, then choose to add or delete.
- **Move a row or column**: Touch and hold a row or column selection handle, then drag it to a new position.
- **See more columns**: If the table becomes wider than your screen, swipe right or left on the table to see all the columns.

To remove the table and convert its contents to text, tap a cell in the table, tap ⊞⊙, then tap Convert to Text.

Take action on addresses, phone numbers, dates, and more

In your notes, a yellow underline appears below text that's recognized as a street or email address, phone number, date, or other data. Tap the underlined text to take action on it. For example, you can see a street address in Maps, compose an email, call a phone number, or add a calendar event.

Note: Data detection is available when the system language of your iPhone is set to a supported language in Settings ⚙ > General > Language & Region.

Draw or write in Notes on iPhone

Use the Notes app ▭ to draw a sketch or jot a handwritten note with your finger. You can choose from a variety of Markup tools and colors and draw straight lines with the ruler.

Draw or write in a note

1. Tap Ⓐ, then draw or write with your finger.
2. Do any of the following:
   o **Change color or tools**: Use the Markup tools.
   o **Adjust the handwriting area**: Drag the resize handle (on the left) up or down.

Tip: You can search handwritten text (in supported languages) in Notes. If the note doesn't have a title, the first line of handwritten text becomes the suggested title. To edit the title, scroll to the top of the note, then tap Edit.

Select and edit drawings and handwriting

1. In the Markup toolbar, tap the Lasso tool ⌇ (between the eraser and ruler).
2. Touch and hold to select drawings and handwriting, then drag to expand the selection. Adjust the selection by dragging the handles if necessary.
3. Tap the selection, then choose Cut, Copy, Delete, Duplicate, Copy as Text, Insert Space Above, Translate, or Straighten.
   If you choose Copy as Text, you can paste the transcribed text in another note or another app.

Show lines or grids in notes

- **In an existing note**: Tap ⋯, tap Lines & Grids, then choose a style.

- **Choose the default style for all new notes**: Go to Settings ⚙ > Notes > Lines & Grids.

Scan text and documents in Notes using the iPhone camera

In the Notes app ▭, you can use the camera to scan text and documents.

Scan text into a note

You can insert scanned text using the camera (on supported models; in supported languages).

- In a note, tap 📷, then tap Scan Text.
- Position iPhone so that the text appears within the camera frame.

- After the yellow frame appears around detected text, tap ⊡.
- Drag or use grab points to select text, then tap Insert.

Scan a document

1. In a note, tap 📷, then choose Scan Documents.
2. Position iPhone so that the document page appears on the screen; iPhone automatically captures the page.

To manually capture the page, tap ◯ or press a volume button. To turn the flash on or off, tap ⚡.

3. Scan additional pages, then tap Save when you're done.
4. To make changes to the saved document, tap it, then do any of the following:

   - Add more pages: Tap ⊕.
   - Crop the image: Tap ⌐.
   - **Apply a filter**: Tap ⊛, then choose to scan the page as a color, grayscale, or black-and-white document, or as a photo.
   - Rotate the image: Tap ▢.
   - **Mark up the document**: Tap ⬆, tap Ⓐ, then use the Markup tools to add annotations or your signature.
   - Delete the scan: Tap 🗑.

Add photos, videos, and more to notes on iPhone

In the Notes app ▢, you can add photos, videos, and info from other apps, such as maps, links, and documents, to a note.

Add a photo or video

1. In a note, tap 📷.
2. Choose a photo or video from your photo library, or take a new photo or video.
3. To change the preview size of attachments, touch and hold an attachment, then tap Small Images or Large Images.

Tip: To draw on a photo, tap the photo, then tap Ⓐ.

To save photos and videos taken in Notes to the Photos app, go to Settings ⚙ > Notes, then turn on Save to Photos.

Add info from another app to a note

You can add information from another app as an attachment to a note—for example, a location in Maps, a webpage in Safari, a PDF in Files, or a screenshot.

1. In the other app, open the item you want to share (for example, a map or webpage).
2. Tap Share or ⬆, then tap Notes or Add to Quick Note.

View all attachments in Notes

1. Above the notes list, tap ⋯, then tap View Attachments to see thumbnails of drawings, photos, links, documents, and other attachments. (Attachments in locked notes aren't shown.)
2. To go to a note with a specific attachment, tap the attachment thumbnail, then tap Show in Note.

Create Quick Notes anywhere on iPhone

You can use Quick Notes to jot down information over any app or screen on iPhone. Add links, images, tags, and mentions to a Quick Note so you can get to important names, numbers, and ideas easily. When you highlight text in Safari or add a link from an app, you see a Quick Note thumbnail next time you visit the site, taking you right to what you were viewing before.

You can access all your Quick Notes in the Notes app ⬜. And when you make a Quick Note on your iPhone, you can see the note on your iPad and Mac, too.

Make a Quick Note

To start a Quick Note from any app, do any of the following:

- Tap ⬆️, then tap Add to Quick Note.
- Open Control Center, then tap 〽️.

  (If you don't see 〽️, add it to Control Center—go to Settings ⚙️ > Control Center, then choose Quick Note.)

View and organize Quick Notes

To view all your Quick Notes in the Notes app, tap Quick Notes in the folders list.

Note: You can't lock a Quick Note unless you move it to a different folder.

If you move an individual Quick Note to a different folder, it becomes a standard note and no longer appears as a Quick Note in other apps.

Search your notes on iPhone

In the Notes app ⬜, you can search all your notes for typed and handwritten text, objects in images, and text in scanned documents. You can also search for text within a note.

Search for text, objects, and more in all your notes

You can search for tags, typed and handwritten text, objects that appear in images, and text in scanned documents.

1. Swipe down on the notes list to reveal the search field.
2. Tap the search field, then enter what you're looking for. You can also choose a suggested search, such as "Notes with Drawings," then enter additional text to refine your search.

If a note is locked, only its title appears in the search results. The search includes handwritten text (in supported languages), photos, and scanned documents.

Search within a note for typed and handwritten text

1. Open the note you want to search.
2. Tap ⋯, then tap Find in Note.
3. Type the text you're looking for in the search field.

Organize your notes in folders on iPhone

In the Notes app [image], you can organize your notes into folders and pin the important notes to the top of the notes list.

Create, rename, move, or delete a folder

In the folders list, do any of the following:

- **Create a folder**: Tap [image], choose an account (if you have more than one), tap New Folder, then enter a name.
- **Create a subfolder**: Touch and hold a folder, then drag it onto another folder.
- **Rename a folder**: Touch and hold a folder, tap Rename, then enter a new name.
- **Move a folder**: Swipe left on the folder, tap [image], then choose a new location. Or touch and hold the folder, then drag it to a new location. The folder becomes a subfolder if you drag it onto another folder.
- **Delete a folder**: Swipe left on the folder, then tap [image]. Or touch and hold the folder, then tap Delete.
  If you change your mind, open the Recently Deleted folder to recover the notes.

Pin notes

To pin an important note to the top of the notes list, touch and hold the note, then tap Pin Note. Or swipe right on the note, then tap the pin.

Sort and change the folder view

In the notes list, tap [image], then do any of the following:

- **Change the folder view**: Choose View as Gallery or View as List.
- **Group the notes by date**: Tap Group By Date, then tap On.

  To group all your notes by date by default, go to Settings [image] > Notes, then turn on Group Notes By Date.
- **Change the sort order of a folder**: Tap "Sort by," then choose Date Edited, Date Created, or Title. You can also reverse the sort order—for example, Oldest First or Newest First.

To choose a default sorting method for all your folders, go to Settings [image] > Notes > Sort Notes By.

Move a note to another folder

Swipe left on the note, then tap [image]. Or touch and hold the note, tap Move, then choose a folder.

Delete a note

Swipe left on the note, then tap [image]. Or touch and hold the note, then tap Delete.

If you change your mind, open the Recently Deleted folder to recover the note.

Organize your notes with tags on iPhone

In the Notes app ⬚, you can use tags as a fast and flexible way to categorize and organize your notes. You can add one or more tags to a note, such as #shopping and #work, and easily search and filter your notes across folders using the Tag Browser or Smart Folders.

Add tags to notes

When you create or edit a note, type # followed by the tag name or choose a tag from the menu above the keyboard. A tag can be only one word, but you can use dashes and underscores to combine words. You can add multiple tags to a note.

Rename or delete a tag

Below Tags at the bottom of the screen, touch and hold a tag, then tap Rename Tag or Delete Tag.

When you delete a tag, it's also removed from all Smart Folders that use it.

View notes with tags

Below Tags at the bottom of the screen, do any of the following:

- View all notes with tags: Tap All Tags.
- **View notes with specific tags**: Tap one or more tags, then choose to view notes matching any or all of the selected tags.

Organize your notes with Smart Folders on iPhone

In the Notes app ⬚, you can easily search and filter your notes across folders using Smart Folders.

Create a Smart Folder

1. Tap ⬚, choose an account (if you have more than one), enter a name, then tap Make Into Smart Folder.
2. Choose one or more filters, then choose to include notes matching any or all of the selected filters. You can filter by tags, dates, mentions, and more.

You can also create a Smart Folder when viewing a list of tagged notes; tap ⋯, then tap Create Smart Folder.

Convert a folder to a Smart Folder

When viewing the folder you want to convert, tap ⋯, scroll to the bottom, then tap Convert to Smart Folder.

When you convert a folder, its notes are moved to the Notes folder and tagged with the name of the Smart Folder.

Note: You can't convert a shared folder, a folder with a subfolder, or a folder that contains locked notes.

Edit a Smart Folder

Touch and hold a Smart Folder, then tap Edit Smart Folder. You can change the name or filters.

Share notes and collaborate on iPhone

In the Notes app ⬜, you can send a copy of a note to a friend. You can also invite people to collaborate on a note or on a folder of notes in iCloud, and everyone will see the latest changes.

Share a copy of a note

1. Open the note you want to share.
2. Tap ⬆, choose Send Copy, then choose how to send your note.

Collaborate on a note or folder of notes using iCloud

You can share a note or folder of notes and collaborate with people who use iCloud. You set permissions for other collaborators (such as allowing them to edit notes, add attachments, and create subfolders), and all the collaborators can see everyone's changes. Everyone you collaborate with must be signed in with their Apple ID and have Notes turned on in iCloud settings.

Note: You can't collaborate on a locked note or on a folder with locked notes.

1. Do one of the following:
    o In the notes list, swipe left on the note you want to share, then tap 👥.
    o Open the note you want to share, then tap ⬆.
    o In the folder list, swipe left on the folder you want to share, then tap 👥.
    o Open the folder you want to share, tap ⋯, then tap Share Folder.
2. Choose Collaborate.
3. To change the access and permissions, tap the share options below Collaborate. You can set any of the following:
    o Allow access only to people you invite or to anyone with the link.
    o Give collaborators permission to make changes or view only.
    o Allow others to invite new collaborators (available only when collaborators have permission to make changes).
4. Choose how to send your invitation (for example, using Messages or Mail).

If you send the invitation in Messages, you get activity updates in the Messages conversation when someone makes changes in the shared note. Tap the updates to go to the shared note.

View activity in a note

In the notes list, an orange dot to the left of a note title indicates the note has changed since you last looked at it.

1. Open the note, then swipe right on the note or swipe up on the Activity card to see who made changes and when.
2. To adjust how the activity is shown, tap 👥, then choose any of the following:
    o **Show Updates**: Shows changes made since you last opened the note.
    o **Show All Activity**: Shows all activity in the note.
    o **Show Highlights**: Shows names, dates, and changes made by each collaborator.

Tip: To mention a collaborator and notify them of important updates, type an @ sign followed by their name.

View activity in a folder

Touch and hold the folder, then tap Show Folder Activity.

Change sharing settings

- **Manage a shared note**: Tap ⊘, then tap Manage Shared Note.
- **Manage a shared folder**: Tap ⋯, then tap Manage Shared Folder.
- **Remove people**: Tap the collaborator you want to remove, then tap Remove Access.
- **Change access and permission settings**: To change the settings for all collaborators, tap Share Options. To change the settings for an individual collaborator, tap their name.
- **Stop sharing**: When you choose this option, the shared note or folder is deleted from the devices of the other participants.

Lock your notes on iPhone

In the Notes app ⬜, you can lock notes to protect your sensitive information. You can access your locked notes using your device passcode or a custom password. If you have multiple Notes accounts, you choose the locking method for each account (for example, your iCloud account).

Lock notes with your device passcode

If you use your device passcode to access locked notes, you don't have to create and remember a separate password, which reduces the chances of losing access to your locked notes. If you use your device passcode, you can also use Face ID to access your locked notes.

If you have multiple devices where you're signed in with the same Apple ID, you use each device's passcode (or login password for a Mac) to access your locked notes on that device.

To access notes locked with a device passcode, you must be using iOS 16 or later. On devices with an earlier version of the OS, you won't be able to access the locked notes.

1. Go to Settings ⚙ > Notes > Password.
2. If you have multiple accounts, choose the account you want to set a password for.
3. Tap Use Device Passcode.
4. For added convenience, you can also turn on Face ID.

Lock notes with a custom password

Creating a custom password for locked notes can provide additional security, but if you forget the password, you may lose access to your locked notes.

You use your custom password to access your locked notes on all devices where you're signed in with the same Apple ID. If you have more than one iCloud account or an "On my iPhone" account, you can set a different custom password for each account.

To access notes locked with a custom password, you must be using iOS 9.3, iPadOS 13, OS X 10.11.4, or later. On devices with an earlier version of the OS, you won't see the notes.

1. Go to Settings ⚙ > Notes > Password.
2. If you have multiple accounts, choose the account you want to set a password for.
3. Tap Use Custom Password.

4. For added convenience, you can also turn on Face ID.
Don't rely on Face ID as the only means of unlocking your notes. If you update your Face ID settings, or want to change your Notes password, you have to reenter your Notes password.

Important: If you forget your custom password, and you can't use Face ID to access your locked notes, Apple can't help you regain access to those notes.

You can reset your custom password, but this doesn't give you access to previously locked notes. The new custom password applies to all notes you lock from now on. Go to Settings > Notes > Password > Reset Password.

Change the locking method

If you're using a custom password, you can switch to using your device passcode. Go to Settings > Notes > Password, choose an account (if you have more than one), then tap Use Device Passcode.

When you change your locking method, notes that you can access using the previous method begin using the new method.

Lock a note

You can only lock notes on your device and notes in iCloud. You can't lock notes that have PDFs, audio, video, Keynote, Pages, or Numbers documents attached; notes that sync with other accounts; or Quick Notes. You can't lock an iCloud note that has collaborators.

1. Open the note, then tap ⋯.
2. Tap Lock.

When a note is locked, the title remains visible in the notes list.

To remove a lock from a note, tap ⋯, then tap Remove.

Open your locked notes

Opening one locked note opens all your locked notes in the same account for several minutes so you can easily jump into another note or copy and paste information from other apps.

1. Tap the locked note, then tap View Note.
2. To open the note, use Face ID your device passcode, or your Notes password.

To lock your notes again, do any of the following:

- Tap the lock icon at the top of the screen.
- Tap Lock Now at the bottom of the notes list.
- Close the Notes app.
- Lock your iPhone.

Change your Notes settings on iPhone

You can customize your preferences for the Notes app in Settings. Choose the default account for new notes, set a password, and more.

From the Home Screen or App Library, go to Settings > Notes, then adjust any of the settings. For example:

- **Default Account**: Choose the default account for Siri and the Notes widget.
- **Password**: Lock important notes.
- **Sort Notes By**: Choose Date Edited, Date Created, or Title.
- **Lines & Grids**: Choose a line or grid style for handwriting in new notes.
- **Save to Photos**: Save photos and videos taken in Notes to the Photos app.
- **Access Notes from Lock Screen**: Choose Always Create New Note or Resume Last Note. Or turn it off to prevent access from the Lock Screen.

Phone

Make a call on iPhone

To start a call in the Phone app 📞, dial the number on the keypad, tap a favorite or recent call, or choose a number in your contacts list.

Dial a number

Siri: Say "call" or "dial" followed by a number. Speak each digit separately—for example, "four one five, five five five…." For the 800 area code in the U.S., you can say "eight hundred."

Or do the following:

1. Tap Keypad.

2. Do any of the following:
   - **Use a different line**: On models with Dual SIM, tap the line at the top, then choose a line.
   - Enter the number using the keypad: If you make a mistake, tap ✕.
   - **Redial the last number**: Tap 📞 to see the last number you dialed, then tap 📞 to call that number.
   - **Paste a number you've copied**: Tap the phone number field above the keypad, then tap Paste.
   - **Enter a soft (2-second) pause**: Touch and hold the star (*) key until a comma appears.

- Enter a hard pause (to pause dialing until you tap the Dial button): Touch and hold the pound (#) key until a semicolon appears.
- **Enter a "+" for international calls**: Touch and hold the "0" key until "+" appears.

3. Tap 📞 to start the call.

To end the call, tap 🔴 .

Call your favorites

1. Tap Favorites, then choose one to make a call.
   On models with Dual SIM, iPhone chooses the line for the call in the following order:
   - The preferred line for this contact (if set)
   - The line used for the last call to or from this contact
   - The default voice line
2. To manage your Favorites list, do any of the following:

   - Add a favorite: Tap ➕ , then choose a contact.
   - Rearrange or delete favorites: Tap Edit.

Redial or return a recent call

Siri: Say something like: "Redial that last number" or "Return my last call."

You can also do the following:

1. Tap Recents, then choose one to make a call.

2. To get more info about a call and the caller, tap ⓘ .
   A red badge indicates the number of missed calls.

Call someone on your contacts list

Siri: Say something like: "Call Eliza's mobile."

Or do the following:

1. In the Phone app, tap Contacts.
2. Tap the contact, then tap the phone number you want to call.

On models with Dual SIM, the default voice line is used for the call unless you set a preferred line for this contact.

Change your outgoing call settings

1. Go to Settings ⚙ > Phone.
2. Do any of the following:
   - **Turn on Show My Caller ID**: (GSM) Your phone number is shown in My Number. For FaceTime calls, your phone number is displayed even if caller ID is turned off.
   - **Turn on Dial Assist for international calls**: (GSM) When Dial Assist is turned on, iPhone automatically adds the correct international or local prefix when you call your contacts and favorites.
   For information about making international calls (including rates and other charges that may apply), contact your carrier.

Answer or decline incoming calls on iPhone

295

You can answer, silence, or decline an incoming call. If you decline a call, it goes to voicemail. You can respond with a text or remind yourself to return the call.

Answer a call

Do one of the following:

- Tap .
- If iPhone is locked, drag the slider.

Tip: You can have Siri announce incoming calls, which you can accept or decline using your voice.

Silence a call

Press the side button or either volume button.

You can still answer a silenced call until it goes to voicemail.

Decline a call and send it directly to voicemail

Do one of the following:

- Press the side button twice quickly.
- Tap .
- Swipe up on the call banner.

You can also swipe down on the call banner for more options.

Do any of the following:

- Tap Remind Me, then choose when you want a reminder to return the call.
- Tap Message, then choose a default reply or tap Custom.

  To create your own default replies, go to Settings > Phone > Respond with Text, then tap any default message and replace it with your own text.

Note: In some countries or regions, declined calls are disconnected without being sent to voicemail.

While on a call on iPhone

When you're on a phone call, you can switch the audio to the speaker or a Bluetooth device. If you get another incoming call, you can respond or ignore it.

Adjust the audio during a call

To change the volume, press the volume buttons on the side of iPhone. Or swipe down on the call banner, then do any of the following:

- **Mute**: Tap the mute button.
- **Put the call on hold**: Touch and hold the mute button.
- **Talk handsfree**: Tap the audio button, then choose an audio destination.

Use another app while on a call

1. Go to the Home Screen, then open the app.
2. To return to the call, tap the green call indicator at the top of the screen.

Respond to a second call on the same line

If you're on a call and receive a second call, do one the following:

- Ignore the call and send it to voicemail: Tap Ignore.
- **End the first call and answer the new one**: When using a GSM network, tap End + Accept. With a CDMA network, tap End and when the second call rings back, tap Accept, or drag the slider if iPhone is locked.
- **Put the first call on hold and answer the new one**: Tap Hold + Accept. With a call on hold, tap Swap to switch between calls, or tap Merge Calls to talk with both parties at once.

Note: With CDMA, you can't switch between calls if the second call was outgoing, but you can merge the calls. You can't merge calls if the second call was incoming. If you end the second call or the merged call, both calls are terminated.

On models with Dual SIM, note the following:

- Wi-Fi Calling must be turned on for a line to enable that line to receive calls while the other line is in use for a call. If you receive a call on one line while the other is in use for a call, and no Wi-Fi connection is available, iPhone uses the cellular data of the line that's in use for the call to receive the other line's call. Charges may apply. The line that's in use for the call must be permitted for data use in your Cellular Data settings (either as the default line, or as the non-default line with Allow Cellular Data Switching turned on) to receive the other line's call.
- If you don't turn on Wi-Fi Calling for a line, any incoming phone calls on that line (including calls from emergency services) go directly to voicemail (if available from your carrier) when the other line is in use; you won't receive missed call notifications. If you set up conditional call forwarding (if available from your carrier) from one line to another when a line is busy or not in service, the calls don't go to voicemail; contact your carrier for setup information.

Start a conference call

With GSM, you can set up a conference call with up to five people (depending on your carrier).

Note: Conference calls may not be available if your call is using VoLTE (Voice over LTE) or Wi-Fi Calling.

1. While on a call, tap Add Call, make another call, then Tap Merge Calls. Repeat to add more people to the conference.
2. During the conference call, do any of the following:
   - **Talk privately with one person**: Tap ⓘ, then tap Private next to the person. Tap Merge Calls to resume the conference.
   - **Add an incoming caller on the same line**: Tap Hold Call + Answer, then tap Merge Calls.
   - **Drop one person**: Tap ⓘ next to a person, then tap End.

Check your voicemail on iPhone

In the Phone app 📞, Visual Voicemail (available from select carriers) shows a list of your messages. You can choose which ones to play and delete without listening to all of them. A badge on the Voicemail icon indicates the number of unheard messages.

Voicemail transcription (beta; available only in certain countries or regions) shows your messages transcribed into text. Transcription is limited to voicemails in English received on your iPhone with iOS 10 or later. Transcription depends on the quality of the recording.

Note: Voicemail, Visual Voicemail, and Voicemail transcription are available from select carriers in select countries or regions.

Set up voicemail

The first time you tap Voicemail, you're asked to create a voicemail password and record your voicemail greeting.

1. Tap Voicemail, then tap Set Up Now.
2. Create a voicemail password.
3. Choose a greeting—Default or Custom; if you choose Custom, you can record a new greeting.

Play, share, or delete a voicemail message

Siri: Say something like: "Play the voicemail from Eliza."

Or do the following:

1. Tap Voicemail, then tap a message.
2. Do any of the following:

    o **Play the message**: Tap ▶ .
       Messages are saved until you delete them or your carrier erases them.

    o Share the message: Tap 📤 .

    o **Delete the message**: Tap 🗑 .
       Important: In some countries or regions, deleted messages may be permanently erased by your carrier. Your voice messages may also be deleted if you change your SIM card.

To recover a deleted message, tap Deleted Messages, tap the message, then tap Undelete.

Check your messages when Visual Voicemail isn't available

- **On your iPhone**: Tap Voicemail, then follow the instructions.
- **On another phone**: Dial your own mobile number, press * or # (depending on your carrier) to bypass your greeting, then enter your voicemail password.

Change your voicemail settings

- **Change your greeting**: Tap Voicemail, then tap Greeting.

- **Change your voicemail password**: Go to Settings 🔘 > Phone > Change Voicemail Password, then enter the new password.
  If you forgot your voicemail password, contact your wireless carrier.
- **Change the alert for new voicemail**: Go to Settings > Sounds & Haptics or Settings > Sounds.

Select ringtones and vibrations on iPhone

You can set the default ringtone and assign distinctive ringtones to certain people. You can also use vibrations and turn the ringer off.

Change the alert tones and vibrations

iPhone comes with ringtones that play for incoming calls. You can also purchase more ringtones in the iTunes Store.

Assign a different ringtone to a contact

1. Open the Contacts app 📇.
2. Select a contact, tap Edit, tap Ringtone, then choose a ringtone.

Turn the ringer on or off

Flip the Ring/Silent switch to turn silent mode on or off. Clock alarms still play when silent mode is turned on.

To temporarily silence incoming calls, Turn on or schedule a Focus on iPhone.

Make calls using Wi-Fi on iPhone

When your iPhone has a low cellular signal, use Wi-Fi Calling to make and receive calls through a Wi-Fi network.

1. On your iPhone, go to Settings ⚙ > Cellular.
2. If your iPhone has Dual SIM, choose a line (below SIMs).
3. Tap Wi-Fi Calling, then turn on Wi-Fi Calling on This iPhone.
4. Enter or confirm your address for emergency services.

Note: Emergency calls on your iPhone are routed through cellular service when available. In the event that cellular service isn't available, and you have enabled Wi-Fi Calling, emergency calls may be made over Wi-Fi, and your device's location information may be used for emergency calls to aid response efforts, regardless of whether you enable Location Services. Some carriers may use the address you registered with the carrier when signing up for Wi-Fi Calling as your location. When connected to Wi-Fi calling, your iPhone may not receive emergency alerts.

When Wi-Fi Calling is available, "Wi-Fi" is displayed after your carrier name in the status bar, and all your calls go through Wi-Fi.

Note: If the Wi-Fi connection is lost when you make calls, calls switch automatically to your carrier's cellular network using VoLTE (Voice over LTE), if available and turned on. Contact your carrier for feature availability.

Set up call forwarding and call waiting on iPhone

You can set up call forwarding and call waiting on iPhone if you have cellular service through a GSM network.

If you have cellular service through a CDMA network, contact your carrier for information about enabling and using these features.

1. Go to Settings ⚙ > Phone.
2. Tap any of the following:

- ○ **Call Forwarding**: ↱ appears in the status bar when call forwarding is on. You must be in range of the cellular network when you set iPhone to forward calls, or calls won't be forwarded.
  On models with Dual SIM, choose a line.
- ○ **Call Waiting**: If you're on a call and call waiting is turned off, incoming calls go directly to voicemail.

On models with Dual SIM, call waiting works only for incoming calls on the same line, unless the other line has Wi-Fi calling enabled and a data connection is available.

For information about conditional call forwarding (if available from your carrier) when the line is busy or not in service, contact your carrier for setup information.

Avoid unwanted calls on iPhone

You can avoid unwanted calls by blocking certain people and sending unknown and spam callers directly to voicemail.

Block voice calls, FaceTime calls, and messages from certain people

In the Phone app 📞, do any of the following.

- Tap Favorites, Recents, or Voicemail. Tap ⓘ next to the number or contact you want to block, scroll down, then tap Block this Caller.
- Tap Contacts, tap the contact you want to block, scroll down, then tap Block this Caller.

Manage your blocked contacts

1. Go to Settings ⚙ > Phone > Blocked Contacts.
2. Tap Edit.

Send unknown and spam callers to voicemail

Go to Settings ⚙ > Phone, then tap any of the following:

- **Silence Unknown Callers**: You get notifications for calls from people in your contacts, recent outgoing calls, and Siri Suggestions.
- **Call Blocking & Identification**: Turn on Silence Junk Callers (available with certain carriers) to silence calls identified by your carrier as potential spam or fraud.

Photos

View photos in the Photos app on iPhone

Use the Photos app 🌸 to find and view all of the photos and videos on your iPhone.

How photos and videos are organized in Photos

You navigate Photos using the Library, For You, Albums, and Search buttons at the bottom of the screen.

- **Library**: Browse your photos and videos organized by days, months, years, and all photos.
- **For You**: View your memories, shared photos, featured photos, and sharing suggestions in a personalized feed.
- **Albums**: View albums you created or shared, and your photos organized automatically by categories—for example, People & Places and Media Types.
- **Search**: Type in the search field to search for photos by date, location, caption, or objects they contain. Or browse photos already grouped by important events, people, places, and categories.

Browse photos in your library

To browse your photos and videos by when they were taken, tap Library, then select any of the following:

- **Years**: Quickly locate a specific year in your photo library.
- **Months**: View collections of photos that you took throughout a month, organized by significant events—like a family outing, social occasion, birthday party, or trip.
- **Days**: View your best photos in chronological order, grouped by the time or place the photos were taken.
- **All Photos**: View all of your photos and videos.

Tip: When viewing All Photos, pinch the screen to zoom in or out. You can also tap ⚫⚫⚫ to zoom in or out, view photos by aspect ratio or square, filter photos, or see photos on a map.

Years, Months, and Days views are curated to show your best shots, and visual clutter like similar photos, screenshots, whiteboards, and receipts aren't shown. To see every photo and video, tap All Photos.

View individual photos

Tap a photo to view it in full screen on your iPhone.

Double-tap or pinch out to zoom in on the photo—drag to see other parts of the photo; double-tap or pinch closed to zoom back out.

Tap ♡ to add the photo to your Favorites album.

Tip: When viewing a Live Photo ◎ , touch and hold the photo to play it.

Tap ‹ or drag the photo down to continue browsing or return to the search results.

See photo and video information

To see saved metadata information about a photo or video, open it, then tap ⓘ or swipe up. Depending on the photo or video, you see the following details:

- People identified in the photo
- A caption field to describe the photo or video, and make it easier to find in Search
- Items detected by Visual Look Up
- Whether the photo was shared with you in Messages or another app
- The date and time the photo or video was taken; tap Adjust to edit the date and time
- Camera metadata such as lens, shutter speed, file size, and more

- Where the photo or video was taken; tap the link to view the location in Maps; tap Adjust to edit the location

Play videos and slideshows in the Photos app on iPhone

Use the Photos app ![icon] to play videos you've recorded or saved on your iPhone. You can also create slideshows of the photos, videos, and Live Photos in your library.

Play a video

As you browse photos and videos in the Photos app, tap a video to play it on your iPhone. While it plays, you can do any of the following:

- Tap the player controls below the video to pause, unmute, favorite, share, delete, or see video information; tap the screen to hide the player controls.
- Double-tap the screen to switch between full screen and fit-to-screen.
- Touch and hold the frame viewer at the bottom of the screen to pause the video, then slide the viewer left or right to move back or forward.

Make and play a slideshow

You can create a slideshow to view a collection of photos and videos that you choose from your library. Slideshows are automatically formatted and set to music.

1. Tap Library, then view photos by All Photos or Days.
2. Tap Select.
3. Tap each photo you want to include in the slideshow, then tap ⋯.
4. Tap Slideshow from the list of options.
   To change the slideshow theme, music, and more, tap the screen while the slideshow plays, then tap Options.

Note: You can also make a slideshow from an album. Tap Albums, tap the album you want to create a slideshow from, then follow the steps above.

Delete or hide photos and videos on iPhone

In the Photos app ![icon], you can delete photos and videos from your iPhone or hide them in the Hidden album. You can also recover photos you recently deleted. Photos you delete and hide are saved in the Hidden and Recently Deleted albums, which you unlock using your iPhone authentication method.

When you use iCloud Photos on iPhone, any photos you delete or hide are synced across your other devices.

Delete or hide a photo or video

In Photos, tap a photo or video, then do either of the following:

- **Delete**: Tap 🗑 to delete a photo from your iPhone and other devices using the same iCloud Photos account.
  Deleted photos and videos are kept in the Recently Deleted album for 30 days, where you can recover or permanently remove them from all devices.

- **Hide**: Tap ⓛ, then tap Hide in the list of options.
  Hidden photos are moved to the Hidden album. You can't view them anywhere else.

  To turn off the Hidden album so it doesn't appear in Albums, go to Settings ⚙ >
  Photos, then turn off Hidden Album.

Delete or hide multiple photos and videos

While viewing photos in an album or in the Days or All Photos view in your library, do either of
the following:

- **Delete**: Tap Select, tap or drag your finger on the screen to select the items you want to
  delete, then tap 🗑.
- **Hide**: Tap Select, tap or drag your finger on the screen to select the items you want to
  hide, tap ⓛ, then tap Hide.

Recover or permanently delete deleted photos

To recover deleted photos, or to permanently delete them, do the following:

1. Tap Albums, then tap Recently Deleted under Utilities.
2. Tap Select, then choose the photos and videos you want to recover or delete.
3. Choose Recover or Delete at the bottom of the screen.

Unlock Recently Deleted and Hidden albums

The Recently Deleted and Hidden albums are locked by default. You unlock these albums using
your iPhone authentication method—Face ID or your passcode.

To change the default setting from locked to unlocked, go to Settings ⚙ > Photos, then turn off
Use Passcode.

Edit photos and videos on iPhone

After you take a photo or video, use the tools in the Photos app 🌸 to edit it on your iPhone.
You can adjust the light and color, crop, rotate, add a filter, and more. If you don't like how your
changes look, tap Cancel to revert back to the original.

When you use iCloud Photos, any edits you make to your photos and videos are saved across
all your devices.

Adjust light and color

1. In Photos, tap a photo or video thumbnail to view it in full screen.
2. Tap Edit, then swipe left under the photo to view the effects you can edit such as
   Exposure, Brilliance, Highlights, and Shadows.
3. Tap the effect you want to edit, then drag the slider to make precise adjustments.
   The level of adjustment you make for each effect is indicated by the outline around the
   button, so you can see at a glance which effects have been increased or decreased. Tap
   the effect button to toggle between the edited effect and the original.
4. Tap Done to save your edits, or if you don't like your changes, tap Cancel, then tap
   Discard Changes.

Tip: Tap 🪄 to automatically edit your photos or videos with effects.

Crop, rotate, or flip a photo or video

1. In Photos, tap a photo or video thumbnail to view it in full screen.
2. Tap Edit, tap ⟲, then do any of the following:
   ○ **Crop manually**: Drag the rectangle corners to enclose the area you want to keep in the photo, or you can pinch the photo open or closed.
   ○ **Crop to a standard preset ratio**: Tap ⊞, then choose an option such as square, 16:9, or 5:4.
   ○ **Rotate**: Tap ⟲ to rotate the photo 90 degrees.
   ○ **Flip**: Tap ▲▲ to flip the image horizontally.
3. Tap Done to save your edits, or if you don't like your changes, tap Cancel, then tap Discard Changes.

Straighten and adjust perspective

1. In Photos, tap a photo or video thumbnail to view it in full screen.
2. Tap Edit, then tap ⟲.
3. Swipe left under the photo to view the effects you can edit: Straighten, Vertical, or Horizontal.
4. Tap the effect you want to edit, then drag the slider to make precise adjustments.
   The level of adjustment you make for each effect is displayed by the outline around the button, so you can see at a glance which effects have been increased or decreased. Tap the button to toggle between the edited effect and the original.
5. Tap Done to save your edits, or if you don't like your changes, tap Cancel, then tap Discard Changes.

Apply filter effects

1. In Photos, tap a photo or video thumbnail to view it in full screen.
2. Tap Edit, then tap ⦿ to apply filter effects such as Vivid, Dramatic, or Silvertone.
3. Tap a filter, then drag the slider to adjust the effect.
   To compare the edited photo to the original, tap the photo.
4. Tap Done to save your edits, or if you don't like your changes, tap Cancel, then tap Discard Changes.

Undo and redo edits

As you edit a photo or video, tap ↺ and ↻ at the top of the screen to undo and redo multiple edit steps.

Tip: You can tap the photo or video to compare the edited version to the original.

Copy and paste edits to multiple photos

You can copy the edits you made to one photo (or video) and paste them onto another photo, or a batch or photos, all at once.

1. Open the photo or video that contains the edits you want to copy.
2. Tap ⋯, then tap Copy Edits.

3. Tap $\langle$ to return to your library.
4. Tap Select, then tap the thumbnails of the photos you want to paste the edits onto. Or, open a single photo or video.
5. Tap ⊙, then tap Paste Edits.

Revert an edited photo or video

After you edit a photo or video and save your changes, you can revert to the original.

1. Open the edited photo or video, then tap ⊙.
2. Tap Revert to Original.

Change the date, time, or location

You can change the date, time, and location that's stored within the photo or video's metadata information.

1. Open the photo or video, then tap ⊙.
2. Tap Adjust Date & Time or Adjust Location.
3. Enter the new information, then tap Adjust.

To change the date, time, or location of a batch of photos, tap Select, tap the thumbnails you want to change, then follow the steps above.

You can revert a photo or video to its original date, time, or location. Tap ⊙, tap Adjust Date & Time or Adjust Location, then tap Revert.

Write or draw on a photo

1. In Photos, tap a photo to view it in full screen.
2. Tap Edit, then tap Ⓐ.
3. Annotate the photo using the different drawing tools and colors. Tap ＋ to magnify or add a caption, text, shapes, or even your signature.
4. Tap Done to save your edits, or if you don't like your changes, tap Cancel.

Trim video length and adjust slow motion on iPhone

In the Photos app ❋, you can trim a video you recorded on your iPhone to change where it starts and stops. You can also adjust the portion of a video that appears in slow motion when you record in Slo-mo mode.

Trim a video

1. In Photos, open the video, then tap Edit.
2. Drag either end of the frame viewer below the video to change the start and stop times, then tap Done.
3. Tap Save Video to save only the trimmed video, or Save Video as New Clip to save both versions of the video.

To undo the trim after you save, open the video, tap Edit, then tap Revert.

Note: A video saved as a new clip can't be reverted to the original.

Change the slow-motion section of a video shot in Slo-mo mode

1. Open a video shot in Slo-mo mode, then tap Edit.
2. Drag the white vertical bars beneath the frame viewer to set where the video is played in slow motion.

Edit Cinematic mode videos on your iPhone

Turn off the Cinematic effect

1. In Photos, open a video you recorded in Cinematic mode, then tap Edit.
2. Tap Cinematic at the top of the screen, then tap Done.

Repeat these steps to turn Cinematic mode back on.

Change the focus subject in a Cinematic mode video

Camera automatically identifies where to focus while you record in Cinematic mode and can automatically change focus if a new subject is identified. You can also change the focus subject manually.

1. In Photos, open a video you recorded in Cinematic mode, then tap Edit.
   White dots under the frame viewer indicate where Camera automatically changed the focus while recording. Yellow dots indicate where the focus was manually changed.
2. Play the video, or slide the white vertical bar in the frame viewer, to the point where you want to change the focus.
3. Tap the new subject, outlined in yellow, on the screen to change the focus; double tap to set automatic focus tracking on the subject.
   A yellow dot appears under the frame viewer to indicate the focus was changed.
   Note: You can also touch and hold the screen to lock the focus at a specific distance from the camera.
4. Repeat the steps above to change focus points throughout the video.
   To remove a manual focus change, tap the yellow dot under the frame viewer, then tap 🗑.
5. Tap Done to save your changes.

Tap ⌞·⌝ to toggle between Camera's automatic focus tracking and your manually selected focus points.

After you save your changes, you can revert a Cinematic mode video to the original if you don't like your edits. Open the video, tap Edit, then tap Revert.

Adjust the depth of field in a Cinematic mode video

1. In Photos, open a video you recorded in Cinematic mode, then tap Edit.
2. Tap 🄵 at the top of the screen.
   A slider appears below the video.
3. Drag the slider left or right to adjust the depth of field effect, then tap Done.

To undo the change after you save, open the video, tap Edit, then tap Revert.

Export Cinematic mode videos to your Mac

306

You can use AirDrop to transfer Cinematic mode videos—with depth and focus metadata—from your iPhone to your Mac to edit in other apps.

1. In Photos, open the Cinematic mode video, then tap ⬆.
2. Tap Options at the top of the screen, turn on All Photos Data, then tap Done.
3. Tap AirDrop, then tap the device you want to share with (make sure the device you're sharing with has AirDrop turned on).

Edit Live Photos on iPhone

In the Photos app 🌸, you can edit Live Photos, change the key photo, and add fun effects like Bounce and Loop.

Edit a Live Photo

In addition to using the photo editing tools (like adding filters or cropping a photo) you can also change the key photo, trim the length, or mute the sound in your Live Photos.

1. Open the Live Photo and tap Edit.
2. Tap ◎, then do any of the following:
   - **Set a key photo**: Move the white frame on the frame viewer, tap Make Key Photo, then tap Done.
   - **Trim a Live Photo**: Drag either end of the frame viewer to choose the frames the Live Photo plays.
   - **Make a still photo**: Tap the Live button at the top of the screen to turn off the Live feature. The Live Photo becomes a still of its key photo.
   - **Mute a Live Photo**: Tap 🔊 at the top of the screen. Tap again to unmute.

Add effects to a Live Photo

You can add effects to Live Photos to turn them into fun videos.

1. Open the Live Photo.
2. Tap ◎ Live in the top-left corner, then choose one of the following:
   - **Live**: Applies the Live video playback feature.
   - **Loop**: Repeats the action in a continuous looping video.
   - **Bounce**: Rewinds the action backward and forward.
   - **Long Exposure**: Simulates a DSLR-like long exposure effect by blurring motion.
   - **Off**: Turns off the Live video playback feature or applied effect.

Edit Portrait mode photos on iPhone

In the Photos app 🌸, you can change and adjust the lighting effects of the photos you take in Portrait mode.

Edit Portrait Lighting effects in Portrait mode photos

On models that support Portrait Lighting, you can apply, change, or remove the Portrait Lighting effects in Portrait mode photos.

1. Tap any photo taken in Portrait mode to view it in full screen.

2. Tap Edit, touch ⬡ below the photo, then drag to choose a lighting effect.
   - **Natural Light**: The face is in sharp focus against a blurred background.
   - **Studio Light**: The face is brightly lit, and the photo has an overall clean look.
   - **Contour Light**: The face has dramatic shadows with highlights and lowlights.
   - **Stage Light**: The face is spotlit against a deep black background.
   - **Stage Light Mono**: The effect is like Stage Light, but the photo is in classic black and white.
   - **High-Key Light Mono**: Creates a grayscale subject on a white background.

3. Drag the slider left or right to adjust the intensity of the lighting effect.
4. Tap Done to save your changes.

To undo the Portrait Lighting effect after you save, tap Edit, then tap Revert to go back to the original lighting.

Note: To remove the Portrait effect from a photo, tap Portrait at the top of the screen.

Adjust Depth Control in Portrait mode photos

Use the Depth Control slider to adjust the level of background blur in your Portrait mode photos.

1. Tap any photo taken in Portrait mode to view it in full screen.

2. Tap Edit, then tap 𝑓 at the top of the screen.
   A slider appears below the photo.
3. Drag the slider left or right to adjust the background blur effect.
4. Tap Done to save your changes.

Use albums in Photos on iPhone

Use albums in the Photos app 🌸 to view and organize your photos and videos. Tap Albums to view your photos and videos organized into different categories and media types, like Videos, Portrait, and Slo-mo. You can also look at your photos arranged on a world map in the Places album, or browse your photos based on who's in them in the People album.

The Recents album shows your entire photo collection in the order that you added them to your library and the Favorites album shows photos and videos that you marked as favorites.

If you use iCloud Photos, albums are stored in iCloud. They're up to date and accessible on devices where you're signed in with the same Apple ID.

Create a new album

1. Tap Albums at the bottom of the screen.

2. Tap ➕, then choose New Album.
3. Name the album, then tap Save.
4. Tap the photos you want to add to the album, then tap Add.

Add a photo or video to an album

1. Open the photo or video in full screen, then tap ⊙.
2. Tap Add to Album, then do one of the following:
   - **Start a new album**: Tap New Album, then give the album a name.
   - **Add to an existing album**: Tap an existing album under My Albums.

Add multiple photos and videos to an album

1. When viewing multiple thumbnails, tap Select at the top of the screen.
2. Tap the photo and video thumbnails you want to add, then tap ⊙.
3. Tap Add to Album, then do one of the following:
   - **Start a new album**: Tap New Album, then give the album a name.
   - **Add to an existing album**: Tap an existing album under My Albums.

Remove photos and videos from an album

1. Open the album, then tap the photo or video you want to remove to view it in full screen.
2. Tap 🗑, then choose one of the following:
   - **Remove from Album**: The photo is removed from that album, but remains in other albums and your library.
   - **Delete from Library**: The photo is removed from all albums and your library and moves to the Recently Deleted album.

To remove multiple photos or videos from an album, tap Select, tap the photo and video thumbnails you want to remove, then tap 🗑.

Edit and organize albums on iPhone

You can rename, rearrange, and delete albums in the Photos app ✳. You can also create folders to contain multiple albums. For example, you could create a folder named "Vacations," and then create multiple albums within the folder of all your vacations. You can also create folders inside folders.

Rename, rearrange, and delete albums

1. Tap Albums, then tap See All.
2. Tap Edit, then do any of the following:
   - **Rename**: Tap the album name, then enter a new name.
   - **Rearrange**: Touch and hold the album's thumbnail, then drag it to a new location.
   - **Delete**: Tap ⊖.
3. Tap Done.

Albums that Photos creates for you, such as Recents, People, and Places, can't be deleted.

Organize albums in folders

1. Tap Albums, then tap +.
2. Choose New Folder.
3. Name the folder, then tap Save.
4. Open the folder, tap Edit, then tap + to create a new album or folder inside the folder.

309

Filter and sort photos and videos in albums on iPhone

You can filter and sort photos and videos in the albums you create in the Photos app ✳. For example, you can filter an album to show only videos, only photos, or photos and videos you marked as favorites. You can also sort photos and videos in an album by newest to oldest, oldest to newest, or in a custom order.

Filter photos and videos in an album

1. Open an album, then tap ⋯ .
2. Tap Filter, then choose how you want to filter the photos and videos in the album.
3. Tap Done.

To remove a filter from an album, tap ⊜ , tap All Items, then tap Done.

Sort photos and videos in an album

1. Open an album, then tap ⋯ .
2. Tap Sort, then choose how you want to sort the photos and videos in the album.

To move an individual photo, touch and hold the thumbnail, then drag it to a new location for a custom sort.

Duplicate and copy photos and videos on iPhone

In the Photos app ✳ on iPhone, you can duplicate a photo or video while preserving the original version. You can also copy a photo and then paste it into another document such as an email, text message, or presentation.

Duplicate a photo or video

1. Open a photo or video, then tap ⊙ .
2. Tap Duplicate.

A duplicate copy appears next to the original in your library.

Duplicate multiple photos or videos

1. Tap Library, then tap All Photos or Days.
2. Tap Select, then tap the thumbnails you want to duplicate.
3. Tap ⊙ , then tap Duplicate.

Copy a photo

1. Open a photo, then tap ⊙ .
2. Tap Copy, then paste the photo into another document.

Copy multiple photos or videos

1. Tap Library, then tap All Photos or Days.
2. Tap Select, then tap the thumbnails you want to copy.
3. Tap ⊙ , then tap Copy.

4. Paste the copies into another document.

Find and delete duplicate photos and videos on iPhone

The Photos app 🌸 identifies duplicate photos and videos in your photo library in the Duplicates album. You can merge duplicate photos and videos to save space and clean up your library.

1. Tap Albums, then tap Duplicates below Utilities.
   Duplicate photos and videos appear next to each other.
2. Tap Merge to combine the duplicates, then tap Merge [number] Items.
   Merging combines the highest quality version and all of the relevant data across the duplicates, and keeps that one in your library. The remaining duplicates are moved to the Recently Deleted album.

If you don't have any duplicate photos or videos in your library, the Duplicates album doesn't appear.

Search for photos on iPhone

When you tap Search in the Photos app 🌸 , you see suggestions for people, places, and photo categories to help you find what you're looking for, or rediscover a moment you forgot about. You can also type a keyword into the search field—for example, a person's name, date, or location—to help you find a specific photo.

Tap Search, then tap the search field at the top of the screen to search by any of the following:

- Date (month or year)
- Place (city or state)
- Business names (museums, for example)
- Category (beach or sunset, for example)
- Events (sports games or concerts, for example)
- A person identified in your People album
- Text (an email address or phone number, for example)
- Caption

Tip: Looking for something more specific? Refine your search with multiple keywords—simply keep adding keywords until you find the right photo. Search also suggests keywords to add to your search.

Find and identify people in Photos on iPhone

The Photos app 🌸 recognizes faces in your photos and sorts them in the People album. When you add names to the faces, you can search for photos by a person's name.

Name a person in a photo

When you identify a person in a photo, they're automatically added to your People album and identified in other photos in your library.

1. Open a photo of the person, then tap ⓘ or swipe up to see the photo details. People identified in the photo appear in the bottom-left corner of the photo. Unnamed people have a question mark next to their picture.
2. Tap the face of a person with a question mark next to their photo to identify them, then tap Tag with Name.
3. Type their name, tap Next, then tap Done.

Name a person in your People album

1. Tap the People album, then tap the face of the person whose name you want to add.
2. Tap Add Name at the top of the screen, then enter the person's name.
3. Tap Next.
   If a face is identified as two or more people in the People album, tap Select, tap each instance of the person, then tap Merge.
4. Tap Done.

Find photos of a specific person

To find photos of a specific person, do either of the following:

- Tap Albums, tap the People album, then tap the face of a person to see all of the photos they're in.
- Tap Search, then enter a person's name in the search field.

Set a person's key photo

1. Tap the People album, then tap the face of a person.
2. Tap Select, then tap Show Faces.
3. Choose the photo you want to set as the key photo.
4. Tap ⬆️, then tap Make Key Photo.

Favorite a person

Mark the people that you interact with the most as a favorite so that it's easier to find them.

1. Tap the People album.
2. Tap ♡ next to the person's photo.
   To favorite multiple people at once, tap Select, tap each person that you want to favorite, then tap Favorite at the bottom of the screen.

Fix misidentifications

1. Tap the People album, then tap the face of a person.
2. Tap Select, then tap Show Faces.
3. Tap the misidentified face.
4. Tap ⬆️, then tap Not This Person.

Sort people alphabetically or manually in the People album

1. Tap the People album.
2. Tap ⋯ , tap ⇅ then choose one of the following:
   ○ Sort people alphabetically: Tap Name.
   ○ Sort people manually: Tap Custom Order, then touch and hold the photo of person and drag it to a new position.

Feature a person in your People album less frequently

You can make photos of certain people less likely to appear in your memories and featured photos, and in the Photos widget.

1. Open the People album, then tap the face of the person you want to see less often.
2. Tap ⬤, then tap Feature [name] Less.
3. Choose Feature This Person Less or Never Feature This Person, then tap Confirm.

Remove a person from your People album

1. Tap the People album, then tap the face of the person you want to remove.
2. Tap ⬤, then tap Remove [name] from People.

When you use iCloud Photos, your People album is kept up to date on all your devices that meet these minimum system requirements: iOS 11, iPadOS 13, or macOS 10.13. (You must be signed in with the same Apple ID on all the devices.)

Browse photos by location on iPhone

The Photos app 🌸 creates collections of your photos and videos in the Places album based on where they were taken. View photos taken in a specific location, or look for photos taken nearby. See a collection of all your places on a map, or even watch a memory of a certain place.

Browse photos by location

1. Tap Albums, then tap the Places album.
2. Select Map or Grid view.
   Only pictures and videos that have embedded location information (GPS data) are included.

Tip: Pinch the map to zoom in and out, or drag to see more locations.

See where a photo was taken

1. Open a photo, then swipe up to see photo information.
2. Tap the map or address link to see more details.

Watch a location-based memory

1. Tap Albums, tap the Places album, then tap Grid.
2. Find a location with several images, then tap the location heading.
3. Tap ▶.

Share photos and videos on iPhone

You can share photos and videos from the Photos app 🌸 in Mail or Messages, or other apps you install. Photos even selects your best photos from an event and recommends people you may want to share them with.

Share photos and videos

- **Share a single photo or video**: Open the photo or video, tap ⬆️, then choose a share option.
- **Share multiple photos or videos**: When viewing a screen with multiple thumbnails, tap Select, then tap the thumbnail of the photos and videos you want to share. Tap ⬆️, then choose a share option.
- **Share photos or videos from a day or month**: Tap Library, tap Days or Months, tap ⚫⚫⚫, then tap Share Photos and choose a share option.

When iCloud Photos is turned on, you can share multiple full-quality photos with an iCloud link. iCloud links remain available for 30 days, can be viewed by anyone, and can be shared using any app, such as Messages or Mail.

You can also use Shared Albums to share photos and videos with just the people you choose.

Note: The size limit of attachments is determined by your service provider. For devices or services that don't support Live Photos, a Live Photo is shared as a still photo.

Share photos with Sharing Suggestions

Sharing Suggestions recommends a set of photos from an event that you may want to share and, based on the people in the photos, who you may want to share them with. The people you share with receive a message with a link to iCloud.com to view your photos. Your shared collection is active for 30 days, but you can stop sharing the collection at any time.

Photos identifies the people in your photos using the identifications you set up in the People album. If a person in the suggested photos isn't identified in your People album, you're prompted to create a contact for them before you can share the photos.

After you share your photos, the recipients are prompted to share their photos from the event with you. iCloud Photos must be turned on to see Sharing Suggestions, but the photos you share can be viewed by anyone.

1. Tap For You, then tap a photo collection below Sharing Suggestions.
   Tap Select if you want to remove any photos from the collection.
2. Tap Next, then tap Share in Messages.
   Photos suggests sharing the photos you took with the people who were also at the event. You can choose who to share with, as well as add others.
3. Tap ⬆️.

To remove a photo collection from Sharing Suggestions, tap the collection, tap ⚫⚫⚫, then tap Remove Sharing Suggestion.

To stop sharing a link you already sent, tap For You, then tap the collection below iCloud Links. Tap ⚫⚫⚫, then tap Stop Sharing.

Save or share a photo or video you receive

- **From email**: Tap to download the item if necessary, then tap ⬆️. Or, touch and hold the item, then choose a sharing or saving option.

- **From a text message**: Tap the photo or video in the conversation, tap ⬆️, then choose a sharing or saving option. You can also tap ⬇️ in the Messages conversation to save the photo or video directly to your Photos library.
- **From an iCloud link**: Tap ⬇️ in the Messages conversation to save the collection directly to your Photos library. To share the collection, open Photos, tap For You, then tap the collection under iCloud Links. Tap ●●●, then tap Share.

View photos and videos shared with you on iPhone

When someone shares photos and videos with you using the Messages app, you can easily find them in the Shared with You section in the Photos app ❋. (Automatic Sharing and Photos must be turned on in Settings ⚙ > Messages > Shared with You, and your friend must be in your contacts.)

1. Tap For You, then scroll down to Shared with You.
2. Do any of the following:
   o Tap a photo to view it in full screen, save it to your library, share it, or delete it.
   o Tap See All to view all photos shared with you.
   o Tap the name of the person who shared the photo, then reply to them using the Messages app.

You can also tap Library, then tap All Photos to see photos and videos shared with you in Messages. These photos and videos have a chat bubble in the bottom-left corner of the thumbnail. Tap the thumbnail to share the photo or video, save it to your library, or delete it. To hide photos and videos shared with you in Messages, tap ●●●, then tap Your Photos Only.

Note: Photos and videos you don't save from a Messages conversation are deleted in Shared with You and your library if the conversation in Messages is deleted.

To turn off Shared with You, go to Settings > Messages > Shared with You, then turn off Photos (green is on).

Interact with text and subjects in Photos on iPhone

When you view a photo in the Photos app ❋, you can interact with the text and subjects that appear within the photo. Use Live Text to share text, translate languages, convert currencies, and more. With Visual Look Up, you can identify and learn about popular landmarks, statues, art, plants, pets, and more. You can also lift the subject of a photo away from the background to copy and share it in other documents and apps.

These features are available on iPhone XS, iPhone XR, and later.

Use Live Text

1. Open a photo or pause a video that contains text.
2. Tap ⬚, then touch and hold the selected text.
3. Use the grab points to select specific text, then do any of the following:

315

- o **Copy Text**: Copy text to paste into another app such as Notes or Messages.
- o **Select All**: Select all the text within the frame.
- o **Look Up**: Show personalized web suggestions.
- o **Translate**: Translate text.
- o **Search the web**: Look up the selected text on the web.
- o **Share**: Share text using AirDrop, Messages, Mail, or other available options.
4. Depending on the content of the photo, you can also tap a quick action at the bottom of the screen to do things like make a phone call, visit a website, start an email, convert currencies, and more.
5. Tap ⌐⌐⌐ to return to the photo or video.

Live Text isn't available in all regions or languages.

Use Visual Look Up

Learn more about popular landmarks, art, statues, plants, pets, birds, insects, and spiders that appear in your photos.

1. Open a photo in full screen; ⓘ indicates Visual Look Up information is available for that photo.
2. Swipe up on the photo or tap ⓘ.
3. Tap the icon that appears on the photo or at the top of the photo information window to view Siri Knowledge and more information about the object.

Visual Look Up isn't available in all regions or languages.

Lift a subject from the photo background

You can lift the subject of a photo away from the background so you can copy and share it in other documents and apps.

1. Open a photo.
2. Touch and briefly hold the subject of the photo. When it's outlined, do one of the following:
   - o Tap Copy, then paste the subject into an email, text message, or note.
   - o Tap Share, then choose a sharing option, such as AirDrop, Messages, or Mail.

Watch memories in Photos on iPhone

The Memories feature in the Photos app 🌸 creates a personalized collection of photos and videos that are set to music and you watch like a movie. Each memory features a significant person, place, or event from your Photos library. You can also create your own memories and share them with your friends and family.

Play a memory

1. Open Photos, then tap For You.
2. Swipe left below Memories, or tap See All to browse through your memories.
3. Tap a memory to play it. As you watch, you can do any of the following:
   - o **Pause**: Touch and hold the screen, or tap the screen, then tap ❚❚ at the bottom of the screen.

- **Go backward or forward**: Swipe left or right on the screen, or tap the screen, then slide the frames at the bottom of the screen.
- **Restart a video**: Tap the left side of the screen while the video plays.

Create a memory

You can create your own memory from an event, a specific day in your library, or an album.

1. Tap Library, tap Days or Months, then tap ⚫. Or, tap Albums, open an album, then tap ⚫.

2. Tap Play Memory Video.

Share a memory

1. Tap For You, then play the memory you want to share.

2. While the memory plays, tap the screen, tap 📤, then choose how you want to share.

Share photos from a memory

You can share multiple or individual photos from a memory.

1. Tap a memory to play it.

2. While the memory plays, tap the screen, then tap ⚏.

3. Tap ⊙, tap Select, then tap the photos you want to share.

4. Tap 📤, then choose how you want to share.

Add a memory to Favorites

Tap For You, then tap ♡ in the top-right corner of the memory. Or, while a memory is playing, tap the screen, tap ⊙, then tap Add To Favorites.

To view your favorite memories, tap For You, tap See All next to Memories, then tap Favorites.

Personalize your memories in Photos on iPhone

In the Photos app 🏵, you can edit your memories to make them even more personal. Try out Memory mixes, which lets you apply different songs with a matching photographic look. You can also choose new songs, edit the title of a memory, change the length, and remove photos. Apple Music subscribers can add from the millions of songs available in the Apple Music library.

Add a Memory mix

Memory mixes are curated combinations of different songs, pacing, and styles that change the look and feel of a memory.

1. Tap For You, then tap a memory to play it.

2. Tap the screen, then tap 🎵.
3. Swipe left to view different Memory mixes.
4. Tap the screen to apply a Memory mix.

Change the Memory look

Use Memory looks to apply consistent color and style adjustments to all the photos in a memory.

1. Play a memory, then tap the screen.
2. Tap ✨🎵, then tap ⊛.
3. Tap a Memory look, then tap Done.

Change the memory's music

You can change a memory's music by choosing from memory soundtracks or Apple Music's suggested songs. Apple Music subscribers can also access their Apple Music library and view suggested songs based on musical preferences or the content of the memory.

1. Play a memory, then tap the screen.
2. Tap ✨🎵, then tap 🎵⊕.

    Apple Music subscribers can tap 🔍 to search for songs in the Apple Music library.
3. Tap a song, then tap Done.

Edit the memory title and subtitle

You can change or edit the title and subtitle of a memory.

1. Tap ⋯ in the top-right corner of the memory, then tap Change Title.
2. Enter the new title or subtitle in the text field, then tap Save.

Change the length of a memory

Depending on the number of photos in a memory, you can change the length of a memory to be short, medium, or long.

1. Play a memory, then tap the screen.
2. Tap ⋯, then tap Short, Medium, or Long.

Add or remove photos from a memory

1. Play a memory, then tap the screen.
2. Tap ⋯, then tap Manage Photos.
3. Tap photos without a checkmark to add them to the memory; tap photos with a checkmark to remove them from the memory.
4. Tap Done.

Delete a memory

1. Tap For You, then tap ⋯ in the top-right corner of the memory you want to delete.
2. Tap Delete Memory.

Feature certain content less frequently in memories

You can make certain people and photos less likely to appear in your memories and featured photos, and in the Photos widget.

1. Tap For You, then tap ⋯ in the top-right corner of the memory.
2. Tap Feature Less, then choose to feature fewer photos of a specific person, date, or place from that memory.

Manage memories and featured photos in Photos on iPhone

The Photos app ❋ can show certain people, places, days, and holidays less frequently or not at all in your memories and featured photos and in the Photos widget. You can also turn off memories and featured photos in the Photos app and widget on your iPhone Home Screen.

Show a person less frequently or not at all

1. Open a photo of the person you want to show less often.
2. Tap ⊙, then tap Feature This Person Less.
3. Choose Feature This Person Less or Never Feature This Person, then tap Confirm.

Note: You can also show a person less often if they appear in your People album.

Show certain content less frequently in memories

1. Tap ⬤ at the top of the memory.
2. Tap Feature Less, then depending on the memory, tap one of the following:
   o Feature a Person Less
   o Feature This Place Less
   o Feature This Holiday Less
   o Feature This Day Less
   o Feature These Days Less
3. If you choose Feature a Person Less, select the person you want to show fewer photos of, then tap Next. Choose Feature This Person Less or Never Feature This Person, then tap Confirm.

Tip: To turn off all memories that feature holiday events in your home country or region, go to Settings ⚙ > Photos, then turn off Show Holiday Events.

Note: If you choose to feature a person less often, but then want to see that person again, you need to reset your Memories settings. Go to Settings > Photos, tap Reset Suggested Memories, then tap Reset to confirm.

Turn off Memories and Featured Photos

You can turn off the Memories and Featured Photos features in the For You section of the Photos app and the Photos widget. Go to Settings ⚙ > Photos, then turn off Show Featured Content.

Use iCloud Photos on iPhone

You can use iCloud Photos to keep the photos and videos in your Photos app securely stored in iCloud, and in sync on your iPhone, iPad, iPod touch, Mac, Apple TV, and Windows computer. You can also access your iCloud photos and videos in a web browser. The photos and videos you take are uploaded automatically and stored in their original format at full resolution. Any changes you make to your Photos collection on one device are reflected on your other devices too.

To use iCloud Photos, make sure that you sign in with the same Apple ID on all devices and that your devices meet these minimum system requirements: iOS 8.3, iPadOS 13.1, macOS 10.10.3, or a PC with iCloud for Windows 7.x.

Turn on iCloud Photos

1. Tap Settings ⚙, then tap [your name].
2. Tap iCloud.
3. Tap Photos, then turn on Sync this iPhone.

Save space on your iPhone

iCloud Photos can help you make the most of the storage space on your iPhone. When Optimize iPhone Storage is turned on, all your full-resolution photos and videos are stored in iCloud in their original formats, with storage-saving versions kept on your iPhone as space is needed.

Optimize iPhone Storage is turned on by default. To turn it off, go to Settings ⚙ > [your name] > iCloud > Photos, then tap Optimize iPhone Storage.

Get more iCloud storage

If your uploaded photos and videos exceed your storage plan, you can upgrade to iCloud+ for more storage and additional features.

Use iCloud Shared Albums with iPhone

With Shared Albums in the Photos app 🌸, you can share photos and videos with just the people you choose. They can also add their own photos, videos, and comments. Shared Albums works with or without iCloud Photos and My Photo Stream.

Turn on Shared Albums

Go to Settings ⚙ > [your name] > iCloud > Photos, then turn on Shared Albums.

Create a new shared album

1. Tap Albums, tap ＋, then tap New Shared Album.
2. Give the album a name, then tap Next.
3. Choose people to invite, or type an email address or phone number, then tap Create.

Turn on public viewing in iCloud

1. Tap Albums, then select a shared album.
2. Tap 👥, then turn on Public Website.

When Public Website is on, anyone with the URL can view the album.

Add photos and videos to a shared album

1. Tap Albums, select a shared album, then tap ＋.
2. Select all the items you want to add, then tap Done.
3. Add a comment (optional), then tap Post.

Manage subscribers and notifications

Select the shared album, tap ⊘, then do any of the following:

- **Add subscribers**: Tap Invite People, then enter the names of the subscribers you want to add.
  Subscribers can add photos and videos to the album. Turn off the Subscribers Can Post button so only you can add photos and videos.
- **Remove subscribers**: Tap the name of the subscriber, then tap Remove Subscriber.
- **Turn notifications off**: Tap the Notifications button. Tap again to turn notifications on.

Delete photos, videos, and comments from a shared album

You must be the owner of the shared album to delete photos or videos.

- **Delete photos and videos**: In a shared album, tap Select. Select the photos or videos you want to delete, then tap 🗑.
- **Delete comments**: While viewing the comment in a shared photo, touch and hold, then tap Delete.

Rename a shared album

1. In Albums, scroll to Shared Albums, then tap See All.
2. Tap Edit, then tap the name of the album and enter a new one.

Subscribe to a shared album

When you receive an invitation, tap ☁, then tap Accept. You can also accept an invitation in an email.

Note: To use Shared Albums, your iPhone must be connected to the internet. Shared Albums works over both Wi-Fi and cellular networks. Cellular data charges may apply.

Import photos and videos on iPhone

You can import photos and videos directly to the Photos app 🌼 from a digital camera, an SD memory card, or another iPhone, iPad, or iPod touch that has a camera. Use the Lightning to USB Camera Adapter or the Lightning to SD Card Camera Reader (both sold separately).

1. Insert the camera adapter or card reader into the Lightning connector on iPhone.
2. Do one of the following:
   - **Connect a camera**: Use the USB cable that came with the camera to connect the camera to the camera adapter. Turn on the camera, then make sure it's in transfer mode. For more information, see the documentation that came with the camera.
   - **Insert an SD memory card into the card reader**: Don't force the card into the slot on the reader; it fits only one way.
   - **Connect an iPhone, iPad, or iPod touch**: Use the USB cable that came with the device to connect it to the camera adapter. Turn on and unlock the device.
3. Open Photos on your iPhone, then tap Import.
4. Select the photos and videos you want to import, then select your import destination.
   - **Import all items**: Tap Import All.
   - **Import just some items**: Tap the items you want to import (a checkmark appears for each), tap Import, then tap Import Selected.

321

5. After the photos and videos have been imported, keep or delete them on the camera, card, iPhone, iPad, or iPod touch.
6. Disconnect the camera adapter or card reader.

Print photos on iPhone to an AirPrint-enabled printer

Print your photos directly from the Photos app ✿ on your iPhone with any AirPrint-enabled device.

- **Print a single photo**: While viewing the photo, tap ⬆, then tap Print.
- **Print multiple photos**: While viewing photos, tap Select, select each photo you want to print, tap ⬆, then tap Print.

Podcasts

Find podcasts on iPhone

Use the Podcasts app 🎙 to find shows about science, news, politics, comedy, and more. If you find a show you like, you can follow it to add it to your library. Then you can easily listen offline, get notified about new episodes, and more.

Note: Shows may offer paid subscriptions that give you access to exclusive shows and episodes, new releases, episodes without ads, and more.

Find podcasts

- **Search by title, person, or topic**: Tap Search at the bottom right of the screen, then enter what you're looking for into the search bar on the top of the screen.
- **Discover new shows**: Tap Browse at the bottom of the screen to see New & Noteworthy, featured shows, and the Apple editorial collections. You can also tap Search to see Top Charts and browse by categories.
  Tip: When you listen to episodes, personalized recommendations appear on the Listen Now screen (below Up Next) to help you discover your next show.
- **Add shows by URL**: Tap Library, tap ⋯ then tap Add a Show by URL.
  Note: The URL must be in RSS format.

View shared podcasts

When a friend shares a show with you in Messages, you can easily find it in Shared with You in Podcasts. (Podcasts must be turned on in Settings ⚙ > Messages > Shared with You, and your friend must be in your contacts.)

To view shared Podcasts, tap Listen Now, then scroll to the Shared with You section.

Browse episodes within a specific podcast

1. Tap a podcast to see its information page.
2. Scroll to see recent episodes or tap See All (if available).

Listen to podcasts on iPhone

In the Podcasts app ⦿ , you can play an episode, listen to an episode when you're offline, set a sleep timer, and use the playback controls.

Play a podcast

- Tap an episode.
  To pick up where you left off in a show or resume playing a previous episode, tap Listen Now, then scroll to the bottom of the screen and tap an episode below Recently Played.

Tip: To jump to a specific time in the episode, drag the slider below the show's artwork.

Set a sleep timer

You can set a sleep timer so that playback stops automatically after a specified period of time.

1. Tap the player at the bottom of the screen to open the Now Playing screen.
2. Tap 🌙 in the lower right of the screen.

Use the playback controls

Open the Now Playing screen, then use any of the following controls.

Control	Description
▶	Play
❚❚	Pause
⟲15	Jump back 15 seconds To change the number of seconds you skip back, go to Settings > Podcasts, then tap Back.
⟳30	Jump forward 30 seconds To change the number of seconds you skip forward, go to Settings > Podcasts, then tap Forward.
1×	Choose a faster or slower playback speed
⦿	Stream the audio to other devices
•••	Choose more actions such as sharing or downloading the episode

	Set a timer for podcasts to stop playing

Follow your favorite podcasts on iPhone

When you find a show you like, follow it to add it to your library so you can get notified about new episodes, change the playback order, and more.

Follow a podcast

When you follow a podcast, it's added to your library.

1. Tap a show to see its information page.
2. Tap ⊕.
    Or you can touch and hold a show's artwork on the Browse tab, then tap Follow.

Unfollow a podcast

1. Tap a show to see its information page.
2. Tap ⋯ in the top-right corner of the screen, then tap Unfollow.

Get notifications for new episodes

Get notified when new episodes are available for podcasts you follow.

1. Tap Listen Now.
2. Tap 👤 or your profile picture.
3. Tap Notifications, then turn Notifications on or off.

Limit the number of downloads from each podcast

1. Tap Library to see podcasts you follow, then tap a show to see its information page.
2. Tap ⋯, then tap Settings.
3. Tap Limit Downloads, then select an option to limit downloads by number or time.

Organize your podcast library on iPhone

Use Library to customize the podcasts you follow, catch up on the latest episodes, and create your own stations.

*   **Shows**: Tap to see shows that are in your library. If you downloaded or saved individual episodes from podcasts you don't follow, tap All to see them. Tap Followed to view only shows you follow. You can tap any show to see the information page or the episodes in your library.
*   **Saved**: Episodes you marked as 🔖 appear in this tab.
*   **Downloaded**: Episodes you download appear here. You can listen to these episodes without an internet connection.
*   **Latest Episodes**: The most recent episodes from each show you follow are displayed here. To change how long episodes stay in this playlist, tap ⋯.

Filter episodes by unplayed, saved, downloaded, and season

1. Tap a show to see its information page.

2. Tap Episodes (or the current filter) above the list of episodes.
3. Choose an option, like Unplayed or Season 1.

Note: Some filter options, such as Unplayed, Downloaded, Saved, and Played, are only available for shows that you follow or shows with saved or downloaded episodes.

Create your own station

Group your shows into stations (similar to a music playlist) based on themes like news, comedy, or morning commute podcasts. Episodes from the podcasts you choose are automatically added to your station regularly.

1. Tap Library, then tap ••• in the top-right corner.
2. Tap New Station, then add a title.
3. Tap Choose Podcasts.

Tip: To adjust the number of episodes from each podcast that are added to your station, tap the station you want to change, tap Station Settings, then tap Episodes.

Change the episode playback order

1. Tap Library, then tap a show to see its information page.
2. Tap ••• , then tap Settings.
3. Choose an option, like Oldest to Newest.

Limit the number of downloads from each podcast

1. Tap Library to see podcasts you follow, then tap a show to see its information page.
2. Tap ••• , then tap Settings.
3. Tap Limit Downloads, then select an option to limit downloads by number or time.

Mark an episode as played

1. Tap Library, then tap a show.
2. Swipe right on an episode, then tap Played.

If you're already looking at a specific episode, tap ••• , then tap Mark as Played.

Hide episodes you've already played

1. Tap Library, then tap a show to see its information page.
2. Tap ••• , then tap Hide Played Episodes.

To automatically hide all episodes you've already played, go to Settings > Podcasts, then turn on Hide Played Episodes.

Download, save, and share podcast episodes on iPhone

In the Podcasts app ⓦ , you can download, save, and share podcast episodes.

Save and download an episode

Download an episode so you can play it when you're offline.

1. Tap Library, then tap a show to see its information page.

2. Swipe left on an episode, then tap ⊙ or ▣ .

When you save an episode, it's automatically downloaded so you can listen to it offline. To turn off this option, go to Settings > Podcasts, then turn off Download When Saving.

Remove a downloaded episode

1. Tap Library, then tap a show to see its information page.
2. Swipe left on an episode, then tap Remove Download or Unsave. If you're looking at a specific episode, tap ⚫.

Remove all downloaded episodes from a show

1. Tap Library.
2. Tap Shows, then tap a show to see its information page.
3. Tap ⚫, then tap Remove Downloads.

Tip: You can also remove all downloaded episodes from a show by going to Settings ⚙ > General > iPhone Storage > Podcasts, then tapping Edit.

Remove all downloaded episodes

1. Tap Library, then tap Downloaded.
2. Tap ⚫, then tap Remove All Downloads.

Share a podcast show or episode

1. Tap Library, then tap a show to see its information page. If you want to share a specific episode of that show, tap the episode.
2. Tap ⚫ in the top-right corner of the screen, then tap Share Show. To share a specific episode of a show, tap ⚫ next to the episode, then tap Share Episode.

Subscribe to a show or channel on iPhone

In the Podcasts app ⊙, subscribe to, change, cancel, and share your podcasts subscriptions. Paid subscriptions allow you to support the shows you love, and they often include premium extras, early access to new episodes, or ad-free listening.

Note: Not all subscriptions and channels are available in all countries, regions, or languages.

Subscribe to a show or channel

1. Select the show or channel you want to subscribe to.
   When you subscribe to a show, you automatically follow it.
2. Tap the subscription button (if available).

Change or cancel your subscriptions

1. Tap Listen Now.
2. Tap ⊙ or your profile picture, then tap Manage Subscriptions.
3. Tap a subscription to change or cancel it.

Share Apple Podcasts subscriptions

When you subscribe to podcasts channels, you can use Family Sharing to share your subscriptions with up to five other family members. Your family group members will automatically have access to the channels you subscribe to.

If you join a family group and a family group member subscribes to a show you already subscribe to, your subscription isn't renewed on your next billing date; instead, you use the group's subscription. If you join a family group that doesn't subscribe, the group uses your subscription.

Note: To stop sharing a show subscription with a family group, you can cancel the subscription or Leave a Family Sharing group.

Change your download settings for Podcasts on iPhone

Podcasts you follow are automatically downloaded to your Apple device. Episodes you've played are automatically deleted from your device. You can change those settings, and adjust other download options.

Turn automatic downloads on or off

1. Go to Settings 🔘 > Podcasts.
2. Turn Enable When Following (under Automatic Downloads) off or on.

Tip: To automatically download a particular podcast, open the Podcasts app 🔘, touch and hold the show's artwork on the Library screen, tap Settings, then turn on Automatic Downloads.

Remove downloaded podcasts after you listen to them

1. Go to Settings 🔘 > Podcasts.
2. Turn on Remove Played Downloads (under Episode Downloads).
   Or, to adjust this setting for a particular podcast you follow, touch and hold the show's artwork on the Library screen, tap Settings, then turn on Remove Played Downloads.

Limit how much cellular data is used when downloading podcasts

Go to Settings 🔘 > Podcasts, then choose any of the following:

- Block downloads over cellular data when downloading podcasts that you follow: Turn on Block Downloads Over Cellular.
- Ask to be notified when an episode will use cellular data to download: Tap Cellular Downloads, then choose an option.

Turn off automatic syncing across Apple devices

By default, your podcasts are kept up to date across all of your Apple devices. You can turn off this setting.

1. Go to Settings 🔘 > Podcasts.
2. Turn off Sync Podcasts.

Reminders

Set up Reminders accounts on iPhone

If you use the Reminders app ⋮☐ with different accounts (such as iCloud, Microsoft Exchange, Google, or Yahoo), you can manage all your to-do lists in one place. Your reminders stay up to date on all your devices that use the same accounts.

Add your reminders stored in iCloud

Go to Settings ⚙ > [your name] > iCloud > Show All, then turn on Reminders.

Your reminders stored in iCloud—and any changes you make to them—appear on your iPhone, iPad, Apple Watch, and Mac where you're signed in with the same Apple ID.

Upgrade your reminders stored in iCloud

1. Go to Settings ⚙ > [your name] > iCloud > Show All, then make sure Reminders is turned on.
2. Open the Reminders app.
3. On the Welcome to Reminders screen, choose one of the following options:
   o **Upgrade Now**: Begin the upgrade process.
   o **Upgrade Later**: A blue Upgrade button appears above your lists; tap it when you're ready to upgrade your reminders.

Note: Upgraded reminders aren't backward compatible with the Reminders app in earlier versions of iOS and macOS.

Add other Reminders accounts

You can use the Reminders app to manage your reminders from other accounts, such as Microsoft Exchange, Google, and Yahoo.

1. Go to Settings ⚙ > Reminders > Accounts > Add Account.
2. Do any of the following:
   o Choose an account provider, then sign in to your account.
   o If your account provider isn't listed, tap Other, tap Add CalDAV Account, then enter your server and account information.

Note: Some Reminders features described in this guide aren't available in accounts from other providers.

To stop using an account, go to Settings > Reminders > Accounts, tap the account, then turn off Reminders. Reminders from the account no longer appear on your iPhone.

Add items to a list in Reminders on iPhone

In the Reminders app ⋮☐ , you can easily make to-do lists for things like grocery shopping, tasks around the house, and projects at work. When you add an item to a list, you can attach images; set flags; get alerts based on time, date, and location; and more.

Note: All Reminders features described in this guide are available when you use upgraded reminders. Some features aren't available when using other accounts.

Start a new list

328

1. Tap Add List, then choose an account (if you have more than one). If you don't see Add List, tap Lists at the top left.
2. Enter a name, then choose a color and symbol for the list.

Add an item to a list

1. Choose a list, tap New Reminder, then enter text.
2. Tap Add Note, then enter any additional information.

Siri: Say something like: "Add artichokes to my groceries list."

Set when and where to be reminded

You can be reminded on a certain date, at a specific time or location, or when you're texting someone in Messages.

- Schedule a date and time: Tap ⚬📅.

- **Add a location**: Tap ◁, then choose where you want to be reminded—for example, when you arrive home or get into a car with a Bluetooth connection to your iPhone. **Note**: To receive location-based reminders, you must allow Reminders to use your precise location. Go to Settings ⚙ > Privacy & Security > Location Services. Turn on Location Services, tap Reminders, choose While Using the App, then turn on Precise Location.

- **Get a reminder in Messages**: Tap ⓘ, turn on When Messaging, then choose someone from your contacts list. The reminder appears the next time you chat with that person in Messages.

Set a flag and priority

- Flag an important item: Tap ⚑.

- **Set a priority**: Tap ⓘ, tap Priority, then choose Low, Medium, or High.

Add a photo or scan a document

1. Tap 📷.
2. Do any of the following:
   - Take a new photo.
   - Choose a photo from your photo library.
   - Scan a document.
   - Scan and insert text.

Edit the item details

Tap the item, then tap ⓘ.

Edit and manage a list in Reminders on iPhone

In the Reminders app ▤, you can easily edit and manage the items in a list.

Note: All Reminders features described in this guide are available when you use upgraded reminders. Some features aren't available when using other accounts.

Mark items as completed

Tap the empty circle next to an item to mark it as completed and hide it.

To unhide completed items, tap ⚬⚬⚬, then tap Show Completed. To delete the completed items, tap Clear.

Edit multiple items at the same time

1. While viewing a list, tap ⚬⚬⚬, tap Select Reminders, then select the items you want to edit. You can also drag two fingers over the items.
2. Use the buttons at the bottom of the screen to add a date and time, move, delete, assign, complete, tag, or flag the selected items.

Create a subtask

Swipe right on the item, then tap Indent. Or drag an item onto another item.

If you complete a main task, the subtasks are also completed. If you delete or move a main task, the subtasks are also deleted or moved.

Sort and reorder items in a list

- **Sort items by due date, creation date, priority, or title**: (not available in the All and Scheduled Smart Lists) In a list, tap ⚬⚬⚬, tap Sort By, then choose an option.

  To reverse the sort order, tap ⚬⚬⚬, tap Sort By, then choose a different option, such as Newest First.
- **Manually reorder items in a list**: Touch and hold an item you want to move, then drag it to a new location.
  The manual order is saved when you re-sort the list by due date, creation date, priority, or title. To revert to the last saved manual order, tap ⚬⚬⚬, tap Sort By, then tap Manual.

When you sort or reorder a list, the new order is applied to the list on your other devices where you're using upgraded reminders. If you sort or reorder a shared list, other participants also see the new order (if they use upgraded reminders).

Delete an item

Swipe left on the item, then tap Delete.

If you change your mind, you can recover the deleted item—tap with three fingers or shake to undo.

Search and organize lists in Reminders on iPhone

In the Reminders app ⠿ , you can arrange items in lists and groups. You can also easily search all your lists for items that contain specific text.

Note: All Reminders features described in this guide are available when you use upgraded reminders. Some features aren't available when using other accounts.

Search for items in all your lists

In the search field above the reminder lists, enter a word or phrase.

Create or edit lists and groups

You can organize your items into lists and groups of lists such as work, school, or shopping. Do any of the following:

- **Create a new list**: Tap Add List, choose an account (if you have more than one), enter a name, then choose a color and symbol for the list.

- **Create a group of lists**: Drag a list onto another list; or tap ⊙, tap Edit Lists, tap Add Group, enter a name, then tap Create.

- **Rearrange lists and groups**: Drag a list or group to a new location. You can even move a list to a different group.

- Change the name and appearance of a list or group: Swipe left on the list or group, then tap ⓘ.

Pin a list for easy access

To pin an important list above the other lists, touch and hold the list, then tap Pin. You can also swipe right on the list, then tap 📌.

You can have a maximum of nine pinned lists.

To change the position of a pinned list, tap ⊙, tap Edit Lists, then drag ☰ to a new position.

Delete a list or a group and their reminders

Swipe left on the list or group, then tap 🗑. When you delete a group, you have the option to keep the lists.

Work with templates in Reminders on iPhone

In the Reminders app ▦, you can save a list as a template to reuse it for routines, packing lists, and more. Create a link to publish and share a template with others, or download templates that others have shared.

Save a list as a template

1. When viewing a list, tap ⊙, then tap Save as Template.
2. Enter a name for the template.
3. Turn on or off Include Completed Reminders, then tap Save.

After you make a template from a list, any changes you make to that list don't affect the template.

Make a new list from a template

1. When viewing your lists, tap ⊙, tap Templates, then tap the name of a template.
2. Enter a name for the list, then tap Create.

Edit or delete a template

Any changes you make to a template don't affect lists previously created from the template.

1. When viewing your lists, tap ⊙, tap Templates, then tap ⓘ next to the template you want to manage.
2. Choose one of the following:
   o **Edit Template**: Add, edit, or delete any items in the template. You can also change the name, color, and icon for the template.
   o **Delete Template**: Remove the template.

Share a template

When you share a template, anyone with the link can download a copy of the template. You can choose whether to keep any dates, tags, or locations in the shared template; images are removed.

1. When viewing your lists, tap ⊙, tap Templates, then tap ⓘ next to the template you want to share.
2. Tap Share Template, then choose a method for sharing.

To manage a shared template, tap ⊙, tap Templates, tap ⓘ, then tap Manage Link.

If you make changes to the template after sharing, you can update the shared version.

Anyone who downloaded the previous version needs to download the template again to get the updates.

If you stop sharing a template, anyone who has already downloaded the template is affected.

Organize your reminders with tags on iPhone

In the Reminders app ⦂, you can use tags as a fast and flexible way to categorize and organize your reminders. You can add one or more tags to a reminder, such as #shopping and #work, and easily search and filter your reminders across lists using the Tag Browser or Smart Lists.

Note: All Reminders features described in this guide are available when you use upgraded reminders. Some features aren't available when using other accounts.

Add tags

When you create or edit an item in a list, type # followed by the tag name or choose a tag from the menu above the keyboard. A tag can be only one word, but you can use dashes and underscores to combine words. You can add multiple tags to an item.

View items with tags

Below Tags at the bottom of the screen, do any of the following:

- View all items with tags: Tap All Tags.
- View items with specific tags: Tap one or more tags, then choose to view notes matching any or all of the selected tags.

Tip: To save this list as a Smart List, tap ⊙, then tap Create Smart List.

Rename or delete a tag

Below Tags at the bottom of the screen, touch and hold a tag, then tap Rename Tag or Delete Tag.

When you delete a tag, it's also removed from all Smart Lists that use it.

Use Smart Lists in Reminders on iPhone

In the Reminders app , you can easily filter your items across lists using Smart Lists. You can create custom Smart Lists to automatically include items filtered by tags, dates, times, locations, flags, and priority. You can choose more than one tag (such as #gardening and #errands) and combine them with other filters.

Note: All Reminders features described in this guide are available when you use upgraded reminders. Some features aren't available when using other accounts.

Organize items automatically using the default Smart Lists

You can view the following default Smart Lists:

- **Today**: Items scheduled for today and overdue items
- **Scheduled**: Items scheduled by date or time
- **Flagged**: Items with a flag
- **Completed**: Items with a checkmark
- **Assigned to Me**: Items assigned to you in shared lists
- **Siri Suggestions**: Suggested items detected in Mail and Messages
- **All**: All items across all your lists

To show, hide, or rearrange the default Smart Lists, tap ⊙, then tap Edit Lists.

Make a custom Smart List

1. Tap Add List, enter a name, choose a color and icon, then tap Make into Smart List.
2. Choose one or more filters, then choose to include items matching any or all of the selected filters. You can filter by tags, dates, locations, and more.

Convert a list to a Smart List

When you convert a list, its items are moved to the top level of the default list and tagged with the name of the Smart List.

Note: You can't convert a shared list.

1. View the list you want to convert.
2. Tap ⊙, tap Show List Info, scroll to the bottom, then tap Convert to Smart List.

Add an item to a Smart List

Choose a list, tap New Reminder, then enter text.

The item inherits the attributes of the Smart List and gets saved to your default list.

Change your Reminders settings on iPhone

You can customize your preferences for the Reminders app ⠿ in Settings. Choose the default list for new items, set a time to see notifications for all-day reminders, and more.

From the Home Screen or App Library, go to Settings ⚙ > Reminders, then adjust any of the settings. For example:

- **Siri & Search**: Allow content in Reminders to appear in Siri Suggestions or search results.
- **Notifications**: Set how you receive notifications, choose the alert style, and have Siri announce notifications.
- **Accounts**: Manage your accounts and how often data is updated.
- **Default List**: Choose the list for new items you create outside of a specific list, such as items you create using Siri.
- **Today Notification**: Set a time to see notifications for all-day reminders that have been assigned a date without a time.
- **Show as Overdue**: The scheduled date turns red for overdue all-day reminders.
- **Include Due Today**: The badge count includes overdue items and items due today.
- **Mute Notifications**: Turn off notifications for assigned items.

Share lists and collaborate in Reminders on iPhone

In the Reminders app ⠿ , use iCloud to share to-do lists. You can collaborate and assign tasks to other people who also use iCloud.

Note: All Reminders features described in this guide are available when you use upgraded reminders. Some features aren't available when using other accounts.

Collaborate on a list using iCloud

You can share a list and collaborate with people who use iCloud. People who accept the invitation can add and edit items, mark items as completed, and all the collaborators can see everyone's changes. Everyone you collaborate with must be signed in with their Apple ID and have Reminders turned on in iCloud settings.

1. While viewing a list, tap ⬆.
2. To change the access and permissions, tap the share options below Collaboration. You can set either of the following:
   o Allow access to only people you invite.
   o Allow others to invite.
3. Choose how to send your invitation (for example, using Messages or Mail).

If you send the invitation in Messages, you get activity updates in the Messages conversation when someone makes changes in the shared note. Tap the updates to go to the shared note.

Assign items in a shared list

When you create or edit a reminder, you can assign it to any person on the list, including yourself. Do any of the following:

- Type @ followed by the person's name or choose a person from the menu above the keyboard.

- Tap ⊖, then choose a person.

Tip: To quickly see all items assigned to you, use the Assigned to Me Smart List.

Print reminders on iPhone

In the Reminders app ⬚ , you can print a list.

1. View the list you want to print.
2. Tap ⋯, then tap Print.

Safari

Browse the web using Safari on iPhone

In the Safari app ⬭ , you can browse the web, view websites, preview website links, translate webpages, and add the Safari app back to your Home Screen if it gets removed. Sign in to iCloud with the same Apple ID on multiple devices to keep your open tabs, bookmarks, history, and Reading List up to date across all your devices.

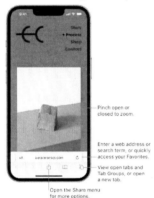

View websites with Safari

You can easily navigate a webpage with a few taps.

- **Get back to the top**: Double-tap the top edge of the screen to quickly return to the top of a long page.
- **See more of the page**: Turn iPhone to landscape orientation.
- **Refresh the page**: Pull down from the top of the page.
- **Share links**: At the bottom of the page, tap ⬆️.

Preview website links

Touch and hold a link in Safari to see a preview of the link without opening the page. To open the link, tap the preview, or choose Open.

To close the preview and stay on the current page, tap anywhere outside the preview.

Touch and hold a link to see the URL and these options.

Translate a webpage or image

When you view a webpage or image that's in another language, you can use Safari to translate the text (not available in all languages or regions).

Tap A A, then tap ⌨ (if translation is available).

Add Safari back to your Home Screen

If you don't see Safari on your Home Screen, you can find it in App Library and add it back.

1. On the Home Screen, swipe left to access App Library.
2. Enter "Safari" in the search field.
3. Press and hold , then tap Add to Home Screen.

Customize your Safari settings on iPhone

In the Safari app , you can change your Safari layout, customize your start page, change the text size on websites, and change display and privacy settings. Sign in to iCloud with the same Apple ID on multiple devices to keep the tabs you have open, your bookmarks, history, and Reading List up to date across all your devices.

Customize your start page

When you open a new tab, you begin on your start page. You can customize your start page with new background images and options.

1. Tap , then tap +.
2. Scroll to the bottom of the page, then tap Edit.
3. Choose options for your start page.
    ○ **Use Start Page on All Devices**: Keep your settings and preferences updated across all Apple devices where you're signed in with your Apple ID.
    ○ **Tab Group Favorites**: Quickly see and open tabs you've marked as favorites.
    ○ **Recently Closed Tabs**: Go back to tabs you previously closed.
    ○ **Favorites**: Display shortcuts to your favorite bookmarked websites.
    ○ **Siri Suggestions**: As you search, allow websites shared in Calendar and other apps to appear.
    ○ **Shared with You**: See links shared with you in Messages, Mail, and more.
    ○ **Frequently Visited**: Go straight to the websites you visit most.

- Privacy Report: Stay updated on how many trackers and websites Safari blocked from tracking you.
- Reading List: Show webpages currently in your Reading List.
- iCloud Tabs: Show open tabs from other Apple devices where you're signed in with the same Apple ID and Safari is turned on in iCloud settings or preferences.
- Background Image: Choose the image you want to appear in the background each time you open a new start page in this Tab Group.

Note: Your custom start page settings are updated on all your Apple devices where you have Use Start Page on All Devices turned on, and you're signed in with the same Apple ID using two-factor authentication.

Change text size

Use the Page Settings button to increase or decrease the text size.

1. Tap AA on the left side of the search field.
2. Tap the large A to increase the font size or the small A to decrease it.

Change display and privacy controls

You can switch to Reader, hide the search field, set privacy controls for a website, and more.

Tap AA, then do any of the following:

- View the webpage without ads or navigation menus: Tap Show Reader (if available).
- Hide the search field: Tap Hide Toolbar (tap the top of the screen to get it back).
- See what the webpage looks like on a desktop computer: Tap Request Desktop Website (if available).
- Set display and privacy controls for each time you visit this website: Tap Website Settings.

Change the layout in Safari on iPhone

In the Safari app , you can choose the layout that works best for you. Depending on the layout, the search field appears at the top (Single Tab layout) or bottom (Tab Bar layout) of the screen.

Go to Settings > Safari, then scroll down to Tabs. Select either Tab Bar or Single Tab.

Search for websites in Safari on iPhone

In the Safari app , enter a URL or a search term to find websites or specific information.

Search the web

1. Enter a search term, phrase, or URL in the search field.
2. Tap a search suggestion, or tap Go on the keyboard to search for exactly what you typed.

If you don't want to see suggested search terms, go to Settings ⚙ > Safari, then turn off Search Engine Suggestions.

Find websites you visited before

Safari search suggestions include your open tabs, bookmarks, and pages you recently visited. For example, if you search for "iPad," the search suggestions include your open tabs related to "iPad" and websites related to "iPad" that you bookmarked or recently visited.

Search within websites

To search within a website, enter the name of a website followed by a search term in the search field. For example, enter "wikipedia einstein" to search Wikipedia for "einstein."

To turn this feature on or off, go to Settings ⚙ > Safari > Quick Website Search.

Access your favorite websites when you search or create a new tab

Go to Settings ⚙ > Safari > Favorites, then select the folder with the favorites you want to see.

Search a webpage

You can find a specific word or phrase on a webpage.

1. Tap ⬆, then tap Find on Page.
2. Enter the word or phrase in the search field.
3. Tap ⌄ to jump to other mentions.

Choose a search engine

Go to Settings ⚙ > Safari > Search Engine.

Use Camera to search for what you see

You can use your Camera to scan text and search online.

Tip: You can use the same feature to look up text and images in your photos.

Use Tab Groups

Open and close tabs in Safari on iPhone

In the Safari app 🧭, use tabs to help you navigate between multiple open webpages.

Note: If you're using the Single Tab layout, the menus and other items may look different from what's described in this guide.

Open a link in a new tab

Touch and hold the link, then tap Open in New Tab.

To stay on the current tab whenever you open a link in a different tab, go to Settings ⚙ > Safari > Open Links, then tap In Background.

View a tab's history

You can see which webpages you previously visited in this tab. Touch and hold $<$ or $>$.

Close tabs

Tap ⬜, then tap ⊗ in the upper-right corner of a tab to close it.

Tip: To close all tabs in this Tab Group at the same time, touch and hold Done, then tap Close All Tabs.

Open a recently closed tab

Tap ⬜, touch and hold ✛, then choose from the list of recently closed tabs.

Organize your tabs with Tab Groups in Safari on iPhone

In the Safari app 🧭, you can create Tab Groups to keep tabs organized and make them easier to find again later.

Create a new Tab Group

1. Tap ⬜ to view your open tabs.
2. Touch and hold a tab, then choose Move to Tab Group.
3. Tap New Tab Group, then give it a name.

Tip: To move between your Tab Groups, tap ∨ in the bottom center of the screen.

Reorder tabs in a Tab Group

1. Tap ⬜ to view the open tabs in that Tab Group.
2. Touch and hold any tab.
3. In the menu that appears, tap Arrange Tabs By, then choose an option.
   Or, touch and hold the tab, then drag it where you want it.

Pin a tab at the top of a Tab Group

You can customize your Tab Groups with pinned tabs in each group. The pinned tab stays at the top of the Tab Group.

1. Tap ⬜ to view the open tabs in that Tab Group.
2. Touch and hold the tab you want to pin.
3. In the menu that appears, tap Pin Tab.

Move a tab to another Tab Group

1. Touch and hold ⬜, then tap Move to Tab Group.
2. Choose one of the Tab Groups you created previously, or create a new group.

View your Safari tabs from another Apple device on iPhone

In the Safari app 🧭, you can view the tabs that are open on your other Apple devices and keep tabs and Tab Groups updated across devices.

Note: You must be signed in to iCloud with the same Apple ID on all your devices to manage Safari tabs across your devices.

View tabs that are open on your other Apple devices

Tap ⬚, tap ＋, then scroll to see the tabs open on your other devices at the bottom of the start page.

To close a tab on another Apple device, touch and hold the link, then choose Close.

Note: To view tabs open on your other devices, you must have iCloud Tabs turned on for your start page.

Keep tabs and Tab Groups updated across your devices

Go to Settings ⚙ > [your name] > iCloud > Show All, then make sure Safari is turned on.

Note: To also see tabs open on your Mac, you must have Safari turned on in iCloud settings on your Mac, be signed in with the same Apple ID, and use two-factor authentication.

Share Tab Groups and collaborate in Safari on iPhone

In the Safari app 🧭 , you can share a Tab Group and collaborate with people who use iCloud. You can add and remove people from the Tab Group at any time, and even start a message conversation, phone call, or FaceTime call without leaving Safari. Collaborators can add and remove tabs from the Tab Group, and everyone sees updates in real time.

Everyone you collaborate with must be signed in with their Apple ID, have Safari turned on in iCloud settings, and have two-factor authentication turned on.

Share a Tab Group

1. Tap ⬚ to view the open tabs in that Tab Group.
2. Tap ⬆ at the top-right corner of the Tab Group.
3. Tap Messages, then choose the person or group you want to share it with.

You get activity updates in the Messages conversation when someone makes changes in the shared Tab Group. Tap the updates to go to the shared Tab Group.

Add and remove people from a shared Tab Group

1. Tap 👥 at the top-right corner.
2. Tap Manage Shared Tab Group, then do any of the following:
    o **Add someone**: Tap Share With More People, then invite them using Messages.
    o **Remove someone**: Tap a name, then tap Remove Access.
    o Stop Sharing with everyone: Tap Stop Sharing.

Start a Messages, audio, or video conversation from Safari

You can start a conversation—using Messages, FaceTime audio, or FaceTime video—with everyone that shares the Tab Group, without leaving Safari.

Tap 👥 , then tap message, audio, or video to start the conversation.

Bookmark a website in Safari on iPhone

In the Safari app 🧭 , you can bookmark a website, add a website to Favorites, or add a website icon to the Home Screen to easily revisit later.

Bookmark a favorite website

Touch and hold 📖, then tap Add Bookmark.

View and organize your bookmarks

1. Tap 📖.
2. Tap Edit, then do any of the following:
   - **Create a new folder**: Tap New Folder at the bottom left, enter a name, then tap Done.
   - **Move a bookmark into a folder**: Tap the bookmark, tap below Location, then tap a folder. Tap ‹ to return to your bookmarks.
   - Delete bookmarks: Tap ⊖ .
   - **Rename bookmarks**: Tap the bookmark, enter a new name, then tap Done.
   - **Reorder bookmarks**: Touch and hold ☰, then drag the bookmark to a new location.

See your Mac bookmarks on iPhone

1. Go to Settings ⚙ > [your name] > iCloud.
2. Tap Show All (below Apps Using iCloud), then make sure Safari is turned on.

Note: You must also have Safari turned on in iCloud settings on your Mac and be signed in with the same Apple ID.

Add a website icon to your Home Screen

You can add a website icon to your iPhone Home Screen for quick access.

On the website, tap 📤, scroll down the list of options, then tap Add to Home Screen.

The icon appears only on the device where you add it.

Save webpages to read later in Safari on iPhone

In the Safari app 🧭 , save interesting items in your Reading List so you can revisit them later. You can even save the items in your Reading List to iCloud and read them when you're not connected to the internet.

Add the current webpage to your Reading List

Tap 📤, then tap Add to Reading List.

Tip: To add a linked webpage without opening it, touch and hold the link, then tap Add to Reading List.

View your Reading List

1. Tap 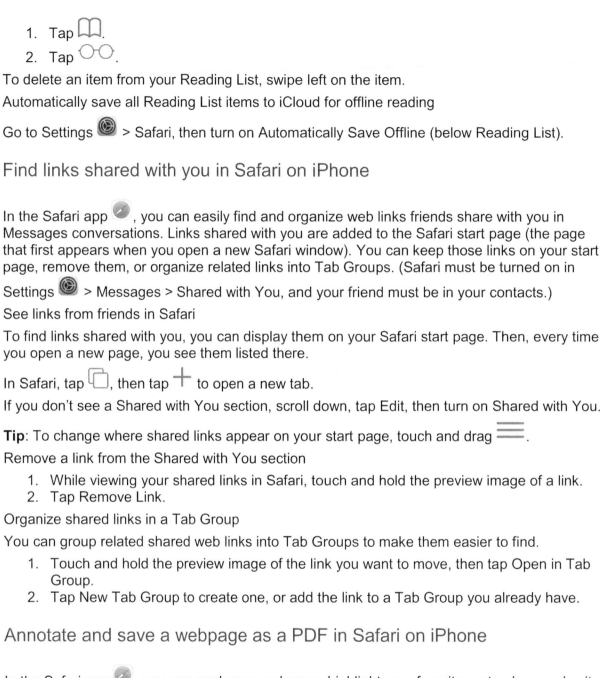.
2. Tap .

To delete an item from your Reading List, swipe left on the item.

Automatically save all Reading List items to iCloud for offline reading

Go to Settings > Safari, then turn on Automatically Save Offline (below Reading List).

Find links shared with you in Safari on iPhone

In the Safari app , you can easily find and organize web links friends share with you in Messages conversations. Links shared with you are added to the Safari start page (the page that first appears when you open a new Safari window). You can keep those links on your start page, remove them, or organize related links into Tab Groups. (Safari must be turned on in Settings > Messages > Shared with You, and your friend must be in your contacts.)

See links from friends in Safari

To find links shared with you, you can display them on your Safari start page. Then, every time you open a new page, you see them listed there.

In Safari, tap , then tap ┼ to open a new tab.

If you don't see a Shared with You section, scroll down, tap Edit, then turn on Shared with You.

Tip: To change where shared links appear on your start page, touch and drag .

Remove a link from the Shared with You section

1. While viewing your shared links in Safari, touch and hold the preview image of a link.
2. Tap Remove Link.

Organize shared links in a Tab Group

You can group related shared web links into Tab Groups to make them easier to find.

1. Touch and hold the preview image of the link you want to move, then tap Open in Tab Group.
2. Tap New Tab Group to create one, or add the link to a Tab Group you already have.

Annotate and save a webpage as a PDF in Safari on iPhone

In the Safari app , you can mark up a webpage, highlight your favorite parts, draw and write notes, and share your document as a PDF with others.

1. Tap .
2. Tap Markup , then use the tools to annotate the webpage.
3. Tap Done, then follow the onscreen instructions to save the page as a PDF.

Automatically fill in your information in Safari on iPhone

In the Safari app ![icon], use AutoFill to automatically fill in credit card information, contact information, and user names and passwords.

Set up AutoFill

You can save your personal information or credit card number on your iPhone to speed up filling in online forms and making purchases.

1. Go to Settings ![icon] > Safari > AutoFill.
2. Do any of the following:
   - **Set up contact info**: Turn on Use Contact Info, tap My Info, then choose your contact card. The contact information from that card is entered when you tap AutoFill on webpages in Safari.
   - **Set up credit card info**: Turn on Credit Cards, tap Saved Credit Cards, then tap Add Credit Card. Enter your credit card information into the fields provided or tap Use Camera to enter the information without typing.

You can also save the credit card information when you make an online purchase.

Fill in your contact information automatically

You can quickly add your personal information to online forms using AutoFill.

1. In a form on a website that supports AutoFill, tap a blank field.
2. Tap AutoFill Contact above the keyboard, then select a contact.
3. Tap any field to make changes.
4. When all the information is correct, tap Done.
5. Follow the onscreen instructions to submit the form.

Note: You can AutoFill another person's information from your contact list. For example, if you're purchasing a gift and shipping it to a friend, you can use AutoFill to enter their address. Tap AutoFill Contact, tap Other Contact, then choose their contact card.

Fill in your credit card information automatically

After you add a credit card, you can use AutoFill to make online purchases without having to enter your full credit card number.

1. Tap the credit card information field, then tap AutoFill Credit Card above the keyboard.
2. Tap the saved credit card you want to use, or tap Use Camera to take a picture of the front of the card.
   Tip: After you enter a new card in Safari, you can save it to Wallet.

For greater security of your credit card information, use a passcode for iPhone.

Automatically fill in strong passwords

When you sign up for services on websites and in apps, you can let iPhone create and save strong passwords for many of your accounts.

Turn off AutoFill

You can turn off AutoFill for your contact or credit card information, and for passwords. This is helpful in situations where you don't want your contact or credit card information to be readily available—for example if you share a device with others.

- Turn off AutoFill for your contact or credit card information: Go to Settings ⚙ > Safari > AutoFill, then turn off either option.
- Turn off AutoFill for passwords: Go to Settings > Passwords, unlock the screen, tap AutoFill Passwords, then turn off AutoFill Passwords.

Get extensions to customize Safari on iPhone

In the Safari app 🧭, you can install extensions to customize the way your browser works. For example, extensions can help you find coupons when shopping, block content on websites, give you access to features from other apps, and more.

View and add Safari extensions

1. Go to Settings ⚙ > Safari, then tap Extensions.
2. Tap More Extensions to browse through extensions in the App Store.
3. When you find one you want, tap the price, or if the app is free, tap Get, then follow the onscreen instructions.

Manage your extensions

Tap AA on the left side of the search field, then tap Manage Extensions. Select or deselect each extension to turn that extension on or off.

Use extensions

Extensions access the content of the websites you visit. You can change how much access you give each extension:

1. Tap AA on the left side of the search field, then tap the extension you want to give permissions to.
2. Choose how much access to give each extension.
   Important: Check which extensions you have installed and make sure you're familiar with what they do.

Remove an extension

1. Swipe down on the Home Screen, then search for the extension you want to remove.
2. Touch and hold the extension icon, tap Delete app, then follow the onscreen instructions.

Hide ads and distractions in Safari on iPhone

In the Safari app 🧭, use Reader to hide ads, navigation menus, or other distracting items.

Show Reader

Reader formats a webpage to show just the relevant text and images.

Tap AA, then tap Show Reader.

To return to the full page, tap AA, then tap Hide Reader.

Note: If Show Reader is dimmed, Reader isn't available for that page.

Automatically use Reader for a website

1. On a supported website, tap A A, then tap Website Settings.
2. Turn on Use Reader Automatically.

Note: To automatically use Reader for all websites that support it, go to Settings ⚙ > Safari > Reader.

Block pop-ups

Go to Settings ⚙ > Safari, then turn on Block Pop-ups.

Privacy and Security

Browse privately in Safari on iPhone

You can view the Privacy Report and adjust settings in the Safari app 🧭 to keep your browsing activities private, and help protect yourself from malicious websites.

Visit sites privately

You can use Private Browsing Mode to open private tabs, which don't appear in History on iPhone or in the list of tabs on your other devices.

1. Tap ⧉.
2. Tap ⌄ in the center of the tab bar at the bottom of the screen, then tap Private.
   Tabs in the Private Tab Group aren't shared with your other Apple devices, even if you're signed in with the same Apple ID.

You can easily confirm that you're in Private Browsing Mode by checking that the search field bar is gray or displays the word Private.

To hide the sites and exit Private Browsing Mode, tap ⧉, then tap ⌄ to open a different Tab Group from the menu at the bottom of your screen. The private sites reappear the next time you use Private Browsing Mode.

To close private tabs, tap ⧉, then swipe left on each of the tabs you want to close.

View the Privacy Report

Safari helps prevent trackers from following you across websites and viewing your IP address. You can review the Privacy Report to see a summary of trackers that have been encountered and prevented by Intelligent Tracking Prevention on the current webpage you're visiting. You can also review and adjust Safari settings to keep your browsing activities private from others who use the same device, and help protect yourself from malicious websites.

To view the Privacy Report, tap A A, then tap Privacy Report 🛡.

Use iCloud Private Relay to browse the web with more privacy

When you subscribe to iCloud+, you can use iCloud Private Relay (beta) to help prevent websites and network providers from creating a detailed profile about you. When iCloud Private Relay is turned on, the traffic leaving your iPhone is encrypted and sent through two separate internet relays. This prevents websites from seeing your IP address and exact location while it prevents network providers from collecting your browsing activity in Safari.

Control privacy and security settings for Safari

Go to Settings ⚙ > Safari, then below Privacy & Security, turn any of the following on or off:

- **Prevent Cross-Site Tracking**: Safari limits third-party cookies and data by default. Turn this option off to allow cross-site tracking.
- **Hide IP address**: Safari automatically protects your IP address from known trackers. For eligible iCloud+ subscribers, your IP address is protected from trackers and websites as you browse in Safari. If this option is off, your IP address isn't hidden.
- **Block All Cookies**: Turn this option on to prevent websites from adding cookies to your iPhone. (To remove cookies already on iPhone, go to Settings > Safari > Clear History and Website Data.)
- **Fraudulent Website Warning**: Safari displays a warning if you're visiting a suspected phishing website. Turn this option off if you don't want to be warned of fraudulent websites.
- **Privacy Preserving Ad Measurement**: This prevents websites from viewing your personal information to serve you targeted ads.
- **Check for Apple Pay**: Websites that use Apple Pay can check to see if you have Apple Pay enabled on your device. Turn this option off to prevent websites from checking if you have Apple Pay.

When you visit a website using Safari that isn't secure, a warning appears in the Safari search field.

Clear your cache in Safari on iPhone

In the Safari app 🧭, you can erase your browsing history and data to clear the cache on your iPhone. This removes the history of websites you visited and recent searches from your device. This process also removes the cookies and permissions you granted to websites to use your location or send you notifications.

Note: Clearing your browsing history in Safari doesn't clear any browsing histories kept independently by websites you visited.

1. Tap 📖, then tap 🕐.
2. Tap Clear in the bottom-right corner, then choose how much of your browsing history to clear.

Use passkeys in Safari on iPhone

In the Safari app 🧭, you can use Face ID to securely sign in to supporting websites.

Use Hide My Email in Safari on iPhone

When you subscribe to iCloud+, you can use Hide My Email to keep your personal email address private. With Hide My Email, you can generate unique, random email addresses that forward to your personal email account, so you don't have to share your real email address when filling out forms on the web or signing up for newsletters.

1. When you're asked for your email address on a website, tap the email field.
2. Tap Hide My Email above the keyboard.
   The Hide My Email screen suggests a new, randomly generated Hide My Email address.
3. If you don't want to use the suggested address, tap ↻ to get a new randomly generated email address.
4. To use the suggested address, tap Continue.

Shortcuts

Use Shortcuts to automate tasks on iPhone

The Shortcuts app ▨ lets you automate tasks you do often with just a tap or by asking Siri. Create shortcuts to get directions to the next event in your Calendar, move text from one app to another, and more. Choose ready-made shortcuts from the Gallery or build your own using different apps to run multiple steps in a task.

Stocks

Check stocks on iPhone

Use the Stocks app ▨ to track market activity and view the performance of stocks you follow.

Siri: Say something like: "How are the markets doing?" or "How's Apple stock today?"

Check stocks

1. Open the Stocks app, then tap a ticker symbol in the My Symbols watchlist for more details.
2. To search for a specific stock, enter a ticker symbol, company name, fund name, or index in the search field at the top of the screen, then tap the symbol in the search results.

Manage symbols in the My Symbols watchlist

When you first open the Stocks app, a list of ticker symbols appears on the screen; this is called the My Symbols watchlist. You can update and manage the My Symbols watchlist and create your own watchlists.

Tap a symbol to view its most recent price, daily percentage change, market capitalization value, and more.

To make changes to the My Symbols watchlist, do any of the following:

- **Add a symbol**: In the search field. enter a ticker symbol, company name, fund name, or index. In the search results, tap ⊕, then tap Done.
- **Delete a symbol**: Swipe left on the symbol in your watchlist.
  Note: If you delete a symbol from the My Symbols watchlist, that symbol is also deleted from your other watchlists.
- **Reorder symbols**: Touch and hold a symbol in your watchlist, then drag it to a new position.
- **Show currency**: Tap ⊙, then tap Show Currency to display the currency the stock is traded in.
- **Share a symbol**: Swipe left on a symbol in your watchlist, tap ⬆, then choose a sharing option, such as Messages or Mail.

View charts, details, and news

You can view interactive charts, performance details, and related news stories about the ticker symbols in your watchlist and the symbols you search for.

Tip: Touch and hold a ticker symbol in your watchlist to see a quick view of the stock's performance.

1. Tap a symbol you want to see more details about, then do any of the following:
   - **View the performance over time**: Tap an option from the time range selections at the top of the chart.
   - **View the value for a specific date or time**: Touch and hold the chart with one finger.
   - **View the difference in value over time**: Touch and hold the chart with two fingers.
   - **View more details**: Swipe the data below the chart to see additional details like 52-week high and low, Beta, EPS, and average trading volume.
   - Read news: Swipe up to see additional news stories, then tap a story.
2. To return to your watchlist, tap ⊗.

Manage multiple watchlists in Stocks on iPhone

You can create your own watchlists in the Stocks app 📈 to organize the stocks you follow according to categories such as tech, energy, or entertainment. Switch between watchlists; edit, update, and delete them; and view them in the Stocks app on your other devices. Any symbols you add to a custom watchlist are also added to the My Symbols watchlist.

Create a new watchlist

1. Tap My Symbols, then tap New Watchlist.
2. Name the watchlist, then tap Save.

To switch between your watchlists, tap My Symbols or the name of the current watchlist you're viewing, then tap the name of the watchlist you want to see.

Add symbols to a watchlist

1. In the search field, enter the name of a ticker symbol, company, fund, or index.

2. Tap $+$, then tap Done.

   Tip: You can easily add a symbol that's in one watchlist to another watchlist. Swipe left on the symbol, tap ⋮☰, select a watchlist, then tap Done.

Each symbol you add to a new watchlist is also added to the My Symbols watchlist.

Remove symbols from a watchlist

To remove a symbol from a watchlist, swipe left on the symbol.

When you remove a symbol from a watchlist that you created, that symbol remains in the My Symbols watchlist.

Delete, reorder, and rename watchlists

Tap the name of the watchlist at the top of the screen, tap Manage Watchlists, then do any of the following:

- **Delete a watchlist**: Tap ⊖ next to the symbol, tap 🗑, then tap Delete.

- **Reorder your watchlists**: Touch and hold ☰, then drag the watchlist to a new position.

- **Rename a watchlist**: Tap ✎, type a new name, then tap Save.

View your watchlists across devices

You can view your watchlists on your iPhone, iPad, iPod touch, and Mac when you're signed in with the same Apple ID.

- **On your iPhone, iPad, and iPod touch**: Go to Settings ⚙ > [your name] > iCloud > Show All, then turn on Stocks.

- **On a Mac with macOS 10.15 or later**: Choose Apple menu > System Preferences > Apple ID, select iCloud, then turn on Stocks.

- **On a Mac with macOS 10.14 or earlier**: Choose Apple menu > System Preferences > iCloud, then turn on Stocks.

Read business news in Stocks on iPhone

In the Stocks app 📈, you can read business stories and listen to audio stories that highlight the current news driving the market. In countries where Apple News is available, you also see stories selected by the Apple News editors and stories from Apple News+. (Apple News and Apple News+ content isn't available in all countries or regions.)

Read a story

1. Open Stocks, then swipe up on Business News or Top Stories to view stories. Stories about companies in your watchlist are grouped by ticker symbol.

2. Tap a story to read it. While viewing a story, you have these options:

   o **Return to your newsfeed in Stocks**: Tap ‹ or Done in the top-left corner.
   o See more stories from the publication in Apple News: Tap the publisher logo at the top of the screen.

- Save the story to Apple News: Tap ⬜ in the top-left corner.
  Note: In order to save stories to Apple News, make sure you're signed in with your Apple ID, then go to Settings ⚙ > [your name] > iCloud > Show All, and turn on News.
- Change the text size: Tap AA in the top-right corner, then tap the smaller or larger letter to change the text size in the story.
- Share the story: Tap ⬤ in the top-right corner, tap Share Story, then choose a sharing option, such as Messages or Mail.

Note: If you tap an Apple News+ story and you're not an Apple News+ subscriber, tap the subscribe or free trial button, then follow the onscreen instructions.

Stories from publications you have blocked in Apple News don't appear in the newsfeed.

Listen to audio stories

Some news stories include an audio version that you can listen to in the Stocks app or listen to later in the News app (not available in all countries or regions).

1. To listen to the audio version of a story, tap Play Now. Or, tap the story to read it, then tap Play Now at the top of the story.
2. Use the mini player at the bottom of the screen to pause the story or jump back 15 seconds. To open the full-screen player, tap the mini player.
3. To return to the mini player, swipe down to minimize the full-screen player.
4. To close the mini player, touch and hold the player, then tap Close Audio Player.

Add an audio story from Stocks to your News queue

If you subscribe to Apple News+, you can add an audio story from Stocks to your Up Next queue in News.

1. Make sure you're signed in with your Apple ID, then go to Settings ⚙ > [your name] > iCloud > Show All, and turn on News.
2. Do either of the following:
   - Add from a Stocks newsfeed: Touch and hold the story, tap Play Later in News, then choose Play Next or Play Last.
   - Add from the story: Open the story, then touch and hold Play Now at the top of the story. Tap Play Later in News, then choose Play Next or Play Last.

Add earnings reports to your calendar in Stocks on iPhone

In the Stocks app 📈, you can see when a company has an upcoming earnings report and add it as an event in the Calendar app.

Add an earnings report event to your calendar

If a stock has an upcoming earnings report, you can add it in the Calendar app and be reminded on the day that it's happening.

1. Tap a ticker symbol in your watchlist, or use the search field to search for a symbol.
2. If an earnings report is upcoming, tap Add to Calendar, then tap Add.

The earnings report is saved as an all-day event in the Calendar app. Calendar sends you an event reminder on the day of the earnings report.

Delete an earnings report event from your calendar

1. Open the Stocks app, then tap the ticker symbol in your watchlist or use the search field to search for the symbol.
2. Tap Edit, then tap Delete Event.

Add a Stocks widget to your iPhone Home Screen

Use a Stocks widget to check stocks at a glance on your iPhone Home Screen. You can choose the size of the Stocks widget and the amount of information the widget displays—choose one of the options to monitor several symbols, or the option to monitor the performance of a single symbol.

Change the widget display

After you add a Stocks widget to your Home Screen, you can change the symbol or watchlist that appears in the widget.

1. Touch and hold the widget.
2. Tap Edit Widget.
3. Depending on the widget option, select the symbol, watchlist, or watchlist details you want to display.

You can add multiple Stocks widgets to your iPhone Home Screen.

Tips

Get tips on iPhone

In the Tips app , see collections of tips that help you get the most from iPhone.

Get Tips

In the Tips app, you can learn how to personalize your Lock Screen, add widgets, unsend an email, take a screenshot, and much more. New tips are added frequently.

To start learning, tap a collection, then tap a tip.

Get notified when new tips arrive

1. Go to Settings > Notifications.
2. Tap Tips below Notification Style, then turn on Allow Notifications.
3. Choose options for the location and style of tip notifications, when they should appear, and more.

Translate

Translate text, voice, and conversations on iPhone

In the Translate app 📱, you can translate text, voice, and conversations between any of the supported languages. You can download languages to translate entirely on a device, even without an internet connection.

Note: Translation is available for supported languages.

Translate text or your voice

1. Tap Translation, select the languages to translate between, then do any of the following:
    - Tap "Enter text," type a phrase, then tap Go.
    - Tap 🎤 , then say a phrase.
2. When the translation is shown, do any of the following:
    - Play the audio translation: Tap ▶ .
    - Save the translation as a favorite: Tap ☆ .
    - Look up a word in the dictionary: Tap ⬜, then tap a word to see its definition.
    - Show the translation to someone else: Tap ↖↘ .

Tip: To view your recent history, swipe the translation down.

Translate a conversation

iPhone shows the translated text bubbles from both sides of the conversation. Conversations work for downloaded languages when you don't have an internet connection or On-Device Mode is turned on.

1. Tap Conversation.
2. Tap 🎤 , then speak in one of the two languages.

Tip: You can translate a conversation without tapping the microphone button before each person speaks. Tap ⋯ , tap Auto Translate, then tap 🎤 to start the conversation. iPhone automatically detects when you start speaking and when you stop.

When chatting face-to-face, tap ⬜, then tap Face to Face so that each person can see the conversation from their own side.

Download languages for offline translation or On-Device Mode

Download languages to translate when you don't have an internet connection or when On-Device Mode is turned on.

1. Go to Settings ⚙ > Translate.
2. Tap Downloaded Languages, then tap ⬇ next to the languages you want to download.
3. Turn On-Device Mode on.

Choose the languages you want to translate between

In the Translate app 🗨, you can choose which languages you want to translate and switch translations.

1. Tap the arrows ⌄ next to the two languages to choose the languages you want to translate between.
2. Tap one of the languages to indicate the input language.

   A blue dot ● appears next to the language that you want to translate.

To switch the input language, tap the other language.

Translate text in apps on iPhone

On iPhone, you can translate text in apps such as Photos, Safari, Messages, Mail, supported third-party apps, and more.

Note: Translation is available for supported languages.

Translate text in apps

You can select any text to translate in apps such as Safari, Messages, Mail, supported third-party apps, and more. When you enter text on your iPhone, you can even replace what you wrote with a translation.

1. Select the text you want to translate, then tap Translate.

   If you don't see Translate, tap ❯ to see more options.
2. Below the text translation, choose any of the following:
   o **Replace with Translation**: Replace your original text with the translation (available only when entering text).
   o **Copy Translation**: Copy and paste the translation somewhere else, such as a different app.
   o **Change Language**: Choose any of the supported languages for the original text and the translation.
   o **Add to Favorites**: Add the translation to a list of favorites.
   o **Open in Translate**: Do more with the translation in the Translate app.
   o **Listen to Original Text**: Tap more, then tap ▶ to listen to the original text.

- ○ **Listen to Translated Text**: Tap ▶ to listen to the translated text.

Translate text in photos

When you view a photo that includes text, tap ⬚, touch and hold the text you want to translate, then tap Translate.

If you don't see Translate, tap ❯ to see more options.

Translate text with the iPhone camera

On iPhone, you can use the iPhone camera to translate text around you—like a restaurant menu or a recipe.

Note: Translation is available for supported languages.

You can translate text using the iPhone camera.

1. Open the Camera app 📷, then position iPhone so that the text appears on the screen.
2. When the yellow frame appears around detected text, tap ⬚.
3. Select the text to translate, then tap Translate.

    If you don't see Translate, tap ❯ to see more options.
4. Below the text translation, choose any of the following:
    - ○ **Copy Translation**: You can paste the translation somewhere else, such as a different app.
    - ○ **Change Language**: Choose any of the supported languages for the original text and the translation.
    - ○ **Add to Favorites**: Add the translation to a list of favorites.
    - ○ **Open in Translate**: Do more with the translation in the Translate app.
    - ○ **Listen to Original Text**: Tap more, then tap ▶ to listen to the original text.
    - ○ **Listen to Translated Text**: Tap ▶ to listen to the translated text.

Translate text with the camera view in Translate on iPhone

In the Translate app 🅰, you can use the camera view to translate text around you. You can also translate text in the photos from your photo library, right from Translate.

Translate text using the camera view

1. Tap Camera.
2. At the top of the screen, select the languages you want to translate between.
3. Position iPhone so that the text you want to translate appears in the camera view.
4. Tap ○ to pause the view and see the translations.
    You can zoom in to get a closer look at the overlaid translations.
5. Tap an overlaid translation to show the translation card, then choose any of the following:

- ○ **Copy Translation**: You can paste the translation somewhere else, such as a different app.
- ○ **Add to Favorites**: Add the translation to a list of favorites.
- ○ **Listen to Original Text**: Tap more, then tap ▶ to listen to the original text.
- ○ **Listen to Translated Text**: Tap ▶ to listen to the translated text.

Translate text in photos from your photo library

1. Tap Camera.
2. At the top of the screen, select the languages you want to translate between.
3. Tap 🖼, then select a photo that contains text from your photo library.

Share and save translated text

After translating text with the camera view, tap ⬆, then do any of the following:

- **Share the translation**: Choose a share option.
- Save the translation as an image: Tap Save Image.

TV

Connect apps and add your TV provider to the Apple TV app on iPhone

With the Apple TV app 📺, you can watch shows and movies from streaming services and cable and satellite providers. The Apple TV app is on your iPhone, iPad, Mac, Apple TV, and supported smart TVs and streaming devices, so you can watch at home or wherever you go.

Note: The availability of the Apple TV app and its features and services (such as Apple TV+, Apple TV channels, sports, and supported apps) varies by country or region.

Connect video streaming apps

The Apple TV app recommends new content or the next episode in a series you watch from a connected app (supported streaming apps only). Connected apps appear in the Apple TV app on all your devices where you're signed in with your Apple ID.

To connect or disconnect supported streaming apps, do the following:

1. Tap Watch Now, then tap 👤 or your profile picture at the top right.
2. Tap Connected Apps.

Add your cable or satellite service to the Apple TV app

Single sign-on provides immediate access to all the supported video apps in your subscription package.

1. Go to Settings ⚙ > TV Provider.
2. Choose your TV provider, then sign in with your provider credentials.

If your TV provider isn't listed, sign in directly from the app you want to use.

Subscribe to Apple TV+ and Apple TV channels on iPhone

In the Apple TV app 📺, you can subscribe to Apple TV+ and Apple TV channels. Apple TV+ is a subscription streaming service featuring Apple Originals—award-winning series, compelling dramas, groundbreaking documentaries, kids' entertainment, comedies, and more—with new items added every month. Apple TV channels let you easily subscribe to just the channels you watch—like Paramount+, Showtime, and more.

A subscription gives you access to content on demand on iPhone, iPad, Mac, Apple TV, and supported smart TVs and streaming devices. You can also download content to watch offline on iPhone, iPad, and Mac.

You can choose to bundle your Apple TV+ subscription with other Apple services by subscribing to Apple One. S

Note: Apple One, Apple TV+, and Apple TV channels aren't available in all countries or regions.

Subscribe to Apple TV+

1. Tap Originals, then tap the subscription button.
2. Review the free trial (if eligible) and subscription details, then follow the onscreen instructions.

Subscribe to Apple TV channels

You can subscribe to premium channels such as Paramount+ and Showtime, all in one place. If you use Family Sharing, up to five other family members can share the subscription for no additional charge.

1. Tap Watch Now, scroll down to the Channels row, then tap a channel.
2. Tap the subscription button, review the free trial (if eligible) and subscription details, then follow the onscreen instructions.

Change or cancel your subscriptions to Apple TV+ or Apple TV channels

1. Tap Watch Now, then tap 👤 or your profile picture at the top right.
2. Tap Manage Subscriptions.

Share Apple TV+ and Apple TV channels with family members

When you subscribe to Apple One, Apple TV+, or Apple TV channels, you can use Family Sharing to share your subscriptions with up to five other family members. Your family group members don't need to do anything—a shared subscription is available to them the first time they open the Apple TV app after your subscription begins.

If you join a family group that subscribes to Apple TV+ or Apple One, and you already subscribe, your subscription isn't renewed on your next billing date; instead, you use the group's subscription. If you join a family group that doesn't subscribe, the group uses your subscription.

Note: To stop sharing Apple One, Apple TV+, or Apple TV channels with a family group, you can cancel the subscription, leave or remove a member from a Family Sharing group, or (if you're the family group organizer), stop using Family Sharing.

Get shows, movies, and more in the Apple TV app on iPhone

The Apple TV app brings your favorite shows, movies, and sports together in one place. Quickly find and watch your favorites, pick up where you left off with Up Next, or discover something new—personalized just for you.

Note: The availability of Apple Media Services varies by country or region..

Discover shows and movies

In the Apple TV app, tap Watch Now, then do any of the following:

- **Get recommendations**: Browse the What to Watch row for editorial recommendations that are personalized for you. Many rows throughout the app feature personalized recommendations based on your channel subscriptions, supported apps, purchases, and viewing interests.
- **Browse Apple TV channels**: Scroll down to browse channels you subscribe to. In the Channels row, browse other available channels, then tap a channel to explore its titles.
- See movies, shows, and episodes sent by friends in Messages: Scroll down to the Shared with You row.

Use the Up Next queue

In the Up Next row, you can find titles you recently added, rented, or purchased, catch the next episode in a series you've been watching, or resume what you're watching from the moment you left off.

Do any of the following:

- **Add an item to Up Next**: Touch and hold the item, then tap Add to Up Next.
- Remove an item from Up Next: Touch and hold the item, then tap Remove from Up Next.
- **Continue watching on another device**: You can see your Up Next queue in the Apple TV app on your iPhone, iPad, Mac, Apple TV, or supported smart TV where you're signed in with your Apple ID.

Browse Apple TV+

Discover Apple Originals—award-winning series, compelling dramas, groundbreaking documentaries, kids' entertainment, comedies, and more—with new items added every month.

Tap Originals, then do any of the following:

- **See what's up next**: In the Up Next row, find titles you recently added, play the next episode in a series, or continue watching where you left off.
- **Browse a collection**: Swipe left on the collection or tap See All.
- See descriptions and ratings: Tap an item.

Search for shows, movies, and more

Tap Search, then enter what you're looking for in the search field. You can search by title, sport, team, cast member, Apple TV channel, or topic (such as "car chase").

Stream or download content

Content from Apple TV+ and Apple TV channels play in the Apple TV app, while content from other providers plays in their video app.

1. Tap an item to see its details.
2. Choose any of the following options (not all options are available for all titles):

- **Watch Apple TV+ or Apple TV channels**: Tap Play. If you're not a current subscriber, tap Try It Free (available for eligible Apple ID accounts) or Subscribe.
- **Choose a different video app**: If the title is available from multiple apps, scroll down to How To Watch, then choose an app.
- **Download**: Tap ↓ . You can find the downloaded item in your library and watch it even when iPhone isn't connected to the internet.

Buy, rent, or pre-order items

1. Tap Store, then tap TV Shows or Movies.
2. Choose any of the following options (not all options are available for all titles):
   - **Buy**: Purchased items are added to your library.
   - **Rent**: When you rent a movie, you have 30 days to start watching it. After you start watching the movie, you can play it as many times as you want for 48 hours, after which the rental period ends. When the rental period ends, the movie is deleted.
   - **Pre-order**: When the pre-ordered item becomes available, your payment method is billed, and you receive an email notification. If you turned on automatic downloads, the item is automatically downloaded to your iPhone.
3. Confirm your selection, then complete the payment or pre-order, as applicable.

You can find your purchases and rentals in your library and play them in the Apple TV app.

Watch sports in the Apple TV app on iPhone

In the Apple TV app , the Sports row gives you access to a wide array of live and scheduled sports events (U.S. and Canada only).

You can see games in progress with up-to-the-minute scores, or browse upcoming games and add them to Up Next. You can also receive notifications about upcoming events and see live scores for your favorite teams with My Sports.

Explore sports

1. Tap Watch Now, then scroll down to the Sports row.
2. Do any of the following:
   - Browse current and upcoming games.
   - Tap Live Sports. Scroll down to browse football, baseball, basketball, and more. To filter by sport, scroll down to the Browse row, then tap a sport.

Watch a live game

Tap the game, then tap Live Now. Or scroll down to How to Watch, then choose an app.

Select games may show the current score and play-by-play updates on the game page.

To hide the scores of live games, go to Settings > TV, then turn off Show Sports Scores.

Follow your favorite teams with My Sports

My Sports lets you follow your favorite teams; access scores, schedules, and standings for the top professional and college leagues; and watch highlights. In the Apple TV app, add your favorite teams to My Sports to see their games in Up Next and receive notifications when they're playing.

1. Tap Watch Now, scroll down to the Sports row, then tap Live Sports.
2. Scroll to the bottom, then tap Follow Your Teams.
3. Tap Turn On.

When you turn on syncing for My Sports, the teams you follow in Apple TV are automatically followed in Apple News and other supported apps.

Note: My Sports in the Apple TV app lets you follow sports teams. Apple News lets you follow sports teams, as well as sports leagues and athletes.

Control playback in the Apple TV app on iPhone

In the Apple TV app , you can use the playback controls to play, pause, skip backward or forward, and more. When you watch with your friends using SharePlay (iOS 15.1 or later), the playback controls are shared by everyone on the FaceTime call.

Use the playback controls

During playback, tap the screen to show the controls.

Control	Description
▶	Play
❚❚	Pause
↺	Skip backward 10 seconds; touch and hold to rewind
↻	Skip forward 10 seconds; touch and hold to fast-forward
⟀	Stream the video to other devices
⋯	Change the playback speed, display subtitles and closed captions, change the language, and more (features subject to availability)
⧉	Start Picture in Picture—you can continue to watch the video while you use another app
✕	Stop playback

Watch together using SharePlay in the Apple TV app on iPhone

In the Apple TV app ⬛, you can stream TV shows and movies in sync with friends and family while on a FaceTime call together using SharePlay. The controls are shared so anyone on the call can pause, rewind, or fast forward. With smart volume, media audio is adjusted automatically, so you can continue to chat while watching. (Settings like subtitles and volume are controlled separately by each person.)

Note: Some apps that support SharePlay require a subscription. To watch a movie or TV show together, every participant needs to have access to the content, through either a subscription or purchase, on a device that meets the minimum system requirements.

SharePlay may not support the sharing of some movies or TV shows across different countries or regions. FaceTime, some FaceTime features, and other Apple services may not be available in all countries or regions.

Start SharePlay in the Apple TV app

You can start a FaceTime call in the Apple TV app while you're browsing or watching video content, and share the item in sync with others using SharePlay. Everyone on the call needs to have access to the content on their own device (for example, through a subscription or purchase).

1. Find a show or movie you want to share, then tap the item to see its details.
2. Tap ⬆, then tap SharePlay.
3. In the To field, enter the contacts you want to share with, then tap FaceTime.
4. When the FaceTime call connects, tap Start or Play to begin using SharePlay. To begin viewing, recipients tap Open.

Note: If the content requires a subscription, people who aren't subscribers can subscribe before watching.

Send what you're watching in SharePlay to Apple TV

After the video starts playing, you can stream it to your Apple TV to enjoy on the big screen. Tap ⬛, then choose Apple TV as the playback destination.

The video plays in sync on Apple TV, and you can keep the conversation going on your iPhone.

Manage your library in the Apple TV app on iPhone

In the Apple TV app ⬛, your library contains shows and movies you purchased, rented, and downloaded. If you use Family Sharing, you can also view purchases made by family members.

Browse your library

Tap Library, then tap TV Shows, Movies, or Genres.

Watch a movie you rented

1. Tap Library, tap Rentals, then tap a movie.
2. Do any of the following:

   ○ **Play**: Tap ▶. The time remaining in the rental period is shown.

   ○ **Download**: Tap ↓ to watch the item later when iPhone isn't connected to the internet.

Share purchases made by family members

If you use Family Sharing, you and your family members can share purchases in the Apple TV app.

Tap Library, tap Family Sharing, then choose a family member.

Remove a downloaded item

1. Tap Library, then tap Downloaded.
2. Swipe left on the item you want to remove, then tap Delete.

Removing an item from iPhone doesn't delete it from your purchases in iCloud. You can download the item to iPhone again later.

Change the Apple TV app settings on iPhone

You can adjust streaming and download settings for the Apple TV app . You can also change how the Apple TV app uses your viewing history to provide personalized recommendations.

Change streaming and download options

1. Go to Settings > TV.
2. Choose streaming options:
   - **Use Cellular Data**: Turn off to limit streaming to Wi-Fi connections.
   - **Cellular**: Choose High Quality or Automatic.
   - **Wi-Fi**: Choose High Quality or Data Saver.
     High Quality requires a faster internet connection and uses more data.
3. Choose download options:
   - **Use Cellular Data**: Turn off to limit downloads to Wi-Fi connections.
   - **Cellular**: Choose High Quality or Fast Downloads.
   - **Wi-Fi**: Choose High Quality or Fast Downloads.
     High Quality results in slower downloads and uses more data.
   - **Languages**: Choose a language. Each added audio language increases the download size. To remove a language, swipe left on the language you want to remove, then tap Delete.

The default language is the primary language for your country or region. If you turned on Audio Descriptions in Settings > Accessibility, audio descriptions are also downloaded.

Use or clear your viewing history

By default, what you watch on your iPhone affects your personalized recommendations and Up Next queue on all your devices where you're signed in with your Apple ID.

You can do any of the following:

- **Clear your viewing history**: Tap Watch Now, tap or your profile picture at the top right, then tap Clear Play History.

- Turn off personalization features based on your viewing history: Go to Settings > TV, then turn off Use Play History.

Voice Memos

Make a recording in Voice Memos on iPhone

With the Voice Memos app 🎙 (located in the Utilities folder), you can use iPhone as a portable recording device to record personal notes, classroom lectures, musical ideas, and more. You can fine-tune your recordings with editing tools like trim, replace, and resume.

Note: To make the Voice Memos app easier to find and open, you can move it from the Utilities folder to the Home Screen.

Record voice memos using the built-in microphone, a supported headset, or an external microphone.

When Voice Memos is turned on in iCloud settings or iCloud preferences, your recordings appear and update automatically on your iPhone, iPad, and Mac where you're signed in with the same Apple ID.

Make a basic recording

1. To begin recording, tap ⚪.
   To adjust the recording level, move the microphone closer to or farther from what you're recording.
2. Tap ⏺ to finish recording.

Your recording is saved with the name New Recording or the name of your location, if Location Services is turned on in Settings ⚙ > Privacy & Security. To change the name, tap the recording, then tap the name and type a new one.

To fine-tune your recording, see Edit a recording in Voice Memos.

Note: For your privacy, when you use Voice Memos to make recordings, an orange dot appears at the top of your screen to indicate your microphone is in use.

Use the advanced recording features

You can make a recording in parts, pausing and resuming as you record.

1. To begin recording, tap ⚪.
   To adjust the recording level, move the microphone closer to or farther away from what you're recording.
   To see more details while you're recording, swipe up from the top of the waveform.
2. Tap ⏸ to stop recording; tap Resume to continue.
3. To review your recording, tap ▶.
   To change where playback begins, drag the waveform left or right across the playhead before you tap ▶.
4. To save the recording, tap Done.

Your recording is saved with the name New Recording or the name of your location, if Location Services is turned on in Settings  > Privacy & Security. To change the name, tap the recording, then tap the name and type a new one.

Mute the start and stop tones

While recording, use the iPhone volume down button to turn the volume all the way down.

Use another app while recording

While you're recording in Voice Memos, you can go to the Home Screen, open another app, and use the other app, as long as it doesn't play audio on your device. If the app starts playing audio, Voice Memos stops recording.

On iPhone 14 Pro and iPhone 14 Pro Max, you can see your recording in progress in the Dynamic Island at the top of the Home Screen and in other apps. You can tap the Dynamic Island to navigate back to Voice Memos.

A Voice Memos recording showing in the Dynamic Island

You can touch and hold the Dynamic Island to expand it. When you expand it, the Stop button appears in it, allowing you to stop recording without returning to Voice Memos.

If Voice Memos is turned on in iCloud settings or iCloud preferences, your recording is saved in iCloud and appears automatically on your iPhone, iPad, and Mac where you're signed in with the same Apple ID.

Recordings using the built-in microphone are mono, but you can record stereo using an external stereo microphone that works with iPhone. Look for accessories marked with the Apple "Made for iPhone" or "Works with iPhone" logo.

Play a recording in Voice Memos on iPhone

In the Voice Memos app 📻, tap a recording and use the playback controls to listen to it.

Drag to go to a specific place in the recording.

Tap to play.

Control	Description
▶	Play
⏸	Pause
⟲15	Skip backward 15 seconds
⟳15	Skip forward 15 seconds

Tip: While the recording is open, you can tap its name to rename it.

Change the playback speed

You can play a recording at a faster or slower speed.

1. In the list of recordings, tap the recording you want to play.
2. Tap ≡, then drag the slider toward the tortoise 🐢 for a slower speed, or toward the rabbit 🐰 for a faster speed.
3. Tap ✕, then tap ▶ to play the recording.

Note: Changing the playback speed doesn't change the recording itself, only how fast it plays.

Enhance a recording

When playing a recording, you can enhance it to reduce background noise and echo.

1. In the list of recordings, tap the recording you want to enhance.
2. Tap ≡, then turn on Enhance Recording.

3. Tap ⊗, then tap ▶ to play the recording.

Note: Turning on Enhance Recording doesn't change the recording itself, only how it sounds when you play it.

Skip over gaps when playing back a recording

Voice Memos can analyze your audio and automatically skip over gaps when playing it.

1. Tap the recording you want to play.
2. Tap ⚏, then turn on Skip Silence.
3. Tap ⊗, then tap ▶ to play the recording.

Note: Turning on Skip Silence doesn't change the recording itself, only how it sounds when you play it.

Turn off the playback options

To return all the playback options to their original settings, tap ⚏, then tap Reset.

Edit or delete a recording in Voice Memos on iPhone

In the Voice Memos app ⬛, you can use the editing tools to fine-tune your recordings. You can remove parts you don't want, record over parts, or replace an entire recording. You can also delete a recording you no longer need.

Trim the excess

1. In the list of recordings, tap the recording you want to edit, tap ⋯, then tap Edit Recording.
2. Tap ⎍ at the top right, then drag the yellow trim handles to enclose the section you want to keep or delete.
   You can pinch open to zoom in on the waveform for more precise editing.

   To check your selection, tap ▶ .
3. To keep the selection (and delete the rest of the recording), tap Trim, or to delete the selection, tap Delete.
4. Tap Save, then tap Done.

Replace a recording

1. In the list of recordings, tap the recording you want to replace, tap ⋯, then tap Edit Recording.
2. Drag the waveform to position the playhead where you want to start recording new audio.
   You can pinch open to zoom in on the waveform for more precise placement.
3. Tap Replace to begin recording (the waveform turns red as you record).

   Tap ⏸ to pause; tap Resume to continue.

4. To check your recording, tap ▶ .
5. Tap Done to save the changes.

Delete a recording

Do one of the following:

- In the list of recordings, tap the recording you want to delete, then tap 🗑.
- Tap Edit above the list of recordings, select one or more recordings, then tap Delete.

Deleted recordings move to the Recently Deleted folder, where they're kept for 30 days by default. To change how long deleted recordings are kept, go to Settings ⚙ > Voice Memos > Clear Deleted, then select an option.

Recover or erase a deleted recording

1. Tap the Recently Deleted folder, then tap the recording you want to recover or erase.
2. Do any of the following:
   - Recover the selected recording: Tap Recover.
   - **Recover everything in the Recently Deleted folder**: Tap Edit above the Recently Deleted list, then tap Recover All.
   - **Delete everything in the Recently Deleted folder**: Tap Edit above the Recently Deleted list, then tap Delete All.

Keep recordings up to date in Voice Memos on iPhone

With the Voice Memos app 📱 and iCloud, your audio recordings appear and are kept up to date automatically on your iPhone, iPad, and Mac (where you're signed in with the same Apple ID and Voice Memos is turned on in iCloud settings or preferences).

To turn on Voice Memos in iCloud on your devices, do the following:

- **iOS or iPadOS**: Go to Settings ⚙ > [your name] > iCloud > Show All, then turn on Voice Memos.

- **macOS 10.15–12.5:** Choose Apple menu > System Preferences, then click Apple ID. Click iCloud in the sidebar, then select iCloud Drive. Click Options next to iCloud Drive, click Documents, then select Voice Memos.

- **macOS 10.14 or earlier**: Choose Apple menu > System Preferences, then click iCloud. Select iCloud Drive, click Options, then select Voice Memos.

Organize recordings in Voice Memos on iPhone

In the Voice Memos app 📱, you can mark recordings as favorites and organize your recordings into folders.

Note: Apple Watch recordings, recently deleted recordings, and favorites are grouped into Smart Folders—folders that automatically gather files by type and subject matter.

Mark recordings as favorites

Do one of the following:

- In the list of recordings, tap the recording you want to mark as a favorite, tap ⋯ , then tap ♡ .
- Tap Edit above the list of recordings, select one or more recordings, tap Move, then tap favorites.

Recordings marked as favorites automatically appear in the Favorites folder.

Organize recordings into folders

You can group related recordings together into folders so you can locate them easily.

1. Tap Edit above the list of recordings.
2. Select one or more recordings, then tap Move.
3. If you want to create a new folder for the recordings, tap ⊡⊕ , then type a name for the folder.
4. Tap the folder where you want to store the selected recordings.

To view your folders, tap ‹ ; tap a folder to check its contents.

To return to the list of recordings, tap All Recordings above the folders.

Delete or reorder folders

1. Tap ‹ to go to the list of folders.
2. Tap Edit above the folders, then do any of the following:
   ○ **Delete a folder**: Tap ⊖ next to the folder, then tap 🗑 .
   ○ Change the order of the folders: Drag ≡ next to any folder.
3. Tap Done.

Search for or rename a recording in Voice Memos on iPhone

You can search for your recordings in the Voice Memos app 📱, and rename any recording.

Search for a recording

1. In the Voice Memos list, swipe down to reveal the search field.
2. Tap the search field, enter part or all of the recording name, then tap Search.

Rename a recording

A recording is initially saved with the name New Recording or the name of your location, if Location Services is turned on in Settings ⚙ > Privacy & Security.

To change the name, tap the recording, tap the name, then type a new one.

Share a recording in Voice Memos on iPhone

In the Voice Memos app 📱, you can share one or more recordings with others (or send it to your Mac or another device) using AirDrop, Mail, Messages, and more.

Share a recording

1. In your Voice Memos list, tap a saved recording, then tap ⊙.
2. Tap Share, choose a sharing option, select or enter a recipient, then tap Done or ⬆.

Share more than one recording

1. Tap Edit above the list of recordings, then select the recordings you want to share.
2. Tap 🔼, choose a sharing option, select or enter a recipient, then tap Done or ⬆.

Duplicate a recording in Voice Memos on iPhone

In the Voice Memos app ▌, you can duplicate a recording, which is useful when you need another version of it. You can make changes to the copy, save it, and give it a new name.

In the Voice Memos list, tap a recording, tap ⊙, then tap Duplicate

The copy appears right below the original version in the list and has "copy" added to its name. To change the name, tap it, then type a new one.

Wallet

Keep cards and passes in Wallet on iPhone

Use the Wallet app ▢ to keep your cards and passes in one convenient place for easy access. (Apple Card and Apple Cash are available only in the U.S.)

Wallet can store the following and more:

- Cards for Apple Pay, such as Apple Card and Apple Cash
- Transit cards
- Digital keys
- Driver's license or state ID
- Employee badges
- Student ID cards
- Rewards cards, boarding passes, and event tickets
- Vaccination records

Set up Apple Pay in Wallet on iPhone

Using Apple Pay can be simpler than using a physical card, and safer too. With your cards stored in the Wallet app ▢, you can use Apple Pay to make secure payments in stores, for transit, in apps, and on websites that support Apple Pay. In Messages, use Apple Cash to send and receive money from friends and family and to make purchases from participating businesses.

To set up Apple Pay, add your debit, credit, and prepaid cards to Wallet.

(Apple Card and Apple Cash are available only in the U.S.)

Add a credit or debit card

For other debit and credit cards, do the following:

1. In Wallet, tap ⊕. You may be asked to sign in with your Apple ID.
2. Do one of the following:
   ○ **Add a new card**: Tap Debit or Credit Card, tap Continue, then position your card so that it appears in the frame, or enter the card details manually.
   ○ **Add your previous cards**: Tap Previous Cards, then choose any of cards you previously used. These cards may include the card associated with your Apple ID, cards you use with Apple Pay on your other devices, cards you added to AutoFill, or cards that you removed. Tap Continue, authenticate with Face ID, then enter the CVV number of each card.

Alternatively, you may be able to add your card from the app of the bank or card issuer.

The card issuer determines whether your card is eligible for Apple Pay, and may ask you for additional information to complete the verification process.

Set the default card and rearrange your cards

The first card you add to Wallet becomes your default card for payments. To set a different card as the default, move it to the front of the stack.

1. In Wallet, choose your default card.
2. Touch and hold the card, then drag it to the front of the stack.
3. To reposition another card, touch and hold it, then drag it to a new location.

Note: The availability of Apple Pay and its features varies by country or region.

Use Apple Pay for contactless payments on iPhone

With your Apple Cash, credit, and debit cards stored in the Wallet app 🔲 on iPhone, you can use Apple Pay for secure, contactless payments in stores, restaurants, and more.

Find places that accept Apple Pay

You can use Apple Pay wherever you see contactless payment symbols such as the following:

Siri: Say something like: "Show me coffee shops that take Apple Pay."_

Pay with your default card on an iPhone with Face ID

1. Double-click the side button.
2. When your default card appears, glance at iPhone to authenticate with Face ID, or enter your passcode.
3. Hold the top of your iPhone near the card reader until you see Done and a checkmark on the screen.

Pay with a different card instead of your default card

1. When your default card appears, tap it, then choose another card.

2. Authenticate with Face ID or your passcode.
3. Hold the top of your iPhone near the card reader until you see Done and a checkmark on the screen.

Use a rewards card

At participating stores, you can receive or redeem rewards when you use Apple Pay.

1. Add your rewards card to Wallet.
2. At the payment terminal in the store, present your rewards card by holding iPhone near the contactless reader.
   Apple Pay then switches to your default payment card to pay for the purchase. In some stores, you can apply your rewards card and payment card in one step. In other stores, you need to wait until the terminal or cashier asks for payment.

To have your rewards card appear automatically when you're in the store, tap ⊙ on the card, tap Pass Details, then turn on Automatic Selection.

Note: If you have Location Services turned on, the location of your iPhone at the time you make a payment may be sent to Apple and the card issuer to help prevent fraud.

Use Apple Pay in apps, App Clips, and Safari on iPhone

You can make purchases using Apple Pay in apps, in App Clips, and on the web using Safari wherever you see the Apple Pay button.

Pay in an app, in an App Clip, or on the web

1. During checkout, tap the Apple Pay button.
2. Review the payment information and set any of the following:
   - Credit card
   - Billing and shipping addresses
   - Contact information
   - Frequency and amount of recurring payments (may be available for recurring payments)
3. Complete the payment:
   - Double-click the side button, then glance at iPhone to authenticate with Face ID, or enter your passcode.

Track your orders

You can track your Apple Pay purchases made in apps and on the web from participating merchants.

Tap 📦 to see the order details, shipping status, order management options, and more.

Change your default shipping and contact information

1. Go to Settings ⚙ > Wallet & Apple Pay.
2. Set any of the following:
   - Shipping address
   - Email
   - Phone

Set up and use Apple Cash on iPhone (U.S. only)

With Apple Cash, you can send, request, and receive money in the Wallet app 📧 or Messages app 💬, get cash back from Apple Card transactions, make purchases using Apple Pay, and transfer your Apple Cash balance to your bank account.

Set up Apple Cash

Do any of the following:

- Open the Wallet app, tap the Apple Cash card, then tap Set Up Now.
- Go to Settings ⚙️ > Wallet & Apple Pay, then turn on Apple Cash.
- In Messages, send or accept a payment.

Make purchases with Apple Cash

You can use Apple Cash at locations that accept Visa and support Apple Pay:

- Use Apple Pay for contactless payments
- Use Apple Pay in apps, App Clips, and Safari

Some stores may require a PIN to complete transactions with Apple Cash.

Apple Cash doesn't require a PIN because every payment is authenticated by Face ID or a secure passcode. However, some terminals may still require you to enter a four-digit code to complete the transaction. To see your PIN, tap ⋯, then tap Card Details.

Send or request payments with Apple Cash

1. Tap the Apple Cash card, then tap Send or Request.
2. Enter a recipient or choose a recent contact, then tap Next.
3. Enter the amount, then tap Send or Request.
4. Add a comment if you want, then tap ⬆️.
5. If you're sending a payment, review the information, then authenticate with Face ID or your passcode.

View your balance and transactions

Tap the Apple Cash card to view your balance and latest transactions. Scroll down to see your transactions grouped by year.

You can also do the following:

- **Search your transactions**: Tap 🔍, enter what you're looking for, then tap Search on the keyboard. You can also choose a suggested search, such as a category, merchant, location, or contact, then enter additional text to refine your search.
- **Get a statement**: Tap ⋯, tap Card Details, scroll down, then tap Request Transaction Statement.

Review pending requests

1. Tap the Apple Cash card to view the pending requests.
2. Tap a pending request, then do any of the following:
   - **Send the payment**: Tap Send Money.

- ○ **Hide or decline the request**: Tap ✕, then choose Dismiss Request or Decline Request. If you dismiss the request, you'll receive a reminder one day before the request expires.

Manage your Apple Cash

Tap the Apple Cash card, tap ⊙, then tap any of the following:

- **Add Money**: Add funds from a debit card in Wallet.
- Transfer to Bank
- **Card Number**: View the last four digits of the Device Account Number—the number transmitted to the merchant.
- **Card Details**: Update your bank account information, turn Express Transit on or off, manage Apple Cash Family, and more.
- **Notifications**: Turn notifications on or off.

Set up and use Apple Card on iPhone (U.S. only)

Apple Card is a credit card created by Apple and designed to help you lead a healthier financial life. You can sign up for Apple Card in the Wallet app 🖰 on iPhone in minutes and start using it with Apple Pay right away in stores, in apps, or online worldwide. Apple Card gives you easy-to-understand, real-time views of your latest transactions and balance right in Wallet, and Apple Card support is available anytime by simply sending a text from Messages.

Get Apple Card

1. In Wallet, tap ⊕, then tap Apply for Apple Card.
2. Enter your information, then agree to the terms and conditions to submit your application.
3. Review the details of your Apple Card offer, including the credit limit and APR, then accept or decline the offer.
4. If you accept the terms, you can do any of the following:
   - ○ Set Apple Card as your default card for Apple Pay transactions.
   - ○ Get a titanium Apple Card to use where Apple Pay isn't accepted.

Use Apple Card

You can use Apple Card wherever you use Apple Pay:

- Make contactless payments using Apple Pay
- Pay in apps or on the web using Apple Pay

You can also use Apple Card at locations where Apple Pay isn't accepted:

- In apps, on the web, or over the phone: Tap ⬛₁₂₃ to see the card number, expiration date, and security code. Use this information to make your purchase.
- In stores, restaurants, and other locations: Use the titanium card.

View transactions and statements

1. In Wallet, tap Apple Card.
2. Do any of the following:
    - **Review your transactions**: View your latest transactions, or scroll down to see all your transactions grouped by month and year.
    - **Search your transactions**: Tap Q, enter what you're looking for, then tap Search on the keyboard. You can also choose a suggested search, such as a category, merchant, or location, then enter additional text to refine your search.
    - **See weekly, monthly, or yearly activity**: Tap Activity (below Card Balance) to see your spending grouped in categories such as Shopping, Food & Drinks, and Services. Tap Week, Month, or Year to see a different view. Swipe right to see previous periods.
    - **Get monthly statements**: Tap Card Balance to see the balance, new spending, and payments and credits. Scroll down to see your monthly statements. Tap a statement to see the summary for that month, download a PDF statement, or export transactions to a CSV, OFX, QFX, or QBO file.

Make payments

Tap the Payment button. Or tap ⓧ, tap Card Details, then choose any of the following:

- **Scheduled Payments**: Choose Pay My Bill or Pay Different Amount, enter the payment details (such as the account and date), then authenticate with Face ID or your passcode.
- **Make a Payment**: Drag the checkmark to adjust the payment amount or tap Show Keypad to enter an amount, tap Pay Now or Pay Later, review the payment details (such as the payment account), then authenticate with Face ID or your passcode.

Use the Apple Card widget on your Home screen

With the Apple Card widget, you can see your Apple Card balance, available credit, and spending activity at a glance.

1. Add the Apple Card widget to your Home screen.
2. To see your spending activity for a different time period, touch and hold the widget, tap Edit Widget, then choose Weekly, Monthly, or Yearly.
3. To go to Apple Card in Wallet, tap the widget.

Manage Apple Card, view details, and more

Tap ⓧ, then tap any of the following:

- **Daily Cash**: View the Daily Cash you've received.
- **Card Details**: Share your Apple Card with family members, schedule payments, view your credit limit, and more.
- **Notifications**: Turn notifications on or off.

Manage Apple Pay cards and activity on iPhone

In the Wallet app 🔲, you can manage the cards you use for Apple Pay and review your recent transactions.

View the information for a card and change its settings

For other debit and credit cards, do the following:

1. In Wallet, tap the card.
   Note: The latest transactions may appear, showing authorized amounts that may differ from the amount of the payment charged to your account. For example, a gas station may request an authorization of $99, even though you pumped only $25 worth of gasoline. To see the final charges, see the statement from your card issuer, which includes all Apple Pay transactions.

2. Tap ⊙, then tap any of the following:
   - **Card Number**: View the last four digits of the card number and Device Account Number—the number transmitted to the merchant.
   - **Card Details**: See more information; change the billing address; turn the transaction history on or off; or remove the card from Wallet.
   - **Notifications**: Turn notifications on or off.

Change your Apple Pay settings

1. Go to Settings ⊚ > Wallet & Apple Pay.
2. Choose options such as the following:
   - **Double-Click Side Button**: (on an iPhone with Face ID) Your cards and passes appear on the screen when you double-click the side button.
   - **Allow Payments on Mac**: Allows iPhone to confirm payments on your nearby Mac.

Remove your cards from Apple Pay if your iPhone is lost or stolen

If you turned on Find My iPhone, you can use it to help locate and secure your iPhone.

To remove your cards from Apple Pay, do any of the following:

- **On a Mac or PC:** Sign in to your Apple ID account. In the Devices section, click the lost iPhone. Below the list of cards, click Remove Items.

- **On another iPhone or iPad**: Go to Settings ⊚ > [your name], tap the lost iPhone, then tap Remove Items (below Wallet & Apple Pay).

- Call the issuers of your cards.

If you remove cards, you can add them again later.

Note: If you sign out of iCloud in Settings > [your name], all your credit and debit cards for Apple Pay are removed from iPhone. You can add the cards again the next time you sign in with your Apple ID.

Pay for transit using iPhone

With your transit cards stored in the Wallet app ▢ , you can use your iPhone to pay for your fare.

Add a transit card

1. In Wallet, tap ⊕ , then tap Transit Card.
2. Choose a transit card in the list, or search by location or card name.

Pay for your ride with Express Transit

With Express Transit (available in certain countries or regions), you don't need to authenticate with Face ID or your passcode, and you don't need to wake or unlock your device or open an app.

1. If you have multiple cards for a transit network, set the default Express Transit card in Settings ⚙ > Wallet & Apple Pay > Express Transit Card.
   By default, Express Transit is turned on when you add an eligible card.
2. As you approach a fare gate or board the bus, make sure your device is turned on (it doesn't need to be connected to the internet).
3. Hold the top of your iPhone near the middle of the ticket gate scanner until you feel a vibration.

On models that support Express Cards with power reserve, your Express Cards may be available for up to five hours when your iPhone needs to be charged. To check if Express Cards are available when iPhone needs to be charged, press the side button (doing this often may significantly reduce the power reserve for Express Cards). If you turn off your iPhone, this feature isn't available.

Pay for transit at a fare gate

If you're not using Express Transit, do the following:

1. Make sure your device is turned on (it doesn't need to be connected to the internet).
2. As you approach a fare gate or board a bus, do one of the following:
   - Double-click the side button, then glance at iPhone to authenticate with Face ID, or enter your passcode.
3. Hold the top of your iPhone near the middle of the ticket gate scanner until you feel a vibration.

Manage your transit card

Tap ⋯, then tap any of the following:

- **Add Money**: Tap a preset or enter an amount, then tap Add.
- **Card Number**: View your account number.
- **Card Details**: View your account balance; turn on Service Mode to get help at stations and kiosks; turn Express Transit on or off; or remove the card from Wallet.
- **Notifications**: Turn notifications on or off.

Access your car, home, workplace, and hotel room with keys in Wallet on iPhone

In the Wallet app 📱, you can store keys to your car, home, workplace, and hotel room. iPhone automatically presents the right key when you arrive at your door, allowing you to enter with just a tap using Near Field Communication (NFC). With power reserve mode, your keys work even if the iPhone battery runs low.

Unlock and start your car

With a compatible car and a digital car key in Apple Wallet, you can unlock, lock, and start your car using iPhone or Apple Watch (Series 6 and later). Ultra Wideband provides precise spatial awareness, ensuring that you can't lock your iPhone or Apple Watch in your car or start your vehicle when iPhone or Apple Watch is left outside.

Unlock your home

With some HomeKit-compatible smart locks, you can unlock your door with a home key in Apple Wallet on a supported iPhone or Apple Watch (Series 4 and later). You add a home key to Apple Wallet with the Home app on your iPhone.

When you have a home key on your iPhone or Apple Watch, just place your device near the lock to unlock it. You can use the Home app to share access with other people.

Access your workplace

If you work at a participating corporate office, you can add your employee badge to Apple Wallet, then use your iPhone or Apple Watch Series 3 and later (with watchOS 8.1 or later) to present your badge to readers at your workplace.

Unlock your hotel room

At participating hotels, you can add your room key to Apple Wallet from the hotel provider's app, check in without going to the lobby, and use your iPhone or Apple Watch to unlock your room. Wallet automatically archives your pass after you check out to keep passes organized as you travel.

Use your driver's license or state ID in Wallet on iPhone (U.S. only)

You can easily and securely add your driver's license or state ID to the Wallet app , then use your iPhone or Apple Watch to present your license or ID at select Transportation Security Administration (TSA) security checkpoints and share in apps that require identity verification.

1. In Wallet, tap .
2. Tap Driver's License or State ID, then choose your state. (If your state isn't listed, it might not participate yet.)
3. Choose whether you want to add your license or ID to your iPhone only, or to both your iPhone and paired Apple Watch.
4. Follow the onscreen instructions to scan the front and back of your license or ID, then follow the prompts to confirm your identity.

If you want to add your license or ID to your Apple Watch later, open the Apple Watch app on your iPhone, tap My Watch, then tap Wallet & Apple Pay. Find your license or ID listed below Other Cards on Your iPhone. Tap the Add button next to it, then follow the onscreen instructions.

Present your license or ID at a TSA checkpoint

1. Hold the top of your iPhone near the identity reader.
2. On your iPhone screen, review the information to be shared.
3. To present your license or ID, do the following:
   o Double-click the side button, then authenticate with the Face ID that you used to add your license or ID.

4. A checkmark appears when you successfully present your license or ID.

Share your license or ID in an app

1. When prompted, tap Verify with Apple Wallet or Continue with Apple Wallet.
2. Review the following:
   o The information being requested
   o The information, if any, that will be stored by the app
   o How long ID information will be stored by the app
   o The reason the app is requesting information
3. To share the requested information, do the following:
   o Double-click the side button, then authenticate with the Face ID that you used to add your license or ID.
4. A checkmark appears when you successfully share your license or ID.

Manage your license or ID

In Wallet, tap your license or ID to see where you have presented it. You can also tap ⋯, tap Card Details, then do any of the following:

- View the information on your license or ID (requires authentication with the Face ID that you used to add your license or ID).
- Remove your license or ID.

Use student ID cards in Wallet on iPhone

On supported campuses, you can add your contactless student ID card to the Wallet app , and then use your iPhone to access locations where your student ID card is accepted, such as your dorm, the library, and campus events. You can even pay for laundry, snacks, and meals around campus.

Add your student ID card to Wallet

1. Download the app that supports student ID cards for your school.
2. Open the app, sign in, then add your student ID card to Wallet.

Present your student ID card

- **With Express Mode turned on**: Hold the top of your iPhone near the identity reader until you see Done and a checkmark on the screen.
- **With Express Mode turned off**: Authenticate with Face ID or your passcode, then hold the top of your iPhone near the identity reader until you see Done and a checkmark on the screen.

Manage your student ID card

Tap the card in Wallet, tap ⋯, then tap any of the following:

- **Card Details**: View your name, ID number, and account balance; turn Express Mode on or off; or contact the card issuer.
  On an iPhone that supports Express Cards with power reserve, your Express Card may be available for up to five hours when your iPhone needs to be charged. To check if Express Cards are available when iPhone needs to be charged, press the side button

(doing this often may significantly reduce the power reserve for Express Cards). If you turn off your iPhone, this feature isn't available.

- **Notifications**: Turn notifications on or off.

Add your Apple Account Card to Wallet on iPhone

In the Wallet app ⬛, you can store your Apple Account Card and see the balance on your Apple Account. You can use your account balance to buy products, accessories, apps, games, and more online or in store with Apple Pay.

Add your Apple Account Card

In Wallet, tap ➕, then tap Add Apple Account.

Manage your Apple Account Card

Tap the Apple Account Card, then tap ⓘ.

You can view the card details or remove the card.

Add and use passes in Wallet on iPhone

Use the Wallet app ⬛ to keep rewards cards, coupons, boarding passes, movie and event tickets, and more in one convenient place for easy access. Passes can include useful information, such as the balance on your coffee card, a coupon's expiration date, or boarding information for a flight.

(Apple Card and Apple Cash are available only in the U.S.)

Add a pass

You may be asked to add a pass within an app after you perform an action such as purchasing a ticket. Or, you can tap Add to Apple Wallet when you see it from the following:

- Wallet-enabled apps
- Mail or Messages
- Web browser such as Safari
- AirDrop sharing
- Wallet notification after you use Apple Pay at a supported merchant
- QR code or barcode

   To scan the code, open the Camera app 📷, then position iPhone so that the code appears on the screen.

Present a pass with a QR code or barcode

1. Access the pass in any of the following ways:
   - On the Lock Screen, tap the pass notification. If prompted, authenticate with Face ID or your passcode.
   - If Automatic Selection is turned on for the pass, double-click the side button. If prompted, authenticate with Face ID or your passcode.
   - Open the Wallet app, then tap the pass.

378

2. Present the QR code or barcode to the reader.

Use a contactless pass

1. Access the pass in any of the following ways:
   o On the Lock Screen, tap the pass notification. If prompted, authenticate with Face ID or your passcode.
   o If Automatic Selection is turned on for the pass, double-click the side button. If prompted, authenticate with Face ID or your passcode.
   o Open the Wallet app, then tap the pass.
2. To present the pass, hold the top of your iPhone near the pass reader until you see Done and a checkmark on the screen.

Manage your passes in Wallet on iPhone

In the Wallet app ⬜, you can rearrange, archive, or delete passes, view pass information, and change the settings.

Rearrange your passes

1. In the Wallet stack, touch and hold the pass you want to move.
2. Drag the pass to a new place in the stack.
   The pass order is updated on your iPhone and Apple Watch where you're signed in with your Apple ID.

View the information for a pass and change its settings

1. Tap the pass, tap ⊙, then tap Pass Details.
2. Choose any of the following (not all options are available on all passes):
   o **Automatic Updates**: Allow the pass to receive updates from the issuer.
   o **Suggest on Lock Screen**: Show the pass based on time or location.

     To allow location access, go to Settings ⚙ > Privacy & Security > Location Services > Wallet, then tap While Using the App.
   o **Automatic Selection**: Select the pass where it's requested.
   o **Share Pass**: Send the pass to a friend using Mail or Messages.
   o **Remove Pass**: Delete the pass from all your devices where you're signed in with your Apple ID.
3. Scroll down to view other information such as the associated app, usage details, and terms and conditions.

Change the settings for all your passes

- Keep your passes up to date on your other devices: Go to Settings ⚙ > [your name] > iCloud, then turn on Wallet.
  Note: This setting applies only to passes in Wallet, not to cards you use with Apple Pay.

- Set notification options: Go to Settings ⚙ > Notifications > Wallet.
- Allow access to Wallet when iPhone is locked: Go to Settings > Face ID & Passcode, then turn on Wallet (below Allow Access When Locked).

Archive or remove passes

- **Automatically archive old passes**: Go to Settings ⚙️ > Wallet & Apple Pay, then turn on Hide Expired Passes.
  To show an expired pass, scroll to the bottom of the Wallet stack, tap View Expired Passes, choose the pass, then tap Unhide.
- **Delete a pass**: In Wallet, tap the pass, tap ⋯, tap Pass Details, then tap Remove Pass.

Use COVID-19 vaccination cards in Wallet on iPhone

If you add a verifiable COVID-19 vaccination record (available in certain countries and regions) in the Health app 💜, you can quickly present the vaccination card in the Wallet app ⬛.

Add a vaccination card to Wallet

Do any of the following:

- Download a verifiable COVID-19 vaccination record from a participating healthcare provider or authority, then tap Add to Wallet & Health.
- If you already have a verifiable COVID-19 vaccination record from a supported healthcare provider or authority in the Health app, tap the record, then tap Add to Wallet.

Note: If you have an Apple Watch paired to your iPhone, the vaccination card is also added to and accessible from your Apple Watch (watchOS 8 and later).

Present a vaccination card

1. Double-click the side button.
2. In the Wallet stack, tap the vaccination card. If prompted, authenticate with Face ID or your passcode.

Note: Your vaccination card may contain sensitive information such as your birthdate. To review the information stored on your card, tap ⓘ.

3.   Present the QR code to the reader. You may be asked to verify your identity by presenting a photo ID such as your driver's license.

Manage or remove a vaccination card

Tap the vaccination card, tap ⓘ, then do any of the following:

- **See the immunization details**: Tap Open to see the information in the Health app 💜.
- **Remove the card**: Tap Remove Pass.
  Note: Removing a vaccination card from Wallet doesn't remove the corresponding vaccination record from the Health app. However, if you have an Apple Watch paired to your iPhone, the vaccination card is removed from your Apple Watch.

Weather

Check the weather on iPhone

Use the Weather app to check the weather for your current location. You can view the upcoming hourly and 10-day forecast, see severe weather information, and more.

Siri: Say something like: "What's the weather for today?" or "How windy is it out there?"

Note: Weather uses Location Services to get the forecast for your current location. To make sure Location Services is turned on, go to Settings > Privacy & Security > Location Services > Weather. Turn on Precise Location to increase the accuracy of the forecast in your current location.

Check the local forecast and conditions

When you open Weather, the details for your current location are shown. If you don't see them, tap , then tap My Location.

Scroll down to view weather details such as:

- **Hourly forecast**: Swipe the hourly display left or right.
- **10-day forecast**: View weather conditions, chance of precipitation, and high and low temperatures for the coming days.
  Tip: Tap a day in the 10-day forecast to see that day's hourly temperature forecast, high and low temperatures, and more. Tap to change the displayed weather condition.
- **Severe weather alerts**: View updates for weather events such as winter storms and flash floods (not available in all countries or regions). Tap the alert to read the full government-issued alert.
- **Air quality**: View air quality information; tap to view details about health information and pollutants (not available in all countries or regions).
  Note: The air quality scale appears above the hourly forecast when air quality reaches a particular level for that location. For some locations, the air quality scale always appears above the hourly forecast.
- **Maps**: View a map of temperature, precipitation, or air quality in the area. Tap the map to view it in full screen or to change the map view between temperature, precipitation, and air quality.
- **Additional details**: Scroll down to see additional weather information such as the UV index, sunrise, sunset, wind, precipitation, and more. Tap a weather detail for the extended forecast, daily summary, and data specific to that detail.

Tip: Some weather details include interactive features; drag your finger over the chart to see data values at specific times, tap a day to see data values for that day, or tap to switch the view to a different weather detail.

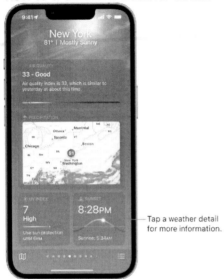

Tap a weather detail for more information.

Switch between Celsius and Fahrenheit

1. Open Weather, then tap ⋮☰.
2. Tap ⬤, then tap Celsius or Fahrenheit.

Send a report about the weather

You can report the weather in your location if it doesn't match what's shown in the Weather app.

1. Open Weather, then tap ⋮☰.
2. Tap ⬤, then tap Report an Issue.
3. Tap the options that best describe the weather conditions in your location.
4. Tap Submit.

Check the weather in other locations on iPhone

Use the Weather app 🌤 to check the weather in other cities and locations. You can also create a saved weather list to quickly check the forecast in places that are important to you.

Siri: Say something like: "What's the weather in Seattle?"

Check the weather in another location

1. Open Weather, then tap ⋮☰ in the bottom-right corner of the screen.
2. Tap the search field at the top of the screen, then enter the name of the city, the zip code, or the airport code.
3. Tap the location in the search results to view the forecast.
4. Tap Cancel to close the forecast, then tap Cancel to clear the search results.

Add a location to your weather list

You can add locations to the weather list to quickly check the weather in places important to you.

1. Open Weather, then tap :≡ in the bottom-right corner of the screen.
2. Tap the search field at the top of the screen, then enter the name of the city, the zip code, or the airport code that you want to add to your list.
3. Tap the location in the search results, then tap Add.

To check the weather in locations you added to your weather list, swipe the iPhone screen left or right when viewing a location, or tap :≡, then tap a location.

Delete and rearrange locations in your weather list

1. Tap :≡ to see your weather list.
2. Do either of the following:
   - **Delete a location**: Swipe left on the location, then tap 🗑. Or, tap •••, then tap Edit List.
   - **Rearrange the order of locations on your list**: Touch and hold the location, then move it up or down. Or, tap •••, then tap Edit List.

Your list of locations stays up to date across your devices when you're signed in with the same Apple ID.

View weather maps on iPhone

You can use the Weather app ☁ to view full-screen temperature, precipitation, and air quality maps in your location or other areas.

View a full-screen weather map

1. Open Weather.
2. Select a location, then do either of the following:
   - Tap 🗺 at the bottom of the screen.
   - Scroll down, then tap the weather map.

Change the map display

1. While viewing a full-screen map, do any of the following to adjust the display:
   - Change the map display to temperature, precipitation, or air quality: Tap ⊗.
   - **Move the map**: Touch the screen and drag your finger.
   - **Zoom in and out**: Pinch the screen.

     While viewing the precipitation map, tap ⌄ to change the view between Next-Hour Forecast and 12-Hour Forecast (not available in all countries or regions).
   - View a different location in your weather list: Tap :≡.
   - Return to your current location: Tap ◁.
   - Add a location to your weather list, view its current conditions, or view it in Maps: Touch and hold the location.
2. Tap Done to return to weather conditions and forecast.

Manage weather notifications on iPhone

You can receive notifications from the Weather app ☁ when precipitation and severe weather events such as tornados and flash floods are about to start or stop in your current location. You can also receive notifications for locations in your weather list (not available in all countries or regions).

Turn on weather notifications for your location

1. Go to Settings ⚙ > Privacy & Security > Location Services > Weather, then tap Always.
2. Turn on Precise Location to receive the most accurate notifications for your current location.
3. Open Weather, then tap ☰ to view your weather list.
4. Tap ⋯, then tap Notifications.
   If prompted, allow notifications from the Weather app.
5. Below Current Location, turn on notifications for Severe Weather and Next-Hour Precipitation (green is on).
6. Tap Done.

Note: Not available in all countries or regions.

Turn on weather notifications for locations in your weather list

1. Open Weather, then tap ☰ to view your weather list.
2. Tap ⋯, then tap Notifications.
   If prompted, allow notifications from the Weather app.
3. Below Your Locations, tap a location, then turn on notifications for Severe Weather and Next-Hour Precipitation (green is on).
4. Tap Done.

Note: Not available in all countries or regions.

Add a Weather widget to your iPhone Home Screen

Use the Weather widget to check the forecast at a glance on your iPhone Home Screen. You can choose the size of the Weather widget and the amount of information displayed.

Learn the weather icons on iPhone

The icons in the Weather app ☁ indicate different weather conditions, like fog or haze. Here's a list of some of the weather icons and what they mean.

Icon	Description
↑	Sunrise

	Sunset
	Clear
	Partly cloudy
	Dust
	Haze
	Smoke
	Fog
	Windy
	Cloudy
	Thunderstorms
	Rain
	Heavy rain
	Drizzle
	Hail
	Tornado

❄	Snow
☁	Scattered snow
☁	Heavy snow/Sleet
🌬	Blowing snow
☁	Cloudy
🌙	Clear

Siri

Use Siri on iPhone

Get everyday tasks done with just your voice. Use Siri to translate a phrase, set an alarm, find a location, report on the weather, and more.

On supported devices, voice input is processed on iPhone, but transcripts of your requests are sent to Apple in order to improve Siri. This data is not associated with your Apple ID and will only be stored for a limited time. You can also opt in to Improve Siri and Dictation. If you opt in, the audio of your interactions with Siri, Dictation, and Translate will be shared with Apple in order to help develop and improve Siri, Dictation, and other language processing features like Translate or Voice Control.

For some requests, iPhone must be connected to the internet. Cellular charges may apply.

Set up Siri

If you didn't set up Siri when you first set up your iPhone, go to Settings > Siri & Search, then do any of the following:

- If you want to activate Siri with your voice: Turn on Listen for "Hey Siri."
- If you want to activate Siri with a button: Turn on Press Side Button for Siri.

Activate Siri with your voice

When you activate Siri with your voice, Siri responds out loud.

1. Say "Hey Siri," then ask a question or make a request.
   For example, say something like "Hey Siri, what's the weather for today?" or "Hey Siri, set an alarm for 8 a.m."

2. To ask another question or make another request, say "Hey Siri" again or tap .

Note: To prevent iPhone from responding to "Hey Siri," place your iPhone face down, or go to Settings > Siri & Search, then turn off Listen for "Hey Siri."

You can also say "Hey Siri" to activate Siri while wearing supported AirPods.

Activate Siri with a button

When you activate Siri with a button, Siri responds silently when iPhone is in silent mode. When silent mode is off, Siri responds out loud.

1. Do one of the following:
   - Press and hold the side button.
   - **EarPods**: Press and hold the center or call button.
   - **CarPlay**: Press and hold the voice command button on the steering wheel.

- Siri Eyes Free: Press and hold the voice command button on your steering wheel.
2. When Siri appears, ask a question or make a request.

For example, say something like "What's 18 percent of 225?" or "Set the timer for 3 minutes."

3. To ask another question or make another request, tap 🌀.

You can also activate Siri with a touch on supported AirPods.

Make a correction if Siri misunderstands you

- **Rephrase your request**: Tap 🌀, then say your request in a different way.
- **Spell out part of your request**: Tap 🌀, then repeat your request by spelling out any words that Siri didn't understand. For example, say "Call," then spell the person's name.
- Change a message before sending it: Say "Change it."
- **Edit your request with text:** If you see your request onscreen, you can edit it. Tap the request, then use the onscreen keyboard.

Type instead of speaking to Siri

1. Go to Settings ⚙ > Accessibility > Siri, then turn on Type to Siri.
2. To type a request, activate Siri, then use the keyboard and text field to ask a question or make a request.

Find out what Siri can do on iPhone

Use Siri on iPhone to get information and perform tasks. Siri and its response appear on top of what you're currently doing, allowing you to refer to information onscreen.

Siri is interactive. When Siri displays a web link, you can tap it to see more information in your default web browser. When the onscreen response from Siri includes buttons or controls, you can tap them to take further action. And you can tap Siri again to ask another question or do an additional task for you.

Below are some examples of what you can use Siri to do. Additional examples appear throughout this guide. You can also discover Siri capabilities on your iPhone and in apps by asking "Hey Siri, what can I do here?"

Use Siri to answer questions

Use Siri to quickly check facts, do calculations, or translate a phrase into another language. Say something like:
- "Hey Siri, what causes a rainbow?"
- "Hey Siri, what does a cat sound like?"
- "Hey Siri, what's the derivative of cosine x?"

Use Siri with apps

You can use Siri to control apps with your voice. Say something like:

- "Hey Siri, set up a meeting with Gordon at 9" to create an event in Calendar.
- "Hey Siri, add artichokes to my groceries list" to add an item to Reminders.
- "Hey Siri, send a message to PoChun saying love you heart emoji" to text with Messages.
- "Hey Siri, what's my update?" to get an update about the weather in your area, the news, your reminders and calendar events, and more.

Use Siri to share information with contacts

You can share onscreen items like photos, webpages, content from Apple Music or Apple Podcasts, Maps locations, and more with people in your contacts.

For example, when looking at a photo in your Photo library, say something like "Hey Siri, send this to mom" to create a new message with the photo.

Tell Siri about yourself on iPhone

You can provide information to Siri—including things like your home and work addresses, and your relationships—for a more personalized experience so you can say things like "Give me driving directions home" and "FaceTime mom."

Tell Siri who you are

1. Open Contacts 📇 , then fill out your contact information.
2. Go to Settings ⚙ > Siri & Search > My Information, then tap your name.

Tell Siri how to say your name

1. Open Contacts 📇 , then tap your contact card.
2. Tap Edit, scroll down and tap "add field," select a pronunciation name field, then type how to say your name.

You can also add a pronunciation for any other contact card in Contacts.

Tell Siri about a relationship

Say something like "Hey Siri, Eliza Block is my wife" or "Hey Siri, Ashley Kamin is my mom."

Keep what Siri knows about you up to date on your Apple devices

On each device, go to Settings ⚙, then sign in with the same Apple ID.

If you use iCloud, your Siri settings stay up to date across your Apple devices using end-to-end encryption.

If you don't want Siri personalization to stay up to date across iPhone and your other devices, you can disable Siri in iCloud settings. Go to Settings > [your name] > iCloud, then turn off Siri.

Note: If you have Location Services turned on, the location of your device at the time you make a request is also sent to Apple to help Siri improve the accuracy of its response to your requests. To deliver relevant responses, Apple may use the IP address of your internet connection to approximate your location by matching it to a geographic region.

Announce calls, messages, and more with Siri on iPhone

Siri can announce calls and notifications from apps like Messages ⬜ on supported headphones and when using CarPlay. You can answer or reply using your voice without needing to say "Hey Siri."

Announce Calls and Announce Notifications also work with supported third-party apps.

Have Siri announce calls

With Announce Calls, Siri identifies incoming phone calls and FaceTime calls, which you can accept or decline using your voice.

1. Go to Settings ⚙ > Siri & Search > Announce Calls, then choose an option.
2. When a call comes in, Siri identifies the caller, and asks if you want to answer the call. Say "yes" to accept the call or "no" to decline it.

Have Siri announce notifications

Siri can automatically announce incoming notifications from apps like Messages and Reminders. Siri automatically enables app notifications for apps that use time-sensitive notifications, but you can change the settings at any time.

1. Go to Settings ⚙ > Siri & Search > Announce Notifications, then turn on Announce Notifications.
2. Tap an app you want Siri to announce notifications from, then turn on Announce Notifications.

For some apps, you can also choose whether to announce all notifications or only time-sensitive notifications.

For apps where you can send a reply, like Messages, Siri repeats what you said, then asks for confirmation before sending your reply. To send replies without waiting for confirmation, turn on Reply Without Confirmation.

Add Siri Shortcuts on iPhone

Apps can offer shortcuts for things you do frequently. You can use Siri to initiate these shortcuts with just your voice.

Some apps have Siri Shortcuts set up automatically. You can also create your own.

Add a suggested shortcut

Tap Add to Siri when you see a suggestion for a shortcut, then follow the onscreen instructions to record a phrase of your choice that performs the shortcut.

You can also use the Shortcuts app to create a new shortcut that uses Siri, or to manage, re-record, and delete existing Siri Shortcuts.

Use a shortcut

Activate Siri, then speak your phrase for the shortcut.

Siri Suggestions on iPhone

Siri makes suggestions for what you might want to do next, such as call into a meeting or confirm an appointment, based on your routines and how you use your apps.

For example, Siri might help when you do any of the following:

- **Glance at the Lock Screen or start a search**: As Siri learns your routines, you get suggestions for just what you need, at just the right time.
- **Create email and events**: When you start adding people to an email or calendar event, Siri suggests the people you included in previous emails or events.
- **Receive calls**: If you get an incoming call from an unknown number, Siri lets you know who might be calling—based on phone numbers included in your emails.
- **Type**: As you enter text, Siri can suggest names of movies, places—anything you viewed on iPhone recently. If you tell a friend you're on your way, Siri can even suggest your estimated arrival time.
- Confirm an appointment or book a flight on a travel website: Siri asks if you want to add it to your calendar.

Turn Siri Suggestions on or off for an app

Siri Suggestions are on by default for your apps. You can turn them off or change the settings at any time.

1. Go to Settings ⚙ > Siri & Search, scroll down, then select an app.
2. Turn settings on or off.

Change where Siri Suggestions appear

Go to Settings ⚙ > Siri & Search, then turn on or off any of the following:

- Allow Notifications
- Show in App Library & Spotlight
- Show When Sharing
- Show When Listening

Your personal information—which is encrypted and remains private—stays up to date across all your devices where you're signed in with the same Apple ID. As Siri learns about you on one device, your experience with Siri is improved on your other devices. If you don't want Siri personalization to update across your devices, you can disable Siri in iCloud settings.

Siri is designed to protect your information, and you can choose what you share.

Use Siri in your car

With CarPlay or Siri Eyes Free, you can keep focused on the road by using Siri to make calls, send text messages, play music that's on your iPhone, get directions, and use other iPhone features.

CarPlay (available in select cars) takes the things you want to do with your iPhone while driving and puts them on your car's built-in display. CarPlay uses Siri, so you can control CarPlay with just your voice.

With Siri Eyes Free (available in select cars), use your voice to control features of your iPhone without looking at or touching iPhone. To connect iPhone to your car, use Bluetooth (refer to the user guide that came with your car if you need to). To activate Siri, press and hold the voice command button on your steering wheel until you hear the Siri tone, then make a request.

Change Siri settings on iPhone

You can change the voice for Siri, prevent access to Siri when your device is locked, and more.

Change when Siri responds

You can customize if Siri responds to your voice or a button press. You can also choose what language Siri responds to.

Go to Settings ⚙ > Siri & Search, then do any of the following:

- Prevent Siri from responding to the voice request "Hey Siri": Turn off Listen for "Hey Siri."
- Prevent access to Siri when iPhone is locked: Turn off Allow Siri When Locked.
- Change the language Siri responds to: Tap Language, then select a new language.

You can also activate Siri by typing.

Change the voice for Siri

You can change the Siri voice (not available for all languages).

1. Go to Settings ⚙ > Siri & Search.
2. Tap Siri Voice, then choose a different variety or voice.

Change how Siri responds

Siri can respond out loud or silently (with text onscreen). You can also see your request onscreen.

Go to Settings ⚙ > Siri & Search, then do any of the following:

- **Change when Siri provides voice responses**: Tap Siri Responses, then choose an option below Spoken Responses.
- **Always see the response from Siri onscreen**: Tap Siri Responses, then turn on Always Show Siri Captions.
- **See your request onscreen**: Tap Siri Responses, then turn on Always Show Speech.

Change Siri settings for Phone, FaceTime, and Messages

You can perform tasks for Phone 📞, FaceTime 📹, and Messages 💬 with just your voice. With Siri, you can hang up calls and skip the confirmation step when sending messages. You can enable these features in Settings.

Go to Settings ⚙ > Siri & Search, then do any of the following:

- **Hang up Phone and FaceTime calls**: Tap Call Hang Up, then turn on Call Hang Up.
- **Send messages without confirmation**: Tap Automatically Send Messages, then turn on Automatically Send Messages.

On supported headphones, Siri can also announce calls, messages, and more.

Change which apps appear in search

You can change which apps appear when you search with Siri.

1. Go to Settings ⚙ > Siri & Search, then scroll down and select an app.
2. Turn settings on or off.

Retrain Siri with your voice

Go to Settings ⚙ > Siri & Search, turn off Listen for "Hey Siri," then turn on Listen for "Hey Siri" again.

iPhone safety features

Contact emergency services on your iPhone

In case of emergency, use your iPhone to quickly call for help. With Emergency SOS, you can quickly and easily call for help and alert your emergency contacts (provided that cellular service is available).

If you share your Medical ID, your iPhone can send your medical information to emergency services when you call or text 911 or use Emergency SOS (U.S. and Canada only).

Note: For emergency help in the U.S., you can send a text message to 911 (not available in all locations).

Dial the emergency number when your iPhone is locked

1. On the Passcode screen, tap Emergency.
2. Dial the emergency number (for example, 911 in the U.S.), then tap 📞 .

Use Emergency SOS (all countries or regions except India)

- Press and hold the side button and either volume button. Continue to hold the buttons when the Emergency SOS slider appears, until iPhone plays a warning sound and starts a countdown. (To skip the countdown, drag the Emergency SOS slider.) When the countdown ends, iPhone calls emergency services.
  Or, you can enable iPhone to start Emergency SOS when you press the side button

After an emergency call ends, your iPhone alerts your emergency contacts with a text message, unless you choose to cancel. Your iPhone sends your current location (if available) and—for a period of time after you enter SOS mode—your emergency contacts receive updates when your location changes.

Use Emergency SOS (India)

- Triple-click the side button. Or, if Accessibility Shortcut is turned on, press and hold the side button and either volume button until the sliders appear, then drag Emergency SOS.

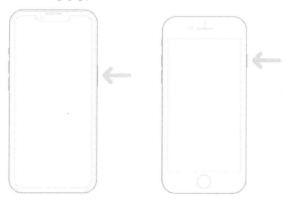

By default, iPhone plays a warning sound, starts a countdown, then calls the emergency services.

After an emergency call ends, your iPhone alerts your emergency contacts with a text message, unless you choose to cancel. Your iPhone sends your current location (if available) and—for a period of time after you enter SOS mode—your emergency contacts receive updates when your location changes.

Change your Emergency SOS settings

1. Go to Settings ⚙ > Emergency SOS.
2. Do any of the following:
   - **Turn Call with Hold on or off**: Press and hold the side and volume buttons to start a countdown to call emergency services.
   - **Turn "Call with 5 presses" on or off**: Rapidly press the side button five times to start a countdown to call emergency services.
   - **Manage your emergency contacts**: In Health, tap Set Up Emergency Contacts or Edit Emergency Contacts.

Important information about emergency calls on iPhone

- Some cellular networks may not accept an emergency call from iPhone if iPhone isn't activated, if iPhone isn't compatible with or configured to operate on a particular cellular network, or (when applicable) if iPhone doesn't have a SIM card or the SIM card is PIN-locked.
- In certain countries or regions, your location information (if determinable) may be accessed by emergency service providers when you make an emergency call.
- Review your carrier's emergency calling information to understand the limits of emergency calling over Wi-Fi.
- With CDMA, when an emergency call ends, iPhone enters emergency call mode for a few minutes to allow a callback from emergency services. During this time, data transmission and text messages are blocked.

- After making an emergency call, certain call features that block or silence incoming calls may be disabled for a short period of time to allow a callback from emergency services. These include Do Not Disturb, Silence Unknown Callers, and Screen Time.
- On an iPhone with Dual SIM, if you don't turn on Wi-Fi Calling for a line, any incoming phone calls on that line (including calls from emergency services) go directly to voicemail (if available from your carrier) when the other line is in use; you won't receive missed call notifications.

If you set up conditional call forwarding (if available from your carrier) from one line to another when a line is busy or not in service, the calls don't go to voicemail; contact your carrier for setup information.

Set up and view your Medical ID

A Medical ID provides information about you that may be important in an emergency, like allergies, medical conditions, and your emergency contacts. Your iPhone and Apple Watch can display this information so that it's available for someone attending to you in an emergency.

Create your Medical ID

Set up a Medical ID in the Health app .

1. Open the Health app on your iPhone.
2. Tap your profile picture at the top right, then tap Medical ID.
3. Tap Get Started or Edit, then enter your information.
4. Below Emergency Contacts, tap Add Emergency Contact, then add your contacts. After an emergency call ends, your iPhone alerts your emergency contacts with a text message, unless you choose to cancel. Your iPhone sends your current location (if available) and—for a period of time after you enter SOS mode—your emergency contacts receive updates when your location changes.
5. Tap Done.

Tip: To view your Medical ID from the Home Screen, touch and hold the Health app icon, then choose Medical ID.

Allow emergency services and first responders to access your Medical ID

The information in your Medical ID can be shared automatically during an emergency call (U.S. and Canada only), and also appears on the Lock Screen of your iPhone and Apple Watch.

1. Open the Health app on your iPhone.
2. Tap your profile picture at the top right, then tap Medical ID.
3. Tap Edit, scroll to the bottom, then turn on Show When Locked and Emergency Call.

Note: A first responder views your Medical ID from the Lock Screen by swiping up, tapping Emergency on the passcode screen, then tapping Medical ID.

Manage Crash Detection on iPhone 14 models

What is Crash Detection?

If your iPhone 14 detects a severe car crash, it can help connect you to emergency services and notify your emergency contacts.

How Crash Detection works

When your iPhone detects a severe car crash, it will display an alert and will automatically initiate an emergency phone call after 20 seconds unless you cancel. If you are unresponsive, your iPhone will play an audio message for emergency services, which informs them that you've been in a severe crash and gives them your latitudinal and longitudinal coordinates with an approximate search radius.

When a crash is detected, Crash Detection won't override any existing emergency calls placed by other means.

Turn Crash Detection on or off

Crash Detection is on by default. You can turn off alerts and automatic emergency calls from Apple after a severe car crash in Settings ⚙ > Emergency SOS, then turn off Call After Severe Crash. If you have third-party apps registered to detect crashes on your device, they will still be notified.

If you have CarPlay or Apple Watch

If your iPhone has Crash Detection turned on and is connected to your vehicle through CarPlay, the Crash Detection features (dialing emergency services) will go through your iPhone.

If you're wearing your Apple Watch at the time of the event, dialing emergency services will be placed by iPhone but Crash Detection features will be routed through Apple Watch.

Reset privacy and security settings in an emergency

You can use Safety Check on iPhone to quickly stop sharing your device access and personal information with others. Safety Check helps you quickly change your passcode and Apple ID password, stop sharing your location with Find My, restrict Messages and FaceTime to the device in your hand, and more.

1. Go to Settings ⚙ > Privacy & Security > Safety Check.
2. Tap Emergency Reset, tap Start Emergency Reset, then follow the onscreen instructions.

You can also use Safety Check to periodically review and update the information you share with people, apps, and devices.

Family Sharing

Set up Family Sharing on iPhone

Family Sharing lets you and up to five other family members share access to Apple services, purchases, an iCloud storage plan, and more. You can even help locate each other's missing devices.

One adult family member—the organizer—invites other family members to participate. When family members join, Family Sharing is set up on everyone's devices automatically. The group then chooses which services and features they want to use and share.

Family Sharing is available on eligible devices.

Create a Family Sharing group

You only need to set up Family Sharing on one device. Then it's available on all your devices that are signed in with the same Apple ID.

1. Go to Settings ⚙️ > [your name] > Family Sharing, then follow the onscreen instructions to set up your Family Sharing group.
2. Add one or more family members. When you add an adult family member, you can designate them as a parent or guardian.
   You can also add family members later.
3. Tap a feature you want to set up for your Family Sharing group, then follow the onscreen instructions.

To set up parental controls or Apple Cash for a child, tap their name, tap the feature, then follow the onscreen instructions.

You can see what you're sharing with your family and adjust sharing settings at any time.

What you can do with Family Sharing

With a Family Sharing group, you can set up or share the following:

- **Apple and App Store subscriptions**: You can share Apple subscriptions, including iCloud+, and eligible App Store subscriptions.
- **Purchases**: You can share items purchased in the App Store, Apple Books, and Apple TV. All purchases are billed to the family organizer.
- **Locations**: When you share your location with your Family Sharing group, all family members, including any new members added later, can use the Find My app 🔵 to see your location and help locate a missing device.
- **Apple Card and Apple Cash**: You can share Apple Card with trusted members of your Family Sharing group or set up an Apple Cash Family account for a child.
- **Parental controls**: You can manage your children's purchases, how they use their Apple devices, and more.

- **A device for your child**: You can set up a new iOS or iPadOS device for a child and customize parental controls.

Tip: You can use Family Checklist to see tips and suggestions for Family Sharing features. Go to Settings ⚙ > [your name] > Family Sharing, then tap Family Checklist.

Add a member to a Family Sharing group on iPhone

With Family Sharing, each family member joins the family group with their own Apple ID.

That way you can share access to subscriptions and other features without sharing personal information like photos or documents.

The family organizer can easily invite family members who have an Apple ID or create an Apple ID for a child who doesn't have one yet.

Add a family member with an Apple ID

The organizer of the Family Sharing group can add a family member who has their own Apple ID.

1. Go to Settings ⚙ > [your name] > Family Sharing, then tap 👤 in the upper-right corner.
2. Tap Invite Others, then follow the onscreen instructions.

You can send the invitation using AirDrop, Messages, or Mail. If you're near the family member, you can also tap Invite in Person and ask the family member to enter their Apple ID and password on your device.

Create an Apple ID for a child

If a child is too young to create their own Apple ID, the organizer, a parent, or a guardian can add the child to the Family Sharing group and create an Apple ID for them.

1. Go to Settings ⚙ > [your name] > Family Sharing.
2. Do one of the following:
   - **If you're the organizer**: Tap 👤, tap Create Child Account.
   Note: If your child already has an Apple ID, tap Invite Others. They can enter their Apple ID password on your device to accept the invitation.

   - If you're a parent or guardian: Tap 👤.
3. Follow the onscreen instructions to finish creating the child account. You can set content restrictions, communication limits, and downtime; share your child's location with all members of the Family Sharing group, including any new members added later; and use Ask to Buy. You can change these settings at any time.

Leave or remove a member from a Family Sharing group on iPhone

In a Family Sharing group, the organizer can remove members or disband the group, and family members who aren't teens with parental controls or children can remove themselves.

Remove a member from a family group

The organizer of a Family Sharing group can remove other members. When a family member is removed, they immediately lose access to shared subscriptions and content purchased by other members.

1. Go to Settings ⚙ > [your name] > Family Sharing.
2. Tap [member's name], then tap Remove [member's name] from Family.

You can't remove a child from your Family Sharing group. However, you can move them to another group or delete their Apple ID.

If you turned on Screen Time for a teen, you need to turn off Screen Time settings before you can remove them from the group.

Leave a Family Sharing group

When you leave a Family Sharing group, you stop sharing your purchases and subscriptions with family members and immediately lose access to any content they've shared.

Note: The organizer can't leave the Family Sharing group. If you want to change the organizer, you must disband the group, and have another adult create a new one.

1. Go to Settings ⚙ > [your name] > Family Sharing.
2. Tap [your name], then tap Stop Using Family Sharing.

Disband a Family Sharing group

When the family organizer turns off Family Sharing, all family members are removed from the group at the same time. When a Family Sharing group is disbanded, all members immediately lose access to the shared content and subscriptions.

Note: If a child is in the Family Sharing group, the organizer must move them to another group or delete their Apple ID before disbanding the group.

1. Go to Settings ⚙ > [your name] > Family Sharing > [your name].
2. Tap Stop Using Family Sharing.

Share Apple and App Store subscriptions with family members on iPhone

When you're in a Family Sharing group, you can share Apple subscriptions and eligible App Store subscriptions with other family members.

If your Family Sharing group has purchase sharing turned on, any subscriptions shared with the group are billed directly to the organizer's default payment method.

Note: Not all services are available in all countries or regions, and some selections are subject to content restrictions set in Screen Time.

Share Apple subscriptions

1. Go to Settings ⚙ > [your name] > Family Sharing.
2. Tap Subscriptions, then do one of the following:
   - Tap a subscription you want to share, then follow the onscreen instructions.
   - Tap Manage Subscriptions, then tap a subscription.

See any of the following to learn more.

- **Apple Arcade**: All members of your family can download and play Apple Arcade games from the App Store. Each player gets a personalized account—your progress is carried over between devices.
- **Apple Fitness+**: All members of your family can access workouts in the Fitness app on their iPhone or iPad.
- **Apple Music**: With a family subscription, each family member gets their own music library and personal recommendations.
- **Apple News+**: All members of your family can read Apple News+ publications for no additional charge.
- **Apple TV+ and Apple TV channels**: Each family member can watch on their iPhone, iPad, iPod touch, Mac, Apple TV, and supported smart TVs and streaming devices, using their own Apple ID and password.
- **iCloud+**: When you share iCloud+, all family members have access to iCloud+ features and storage. For storage, you only share the space—your photos and documents stay private and everyone keeps using their own accounts.

Share App Store subscriptions

You can choose which eligible App Store 🅰 subscriptions you share with family members.

1. Go to Settings ⚙ > [your name] > Subscriptions.
2. Do either of the following:
   - **Share all new subscriptions**: Turn on Share with Family. When you purchase a new subscription that's eligible for sharing, it's shared with your Family Sharing members by default.
   - **Change the settings of a specific subscription**: Tap a subscription, then turn Share with Family on or off.
     If you don't see Share with Family, the subscription isn't eligible for sharing.

Share App Store, Apple TV, and Apple Books purchases with Family Sharing on iPhone

With Family Sharing, the organizer can set up purchase sharing to share App Store, Apple Books, and Apple TV purchases.

The organizer adds a payment method that's shared with the family; when a family member makes a purchase, the organizer is billed. The purchased item is added to the initiating family member's account and eligible purchases are shared with the rest of the family.

The family organizer can also require that children in the family group request approval for purchases or free downloads.

Turn on purchase sharing

When the family organizer turns on purchase sharing, they pay for family members' purchases and must have a valid payment method on file.

1. Go to Settings ⚙ > [your name] > Family Sharing.
2. Tap Purchase Sharing, then follow the onscreen instructions.

Turn off purchase sharing for yourself

You can turn off purchase sharing for yourself. Family Sharing members won't see your purchases, but you can still see items other members have shared with you.

Note: Even though your items aren't shared, any purchases you make still use the shared family payment method.

1. Go to Settings ⚙ > [your name] > Family Sharing, then tap Purchase Sharing.
2. Tap [your name], then turn off Share Purchases.
   If the organizer wants to turn off purchase sharing entirely, they can tap Stop Purchase Sharing.

Share locations with family members and locate their lost devices on iPhone

With Family Sharing, you can share your location with members of your Family Sharing group and help them find lost devices. When the family organizer sets up location sharing in Family Sharing settings, the organizer's location is automatically shared with everyone in the family, including any new members added later. Then, family members can choose whether or not to share their location.

Share your location with family members

When you share locations with your family, they can see your location in Find My. You can also get notified when family members change their locations—for example, if a child leaves school during school hours.

1. Go to Settings > [your name] > Family Sharing, then scroll down and tap Location.
2. Tap the name of a family member you want to share your location with.
   You can repeat this step for each family member you want to share your location with. Each family member receives a message that you're sharing your location and can choose to share their location with you.
   You can stop sharing your location with any family member at any time.

ote: Children and teens with Screen Time turned on may not be able to change their own location sharing settings.

To share your location, you must have Location Services turned on in Settings > Privacy & Security.

Locate a family member's device

After you share your location with members of your Family Sharing group, they can help locate a missing device added to the Find My app.

Your devices are at the top of the list, and your family members' devices are below yours.

Use Apple Cash and Apple Card with Family Sharing on iPhone (U.S. only)

You can use Family Sharing with the Wallet app . The organizer of the Family Sharing group can set up Apple Cash for a child. They can also share Apple Card with trusted members of their Family Sharing group.

Set up Apple Cash Family

The family organizer can set up Apple Cash for a child. They can use Wallet to see the card balance, monitor transactions, and limit who the child can send money to.

1. Go to Settings > [your name] > Family Sharing.
2. Tap the child you want to set up Apple Cash for.
3. Tap Apple Cash, then follow the onscreen instructions.

Set up Apple Card Family

The family organizer can invite one eligible member of their Family Sharing group who is 18 years or older to co-own Apple Card. Members of the Family Sharing group who are 13 years or older can be added as participants.

1. In Wallet , tap Apple Card.

2. Tap ⬤, tap Share My Card, then follow the onscreen instructions.

Set up parental controls with Family Sharing on iPhone

With Family Sharing, the organizer can set up parental controls for children in the Family Sharing group. You can use Screen Time to manage how your children use their Apple devices. You can also turn on Ask to Buy, so children must receive approval for purchases or free downloads.

Customize parental controls during setup

When you add a child to your Family Sharing group or set up a device for a child, you can customize parental controls from the start. You can change those settings at any time.

Follow the onscreen instructions during setup to add any of the following:

- Age-related restrictions for content in apps, books, TV shows, and movies
- Downtime and limits for specific apps
- Restrictions for who your child can communicate with
- Approvals for purchases or free downloads

Set up Screen Time for a child later

Screen Time allows you to manage settings for downtime, app use, contacts, content ratings, and more. To use Screen Time, your child must be using an eligible device.

1. Go to Settings ⚙ > [your name] > Family Sharing > Screen Time.
2. Tap the child you want to set up Screen Time for.
3. Tap Screen Time, then follow the onscreen instructions.

If your child requests more screen time, you can approve or decline the request in Settings

> Screen Time or in Messages 💬.

Turn on Ask to Buy for a child later

When you set up Ask to Buy, a child's purchases must be approved by the family organizer or a parent or guardian in the family group.

1. Go to Settings ⚙ > [your name] > Family Sharing.
2. Tap the child you want to set up Ask to Buy for.
3. Tap Ask To Buy, then follow the onscreen instructions.

Note: Age restrictions for Ask to Buy vary by region. In the United States, the family organizer can turn on Ask to Buy for any family member under age 18; for children under age 13, it's on by default.

Set up a device for a child with Family Sharing on iPhone

With Family Sharing, the organizer, a parent, or a guardian can use Quick Start on their iPhone to set up a new iOS or iPadOS device for a child and customize parental controls.

1. If the child already has an Apple ID, make sure they've been added to the Family Sharing group. If they don't have an Apple ID, you can create an Apple ID for them while adding them to the Family Sharing group.
2. On the new iOS or iPadOS device you want to set up for your child, press and hold the side button or top button until the Apple logo appears.
3. Bring your iPhone next to the device.
4. When you see Set Up New [device] on your iPhone, tap Continue, follow the onscreen instructions, then do one of the following:
   - If you have a child in your family group, tap your child's name.
   - If you need to create a new Apple ID for your child, tap Create New Child Account, then create an Apple ID for your child.
5. Follow the onscreen instructions to finish setting up your child's device. You can set content restrictions, communication limits, and downtime; share your child's location with all members of the Family Sharing group, including any new members added later; and use Ask to Buy. You can change these settings at any time.

Screen Time

Keep track of your screen time on iPhone

You can use Screen Time to get information about how you and your family members spend time on your devices—which apps and websites you use, how often you pick up your device, and more. You can use this information to help you make decisions about managing the time you spend on devices. You can also schedule time away from your screen, set time limits for app use, and more.

Turn on Screen Time

Before you can view your app and device usage, you need to turn on Screen Time.

1. Go to Settings ⚙ > Screen Time.
2. Tap Turn On Screen Time, then tap Continue.
3. Tap This is My iPhone if you're setting up Screen Time for yourself on your iPhone. If you're setting up Screen Time for your child (or family member), tap This is My Child's iPhone.
4. To use Screen Time on all your Apple devices, scroll down, then turn on Share Across Devices.

If you've set up Family Sharing, you can turn on Screen Time for a family member through Family Sharing on your device.

View your Screen Time report

After you turn on Screen Time, you can view a report of your device use with information including how much time you spend using certain kinds of apps, how often you pick up your iPhone and other devices, what apps send you the most notifications, and more.

1. Go to Settings ⚙ > Screen Time.
2. Tap See All Activity, then tap Week to see a summary of your weekly use, or tap Day to see a summary of your daily use.

Use the Screen Time widget to check your device use at a glance

To keep track of your device use from the Home Screen, you can add a widget to your Home Screen for Screen Time. The widget displays information from your Screen Time summary—the larger the widget you add, the more information it displays. You can quickly check your device use by glancing at the widget.

If you set up Screen Time for family members through Family Sharing, you can tap the widget to see a list of the people in your family group. Tap the name of a family member whose report you want to view.

Use Screen Time on all your devices

To share your Screen Time settings and reports across all your devices, make sure you're signed in with the same Apple ID on each device and Share Across Devices is turned on.

1. Go to Settings ⚙ > Screen Time.
2. Scroll down, then turn on Share Across Devices.

Set up Screen Time for yourself on iPhone

With Screen Time, you can manage your app use, schedule time away from your device, and more. You can change or turn off any of these settings at any time.

Schedule time away from the screen

In Screen Time, you can block apps and notifications for periods when you want time away from your devices. For example, you might want to schedule downtime during meals or at bedtime.

1. Go to Settings ⚙ > Screen Time, then turn on Screen Time if you haven't already.
2. Tap Downtime, then turn on Downtime.
3. Select Every Day or Customize Days, then set the start and end times.

Turn on downtime on demand

During downtime, only calls, messages, and apps you choose to allow are available. You can receive calls from contacts you've selected to allow communication with during downtime, and you can use apps you've chosen to allow at all times.

When you turn on downtime on demand, a five-minute reminder is sent before downtime is turned on. It stays on until the end of the day, or until the beginning of your scheduled downtime, if you've scheduled it.

1. Go to Settings ⚙ > Screen Time, then turn on Screen Time if you haven't already.
2. Tap Downtime, then tap Turn On Downtime Until Tomorrow, or Turn On Downtime Until Schedule (if Scheduled is turned on).
   To turn off downtime on demand, tap Turn Off Downtime.

Note: You can also turn on downtime on demand for a family member, either directly on their device, or through Family Sharing on your device.

Set limits for app use

You can set a time limit for a category of apps (for example, Games or Social Networking) and for individual apps.

1. Go to Settings ⚙ > Screen Time, then turn on Screen Time if you haven't already.
2. Tap App Limits, then tap Add Limit.

3. Select one or more app categories.
   To set limits for individual apps, tap the category name to see all the apps in that category, then select the apps you want to limit. If you select multiple categories or apps, the time limit you set applies to all of them.
4. Tap Next, then set the amount of time allowed.
   To set an amount of time for each day, tap Customize Days, then set limits for specific days.
5. When you finish setting limits, tap Add.

To temporarily turn off all app limits, tap App Limits on the App Limits screen. To temporarily turn off a time limit for a specific category, tap the category, then turn off App Limit.

To remove a time limit for a category, tap the category, then tap Delete Limit.

Set communication limits

In Screen Time, you can either allow or block communication—including incoming and outgoing phone calls, FaceTime calls, and messages—from certain contacts in iCloud, either at all times or during certain periods.

1. If you haven't already turned on Contacts in iCloud, go to Settings 🔘 > [your name] > iCloud, then turn on Contacts.
2. Go to Settings 🔘 > Screen Time, then turn on Screen Time if you haven't already.
3. Tap Communication Limits, tap During Screen Time, then select one of the following for communication at all times (other than downtime):
   ○ **Contacts Only**: To allow communication only with your contacts.
   ○ **Contacts & Groups with at Least One Contact**: To allow one-on-one conversations only with people in your contacts and group conversations that include at least one person in your contacts.
   ○ **Everyone**: To allow conversations with anyone, including unknown numbers.
4. Tap Back at the top left, then tap During Downtime.
   The option you selected for During Screen Time is already set here. You can change this setting to Specific Contacts, then choose one of the following:
   ○ **Choose From My Contacts**: To select contacts to allow communication with during Downtime.
   ○ **Add New Contact**: To add a person to your contacts and allow communication with that person during downtime.

If someone who's currently blocked by your Communication Limit settings tries to call you or send you a message, their communication won't go through.

If you try to call or send a message to someone who's currently blocked by your Communication Limit settings, their name or number appears in red in your list of recent calls or messages, and your communication won't go through. You can communicate with them when the communication limit is changed. If the limit applies only to downtime, you receive a Time Limit message. You can resume communication with them when downtime is over.

To resume communication with contacts who are blocked by your Communication Limit settings, change the settings by following the steps above.

Choose apps and contacts you want to allow at all times

In Screen Time, you can specify apps that can be used, and contacts you can communicate with, at all times—even during downtime (for example, in the event of an emergency).

1. Go to Settings ⚙ > Screen Time > Always Allowed.
2. Below Allowed Apps, tap ⊕ or ⊖ next to an app to add or remove it from the Allowed Apps list.
3. To specify contacts you want to allow communication with, tap Contacts.
   The option you selected in Communication Limits appears here. You can change this setting to Specific Contacts, then choose one of the following:
   - **Choose From My Contacts**: To select specific people to allow communication with.
   - **Add New Contact**: To add a new contact and allow communication with that person.
4. Tap Back at the top left.

Set content and privacy restrictions

You can block inappropriate content and set restrictions for iTunes Store and App Store purchases.

1. Go to Settings ⚙ > Screen Time.
2. Tap Content & Privacy Restrictions, then turn on Content & Privacy Restrictions.
   You can also set a passcode that's required before changing settings.
3. Select options to set content allowances for iTunes Store and App Store purchases, app use, content ratings, and more.

Note: To restrict SharePlay in FaceTime calls on your device, go to Settings > Screen Time > Content & Privacy Restrictions > Allowed Apps, then turn off SharePlay. To allow SharePlay, turn it on.

Set up Screen Time for a family member on iPhone

Screen Time lets you see how family members are using their devices, so you can structure the time they spend on them. You can set up Screen Time for a family member on their device or, if you've set up Family Sharing, you can set up Screen Time for a family member through Family Sharing on your device.

Note: As the organizer of a Family Sharing group, when you set up a child account, you can set up content restrictions, communication limits, and downtime. After the child's account is set up, you can change parental control settings at any time in Settings > Screen Time.

Family Sharing has a checklist that reminds the organizer to update the parental control settings as the child gets older.

Set downtime and app limits on a family member's device

1. On your family member's device, go to Settings ⚙ > Screen Time.
2. Tap Turn On Screen Time, tap Continue, then tap This is My Child's iPhone.
3. To schedule downtime for your family member (time away from the screen), enter the start and end times, then tap Set Downtime.
4. To set limits for categories of apps you want to manage for your family member (for example, Games or Social Networking), select the categories.
   To see all the categories, tap Show All Categories.
5. Tap Set, enter an amount of time, then tap Set App Limit.
6. Tap Continue, then enter a Screen Time passcode for managing your family member's Screen Time settings.

Note: You can also turn on downtime on demand for a family member, either directly on their device, or through Family Sharing on your device (if you've set up Family Sharing).

If your child requests more screen time, you can approve or decline the request in Settings > Screen Time or in Messages.

Set communication limits on a family member's device

You can block incoming and outgoing communication on your family member's device—including phone calls, FaceTime calls, and messages—from specific contacts, either at all times or during certain periods.

1. If you haven't already turned on Contacts in iCloud on your family member's device, go to Settings ⚙ > [child's name] > iCloud, then turn on Contacts.
   Note: You can only manage your family member's communication if they're using Contacts in iCloud.
2. On your family member's device, go to Settings ⚙ > Screen Time.
3. If you haven't already turned on Screen Time, tap Turn On Screen Time, tap Continue, then tap This is My Child's iPhone.
4. Tap Communication Limits, then do any of the following:
   - **Limit communication at any time**: Tap During Screen Time, then select Contacts Only, Contacts & Groups with at Least One Contact, or Everyone.
   - **Limit communication during downtime**: Tap During Downtime. The option you selected for During Screen Time is already set here. You can change this setting to Specific Contacts.
     If you select Specific Contacts, then tap either Choose From My Contacts or Add New Contact to select people you want to allow communication with during downtime.
   - **Manage a child's contacts**: If you're using Family Sharing, you can view, edit, add, or delete your child's contacts. Tap Manage [child's name] Contacts.
     If your child already has contacts in iCloud, they receive a notification on their device asking them to approve the request to manage them. If they don't have contacts, they don't get a notification and you can immediately add contacts. When you manage your child's contacts, a new row appears beneath Manage [child's name] Contacts to show how many contacts your child has. Tap the row to view and edit the contacts.

- o **Allow contact editing**: Tap Allow Contact Editing to turn off this option and prevent your child from editing their contacts.
  Turning off contact editing and limiting communication at any time to Contacts Only is a good way to control who your child can communicate with and when they can be contacted.

If someone who's currently blocked by the Communication Limit settings tries to call your family member (by phone or FaceTime), or send them a message, their communication won't go through.

If your family member tries to call or send a message to someone who's currently blocked by the Communication Limit settings, the recipient's name or number appears in red with an hourglass icon, and the communication won't go through. If the limit applies only to downtime, your family member receives a Time Limit message and can resume communication with the contact when downtime is over.

To allow your family member to communicate with contacts who are blocked by the Communication Limit settings, change the settings by following the steps above.

Turn communication safety for messages on or off on a family member's device

When communication safety is turned on in Screen Time, nudity in photos can be detected in the Messages app before the photos are sent or received by your child, and resources are provided to help your child handle the situation (not available in all countries or regions). This feature does not give Apple access to the photos.

1. On your family member's device, go to Settings ⚙ > Screen Time.
2. If you haven't already turned on Screen Time, tap Turn On Screen Time, tap Continue, then tap This is My Child's iPhone.
3. Tap Communication Safety, then turn on Check for Sensitive Photos.

Choose which apps to allow at all times on a family member's device

You can set which apps you want your family member to be able to use at any time.

1. On your family member's device, go to Settings > Screen Time.
2. If you haven't already turned on Screen Time, tap Turn On Screen Time, tap Continue, then tap This is My Child's iPhone.
3. Tap Always Allowed, then tap ⊕ or ⊖ next to an app to add or remove the app from the list.

Note: If your family member needs health or accessibility apps, make sure they're in the Allowed Apps list. If Messages isn't always allowed, your family member may not be able to send or receive messages (including to emergency numbers and contacts) during downtime or after the app limit has expired.

Set content and privacy restrictions on a family member's device

411

You can help ensure that the content on your family member's device is age appropriate by limiting the explicitness ratings in Content & Privacy Restrictions.

1. On your family member's device, go to Settings ⚙ > Screen Time.
2. If you haven't already turned on Screen Time, tap Turn On Screen Time, tap Continue, then tap This is My Child's iPhone.
3. Tap Content & Privacy Restrictions, then turn on Content & Privacy Restrictions.
4. Choose specific content and privacy options.
   Note: To protect your family member's hearing, scroll down, tap Reduce Loud Sounds, then select Don't Allow. (This prevents changes to the maximum headphone volume.)

Note: To restrict SharePlay in FaceTime calls for your family member, go to Settings > Screen Time > Content & Privacy Restrictions > Allowed Apps, then turn off SharePlay. To allow SharePlay, turn it on.

5. Tap ‹ at the top left.

Add or change Screen Time settings for a family member later

Important: If you set up Screen Time for a family member on their device (not through Family Sharing), and you forget the Screen Time passcode, you can use your Apple ID to reset it. However, if you set up Screen Time for a family member on your device through Family Sharing and you forget your Screen Time passcode, you can reset it on your device using your device passcode or Face ID.

Get a report of your device use on iPhone

When you have Screen Time set up, you can get a report of your device use.

1. Go to Settings ⚙ > Screen Time.
2. Tap See All Activity, then do any of the following:
   - Tap Week to see a summary of your weekly use.
   - Tap Day to see a summary of your daily use.

You can also view your summary by tapping a Screen Time Weekly Report notification when one appears on your screen. (If the notification disappears, you can find it in Notification Center.) Alternatively, you can add a Screen Time widget to your Home Screen to check your Screen Time report at a glance.

Accessories

Charging cable for iPhone

Your iPhone includes one of the following charging cables:

USB-C to Lightning Cable

Lightning to USB Cable

You can connect iPhone to a power outlet using a compatible power adapter (sold separately) and the included cable. You can also connect the included cable to your computer's USB port for charging, transferring files, and more.

Power adapters for iPhone

You can connect iPhone to a power outlet using its charging cable (included) and a compatible power adapter (sold separately).

You can use the following Apple USB power adapters to charge iPhone. The size and style may vary depending on the country or region.

Apple 20W USB-C power adapter

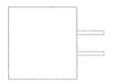

Note: For fast charging, iPhone requires a power adapter with a minimum power output of 20 watts, such as the Apple 20W USB power adapter. If you use a third-party power adapter, it should meet these recommended specifications:

- Frequency: 50 to 60 Hz, single phase
- Line Voltage: 100 to 240 VAC
- Output Voltage/Current: 9 VDC/2.2 A
- Minimum Power Output: 20 W
- Output Port: USB-C

Apple 18W USB-C power adapter

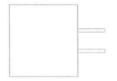

Apple 5W USB power adapter

You can also use Apple USB power adapters for iPad and Mac notebooks to charge iPhone, and you can use third-party power adapters that are compliant with applicable country regulations and international and regional safety standards.

MagSafe chargers and battery packs for iPhone

MagSafe chargers and battery packs snap to the back of iPhone or its MagSafe case or sleeve. The magnets ensure proper alignment for fast wireless charging, and you can hold and use iPhone while it's charging.

Without the magnetic alignment, MagSafe chargers can also charge other iPhone models and AirPods. (AirPods and MagSafe chargers, battery packs, cases, and sleeves are sold separately.)

Charge iPhone or AirPods with MagSafe Charger

1. Connect MagSafe Charger to power using the Apple 20W USB-C power adapter or another compatible power adapter (sold separately).

2. Do one of the following:
   - **iPhone**: Place MagSafe Charger on the back of iPhone or its MagSafe case or sleeve. The charging symbol appears when iPhone starts charging.
   Note: If iPhone Leather Wallet is attached, remove it before placing MagSafe Charger on the back of iPhone.
   - **AirPods (2nd generation) with Wireless Charging Case, AirPods (3rd generation), and AirPods Pro:** Place your AirPods in the charging case, close the lid, then place the case with the status light facing up on the center of MagSafe Charger. When the case is aligned properly with the charger, the status light turns on for several seconds, then turns off while continuing to charge.

Charge iPhone or AirPods and Apple Watch with MagSafe Duo Charger

With MagSafe Duo Charger, you can charge your iPhone or AirPods at the same time you charge your Apple Watch. (MagSafe Duo Charger, Apple Watch, and AirPods are sold separately.)

1. Connect MagSafe Duo Charger to power using the Apple 20W USB-C power adapter or another compatible power adapter (sold separately).

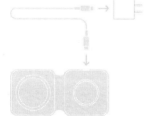

2. To charge iPhone or AirPods, do one of the following:

415

- **iPhone**: Place iPhone face up on the center of the iPhone charging surface. Supported models help you align iPhone with the charger, and the charging symbol appears when iPhone starts charging.

Note: If iPhone Leather Wallet is attached, remove it before placing iPhone on MagSafe Duo Charger.

- **AirPods (2nd generation) with Wireless Charging Case, AirPods (3rd generation), and AirPods Pro**: Place your AirPods in the charging case, close the lid, then place the case with the status light facing up on the center of the iPhone charging surface. When the case is aligned properly with the charger, the status light turns on for several seconds, then turns off while continuing to charge.

3. To charge Apple Watch, do one of the following:
   - With the Apple Watch charging surface lying flat and the Apple Watch band open, place Apple Watch face up on the charging surface.
   - With the Apple Watch charging surface raised, place Apple Watch on its side with its back against the charging surface. Apple Watch automatically goes into Nightstand mode, so you can also use it as an alarm clock.

4. The concave charging surface magnetically snaps to the back of your Apple Watch and aligns it properly. When charging begins, a charging symbol appears on the watch face.

Charge iPhone with MagSafe Battery Pack

MagSafe Battery Pack magnetically attaches to supported models and extends the battery life.

Note: If iPhone Leather Wallet is attached, remove it before placing MagSafe Battery Pack.

- **Charge your iPhone on the go**: Place MagSafe Battery Pack on the back of iPhone or its MagSafe case or sleeve. The charging symbol appears when iPhone starts charging.
- **See the battery status of MagSafe Battery Pack and iPhone**: Check the Batteries widget in Today View or on the Home Screen.
- **Charge MagSafe Battery Pack and iPhone**: With MagSafe Battery Pack on iPhone, connect either device to power using the USB-C to Lightning Cable and Apple 20W USB-C power adapter or another compatible power adapter (minimum power output of 20 watts; sold separately). The status indicator on MagSafe Battery Pack is amber while charging, then turns green when charging is complete.

Note: By default, charging is limited to 90 percent to optimize the lifespan of MagSafe Battery Pack. To remove the charging limit, open Control Center, tap Low Power Mode, then tap Charge past 90%.

You can also charge MagSafe Battery Pack without iPhone.

MagSafe cases and sleeves for iPhone

MagSafe cases and sleeves contain magnets that align iPhone with MagSafe chargers and battery packs. You can even hold and use iPhone while it's charging.

iPhone Leather Sleeve

When iPhone Leather Sleeve covers your iPhone, you can do the following without removing the sleeve:

- **Get the current time**: If the clock window is dark, raise iPhone or tap the window.
- **See the charging status**: When you charge iPhone, the clock window indicates the battery level and its charging status.
- **See who's calling**: When a phone or FaceTime call arrives, the caller's name or number appears in the clock window.
  To answer, remove iPhone from the sleeve, then drag the slider.
  Or without removing iPhone, use your AirPods or Apple Watch (sold separately) to answer the call. (FaceTime video calls are answered with your video paused.)
- **Make an Express Transit payment**: Position the rear top of iPhone within a few centimeters of the contactless reader at the transit gate. A confirmation message appears in the clock window.

If your iPhone is in Express Cards power reserve mode, confirmation messages don't appear in the clock window.

If you carry a separate transit card in iPhone Leather Sleeve, your transit card is used for payment when you position the lower front of iPhone near the contactless reader.

When your iPhone is in iPhone Leather Sleeve, you can also use "Hey Siri," your AirPods, your Apple Watch, and CarPlay to make calls, ask questions, and do tasks that don't require you to look at or touch the iPhone screen.

Note: If you remove your iPhone from the sleeve and see the time for the clock window instead of the Lock Screen, tap in the top-right corner.

Qi-certified wireless chargers for iPhone

You can wirelessly charge iPhone using a Qi-certified charger (sold separately). You can also use a Qi-certified charger to charge AirPods.

Charge iPhone or AirPods with a Qi-certified charger

1. Connect the charger to power. Use the power adapter that came with your charger or a power adapter recommended by the manufacturer.
2. Do one of the following:
   - **iPhone**: Place iPhone face up on the center of the charger. When iPhone is aligned properly with the charger, appears in the status bar.
   - **AirPods (2nd generation) with Wireless Charging Case, AirPods (3rd generation), and AirPods Pro**: Place your AirPods in the charging case, close the lid, then place the case with the status light facing up on the center of the charger. When the case is aligned properly with the charger, the status light turns on for several seconds, then turns off while continuing to charge.

Use AirPods with iPhone

After you pair AirPods with iPhone, you can use AirPods to listen to audio playing on iPhone, make and answer calls, listen and respond to messages, hear reminders when you need them, listen to conversations more easily in noisy environments, and more.

Pair AirPods with your iPhone

1. On iPhone, go to Settings ⚙ > Bluetooth, then turn on Bluetooth.
2. Go to the Home Screen on your iPhone.
3. Do one of the following:
   - **AirPods (1st, 2nd, and 3rd generation) and AirPods Pro**: Open the case with your AirPods inside, then hold it next to your iPhone.
   - **AirPods Max**: Take your AirPods Max out of the Smart Case, then hold AirPods Max next to your iPhone.
4. Follow the onscreen instructions, then tap Done.

Note: If onscreen instructions for pairing your AirPods Max don't appear, go to Settings > Bluetooth, then select your AirPods Max. If the status light doesn't flash white on AirPods Max, press and hold the noise control button until it does.

Your AirPods are automatically paired with all of your supported devices where you're signed in with the same Apple ID (iOS 10, iPadOS 13, macOS 10.12, watchOS 3, or later required).

Use EarPods with iPhone

You can use EarPods (sold separately) to listen to music and videos and to make calls on iPhone. EarPods feature a microphone, volume buttons, and the center button.

Use the center button to answer and end calls, control audio and video playback, and use Siri, even when iPhone is locked.

Center button

Control audio with your EarPods

- **Pause**: Press the center button. Press again to resume playback.
- **Skip forward:** Press the center button twice quickly.
- **Skip backward**: Press the center button three times quickly.

- **Fast-forward**: Press the center button twice quickly and hold.

Manage calls using your EarPods

- **Answer an incoming call**: Press the center button.
- **End the current call**: Press the center button.
- **Switch to an incoming or on-hold call, and put the current call on hold**: Press the center button. Press again to switch back to the first call.

Ask Siri with your EarPods

Press and hold the center button until you hear a beep. Let go, then ask Siri to perform a task or answer your question.

Use Apple Watch with iPhone

Pair Apple Watch with iPhone

On your iPhone, tap the Apple Watch app , then follow the onscreen instructions.

Unlock iPhone with Apple Watch

When you're wearing your Apple Watch (Series 3 and later), you can use it to securely unlock your iPhone when you're wearing a face mask (watchOS 7.4 or later required).

Note: On iPhone 14 models, it's not necessary to use Apple Watch to unlock iPhone when you're wearing a face mask.

To allow Apple Watch to unlock your iPhone, do the following:

1. Go to Settings > Face ID & Passcode.
2. Scroll down, then turn on Apple Watch (below Unlock with Apple Watch).
   If you have more than one watch, turn on the setting for each one.

To unlock your iPhone while you're wearing your Apple Watch and a face mask, raise iPhone or tap its screen to wake it, then glance at your iPhone.

Note: To unlock your iPhone, your Apple Watch must have a passcode, be unlocked and on your wrist, and be close to your iPhone.

Work out with Apple Fitness+

Used in conjunction with Apple Watch, Apple Fitness+ is a subscription service that lets you choose from a catalog of workouts led by expert trainers. While you follow a workout on your iPhone, in-session metrics like heart rate and calories burned (which are captured by your watch) appear on your screen. (watchOS 7.2 or later required; Apple Fitness+ availability varies by country or region.)

Note: With Fitness on iPhone, you can view your active calories and steps, set a move goal, track your progress, and see your movement trends over time—even if you don't have an Apple Watch.

Collect health and fitness data from Apple Watch

Apple Watch can send data about your health and fitness to iPhone for you to view in Health. Apple Watch can also send notifications about high heart rates, low heart rates, loud environmental sounds, and more to your iPhone.

Apple TV, smart TVs, and video displays

Wirelessly stream videos and photos to Apple TV or a smart TV from iPhone

You can use your Apple TV or an AirPlay 2-enabled smart TV to watch videos and view photos streamed from your iPhone.

Play video on Apple TV or an AirPlay 2-enabled smart TV

1. While playing video in the Apple TV app 📺 or another supported video app on your iPhone, tap the screen to show the controls.
2. Tap ⬆️, then choose your Apple TV or AirPlay 2-enabled smart TV as the playback destination.

If an AirPlay passcode appears on the TV screen, enter the passcode on your iPhone.

To change the playback destination, choose a different AirPlay option on your iPhone screen.

Show photos on Apple TV or an AirPlay 2-enabled smart TV

1. In Photos 🌸 on your iPhone, tap a photo, then tap ⬆️.
2. Swipe up, tap ⬆️, then choose your Apple TV or an AirPlay 2-enabled smart TV as the playback destination.

If an AirPlay passcode appears on the TV screen, enter the passcode on your iPhone.

To stop streaming photos, tap ⬆️ near the top of the iPhone screen, then tap Turn off AirPlay.

Turn automatic AirPlay streaming on or off

You can allow your iPhone to discover and automatically connect to any frequently used Apple TV or smart TV when playing content from apps that you regularly use with AirPlay.

Go to Settings ⚙️ > General > AirPlay & Handoff, then choose Automatic, Never, or Ask.

Mirror your iPhone on Apple TV or a smart TV

On Apple TV or a smart TV, you can show whatever appears on your iPhone.

1. Open Control Center on your iPhone.

2. Tap ⬜, then choose your Apple TV or an AirPlay 2-enabled smart TV as the playback destination.

If an AirPlay passcode appears on the TV screen, enter the passcode on your iPhone.

To switch back to iPhone, open Control Center, tap ⬜, then tap Stop Mirroring.

Connect iPhone to a display with a cable

With the appropriate cable or adapter, you can connect your iPhone to a secondary display, like a computer monitor, TV, or projector.

1. Plug a Lightning Digital AV Adapter or Lightning to VGA Adapter into the charging port on the bottom of iPhone.
2. Connect an HDMI or VGA cable to your adapter.
3. Connect the other end of your HDMI or VGA cable to your monitor, TV, or projector.
4. If necessary, switch to the correct video source on your monitor, TV, or projector. If you need help, use your display's manual.

The adapters have an extra port so you can connect the charging cable and charge your iPhone while connected to a monitor, TV, or projector.

Play audio from iPhone on HomePod and AirPlay 2 speakers

You can play audio from iPhone on wireless devices like HomePod, Apple TV, AirPlay 2-enabled smart TVs, and Bluetooth headphones and speakers.

Play audio from iPhone on a wireless device

1. On your iPhone, open an audio app, such as Podcasts 📻 or Music 🎵, then choose an item to play.
2. Tap 📡, then choose a playback destination.

Note: If your AirPlay 2-enabled devices don't appear in the list of playback destinations, make sure they're on the same Wi-Fi network. With a Bluetooth device, the playback destination returns to iPhone if you move the device out of Bluetooth range.

To select the playback destination, you can also tap 📡 on the Lock Screen or in Control Center.

Play audio on multiple AirPlay 2-enabled devices

With AirPlay 2 and iPhone, you can play audio on multiple AirPlay 2-enabled devices connected to the same Wi-Fi network. For example, you can play a party playlist on HomePod speakers in the living room and kitchen, on an Apple TV in the bedroom, and on an AirPlay 2-enabled smart TV in the den.

Siri: Say something like:

- "Stop playing music everywhere"
- "Set the dining room volume to 10 percent"
- "What's playing in the kitchen?"
- "Play a song I like in the kitchen"
- "Add the living room speaker"
- "Remove the music from the kitchen"
- "Move the music to the den"

You can also choose playback destinations from the iPhone screen.

1. Tap 📡 in Control Center, on the Lock Screen, or on the Now Playing screen for the app you're listening to.
2. Select each device you want to use.

Note: Devices arranged in a stereo pair are treated as a single audio device.

Hand off audio from iPhone to HomePod

While playing audio from Music, Podcasts, or another audio app, bring iPhone close to the top of HomePod.

Audio hand off has the following requirements:

- You must be signed in with the same Apple ID on both devices.
- On your iPhone, you've turned on Wi-Fi and Handoff.
- iPhone and HomePod must be in the same HomeKit home and on the same Wi-Fi network.
- Your devices must have Bluetooth turned on in Settings 📲 and be within Bluetooth range of one another (about 33 feet or 10 meters).

To disable Handoff between iPhone and HomePod and other devices, go to Settings > General > AirPlay & Handoff.

Magic Keyboard

Pair Magic Keyboard with iPhone

You can use Magic Keyboard, including Magic Keyboard with Numeric Keypad, to enter text on iPhone. Magic Keyboard connects to iPhone using Bluetooth.

Pair Magic Keyboard

1. Make sure the keyboard is turned on and charged.
2. On iPhone, go to Settings 📲 > Bluetooth, then turn on Bluetooth.
3. Select the device when it appears in the Other Devices list.

Note: If Magic Keyboard is already paired with another device, you must unpair them before you can connect Magic Keyboard to your iPhone. For iPhone, iPad, or iPod touch, see Unpair a Bluetooth device. On macOS 12.5 or earlier, choose Apple menu > System Preferences, click Bluetooth, Control-click the device name, then click Remove.

Reconnect Magic Keyboard to iPhone

Magic Keyboard disconnects when you turn its switch to Off or when you move it or iPhone out of Bluetooth range—about 33 feet (10 meters).

To reconnect, turn the keyboard switch to On, or bring the keyboard and iPhone back into range, then tap any key.

Enter characters with diacritical marks while using Magic Keyboard with iPhone

If your Magic Keyboard doesn't include accents and other diacritical marks for the language you're typing, you can use an Option key modifier or the onscreen keyboard to enter those marks.

Use the Option key to enter a diacritical mark for a character

To enter a character with a diacritical mark, you can press the Option key on Magic Keyboard to select a mark.

1. Do one of the following:
   - Add a language keyboard that supports diacritical marks, then in an app, switch to that language keyboard.
     For example, add the Spanish (Mexico) keyboard, then in an app, press and hold the Control key on Magic Keyboard, then press the Space bar until you select Español (México).
   - Go to Settings ⚙ > General > Keyboard > Hardware Keyboard, then choose an alternative keyboard layout that supports diacritical marks.
     For example, if you have the English (US) language keyboard, tap English (US), then choose U.S. International — PC or ABC — Extended.
2. In an app, press and hold the Option key, then press a key that enters a diacritical mark. For example, the Spanish (Mexico) keyboard and the U.S. International — PC alternative layout support these diacritical marks:
   - Acute accent (for example, é): Option-E.
   - Grave accent (for example, è): Option-`.
   - Tilde (for example, ñ): Option-N.
   - Diaeresis or umlaut (for example, ü): Option-U.
   - Circumflex (for example, ê): Option-I.
3. Press the letter.

For example, to enter ñ using the Spanish (Mexico) keyboard or the U.S. International — PC alternative layout, press Option-N, then type an n.

Note: The ABC - Extended alternative layout also allows you to enter tone marks for typing Mandarin Chinese in Pinyin orthography. For example, to type ǔ in lǚxíng ("travel"), press Option-V, then type a v. In addition, the ABC - Extended layout allows you to type diacritical marks and letters from several different European languages, such as Czech, French, German, Hungarian, and Polish.

Use the onscreen keyboard to enter a diacritical mark

1. To show the onscreen keyboard, press ⏏ on Magic Keyboard.

2. On the onscreen keyboard, touch and hold the letter, number, or symbol on the keyboard that's related to the character you want.
   For example, to enter é, touch and hold the e key.
3. Slide your finger to choose a variant.
4. To hide the onscreen keyboard when you're finished, press ⏏ on Magic Keyboard.

Switch between keyboards with Magic Keyboard and iPhone

With Magic Keyboard, you can switch between the language keyboard for your region, an emoji keyboard, other language keyboards that you add, and the onscreen keyboard.

Switch between language keyboards and the onscreen emoji keyboard

1. On Magic Keyboard, press and hold the Control key.
2. Press the Space bar to cycle between the language keyboard for your region, the emoji keyboard, and any keyboards you added for typing in different languages.

Show or hide the onscreen keyboard

To show the onscreen keyboard, press ⏏ on Magic Keyboard. To hide the onscreen keyboard, press ⏏ again.

Dictate text while using Magic Keyboard with iPhone

You can dictate text instead of typing it on Magic Keyboard.

Note: Dictation may not be available in all languages or in all countries or regions, and features may vary. Cellular data charges may apply.

1. Go to Settings ⚙ > General > Keyboard, turn on Enable Dictation, then choose a dictation shortcut.
2. To insert text by dictating, tap to place the insertion point, then press the dictation shortcut key twice.
3. To use Magic Keyboard again, quickly press the dictation shortcut key twice.

As you speak to insert text, iPhone automatically inserts punctuation for you. You can insert emoji by saying their names (for example, "mind blown emoji" or "happy emoji").

Use shortcuts on Magic Keyboard with iPhone

You can perform searches and use text replacements from anywhere on iPhone without taking your hands away from Magic Keyboard.

- **Open Search**: Press Command-Space.
  Note: You can change the actions that are performed by the Command key (and other modifier keys like Caps Lock). Go to Settings ⚙ > General > Keyboard > Hardware Keyboard, tap Modifier Keys, tap a key, then choose the action you want it to perform.
- **Use text replacements**: You can set up text replacements that enter words or phrases after you type just a few characters. For example, type "omw" to enter "On my way!"

- **Choose additional accessibility keyboard shortcuts**: Go to Settings > Accessibility > Keyboards > Full Keyboard Access, then turn on Full Keyboard Access.

Choose an alternative layout for Magic Keyboard with iPhone

With an alternative keyboard layout, you can enter letters and marks that are different from the ones on Magic Keyboard. For example, with the ABC - Extended keyboard layout, you can type letters and enter diacritical marks for several different European languages and tone marks for Mandarin Chinese in Pinyin.

1. Go to Settings ⚙ > General > Keyboard > Hardware Keyboard.
2. Tap a language at the top of the screen, then choose an alternative layout from the list.

Change typing assistance options for Magic Keyboard with iPhone

You can change Magic Keyboard options for autocorrection, autocapitalization, and more.

Go to Settings ⚙ > General > Keyboard > Hardware Keyboard, then do any of the following:

- **Turn Auto-Capitalization on or off**: When this option is selected, an app supporting this feature capitalizes proper nouns and the first words in sentences as you type.
- **Turn Auto-Correction on or off**: When this option is selected, an app supporting this feature corrects the spelling as you type.
- **Turn "." Shortcut on or off**: When this option is selected, double-tapping the space bar inserts a period followed by a space.
- **Change the action performed by the Command key or other modifier key**: Tap Modifier Keys, tap a key, then choose the action you want it to perform.

Connect external storage devices to iPhone

You can use the Files app 📁 and other supported apps to access files stored on external devices, such as USB drives and SD cards, connected to your iPhone.

Connect a USB drive or an SD card reader

1. Attach the USB drive or SD card reader to the charging port on your iPhone using a compatible connector or adapter.
   You may need the Lightning to USB Camera Adapter, Lightning to USB 3 Camera Adapter, or Lightning to SD Card Camera Reader (all sold separately).
   Note: A USB drive must have only a single data partition, and it must be formatted as FAT, FAT32, exFAT (FAT64), or APFS. To change the formatting of a USB drive, use a Mac or PC.
2. Do any of the following:
   - **Insert an SD memory card into a card reader**: Don't force the card into the slot on the reader; it fits only one way.

Note: You can import photos and videos from the memory card directly to the Photos app.

- ○ **View the contents of the drive or memory card**: In a supported app (for example, Files), tap Browse at the bottom of the screen, then tap the name of the device below Locations. If you don't see Locations, tap Browse again at the bottom of the screen.
- ○ **Disconnect the drive or card reader**: Remove it from the charging port on iPhone.

Note: The Lightning to USB 3 Camera Adapter can be powered with a USB power adapter. This allows you to connect USB devices with higher power requirements, such as external hard drives, to iPhone.

Set up and use Bluetooth accessories on iPhone

Using a Bluetooth connection, you can use third-party devices such as wireless keyboards, headphones, speakers, car kits, game controllers, and more with iPhone.

Note: iPhone must be within about 33 feet (10 meters) of the Bluetooth device.

Pair a Bluetooth headphone, car kit, game controller, or other device

1. Follow the instructions that came with the device to put it in discovery mode.
   Note: To pair AirPods, see the instructions for your model in the "Pair and connect" section in the AirPods User Guide.
2. On iPhone, go to Settings ⚙ > Bluetooth, turn on Bluetooth, then tap the name of the device.

Note: With Siri Eyes Free (available in select cars), you can use your voice to control features of your iPhone without looking at or touching iPhone. Use Bluetooth to pair iPhone to your car (refer to the user guide that came with your car if you need to). To activate Siri, press and hold the voice command button on your steering wheel until you hear the Siri tone, then make a request.

Customize a wireless game controller

After you pair a compatible game controller, you can customize it for supported games from Apple Arcade and the App Store.

1. Go to Settings ⚙ > General > Game Controller.
2. Tap the buttons you want to change.
3. To customize for a specific app, tap Add App.

Note: Apple Arcade availability varies by country or region.

Play audio from iPhone on a Bluetooth audio device

1. On your iPhone, open an audio app, such as Music, then choose an item to play.
2. Tap 🔘, then choose your Bluetooth device.

While audio is playing, you can change the playback destination on the Lock Screen or in Control Center.

The playback destination returns to iPhone if you move the device out of Bluetooth range.

Bypass your Bluetooth device for calls

To use the iPhone receiver or speaker for calls, do any of the following:

- Answer a call by tapping the iPhone screen.
- During a call, tap Audio, then choose iPhone or Speaker Phone.
- Turn off the Bluetooth device, unpair it, or move out of range.
- Go to Settings ⚙️, tap Bluetooth, then turn off Bluetooth.

Unpair a Bluetooth device

Go to Settings ⚙️ > Bluetooth, tap the information button ⓘ next to the name of the device, then tap Forget This Device.

If you don't see the Devices list, make sure Bluetooth is turned on.

If you have AirPods and you tap Forget This Device, they're automatically removed from other devices where you're signed in with the same Apple ID.

Disconnect from Bluetooth devices

To quickly disconnect from all Bluetooth devices without turning Bluetooth off, open Control Center, then tap ❊.

Note: The use of certain accessories with iPhone may affect wireless performance. Not all iOS accessories are fully compatible with iPhone. Turning on airplane mode may eliminate audio interference between iPhone and an accessory. Reorienting or relocating iPhone and the connected accessory may improve wireless performance.

Print from iPhone

Use AirPrint to print wirelessly to an AirPrint-enabled printer from apps such as Mail, Photos, and Safari. Many apps available on the App Store also support AirPrint.

iPhone and the printer must be on the same Wi-Fi network.

See the status of a print job

Open the App Switcher, then tap Print Center.

The badge on the icon shows how many documents are in the queue.

To cancel a print job, select it in Print Center, then tap Cancel Printing.

Print a document

Tap ⬆️, •••, or ↩️ (depending on the app you're using), then tap Print. (Swipe up if you don't see Print.)

Use iPhone with iPad, iPod touch, Mac, and PC

Share your internet connection from iPhone

You can use Personal Hotspot to share a cellular internet connection from your iPhone to other devices. Personal Hotspot is useful when the other devices don't have internet access from a Wi-Fi network.

Note: Personal Hotspot is not available with all carriers. Additional fees may apply. The number of devices that can join your Personal Hotspot at one time depends on your carrier and iPhone model. Contact your carrier for more information.

Set up Personal Hotspot on iPhone

Go to Settings 🔘 > Cellular, tap Set Up Personal Hotspot, then follow the onscreen instructions.

Note: If you don't see Set Up Personal Hotspot as an option, and Cellular Data is turned on in Settings > Cellular, contact your carrier about adding Personal Hotspot to your plan.

You can change the following settings:

- **Change the Wi-Fi password for your Personal Hotspot**: Go to Settings > Personal Hotspot > Wi-Fi Password.
- **Turn off Personal Hotspot and disconnect devices**: Go to Settings > Personal Hotspot, then turn off Allow Others to Join.

If you set up your iPhone to use two SIMs, Personal Hotspot uses the line you select for cellular data.

Connect a Mac or PC to your Personal Hotspot

You can use Wi-Fi, a USB cable, or Bluetooth to connect a Mac or PC to your Personal Hotspot. Do one of the following:

- **Use Wi-Fi to connect from a Mac**: On a Mac, click the Wi-Fi status menu 📶 in the menu bar, then choose your iPhone from the list of available networks.
If asked for a password, enter the password shown in Settings > Personal Hotspot on your iPhone.

  The Wi-Fi status icon 📶 in the menu bar changes to the Personal Hotspot icon 🔗 as long as your Mac remains connected to your Personal Hotspot.
  Note: You can connect your devices to Personal Hotspot without entering a password when you're signed in with the same Apple ID on your Mac and iPhone, you've turned on Bluetooth and Wi-Fi on your iPhone, and you've turned on Bluetooth and Wi-Fi on your Mac.
- **Use Wi-Fi to connect from a PC**: In the Wi-Fi settings on your PC, choose your iPhone, then enter the password shown in Settings > Personal Hotspot on your iPhone.

- **Use USB**: Connect iPhone and your computer with a cable. If you receive an alert that says Trust this Computer?, tap Trust. In your computer's network preferences, choose iPhone, then configure the network settings.

- **Use Bluetooth**: To make sure your iPhone is discoverable, go to Settings ⚙ > Bluetooth and leave the screen showing. On a Mac, use Bluetooth to connect your Mac and iPad. On your iPhone, tap the name of your Mac, then follow the onscreen instructions on your Mac.

On a PC, follow the manufacturer directions to set up a Bluetooth network connection.

Connect iPad, iPod touch, or another iPhone to your Personal Hotspot

On the other device, go to Settings ⚙ > Wi-Fi, then choose your iPhone from the list of available networks.

If asked for a password on the other device, enter the password shown in Settings > Personal Hotspot on your iPhone.

Note: You can connect the devices without entering a password when you're signed in with the same Apple ID on each device, and you've turned on Bluetooth and Wi-Fi on both devices.

When a device is connected, a blue band appears at the top of your iPhone screen. The Personal Hotspot icon � appears in the status bar of the connected device.

With Family Sharing, you can share your Personal Hotspot with any member of your family automatically or after they ask for approval.

When you share a Personal Hotspot from your iPhone, it uses cellular data for the internet connection. To monitor your cellular data network usage, go to Settings > Cellular.

Allow phone calls on your iPad, iPod touch, and Mac

You can make and receive phone calls on your iPad, iPod touch, and Mac by relaying calls through your iPhone.

Note: Cellular charges may apply. Wi-Fi Calling is not available from all carriers.

Allow phone calls on your other devices from iPhone

You first set up your iPhone, and then set up your other devices.

1. On your iPhone, go to Settings ⚙ > Cellular.
2. If your iPhone has Dual SIM, choose a line (below SIMs).
3. Do any of the following:
   - Tap Calls on Other Devices, turn on Allow Calls on Other Devices, then choose the devices on which you'd like to make and receive calls.
     This allows other devices where you're signed in with the same Apple ID to make and receive calls when they're nearby your iPhone and connected to Wi-Fi.

- Tap Wi-Fi Calling, then turn on Add Wi-Fi Calling For Other Devices.
    This allows other devices where you're signed in with the same Apple ID to make and receive calls even when your iPhone isn't nearby.
4. On your other devices, do the following:
    - On your iPad or iPod touch: Go to Settings > FaceTime, then turn on FaceTime and Calls from iPhone. If you're asked, turn on Wi-Fi Calling.
    - On your Mac: Open FaceTime, choose FaceTime > Preferences > Settings, then select Calls from iPhone. If an Upgrade to Wi-Fi Calling button appears, click it, then follow the instructions.

Note: If you enable Wi-Fi Calling, emergency calls may be made over Wi-Fi, and your device's location information may be used for emergency calls to aid response efforts, regardless of whether you enable Location Services. Some carriers may use the address you registered with the carrier when signing up for Wi-Fi Calling as your location.

Make or receive a phone call on your iPad, iPod touch, or Mac

- **Make a call**: Tap or click a phone number in Contacts, Calendar, FaceTime, Messages, Search, or Safari. Or open FaceTime, enter a contact or phone number, then tap ☏.
    If you make a call from another device by relaying it through your iPhone with Dual SIM, the call is made using your default voice line.
- **Receive a call**: Swipe, tap, or click the notification to answer or ignore the call.

Hand off tasks between iPhone and your other devices

With Handoff, you can start something on one device (iPhone, iPad, iPod touch, Mac, or Apple Watch) and then pick it up on another device right where you left off. For example, you can start answering an email on your iPhone, then finish it in Mail on your Mac. You can use Handoff with many Apple apps—for example, Calendar, Contacts, and Safari. Some third-party apps may also work with Handoff.

Hand off from another device to your iPhone

1. Open the App Switcher on iPhone. The Handoff icon of the app you're using on your other device appears at the bottom of the iPhone screen.
2. Tap the Handoff icon to continue working in the app.

Hand off from iPhone to another device

On the other device, click or tap the Handoff icon to continue working in the app.

The Handoff icon of the app you're using on iPhone appears in the following locations on other devices:

- **Mac**: The right end of the Dock (or at the bottom, depending on the Dock position).
- **iPad**: The right end of the Dock.
- **iPhone or iPod touch**: At the bottom of the App Switcher screen.

Turn off Handoff on your devices

- **iPad, iPhone, and iPod touch**: Go to Settings ⚙ > General > AirPlay & Handoff.
- **macOS 12.5 or earlier**: Choose Apple menu > System Preferences, click General, then deselect "Allow Handoff between this Mac and your iCloud devices."

Tip: When Handoff is on, you can use Universal Clipboard to copy and paste text, images, photos, and videos across devices.

Wirelessly stream video, photos, and audio from your iPhone to a Mac

You can use a nearby Mac to watch videos, view photos, and play audio streamed from your iPhone. You can also mirror your iPhone screen to the Mac (macOS 12 or later required).

Set up a Mac to allow streaming from your iPhone

1. On a Mac, choose Apple menu > System Preferences, click Sharing, then select and turn on AirPlay Receiver.
2. Choose an option for "Allow AirPlay for:"
    - To allow only devices where you're signed in with the same Apple ID as on the Mac to stream to the Mac, select "Current user."
    - To allow others, select "Anyone on the same network" or "Everyone."
3. To require a password to use AirPlay with the Mac, select the option, then enter a password in the text field.

If you choose the option "Anyone on the same network" or "Everyone," and someone is signed in to their device with a different Apple ID than on the Mac, an AirPlay request initially requires acceptance on the Mac and verification on the other device. On the Mac, accept the AirPlay request. If the Mac displays an AirPlay code, enter the code on the other device.

Play video from your iPhone on a Mac

1. While playing video in the Apple TV app 📺 or another supported video app on your iPhone, tap the screen to show the controls.
2. Tap ⬆️, then choose the Mac as the playback destination.

To show video playback controls on the Mac, move the pointer over the video playing on the Mac screen.

To change the playback destination, choose a different AirPlay option on your iPhone screen.

Show photos from your iPhone on a Mac

1. In Photos ✺ on your iPhone, tap a photo, then tap ⬆️.
2. Swipe up, tap ⬜, then choose the Mac as the playback destination.

To stop streaming photos, tap ⬜ near the top of the iPhone screen, then tap Turn off AirPlay.

Mirror your iPhone on a Mac

On a Mac, you can view and listen to whatever appears and plays on your iPhone.

1. Open Control Center on your iPhone.
2. Tap 🗗, then choose your Mac as the playback destination.

To switch back to iPhone, open Control Center, tap 🗗, then tap Stop Mirroring.

Play audio from iPhone on Mac

1. On your iPhone, open an audio app, such as Podcasts 🎙️ or Music 🎵, then choose an item to play.
2. Tap 📶, then choose a playback destination.

To select the playback destination, you can also tap 📶 on the Lock Screen or in Control Center.

Wirelessly stream video, photos, and audio from your iPhone to a Mac

You can use a nearby Mac to watch videos, view photos, and play audio streamed from your iPhone. You can also mirror your iPhone screen to the Mac (macOS 12 or later required).

Set up a Mac to allow streaming from your iPhone

1. On a Mac, choose Apple menu > System Preferences, click Sharing, then select and turn on AirPlay Receiver.
2. Choose an option for "Allow AirPlay for:"
    o To allow only devices where you're signed in with the same Apple ID as on the Mac to stream to the Mac, select "Current user."
    o To allow others, select "Anyone on the same network" or "Everyone."
3. To require a password to use AirPlay with the Mac, select the option, then enter a password in the text field.

If you choose the option "Anyone on the same network" or "Everyone," and someone is signed in to their device with a different Apple ID than on the Mac, an AirPlay request initially requires acceptance on the Mac and verification on the other device. On the Mac, accept the AirPlay request. If the Mac displays an AirPlay code, enter the code on the other device.

Play video from your iPhone on a Mac

1. While playing video in the Apple TV app 📺 or another supported video app on your iPhone, tap the screen to show the controls.
2. Tap ⬆, then choose the Mac as the playback destination.

To show video playback controls on the Mac, move the pointer over the video playing on the Mac screen.

To change the playback destination, choose a different AirPlay option on your iPhone screen.

Show photos from your iPhone on a Mac

1. In Photos 🏵 on your iPhone, tap a photo, then tap ⬆.
2. Swipe up, tap ⬆, then choose the Mac as the playback destination.

To stop streaming photos, tap ⬆ near the top of the iPhone screen, then tap Turn off AirPlay.

Mirror your iPhone on a Mac

On a Mac, you can view and listen to whatever appears and plays on your iPhone.

1. Open Control Center on your iPhone.
2. Tap ⬒, then choose your Mac as the playback destination.

To switch back to iPhone, open Control Center, tap ⬒, then tap Stop Mirroring.

Play audio from iPhone on Mac

1. On your iPhone, open an audio app, such as Podcasts 🎙 or Music 🎵, then choose an item to play.
2. Tap 📡, then choose a playback destination.

To select the playback destination, you can also tap 📡 on the Lock Screen or in Control Center.

Cut, copy, and paste between iPhone and other devices

You can use Universal Clipboard to cut or copy content (a block of text or an image, for example) on your iPhone, then paste it on iPad, on another iOS device, or on a Mac, and vice versa.

Copy, cut, or paste

- **Copy**: Pinch closed with three fingers.
- **Cut**: Pinch closed with three fingers two times.
- **Paste**: Pinch open with three fingers.

You can also touch and hold a selection, then tap Cut, Copy, or Paste.

Important: You need to cut, copy, and paste your content within a short period of time.

Connect iPhone and your computer with a cable

Using a USB cable or adapter, you can directly connect iPhone and a Mac or Windows PC.

1. Make sure you have one of the following:
   - Mac with a USB port and OS X 10.9 or later
   - PC with a USB port and Windows 7 or later
2. Connect iPhone to your computer using the charging cable for your iPhone. If the cable isn't compatible with the port on your computer, do one of the following:
   - If your iPhone came with a Lightning to USB Cable and your computer has a USB-C port, connect the USB end of the cable to a USB-C to USB Adapter (sold separately), or use a USB-C to Lightning Cable (sold separately).
   - If your iPhone came with a USB-C to Lightning Cable and your computer has a USB port, use a Lightning to USB Cable (sold separately).
3. The first time you connect the devices, select Trust when asked on iPhone whether to trust this computer.
4. Do any of the following:
   - Set up iPhone for the first time.
   - Share your iPhone internet connection with your computer.
   - Use your computer to erase all content and settings from iPhone.
   - Update iPhone using your computer.
   - Sync content or transfer files between your iPhone and computer.

The iPhone battery charges when iPhone is connected to your computer and your computer is connected to power.

Transfer files between your iPhone and computer

Transfer files wirelessly between your iPhone and computer with email, messages, or AirDrop

The simplest way to manually transfer files is to use email, messages, or AirDrop to wirelessly send files between devices.

Use email to transfer files

Make sure you have an email account on your iPhone and computer, then follow the steps below.

1. Attach one or more files to an email message on your iPhone or computer, then send the email to yourself.

For example, to transfer a photo from your iPhone using Mail, select the item in Photos, tap ⬆️, choose Mail, then send the message to yourself.

2. Open the email and download the attachments on the other device.
   For example, when using Mail on a Mac to receive a file, select the email that includes the attachment, then choose File > Save Attachments.

Note: Depending on your email provider and ISP (internet service provider), there may be size limits to the files you send.

Use text messages to transfer files

Make sure you have messaging set up on your iPhone and computer, then follow the steps below.

1. Attach a file to a message on your iPhone or computer, then send the message to yourself.
   For example, to transfer a photo from your iPhone using Messages, select the photo in Photos, tap ⬆️, choose Messages, then send the message to yourself.
2. Open the message and save the attachment on the other device.

For example, when using Messages on Mac to receive a photo, Control-click the attached photo in a message, then select Add to Photos.

Note: Standard carrier data and text rates may apply. Your carrier may set size limits for attachments. iPhone may compress photo and video attachments when necessary.

Use AirDrop to transfer files

On a Mac (OS X 10.10 or later), you can use AirDrop to send files between it and your iPhone. AirDrop transfers information using Wi-Fi and Bluetooth, and the devices must be nearby. (Be sure you've turned on Wi-Fi and Bluetooth on your Mac, and you've turned on Wi-Fi and Bluetooth on your iPhone.) Transfers are encrypted for security.

To use AirDrop, you must be signed in with your Apple ID on both your iPhone and your Mac.

1. Choose an item on your iPhone or Mac.
2. Tap or click the button (such as ⬆️, Share, AirDrop, or ● ● ●) that displays the app's sharing options.
   For example, to transfer a photo from your iPhone using AirDrop, select the photo in Photos, then tap ⬆️.
3. Tap or click ◉ in the share options, then select your other device.

After an item is sent to your iPhone, you can find it in the app you saved the item to or in the app that automatically opened. After an item is sent to your Mac, you can find it in the app you saved the item to or in the Downloads folder.

Automatically keep your files up to date on your iPhone and computer with iCloud

With iCloud, you can store your files, photos, videos, and more in the cloud so you can access them on all your devices. You see the same information on your iPhone and Mac (OS X 10.10

or later) or Windows PC (Windows 7 or later). You must be signed in with your Apple ID on both your iPhone and your computer.

Note: iCloud provides you with an email account and 5 GB of free storage for your data. For more storage and additional features, you can subscribe to iCloud+.

Set up iCloud on your iPhone

1. On your iPhone, go to Settings 🌐 > [your name].
   If you don't see [your name], tap "Sign in to your [device]," then enter your Apple ID and password.
2. Tap iCloud, then turn on items to keep their data in the cloud.

For example, turn on iCloud Drive to make your files in iCloud Drive available to your computer.

Set up iCloud on your Mac

1. Follow the instructions to set up iCloud features on Mac in the macOS User Guide.
2. Turn on the same items that you turned on for iPhone.

Set up iCloud on your Windows PC

1. Follow the instructions to set up iCloud in the iCloud for Windows User Guide.
2. Turn on the same items that you turned on for iPhone, then click Apply.

You can also access your information in iCloud from anywhere by using a web browser recommended in the Apple Support article System requirements for iCloud and signing in to iCloud.com with your Apple ID.

Transfer files between your iPhone and computer with an external storage device

1. Connect your iPhone or computer to an external storage device, such as a USB drive or SD card.
   To connect to iPhone, you may need a cable adapter.
   The first time you connect the devices, select Trust when asked on iPhone whether to trust this computer.
2. Use a supported app like Files or Pages to copy files to the storage device.
   For example, to copy a file from the Files app on iPhone to the storage device, touch and hold the file, then tap Copy. Tap Browse at the bottom of the screen, then tap the name of the device (below locations). Select a location for the file, touch and hold the screen, then tap Paste.
3. Disconnect the storage device.
4. Connect the storage device to your other device, then copy the files to that device.
   For example, to copy a file to your Mac, click the Finder icon in the Dock to open a Finder window, select the storage device (listed below Locations in the Finder sidebar), navigate to the file, then drag it to a folder on your Mac.

Use a file server to share files between your iPhone and computer

1. Obtain access to a file server, or set up your own computer as a file server.
   For example, if you have a Mac, you can set it up as a file server on a local network, such as your Wi-Fi network.
2. Use the Files app to connect to the server from your iPhone.

   For example, to connect as a Guest user, tap ⬤⬤⬤ at the top of the Browse screen in the Files app, tap Connect to Server, enter the hostname or network address, tap Connect, select Guest, then tap Next.
3. Connect your Mac or Windows PC to the file server (unless your computer is the file server).
   For example, if you have a Mac, you can connect to a file server by navigating to it after selecting Network in the sidebar of a Finder window, or by choosing Go > Connect to Server in the Finder, then entering the server's network address.
4. Use the file server to transfer files between your iPhone and computer.
   For example, to copy a file from iPhone to a Mac file server, touch and hold a file in the Files app on iPhone, then tap Copy. Tap Browse at the bottom of the screen, tap the server in the Browse screen (under Shared), then select a location for the file. Touch and hold the screen, then tap Paste.
5. To disconnect your iPhone from the file server when you're finished, tap ⏏ next to the server in the Browse screen.

Share files between your iPhone and computer with a cloud storage service

You can store files using a service like Box or Dropbox, where you can share the files between your iPhone and computer.

Note: Subscription fees may apply.

1. Set up a cloud storage service to work with your Mac or Windows PC.
   See the instructions from your cloud storage provider.
2. On your iPhone, use the App Store app to download an app for your cloud storage service.
3. Open the downloaded app and follow the onscreen instructions.
4. Open Files, then tap Browse at the bottom of the screen.
5. Tap More Locations (below Locations), then turn on the service.

To access your files on iPhone, open Files, tap Browse at the bottom of the screen, then tap the name of the storage service below Locations. If you don't see Locations, tap Browse again at the bottom of the screen.

Sync content or transfer files between your iPhone and computer with the Finder or iTunes

With a USB or USB-C cable, you can connect your iPhone to a computer with a USB port to do the following:

- Sync supported content like movies and podcasts.
- Transfer files used by iPhone apps that support file sharing.

Depending on your computer, you use either the Finder or iTunes on your computer to sync content and transfer files.

Sync supported content

Syncing with the Finder or iTunes keeps supported content up to date between your iPhone and computer. For example, when you add a movie to your iPhone, you can sync so that the movie also appears on your computer. After you set up syncing between your devices with a cable, you can set them up to sync wirelessly and automatically whenever they're connected to the same Wi-Fi network.

You can sync content like music, movies, TV shows, podcasts, photos, contacts, and calendars.

- To sync content with your Mac (macOS 10.15 or later)
- To sync content with your Windows PC or Mac (macOS 10.14 or earlier)

Transfer files for supported apps

You can transfer files by copying them from one device to the other. For example, you can copy a Pages document created on your iPhone to view or modify on your computer. Only files for iPhone apps that support file sharing can be transferred using the Finder or iTunes. After you connect your iPhone and computer, you can see which of your apps support file sharing. (Note that files you transfer with the Finder or iTunes are not synced.)

- To transfer files with your Mac (macOS 10.15 or later)
- To transfer files with your Windows PC or Mac (macOS 10.14 or earlier)

CarPlay

Connect iPhone to CarPlay

Set up CarPlay by connecting your iPhone and your vehicle using your vehicle's USB port or its wireless capability.

Ensure that Siri is enabled on iPhone

If Siri is not enabled on your iPhone, go to Settings ⚙️ > Siri & Search, then Press Side Button for Siri

Connect using USB

Connect iPhone to your vehicle's USB port using an Apple-approved Lightning to USB cable.

The USB port may be labeled with the CarPlay logo or an image of a smartphone.

Connect wirelessly

1. On a vehicle that supports wireless CarPlay, do one of the following (see your owner's guide for detailed instructions):
    o Press and hold the voice command button on your steering wheel.
    o Make sure your vehicle is in wireless or Bluetooth pairing mode.
2. On your iPhone, go to Settings ⚙️ > General > CarPlay > Available Cars.
3. Choose your vehicle.

Note: Some vehicles that support wireless CarPlay allow you to pair simply by plugging iPhone into your vehicle's USB port using a Lightning to USB cable. If supported, after you start CarPlay using USB, you're asked if you want to pair wireless CarPlay for future use. If you agree, the next time you go for a drive, iPhone connects wirelessly to CarPlay automatically.

Note: After connecting to CarPlay on some electric vehicles, use the Maps app to identify the vehicle for EV routing.

On some vehicle models, CarPlay Home appears automatically when you connect iPhone.

If CarPlay Home doesn't appear, select the CarPlay logo on your vehicle's display.

Use Siri to Control CarPlay

CarPlay uses Siri voice control, so you can ask for what you want. (You can also use your car's built-in controls to control CarPlay.)

Use Siri on CarPlay

1. Do one of the following until Siri beeps:
   - Press and hold the voice command button on the steering wheel.
   - Touch and hold the CarPlay Dashboard ⬛≣ or CarPlay Home ⣿ button on a touchscreen displaying CarPlay.
   - You can also say "Hey Siri" to activate Siri in supported vehicles.
2. Use Siri to ask a question or to do something.
   Siri: Say something like:
   - "Get directions to the nearest coffee shop"
   - "Call Eliza Block"
   - "Play more songs like this one"
   - "Show me the map"
   - "What's my next meeting?"
   - "What's the weather for today?"
   - "Remind me to pack an umbrella when I get home"

Tip: Instead of waiting for Siri to notice that you've stopped talking, you can press and continue to hold the voice command button on the steering wheel while you speak, then release it when you finish.

Siri also makes suggestions in CarPlay for what you might want to do next, such as operate the garage door when you arrive home or drive to your next meeting.

Use your vehicle's built-in controls to control CarPlay

CarPlay works with your vehicle's built-in controls—for example, a touchscreen, a rotary knob, or a touchpad. To learn how to operate your display, see the owner's guide that came with your vehicle. (You can also use Siri to control CarPlay.)

- **Open an app**: Tap the app on the touchscreen, or turn the rotary knob to select the app, then press the knob.
- **Switch between CarPlay Dashboard and CarPlay Home**: CarPlay Dashboard displays several items you likely want to view or control, such as driving directions, audio playback, and suggestions from Siri. CarPlay Home shows all your CarPlay apps organized into pages.

   To go to CarPlay Home, tap ⣿ on the touchscreen, or turn the rotary knob to select ⣿, then press the knob.

   To go to CarPlay Dashboard, tap ⬛≣, or turn the rotary knob to select ⬛≣, then press the knob.
- **Return to your vehicle's Home Screen**: Select the icon with your vehicle's logo if it appears on CarPlay Home.
- **Return to a recently used app**: Tap its icon on the edge of the touchscreen, or turn the rotary knob to the icon, then press the knob.

- **View additional apps**: If you have more than eight apps, some may appear on another page of CarPlay Home. To view them, swipe left on the touchscreen, or turn the rotary knob.
- **Scroll quickly through a list**: Tap the letters in the list on the right side of the touchscreen, or turn the rotary knob.
- **Control audio playback**: Use the audio playback controls on CarPlay Dashboard. Or from CarPlay Home, select Now Playing to view and control the current audio app.

Get turn-by-turn directions with CarPlay

Use Siri or open Maps to get turn-by-turn directions, traffic conditions, and estimated travel time (not available in all regions).

Note: To get directions, iPhone must be connected to the internet, and Location Services must be on.

Find a route

CarPlay generates likely destinations using addresses from your email, text messages, contacts, and calendars—as well as places you frequent. You can also search for a location, use locations you saved as favorites and in collections, and find nearby attractions and services.

Siri: Say something like:

- "Find a gas station"
- "Give me directions home"
- "Take me to the Golden Gate Bridge"
- "Find a charging station"
- "Find coffee near me"

Or you can use your vehicle's built-in controls to open Maps in CarPlay and select a route.

Note: If you're viewing CarPlay Dashboard and Maps doesn't appear in the recent apps list on the left, tap ▦ to see pages of all of your CarPlay apps, including Maps.

1. With Maps open in CarPlay, do one of the following:
   - Select a place you saved as a favorite.
   - Select Destinations, then select a recent destination or scroll to select a destination you saved in a collection.
   - Select Search, then select 🎤 to speak a search phrase, or select ⌨ to use the onscreen keyboard (if available). You can also select a destination from a category of nearby services, such as Parking or Restaurants.
2. If multiple routes appear, use your vehicle's controls to select the route you prefer.
3. To call your destination before you leave, select 📞.
4. To start turn-by-turn directions, select Go.

Maps shows directions from your current location.

When you arrive at your destination and exit your vehicle, a parked car marker appears in Maps on iPhone so you can easily find your way back to your vehicle.

442

Follow turn-by-turn directions

As CarPlay follows your progress, it speaks turn-by-turn directions to your destination.

Do any of the following at any time during your trip:

- **Add a stop to your driving directions**: Select the ETA display at the bottom left, select Add Stop, then choose a destination or use Siri to search for one.
- **End directions at any time**: Say something to Siri like "Stop navigating," or select the estimated time of arrival (ETA) display at the bottom left, then choose End Route.
- **Mute turn-by-turn directions**: Tap ◀)), then choose ◀ to mute all directions.
- Mute turn-by-turn directions, except for alerts and hazards: Tap ◀)), then choose ◀⚠.
- **Make a quick detour**: Say something to Siri like "Find a gas station." Or select the ETA display, select Search, select a suggested service, then choose a destination.
- **Share your ETA**: Select the ETA display at the bottom left, select Share ETA, then choose one or more suggested contacts.

People using devices with iOS 13.1, iPadOS 13.1, or later receive a Maps notification with your ETA, and they can track your progress in Maps. People using devices with earlier versions receive the notification through iMessage. People using other mobile devices receive an SMS message. (Standard carrier data and text rates may apply.)

To stop sending ETA information, select Sharing ETA at the bottom of the CarPlay screen, then choose a contact.

Note: For navigation apps that support the CarPlay Dashboard, Dashboard shows the last navigation app opened if no apps are navigating, the one that is actively navigating, or the last opened and actively navigating app if multiple apps are navigating.

Report traffic incidents in CarPlay

In select regions and countries, you can report accidents, hazards, speed checks, and road work (features vary by region and country).

Report an incident

Siri: Say something like:

- "Report an accident"
- "There's something on the road"
- "There's a speed check here"

Or with turn-by-turn directions showing, you can select 💬 , then choose from one of the available options.

Apple evaluates incoming incident reports. When there's a high level of confidence in the reports, incident markers for Accident, Hazard, and Road Work are displayed in Maps for other users.

Note: Speed checks are not displayed with incident markers. Instead, notifications for speed checks appear when you follow turn-by-turn directions.

Report on the status of a hazard or accident

Incident markers show information about hazards ⚠ and accidents ◈. When you're near their locations, you can report their status.

Siri: Say something like "The hazard is gone" or "Clear the accident."

Or, you can do the following:

1. Select the incident marker.
2. Select Cleared or Still Here.
   Note: You can't clear reports of speed checks.

Apple evaluates incoming incident reports. When there's a high level of confidence in reports that an incident has been cleared, its incident marker is removed from Maps.

Note: Apple is committed to keeping personal information safe and private. To learn more, go to Settings ◉ > Maps, then tap About Apple Maps and Privacy.

Change the map view in CarPlay

Find your location on a map, zoom in and out, and move the map to see the detail you need.

When you follow turn-by-turn directions, you can tap the touchscreen or turn the rotary knob, then do one of the following:

- **Switch between detailed and high-level views**: To see a detailed 3D map with your heading at the top of the screen, select ⌃. To see the route overview in 2D with north at the top of the screen, select ⌀.

- **Zoom in or out**: Select ＋ or ▬.

- **Scroll the map**: Select ✥, then select a direction arrow on one of the edges of the screen. To return to turn-by-turn directions, tap Resume.

On some touchscreens, you can also drag the map to scroll it.

You can also change the map view when not following directions. Tap the touchscreen or turn the rotary knob, then do one of the following:

- **Show your current location**: Tap ⌁ . Your position is marked in the middle of the map.
- **View a 3D map**: Tap 3D. To return to a 2D map, tap 2D.
- **Show your heading at the top of the screen**: Tap ◤ . To resume showing north at the top, tap ⌃
- **Zoom in or out**: Select ✛ or ━ .
- **Scroll the map**: Select ✥ , then select a direction arrow at the edges of the screen. When finished, tap Done.

Make and receive phone calls with CarPlay

Use CarPlay to make phone calls and listen to voicemail from your iPhone.

Siri: Say something like: "Call Eliza."

Or you can use your vehicle's built-in controls to help make a call.

Open Phone in CarPlay, then select an option.

Note: If you're viewing CarPlay Dashboard and Phone doesn't appear in the recent apps list on the left, tap ▦ to see pages of all of your CarPlay apps, including Phone.

Play music with CarPlay

Use Siri or open Music in CarPlay to play music that's available on your iPhone—including songs, artists, albums, playlists, and Radio.

Siri: Say something like:

- "Let's hear the Acoustic playlist"
- "Play 'You Need to Calm Down' by Taylor Swift"
- "Play more songs like this one"
- "Play the rest of this album"
- "Skip this song"
- "Repeat this song"
- "Shuffle this playlist"
- "Tune into ESPN Radio"

If Siri doesn't find what you asked for, be more specific. For example, say "Play the radio station 'Pure Pop'" rather than saying "Play 'Pure Pop.'"

You can also use the controls on your vehicle's steering wheel, buttons on the Now Playing screen, and CarPlay Dashboard to control music playback.

Note: If you're viewing CarPlay Dashboard, tap ▦ to see pages of all of your CarPlay apps, including Music.

Button	Description

❚❚	Pause playback.
▶	Play the current song.
▶▶	Skip to the next song. When pressed and held, fast forward through the current song.
◀◀	Return to the song's beginning. When pressed again, return to the previous song. When pressed and held, rewind through the current song.
⤬	Play songs in random order.
⤶	Continually repeat the current song.
•••	Display controls to create a custom station based on the current song and to rate the current song.
Up Next	Display a list of songs queued for playback. (You can select a song from the list to skip the songs that proceed it.)

On some systems, Now Playing displays only a partial list of choices while you're driving. To choose among options not in the list, select More at the bottom of the screen, or use Siri by pressing and holding the voice command button on your steering wheel.

View your Calendar with CarPlay

Use Siri or open Calendar in CarPlay to view events, appointments, and meetings.

Siri: Say something like: "Do I have a meeting at 10?" or "Where is my 3:30 meeting?"

Upcoming events appear in CarPlay Dashboard. You can also use your vehicle's built-in controls to open Calendar in CarPlay to view upcoming events.

Note: If you're viewing CarPlay Dashboard, tap ▦ to see pages of all of your CarPlay apps, including Calendar.

To see more information about an event, select it. Options may allow you to get directions to the event or phone into it.

Send and receive text messages with CarPlay

Use CarPlay to send, hear, and reply to text messages from your iPhone.

Siri: Say something like:

- "Text my wife"
- "Text Eliza Block I'm in traffic and I'll be 15 minutes late to the meeting"
- "Read my text messages"

Or you can use your vehicle's built-in controls to help send and receive messages. Open Messages in CarPlay, then do one of the following:

- Hear unread messages or respond to a thread: Select a conversation.

- Start a new conversation: Select ☑️ .

- **Automatically send messages**: Skip the confirmation step when sending messages with Siri to send messages automatically, unless you ask to change or cancel it.

  In CarPlay, go to Settings ⚙️ > Siri and Suggestions, then select Automatically Send Messages.

Note: If you're viewing CarPlay Dashboard and Messages doesn't appear in the recent apps list on the left, tap ▦ to see pages of all of your CarPlay apps, including Messages.

Announce incoming text messages with CarPlay

Use CarPlay to have Siri automatically read your incoming text messages and listen for your response.

1. On your iPhone, go to Settings ⚙️ > Siri & Search > Announce Notifications, then turn on Announce Notifications.
2. Tap CarPlay, then choose any of the following:
   - **Announce New Messages**: CarPlay starts your drive with Announce Messages active and reads your incoming text messages aloud.
   - **Silence New Messages**: CarPlay starts your drive with Announce Messages silenced and doesn't read incoming text messages automatically.
   - **Remember Previous Setting**: CarPlay remembers whether Announce Messages were active or silenced from the previous drive.

Note: You can also enable or disable Announce Messages directly in CarPlay by tapping Announce when Siri reads an incoming text message.

Play podcasts with CarPlay

Use CarPlay to play the podcasts that are on your iPhone.

You can use your vehicles's built-in controls to open Podcasts and select a podcast to play.

Note: If you're viewing CarPlay Dashboard, tap ▦ to see pages of all of your CarPlay apps, including Podcasts.

You can also use the controls on your vehicle's steering wheel, the buttons on the Now Playing screen, and CarPlay Dashboard to control podcast playback.

Button	Description
▶	Play
❚❚	Pause
(15)	Jump back 15 seconds
(30)	Jump forward 30 seconds
1×	Choose a faster or slower playback speed

Play audiobooks with CarPlay

Use CarPlay to play the audiobooks that are on your iPhone.

Siri: Say something like: "Play Pride and Prejudice audiobook" or "Rewind 15 seconds."

Or you can use your vehicles's built-in controls to open Audiobooks and select a book to play. You can also use the controls on your vehicle's steering wheel, buttons on the Now Playing screen, and CarPlay Dashboard to control audiobook playback.

Note: If you're viewing CarPlay Dashboard, tap ▦ to see pages of all of your CarPlay apps, including Audiobooks.

Listen to news stories with CarPlay

Use CarPlay to listen to Apple News Today audio briefings and, if you're an Apple News+ subscriber, audio versions of select news stories. (If you aren't a subscriber, you can listen to story previews.)

You can use your vehicles's built-in controls to open News and select a story to play.

Note: If you're viewing CarPlay Dashboard and News doesn't appear in the recent apps list on the left, tap ▦ to see pages of all of your CarPlay apps, including News.

You can also use the controls on your vehicle's steering wheel, the buttons on the Now Playing screen, and CarPlay Dashboard to control playback.

Button	Description
❚❚	Pause playback.
▶	Play the current story.
▶▶	Skip to the next story.
⟲15	Jump back 15 seconds.
1×	Choose a faster or slower playback speed.

Note: CarPlay isn't available in all countries or regions.

Control your home from CarPlay

You can use suggestions from Siri that appear on CarPlay Dashboard or use Siri directly to control HomeKit-enabled accessories, such as garage doors, lights, and door locks.

Siri: Say something like:

- "Open the garage door"
- "Did I leave the garage door open?"
- "Close the garage door"
- "Lock the front door"
- "Turn on the lights"
- "Turn off the lights"

Use other apps with CarPlay

You can use Siri with CarPlay to access many of the apps on iPhone, including Reminders, Clock, Weather, and more.

Siri: Say something like:

- "Remind me to pack an umbrella when I get home"
- "Add milk to my grocery list"
- "Set my alarm for 6:00 a.m. tomorrow"
- "What's the weather for today?"

CarPlay works with select third-party apps that you download to your iPhone. Compatible apps—including audio, navigation, messaging, and voice-calling apps, and apps made by your vehicle manufacturer—show up automatically on CarPlay Home and can be controlled with Siri. For example, you can use Siri to give you directions from your favorite navigation app. CarPlay also works with additional third-party apps for EV charging, parking, and quick food ordering.

Note: Compatible third-party navigation apps appear on CarPlay Dashboard while in use. When you're not actively navigating, or if you're navigating using more than one app, CarPlay Dashboard displays the last compatible navigation app that was used.

Rearrange the icons on CarPlay Home

1. When you're not operating your vehicle, open Settings on your iPhone, go to General > CarPlay, select your vehicle, then tap Customize.
2. Do one of the following:
   - **Move an icon**: Drag ≡ up or down in the list.
   - **Remove an icon**: Tap ⊖ next to the icon, then tap Remove.
     Only icons that have ⊖ next to them can be removed.
   - **Add an icon back to CarPlay**: Below More Apps at the bottom of the page, tap ⊕ next to the icon.

Your icon changes appear on CarPlay Home the next time you connect to CarPlay.

Change settings in CarPlay

In Settings in CarPlay, you can change the Wallpaper, turn on Driving Focus, change how CarPlay looks on the display, turn suggestions in CarPlay Dashboard on or off, and show or hide album art.

Use the Driving Focus with CarPlay

The Driving Focus helps you stay focused on the road. While your iPhone is connected to CarPlay and Driving Focus is on, notifications and text messages are silenced or limited.

1. Open Settings in CarPlay using your vehicle's built-in controls.
   Note: If you're viewing CarPlay Dashboard and Settings doesn't appear in the recent apps list on the left, tap ▦ to see pages of all of your CarPlay apps, including Settings.
2. Go to Driving Focus, then select Activate With CarPlay.

If you receive a Driving Focus notification when you're not driving (for example, when you're a passenger) you can turn it off—tap the notification, then tap "I'm not driving."

Switch the appearance of CarPlay

CarPlay is set to dark appearance by default in most vehicles. If you prefer to have CarPlay automatically switch between dark and light appearance, do the following:

1. Open Settings in CarPlay using your vehicle's built-in controls.
2. Select Appearance.
3. Select Always Dark.

The dark appearance is optimized for viewing in low-light environments, such as at night.

Change the wallpaper in CarPlay

Open Settings in CarPlay using your vehicle's built-in controls, select Wallpaper, then choose one of the available options.

Hide or show suggestions in CarPlay Dashboard

Open Settings in CarPlay using your vehicle's built-in controls, then turn Suggestions in CarPlay off or on.

Hide or show album art

Open Settings in CarPlay using your vehicle's built-in controls, then turn Show Album Art off or on.

Accessibility

Vision

VoiceOver

Turn on and practice VoiceOver on iPhone

With VoiceOver—a gesture-based screen reader—you can use iPhone even if you can't see the screen. VoiceOver gives audible descriptions of what's on your screen—from battery level, to who's calling, to which app your finger is on. You can also adjust the speaking rate and pitch to suit your needs.

When you touch the screen or drag your finger over it, VoiceOver speaks the name of the item your finger is on, including icons and text. To interact with the item, such as a button or link, or to navigate to another item, use VoiceOver gestures.

When you go to a new screen, VoiceOver plays a sound, then selects and speaks the name of the first item on the screen (typically in the top-left corner). VoiceOver tells you when the display changes to landscape or portrait orientation, when the screen becomes dimmed or locked, and what's active on the Lock Screen when you wake iPhone.

Turn VoiceOver on or off

Important: VoiceOver changes the gestures you use to control iPhone. When VoiceOver is on, you must use VoiceOver gestures to operate iPhone.

To turn VoiceOver on or off, use any of the following methods:

- Activate Siri and say "Turn on VoiceOver" or "Turn off VoiceOver."
- Triple-click the side button.
- Use Control Center.
- Go to Settings ⚙ > Accessibility > VoiceOver, then turn the setting on or off.

Learn and practice VoiceOver gestures

You can practice VoiceOver gestures in a special area without affecting iPhone or its settings. When you practice a gesture, VoiceOver describes the gesture and the resulting action.

Try different techniques to discover which works best for you. If a gesture doesn't work, try a quicker movement, especially for a double-tap or swipe gesture. To swipe, try brushing the screen quickly with your finger or fingers. For best results using multifinger gestures, touch the screen with some space between your fingers.

1. Go to Settings ⚙ > Accessibility > VoiceOver.
2. Turn on VoiceOver, tap VoiceOver Practice, then double-tap to start.
3. Practice the following gestures with one, two, three, and four fingers:
   - Tap
   - Double-tap
   - Triple tap
   - Swipe left, right, up, or down

4. When you finish practicing, tap Done, then double-tap to exit.

Change your VoiceOver settings on iPhone

You can customize the settings for VoiceOver, such as the audio options, language, voice, speaking rate, and verbosity.

Adjust the VoiceOver volume and other audio options

- To increase or decrease the volume, press the volume buttons on iPhone.
- To set other audio options, go to Settings 🔘 > Accessibility > VoiceOver > Audio, then set options such as the following:
  - **Sounds & Haptics**: Adjust and preview sound effects and haptics.
  - **Audio Ducking**: Temporarily reduce media playback volume when VoiceOver speaks.
  - **Auto-select Speaker in Call**: Automatically switch to the speaker during a call when you're not holding iPhone to your ear.
  - **Send to HDMI**: Route audio to externally connected devices, such as an instrument amplifier or a DJ mixer.

Set the VoiceOver language

VoiceOver uses the same language you choose for your iPhone. VoiceOver pronunciation of some languages is affected by the Region Format you choose.

1. Go to Settings 🔘 > General > Language & Region.
2. Tap iPhone Language, then choose a language.

Adjust the speaking voice

Go to Settings 🔘 > Accessibility > VoiceOver, then do any of the following:

- **Adjust the speaking rate**: Drag the Speaking Rate slider.
- Choose a voice: Tap Speech > Voice, then choose a voice. To download an enhanced voice, tap ⬇.
- **Adjust the pitch**: Tap Speech, then drag the slider. You can also turn on Use Pitch Change to have VoiceOver use a higher pitch when speaking the first item of a group (such as a list or table) and a lower pitch when speaking the last item of a group.
- **Specify the pronunciation of certain words**: Tap Speech > Pronunciations, tap ＋, enter a phrase, then dictate or spell out how you want the phrase to be pronounced. **Note**: You can dictate only if you turned on Enable Dictation in Settings > General > Keyboards.

Set how much VoiceOver tells you

Go to Settings 🔘 > Accessibility > VoiceOver, then tap any of the following:

- **Verbosity**: Choose options to have VoiceOver speak hints, punctuation, uppercase letters, embedded links, and more. VoiceOver can even confirm rotor actions and tell you when the flashlight is turned on.

To change how VoiceOver speaks punctuation, tap Punctuation, then choose a group. You can also create new groups—for example, a programming group in which "[" is spoken as "left brack."

- **Always Speak Notifications**: VoiceOver reads notifications, including incoming text messages as they occur, even if iPhone is locked. Unacknowledged notifications are repeated when you unlock iPhone.

Customize VoiceOver settings for an activity

You can customize a group of VoiceOver settings for an activity such as programming. Apply the settings automatically when you open certain apps or by adjusting the rotor.

1. Go to Settings ⚙ > Accessibility > VoiceOver > Activities.
2. Choose an existing activity or tap Add Activity.
3. Adjust settings for speech, audio, verbosity, and braille.
4. Choose Apps or Context to automatically apply the settings for this activity.

Use flat or grouped navigation

Go to Settings ⚙ > Accessibility > VoiceOver > Navigation Style, then choose one of the following:

- **Flat**: VoiceOver moves sequentially through each item on the screen when you use the move next and previous commands.
- **Grouped**: VoiceOver moves through items and groups of items on the screen. To move into a group, use a two-finger swipe right. To move out of a group, use a two-finger swipe left.

Adjust VoiceOver visuals

Go to Settings ⚙ > Accessibility > VoiceOver, then turn on any of the following:

- **Large Cursor**: If you have difficulty seeing the black outline around the selected item, you can enlarge and thicken the outline.
- **Caption Panel**: The text spoken by VoiceOver is displayed at the bottom of the screen.

Use Quick Settings to adjust VoiceOver from anywhere on iPhone

When VoiceOver is turned on, you can access Quick Settings by doing a two-finger quadruple tap.

To customize Quick Settings, do the following:

1. Go to Settings ⚙ > Accessibility > VoiceOver > Quick Settings.
2. Choose the settings you want, or drag ≡ to reorder settings.

Learn VoiceOver gestures on iPhone

When VoiceOver is on, standard touchscreen gestures have different effects, and additional gestures let you move around the screen and control individual items. VoiceOver gestures include two-, three-, and four-finger taps and swipes.

You can use different techniques to perform VoiceOver gestures. For example, you can perform a two-finger tap using two fingers on one hand, one finger on each hand, or your thumbs. Instead of selecting an item and double-tapping, you can use a split-tap gesture—touch and hold an item with one finger, then tap the screen with another finger.

Explore and speak items on the screen

To explore the screen, drag your finger over it. VoiceOver speaks the name of each item you touch.

You can also use VoiceOver gestures to explore the screen in order, from top to bottom and left to right.

Action	Gesture
Select and speak an item	Tap or touch the item
Select the next item	Swipe right
Select the previous item	Swipe left
Move into a group of items	Two-finger swipe right
Move out of a group of items	Two-finger swipe left
Select the first item on the screen	Four-finger tap near the top of the screen
Select the last item on the screen	Four-finger tap near the bottom of the screen
Speak the entire screen from the top	Two-finger swipe up
Speak the entire screen from the selected item	Two-finger swipe down
Pause or continue speaking	Two-finger tap

Speak additional information, such as the position within a list or whether text is selected	Three-finger tap

Scroll up, down, left, and right

Use VoiceOver gestures to move to another page.

Action	Gesture
Scroll up one page	Three-finger swipe down
Scroll down one page	Three-finger swipe up
Scroll left one page	Three-finger swipe right
Scroll right one page	Three-finger swipe left

Take action on an item

Use VoiceOver gestures to perform actions on an item.

Action	Gesture
Select an item	Tap
Activate the selected item	Double-tap
Double-tap the selected item	Triple-tap
Drag a slider	Tap the slider to select it, then swipe up or down with one finger; or double-tap and hold the slider until you hear three rising tones, then drag the slider
Start or stop the current action (for example, play or pause music or a video, take a photo in Camera, start or stop a recording, start or stop the stopwatch)	Two-finger double-tap
Dismiss an alert or return to the previous screen	Two-finger scrub (move two fingers back and forth three times quickly, making a "z")

Edit an item's label to make it easier to find	Two-finger double-tap and hold

Tip: As an alternative to selecting an item and double-tapping to activate it, touch and hold an item with one finger, then tap the screen with another.

Use gestures to control VoiceOver

Use these gestures to control VoiceOver.

Action	Gesture
Mute or unmute VoiceOver	Three-finger double tap. If both VoiceOver and Zoom are enabled, use the three-finger triple-tap gesture.
Turn the screen curtain on or off (When the screen curtain is on, the screen contents are active even though the display is turned off.)	Three-finger triple tap. If both VoiceOver and Zoom are enabled, use the three-finger quadruple-tap gesture.
Use a standard gesture	Double-tap and hold your finger on the screen until you hear three rising tones, then make the gesture. When you lift your finger, VoiceOver gestures resume. For example, to drag a volume slider with your finger instead of swiping up and down, select the slider, double-tap and hold, wait for the three tones, then slide left or right.

Open the Item Chooser	Two-finger triple tap.
	To move quickly through the list of items, type a name in the search field, swipe right or left to move through the list alphabetically, or tap the table index to the right of the list and swipe up or down. You can also use handwriting to select an item by writing its name.
	To dismiss the Item Chooser without making a selection, do a two-finger scrub (move two fingers back and forth three times quickly, making a "z").
Open the VoiceOver quick settings	Two-finger quadruple tap.

Use the VoiceOver rotor

You can use the rotor to change VoiceOver settings, jump from one item to the next on the screen, select special input methods such as Braille Screen Input or Handwriting, and more.

Use these gestures to use the rotor.

Action	Gesture
Choose a rotor setting	Two-finger rotation
Move to the previous item or increase (depending on the rotor setting)	Swipe up
Move to the next item or decrease (depending on the rotor setting)	Swipe down

Operate iPhone using VoiceOver gestures

When VoiceOver is on, you need to use special gestures to unlock iPhone, go to the Home Screen, open Control Center, switch apps, and more.

Unlock iPhone

Wake iPhone and glance at it, then drag up from the bottom edge of the screen until you feel a vibration or hear two rising tones.

If prompted, enter your passcode. To avoid having your passcode spoken as you enter it, enter your passcode silently using handwriting mode or type onscreen braille.

Go to the Home Screen

- Drag one finger up from the bottom edge of the screen until you feel a vibration or hear two rising tones, then lift your finger.

Switch to another app

Swipe right or left with four fingers to cycle through the open apps.

Alternatively, you can use the App Switcher:

1. Open the App Switcher using one of the following methods:
   o Drag one finger up from the bottom edge of the screen until you feel the second vibration or hear three tones, then lift your finger.
2. To browse the open apps, swipe left or right until the app you want is selected.
3. Double-tap to open the app.

Open Control Center

- **On an iPhone with Face ID**: Drag one finger down from the top edge of the screen until you feel a vibration or hear the second tone.
- **On all iPhone models**: Tap any item in the status bar, then swipe up with three fingers. Or touch and hold the bottom of the screen until you hear a tone, then swipe up.

To dismiss Control Center, do a two-finger scrub (move two fingers back and forth three times quickly, making a "z").

View notifications

- Drag one finger down from the top edge of the screen until you feel the second vibration or hear the third tone.

To dismiss the notifications screen, do a two-finger scrub (move two fingers back and forth three times quickly, making a "z").

To dismiss the notifications screen, do a two-finger scrub (move two fingers back and forth three times quickly, making a "z").

Speak status bar information

1. Tap the status bar at the top of the screen.
2. Swipe left or right to hear the time, battery state, Wi-Fi signal strength, and more.

Rearrange apps on your Home Screen

Use one of the following methods:

- **Drag and drop**: Tap an icon on the Home Screen, then double-tap and hold your finger on the screen until you hear three rising tones. The item's relative location is described as you drag. Lift your finger when the icon is in its new location. Drag an icon to the edge of the screen to move it to another Home Screen.
- **Move actions**: Tap an app, then swipe down to hear available actions. When you hear "Edit Mode," double-tap to start arranging apps. Find the app you want to move, then swipe down to the Move action and double-tap. Move the VoiceOver cursor to the new destination for the app, then choose from the available actions: Cancel Move, Create New Folder, Add to Folder, Move Before, or Move After.

When you're finished, tap Done, then double-tap.

Search from the Home Screen

1. Tap anywhere on the Home Screen outside the status bar.
2. Swipe down with three fingers.

Control VoiceOver using the rotor on iPhone

You can use the VoiceOver rotor to change how VoiceOver works. You can adjust the VoiceOver volume or speaking rate, move from one item to the next on the screen, select special input methods such as Braille Screen Input or Handwriting, and more.

When you use Magic Keyboard to control VoiceOver, use the rotor to adjust settings such as volume, speech rate, use of pitch or phonetics, typing echo, and reading of punctuation.

Use the VoiceOver rotor

1. When VoiceOver is turned on, rotate two fingers on your screen as if you're turning a dial. If you prefer to use one finger on each hand, simultaneously drag up with one finger and drag down with the other.
   VoiceOver speaks the rotor setting. Keep rotating your fingers to hear more settings. Stop rotating your fingers when you hear the setting you want.
2. Swipe your finger up or down on the screen to use the setting.
   The available rotor settings and their effects depend on what you're doing. For example, if you choose Headings when you're browsing a webpage, swipe down or up to move the VoiceOver cursor to the next or previous heading.

Customize the VoiceOver rotor

1. Go to Settings ⚙ > Accessibility > VoiceOver.
2. Do any of the following:
   - **Add or reorder the rotor settings**: Tap Rotor, then choose the settings you want, or drag ≡ to reorder settings.
   - **Add another language**: Tap Speech > Add New Language (below Rotor Languages), then choose a language.
   - **Have VoiceOver confirm rotor actions**: Tap Verbosity, then turn on Speak Confirmation.

Use the onscreen keyboard with VoiceOver on iPhone

VoiceOver changes how you use the onscreen keyboard when you activate an editable text field. You can enter, select, and delete text; change the keyboard language; and more.

Enter text with the onscreen keyboard

1. Select a text field, then double-tap.
   The insertion point and the onscreen keyboard appear.
2. Enter text using one of the following methods:
   - **Standard typing (default)**: Select a key on the keyboard by swiping left or right, then double-tap to enter the character. Or move your finger around the keyboard to select a key and, while continuing to touch the key with one finger, tap the screen with another finger. VoiceOver speaks the key when it's selected, and again when the character is entered.

- Touch typing: Touch a key on the keyboard to select it, then lift your finger to enter the character. If you touch the wrong key, slide your finger to the key you want. VoiceOver speaks the character for each key as you touch it, but doesn't enter a character until you lift your finger.
- Direct Touch typing: VoiceOver is disabled for the keyboard only, so you can type just as you do when VoiceOver is off.
- Dictation: Use a two-finger double tap on the keyboard to start and stop dictation.

To enter an accented character, use one of the following methods:

- **Standard typing (default)**: Select the plain character, then double-tap and hold until you hear a tone indicating alternate characters have appeared. Drag left or right to select and hear the choices. Release your finger to enter the current selection.
- **Touch typing**: Touch and hold a character until the alternate characters appear.

Edit text with the onscreen keyboard

- **Move the insertion point**: Swipe up or down to move the insertion point forward or backward in the text. Use the rotor to choose whether you want to move the insertion point by character, by word, or by line. To jump to the beginning or end, double-tap the text.

  VoiceOver makes a sound when the insertion point moves, and speaks the character, word, or line that the insertion point moves across. When moving forward by words, the insertion point is placed at the end of each word, before the space or punctuation that follows. When moving backward, the insertion point is placed at the end of the preceding word, before the space or punctuation that follows it.

- **Move the insertion point past the punctuation at the end of a word or sentence**: Use the rotor to switch back to character mode.

  When moving the insertion point by line, VoiceOver speaks each line as you move across it. When moving forward, the insertion point is placed at the beginning of the next line (except when you reach the last line of a paragraph, when the insertion point is moved to the end of the line just spoken). When moving backward, the insertion point is placed at the beginning of the line that's spoken.

- Delete a character: Use ⌫.
- **Select text**: Use one of the following methods.
  - Set the rotor to Text Selection, swipe up or down to choose Character, Word, Line, or Sentence, then swipe left or right to move backward or forward. (You may need to enable Text Selection—go to Settings ⚙ > Accessibility > VoiceOver > Rotor.)
  - Set the rotor to Edit, swipe up or down to choose Select or Select All, then double-tap. If you choose Select, the word closest to the insertion point is selected when you double-tap. To increase or decrease the selection, do a two-finger scrub (move two fingers back and forth three times quickly, making a "z") to dismiss the pop-up menu, then pinch.
- **Cut, copy, or paste**: Set the rotor to Edit, select the text, swipe up or down to choose Cut, Copy, or Paste, then double-tap.

- **Fix misspelled words**: Set the rotor to Misspelled Words, then swipe up or down to jump to the previous or next misspelled word. Swipe left or right to choose a suggested replacement, then double-tap to use the replacement.
- **Undo**: Shake iPhone, swipe left or right to choose the action to undo, then double-tap.

Change the keyboard settings

1. Go to Settings ⚙ > Accessibility > VoiceOver.
2. Tap any of the following:
   - ○ **Typing Style**: You can choose a new style. Or, set the rotor to Typing Mode, then swipe up or down.
   - ○ **Phonetic Feedback**: Speak text character by character. VoiceOver first speaks the character, then its phonetic equivalent—for example, "f" and then "foxtrot."
   - ○ **Typing Feedback**: Choose to speak characters, words, both, or nothing.
   - ○ **Rotor**: Select the settings you want to include in the rotor.
   - ○ **Speech**: Tap Add New Language (below Rotor Languages), then choose a language.
   - ○ **Verbosity**: Tap Deleting Text. To have VoiceOver speak deleted characters in a lower pitch, tap Change Pitch.

Write with your finger using VoiceOver on iPhone

With Handwriting mode, you can enter text by writing characters on the screen with your finger. In addition to normal text entry, use handwriting mode to enter your iPhone passcode silently or to open apps from the Home Screen.

Use handwriting mode

1. Set the rotor to Handwriting.

   If Handwriting isn't in the rotor, go to Settings ⚙ > Accessibility > VoiceOver > Rotor, then add it.
2. To choose a character type (lowercase, numbers, uppercase, or punctuation), swipe up or down with three fingers.
   To hear the selected character type, tap with three fingers.
3. Trace a character on the screen with your finger.
   You can also do any of the following:
   - ○ **Enter an alternate character (a character with an accent, for example)**: Write the character, then swipe up or down with two fingers until you hear the type of character you want.
   - ○ **Enter a space**: Swipe right with two fingers.
   - ○ **Go to a new line**: Swipe right with three fingers.
   - ○ **Delete the previous character**: Swipe left with two fingers.
4. To exit handwriting mode, do a two-finger scrub (move two fingers back and forth three times quickly, making a "z"), or set the rotor to a different setting.

Enter your passcode silently with handwriting mode

1. On the passcode screen, set the rotor to Handwriting.
2. Write the characters of your passcode with your finger.

Select an item on the Home Screen

1. On the Home Screen, set the rotor to Handwriting.
2. Start writing the name of the item with your finger.
   If there are multiple matches, continue to spell the name until it's unique, or swipe up or down with two fingers to choose from the current matches.

Quickly navigate a long list

1. Select the index to the right of the list (for example, next to your Contacts list or in the VoiceOver Item Chooser).
2. Set the rotor to Handwriting, then use your finger to write the letter you want to navigate to.

Use VoiceOver on iPhone with an Apple external keyboard

If you use Magic Keyboard with iPhone, you can use keyboard shortcuts to activate VoiceOver commands.

Additionally, you can use VoiceOver Help to learn the keyboard layout and the actions associated with various key combinations. VoiceOver Help speaks keys and keyboard commands as you type them, without performing the associated action.

Choose the VoiceOver modifier

The modifier is a key or set of keys you press with one or more other keys to enter VoiceOver commands. You can set the modifier to be the Caps Lock key or the Control and Option keys pressed at the same time.

1. Go to Settings ⚙ > Accessibility > VoiceOver > Typing > Modifier Keys.
2. Choose the modifier for VoiceOver commands: the Caps Lock key or the Control and Option keys.
   This modifier is abbreviated as "VO" in the tables below.

VoiceOver keyboard commands

VO = modifier keys

Action	Shortcut
Turn on VoiceOver Help	VO-K
Turn off VoiceOver Help	Esc (Escape)
Select the next or previous item	VO-Right Arrow or VO-Left Arrow
Activate the selected item	VO-Space bar

Touch and hold the selected item	VO-Shift-M
Read from the current position	VO-A
Read from the top	VO-B
Pause or resume reading	Control
Copy the last spoken text to the clipboard	VO-Shift-C
Search for text	VO-F
Mute or unmute VoiceOver	VO-S
Go to the Home Screen	VO-H
Move to the status bar	VO-M
Open the notifications screen	Move to the status bar (VO-M), then Option-Up Arrow
Open Control Center	Move to the status bar (VO-M), then Option-Down Arrow
Open Search	Option-Up Arrow
Open the App Switcher	VO-H-H
Open the Item Chooser	VO-I
Change the label of the selected item	VO-/

Start, stop, or pause an action	VO-Hyphen
Swipe up or down	VO-Up Arrow or VO-Down Arrow
Adjust the rotor	VO-Command-Left Arrow or VO-Command-Right Arrow
Adjust the setting specified by the rotor	VO-Command-Up Arrow or VO-Command-Down Arrow
Turn the screen curtain on or off	VO-Shift-F11
Return to the previous screen	Esc

Quick Nav using the arrow keys

Turn on Quick Nav to control VoiceOver using the arrow keys.

Action	Shortcut
Turn Quick Nav on or off	Left Arrow-Right Arrow
Select the next or previous item	Right Arrow or Left Arrow
Select the next or previous item specified by the rotor	Up Arrow or Down Arrow
Select the first or last item	Control-Up Arrow or Control-Down Arrow
Tap an item	Up Arrow-Down Arrow
Scroll up, down, left, or right	Option-Up Arrow, Option-Down Arrow, Option-Left Arrow, or Option-Right Arrow
Adjust the rotor	Up Arrow-Left Arrow or Up Arrow-Right Arrow

Single-key Quick Nav for web browsing

To navigate a webpage quickly, turn on Quick Nav (VO-Q), then press keys on the keyboard to navigate to specific item types, such as headings or links. To move to the previous item, hold the Shift key as you press a key for the item type.

Item type	Shortcut
Heading	H
Link	L
Text field	R
Button	B
Form control	C
Image	I
Table	T
Static text	S
ARIA landmark	W
List	X
Item of the same type	M
Level 1 heading	1
Level 2 heading	2
Level 3 heading	3
Level 4 heading	4

Level 5 heading	5
Level 6 heading	6

Text editing

Use these commands (with Quick Nav turned off) to work with text. VoiceOver reads the text as you move the insertion point.

Action	Shortcut
Go forward or back one character	Right Arrow or Left Arrow
Go forward or back one word	Option-Right Arrow or Option-Left Arrow
Go up or down one line	Up Arrow or Down Arrow
Go to the beginning or end of the line	Command-Left Arrow or Command-Down Arrow
Go to the beginning or end of the paragraph	Option-Up Arrow or Option-Down Arrow
Go to the previous or next paragraph	Option-Up Arrow or Option-Down Arrow
Go to the top or bottom of the text field	Command-Up Arrow or Command-Down Arrow
Select text as you move	Shift + any of the insertion point movement commands above
Select all text	Command-A
Copy, cut, or paste the selected text	Command-C, Command-X, or Command-V
Undo or redo last change	Command-Z or Shift-Command-Z

Use a braille display with VoiceOver on iPhone

iPhone supports many international braille tables and refreshable braille displays. You can connect a Bluetooth wireless braille display to read VoiceOver output, including contracted and uncontracted braille and equations using Nemeth Code. When you edit text, the braille display shows the text in context, and your edits are automatically converted between braille and printed text. You can also use a braille display with input keys to control your iPhone when VoiceOver is turned on.

Connect a braille display and learn commands to control iPhone

1. Turn on the braille display.
2. On iPhone, go to Settings ⚙ > Bluetooth, turn on Bluetooth, then choose the display.
3. On iPhone, go to Settings > Accessibility > VoiceOver > Braille, then choose the display.
4. To see the braille commands for controlling iPhone, tap More Info, then tap Braille Commands.

Change the braille display settings

1. On iPhone, go to Settings ⚙ > Accessibility > VoiceOver > Braille.
2. Set any of the following:

Setting	Description
Output	Set the braille display output to uncontracted six-dot, uncontracted eight-dot, or contracted braille.
Input	Choose the input method for entering braille on the display—uncontracted six-dot, uncontracted eight-dot, or contracted braille. You can also turn on Automatic Translation.
Braille Screen Input	Choose the input method for entering braille using the screen.
Braille Tables	Add tables to the Braille Table rotor.
Status Cells	Turn on the general and text status cells and choose their location.
Equations use Nemeth Code	Turn on Nemeth Code for mathematical equations.
Show On-screen Keyboard	Display the keyboard on the screen.
Turn Pages when Panning	Automatically turn pages when panning.
Word Wrap	Wrap words to the next line.
Braille Alert Messages	When turned on, your braille display shows an alert message for the specified duration.

Ignore Chord Duration	Adjust the amount of time required before subsequent key presses are recognized as braille chords.
Auto Advance Duration	Adjust this setting to your preferred reading speed.

Output closed captions in braille during media playback

1. On iPhone, go to Settings ⚙ > Accessibility > VoiceOver > Verbosity.
2. Choose Braille or Speech and Braille.

Type braille directly on the iPhone screen using VoiceOver

If you turn on Braille Screen Input, you can use your fingers to enter six-dot or contracted braille directly on the iPhone screen, without a physical braille keyboard.

Enter braille on the screen

1. Set the rotor to Braille Screen Input.

   If you don't see Braille Screen Input in the rotor, go to Settings ⚙ > Accessibility > VoiceOver > Rotor, then select it from the list.
2. Place iPhone in one of the following positions:
   o **Tabletop mode**: Lay iPhone flat in front of you.
   o **Screen away mode**: Hold iPhone with the screen facing away so your fingers curl back to tap the screen.
3. Enter braille characters by tapping the screen with one or more fingers at the same time.

Tip: To have iPhone read dots aloud, tap and hold the dots, then when you hear the timer tones and announcement, release the dots.

To move the entry dots to match your natural finger positions, tap and lift your right three fingers all at once to position dots 4, 5, and 6, followed immediately by your left three fingers for dots 1, 2, and 3.

You can also use gestures to perform actions such as the following:

Action	Gesture
Enter a space	Swipe right with one finger; in screen away mode, swipe to your right
Delete the previous character	Swipe left with one finger
Move to a new line	Swipe right with two fingers
Cycle through spelling suggestions	Swipe up or down with one finger

Enter a carriage return, or send a message (in Messages)	Swipe up with three fingers
Cycle through the braille modes	Swipe left or right with three fingers
Translate immediately (when contractions are enabled)	Swipe down with two fingers
Switch to the next keyboard	Swipe up with two fingers

4.   To exit Braille Screen Input, do a two-finger scrub (move two fingers back and forth three times quickly, making a "z"), or adjust the rotor to another setting.

Change Braille Screen Input settings

1. Go to Settings 🔘 > Accessibility > VoiceOver > Braille > Braille Screen Input.
2. Do any of the following:
   - Set six-dot or contracted braille as the default.
   - Reverse the dot positions for six-dot braille.
3. To view or edit the commands and gestures you can perform when Braille Screen Input is turned on, go to Settings > Accessibility > VoiceOver > Commands > Braille Screen Input.

Customize VoiceOver gestures and keyboard shortcuts on iPhone

You can customize the gestures and keyboard shortcuts that activate VoiceOver commands.

1. Go to Settings 🔘 > Accessibility > VoiceOver > Commands.
2. Tap any of the following:
   - **All Commands**: Navigate to the command you want to customize, then tap Edit, Add Gesture, or Add Keyboard Shortcut.
   - **Touch Gestures**: List the gestures and the associated commands.
   - **Handwriting**: List the gestures for handwriting and the associated commands.
   - **Braille Screen Input**: List the gestures for Braille Screen Input and the associated commands.

To clear your custom gestures and keyboard shortcuts, tap Reset VoiceOver Commands.

Use VoiceOver on iPhone with a pointer device

If you use a pointer device with iPhone, you can adjust how it works with VoiceOver.

1. Go to Settings 🔘 > Accessibility > VoiceOver.
2. Below Pointer Control, tap any of the following:
   - **Pointer**: Set the pointer to ignore, follow, or move the VoiceOver cursor.
   - **Speak Under Pointer**: You can adjust the delay to speak the item under the pointer.

Use VoiceOver for images and videos on iPhone

You can use the Camera and Photos apps with VoiceOver, even if you can't see the screen. VoiceOver can provide image descriptions, and you can even add your own descriptions using Markup.

Take photos and videos in Camera

When you use Camera, VoiceOver describes objects in the viewfinder.

To take a photo or start, pause, or resume a video recording, double-tap the screen with two fingers.

Explore images

When you use the Image Explorer, VoiceOver tells you about people, objects, text, and tables within images. You can navigate receipts and nutrition labels in logical order, or move your finger over a photo to discover a person's position relative to other objects.

1. Go to Settings > Accessibility > VoiceOver > VoiceOver Recognition, then turn on Image Descriptions.
2. In an app such as Photos or Safari, select an image.
3. Swipe up to hear more options, then double-tap when you hear "Explore image features."
4. Move your finger around on the image to find out the position of each object.

Add custom image descriptions

Using Markup, you can add your own descriptions to images. VoiceOver reads your custom descriptions when you use the Image Explorer.

1. In a supported app such as Photos, tap .
2. In the Markup toolbar, tap , then tap Description.
3. Enter your description, then tap Done.

Trim videos in Photos

1. Select the video you want to trim, then double-tap.
2. Select Edit, then double-tap.
3. Select Start or End (on the media scrubber), then swipe up or down to adjust the start or end time.
4. When you're finished, select Done, then double-tap.

Use VoiceOver in apps on iPhone

You can use VoiceOver to interact with apps, even if you can't see the screen. VoiceOver is supported in the built-in Apple apps that came with your iPhone—such as Safari , Maps , and more. With VoiceOver Recognition, you can get descriptions of images and screen elements even on webpages and in apps without accessibility information.

Browse the web in Safari

- **Search the web**: Select the address field, double-tap to invoke the keyboard, then enter a search term, phrase, or URL. Select a search suggestion, then double-tap.
- **Skip to the next element on a webpage**: Set the rotor to the element type—such as headings, links, and form controls—then swipe up or down.
- **Set the rotor settings for web browsing**: Go to Settings 🔘 > Accessibility > VoiceOver > Rotor. Select or deselect items, or drag ☰ up or down to reposition an item.
- **Skip images while navigating**: Go to Settings > Accessibility > VoiceOver > Navigate Images. You can choose to skip all images or only those without descriptions.
- **Reduce page clutter for easier reading and navigation**: In the Safari address field, select the Format Options button, double-tap, select Show Reader View (not available for all webpages), then double-tap.

Navigate in Maps

- **Control how the map tracks your current location**: Select ◁ , then double-tap until you hear the tracking option you want.
  - ○ **Tracking on**: The map automatically centers on your current location.
  - ○ **Tracking on with heading**: The map automatically centers on your current location and rotates so that the heading you're facing is at the top of the screen. In this mode, iPhone speaks street names and points of interest as you approach them.
  - ○ **Tracking off**: The map doesn't automatically center on your current location.
- **Explore the map**: Drag your finger around the screen, or swipe left or right to move to another item.
- **Zoom in or out**: Select the map, set the rotor to Zoom, then swipe up or down with one finger.
- **Pan the map**: Swipe with three fingers.
- **Browse points of interest shown on the map**: Set the rotor to Points of Interest, then swipe up or down with one finger.
- **Follow a road**: Hold your finger down on the road, wait until you hear "pause to follow," then move your finger along the road.
- **Get information about a location**: Select the location (for example, a business, landmark or pin), then double-tap to open the information card. Swipe left or right to hear information such as directions, street address, phone number, business hours, and customer reviews.
- **Get guidance to the starting point**: When you start walking directions in Maps, iPhone guides you in the direction of the starting point using sound and haptic feedback.

Read PDF documents

In the Books 📖 and Files 📁 apps, you can use VoiceOver to read PDF documents. VoiceOver even describes detailed information—such as forms, tables, and lists.

Make and receive phone calls

In the Phone 📞 app, you can use VoiceOver to make and receive calls.

- **Answer or end a call**: Double-tap the screen with two fingers.
  When a phone call is established with VoiceOver on, the screen displays the numeric keypad by default, instead of showing call options.
- **Display call options**: Select the Hide button in the lower-right corner, then double-tap.
- **Display the numeric keypad again**: Select the Keypad button near the center of the screen, then double-tap.

Trim voice memo recordings

In the Voice Memos ⬚ app, you can use VoiceOver to edit recordings.

1. Select the recording you want to trim, then double-tap.
2. Select ⋯, then double-tap.
3. Select Edit Recording, then double-tap.
4. Select ⬚, then double-tap.
5. In the Waveform Overview, select Trim Beginning or Trim End, then swipe up or down to adjust the start or end time.
6. Select Trim, then double-tap.
7. Select Save, then double-tap.
8. Select Done, then double-tap.

Read math equations

VoiceOver can read math equations on the web (encoded using MathML) and in supported Apple apps such as Numbers and Keynote.

- **Hear an equation**: Have VoiceOver read the text as usual. VoiceOver says "math" before it starts reading an equation.
- **Explore the equation**: Double-tap the selected equation to display it in full screen and move through it one element at a time. Swipe left or right to read elements of the equation. Use the rotor to select Symbols, Small Expressions, Medium Expressions, or Large Expressions, then swipe up or down to hear the next element of that size. You can continue to double-tap the selected element to "drill down" into the equation to focus on the selected element, then swipe left or right, or up or down, to read one part at a time.

Equations spoken by VoiceOver can also be output to a braille device using Nemeth Code, as well as the codes used by Unified English Braille, British English, French, and Greek.

Use VoiceOver Recognition on the web or in apps without accessibility information

Note: VoiceOver Recognition should not be relied upon in circumstances where you could be harmed or injured, in high-risk situations, for navigation, or for the diagnosis or treatment of any medical condition.

1. Go to Settings ⚙ > Accessibility > VoiceOver > VoiceOver Recognition.
2. Turn on any of the following:
   - **Image Descriptions**: Get descriptions of images in apps and on the web.
   - **Screen Recognition**: Get descriptions of screen elements in apps.
   - **Text Recognition**: Get descriptions of text found in images.
3. Tap Feedback Style, then choose Speak, Play Sound, or Do Nothing.

Zoom in on the iPhone screen

In many apps, you can zoom in or out on specific items. For example, you can double-tap or pinch to look closer in Photos or expand webpage columns in Safari. You can also use the Zoom feature to magnify the screen no matter what you're doing. You can magnify the entire screen (Full Screen Zoom) or magnify only part of the screen with a resizable lens (Window Zoom). And, you can use Zoom together with VoiceOver.

Set up Zoom

1. Go to Settings ⚙ > Accessibility > Zoom, then turn on Zoom.
2. Adjust any of the following:
   - **Follow Focus**: Track your selections, the text insertion point, and your typing.
   - **Smart Typing**: Switch to Window Zoom when a keyboard appears.
   - **Keyboard Shortcuts**: Control Zoom using shortcuts on an external keyboard.
   - **Zoom Controller**: Turn the controller on, set controller actions, and adjust the color and opacity.
   - **Zoom Region**: Choose Full Screen Zoom or Window Zoom.
   - **Zoom Filter**: Choose None, Inverted, Grayscale, Grayscale Inverted, or Low Light.
   - **Maximum Zoom Level**: Drag the slider to adjust the level.
3. If you use iPhone with a pointer device, you can also set the following below Pointer Control:
   - **Zoom Pan**: Choose Continuous, Centered, or Edges to set how the screen image moves with the pointer.
   - **Adjust Size with Zoom**: Allow the pointer to scale with zoom.
4. To add Zoom to Accessibility Shortcut, go to Settings > Accessibility > Accessibility Shortcut, then tap Zoom.

Use Zoom

1. Double-tap the screen with three fingers or use accessibility shortcuts to turn on Zoom.
2. To see more of the screen, do any of the following:
   - **Adjust the magnification**: Double-tap the screen with three fingers (without lifting your fingers after the second tap), then drag up or down. Or triple-tap with three fingers, then drag the Zoom Level slider.
   - **Move the Zoom lens**: (Window Zoom) Drag the handle at the bottom of the Zoom lens.
   - **Pan to another area**: (Full Screen Zoom) Drag the screen with three fingers.
3. To adjust the settings with the Zoom menu, triple-tap with three fingers, then adjust any of the following:
   - **Choose Region**: Choose Full Screen Zoom or Window Zoom.
   - **Resize Lens**: (Window Zoom) Tap Resize Lens, then drag any of the round handles that appear.
   - **Choose Filter**: Choose Inverted, Grayscale, Grayscale Inverted, or Low Light.
   - **Show Controller**: Show the Zoom Controller.
4. To use the Zoom Controller, do any of the following:
   - **Show the Zoom menu**: Tap the controller.
   - **Zoom in or out**: Double-tap the controller.
   - **Pan**: When zoomed in, drag the controller.

While using Zoom with Magic Keyboard, the Zoom region follows the insertion point, keeping it in the center of the display.

To turn off Zoom, double-tap the screen with three fingers or use accessibility shortcuts.

Adjust the display and text size on iPhone

If you have color blindness or other vision challenges, you can customize the display settings to make the screen easier to see.

Use display accommodations

1. Go to Settings ⚙ > Accessibility > Display & Text Size.
2. Adjust any of the following:
   - **Bold Text**: Display the text in boldface characters.
   - **Larger Text**: Turn on Larger Accessibility Sizes, then adjust the text size using the Font Size slider.
     This setting adjusts to your preferred text size in apps that support Dynamic Type, such as Settings, Calendar, Contacts, Mail, Messages, and Notes.
   - **Button Shapes**: This setting underlines text you can tap.
   - **On/Off Labels**: This setting indicates switches turned on with "1" and switches turned off with "0".
   - **Reduce Transparency**: This setting reduces the transparency and blurs on some backgrounds.
   - **Increase Contrast**: This setting improves the contrast and legibility by altering color and text styling.
     Apps that support Dynamic Type—such as Settings, Calendar, Contacts, Mail, Messages, and Notes—adjust to your preferred text size.
   - **Differentiate Without Color**: This setting replaces user interface items that rely on color to convey information with alternatives.
   - **Smart Invert or Classic Invert**: Smart Invert Colors reverses the colors of the display, except for images, media, and some apps that use dark color styles.
   - **Color Filters**: Tap a filter to apply it. To adjust the intensity or hue, drag the sliders.
   - **Reduce White Point**: This setting reduces the intensity of bright colors.
   - **Auto-Brightness**: This setting automatically adjusts the screen brightness for current light conditions using the built-in ambient light sensor.

Adjust the text size when you're using an app

1. Open Control Center, then tap AA.

   (If you don't see AA, add it to Control Center—go to Settings ⚙ > Control Center, then choose Text Size).
2. Drag the slider up or down to increase or decrease the text size.

To change the text size for all apps, tap All Apps at the bottom of the screen.

Customize iPhone for motion sensitivities

If you have sensitivity to motion effects or screen movement on your iPhone, you can stop or reduce the movement of some screen elements, such as:

- Parallax effect of wallpaper, apps, and alerts
- Screen transitions
- Siri animations
- Typing autocompletion
- Animated effects in Messages

1. Go to Settings ⚙ > Accessibility > Motion.
2. Turn on or off any of the following controls:
    - **Reduce Motion**: Reduces the motion of the user interface, including the parallax effect of icons.
    - **Auto-Play Message Effects**: Allows the Messages app to automatically play full-screen effects. If you turn this setting off, you can still manually play effects by tapping Replay below the message bubble.
    - **Auto-Play Video Previews**: Allows apps such as the App Store to automatically play video previews.
    - **Limit Frame Rate**: Limits the maximum frame rate of the display to 60 frames per second (on models with ProMotion display technology).

Hear iPhone speak the screen, selected text, and typing feedback

Even if VoiceOver is turned off, you can have iPhone speak selected text or the entire screen. iPhone can also provide feedback and speak text corrections and suggestions as you type.

Change the speech settings

1. Go to Settings ⚙ > Accessibility > Spoken Content.
2. Adjust any of the following:
    - **Speak Selection**: To hear text you selected, tap the Speak button.
    - **Speak Screen**: To hear the entire screen, swipe down with two fingers from the top of the screen.
    - **Speech Controller**: Show the controller for quick access to Speak Screen and Speak on Touch.
    - **Highlight Content**: iPhone can highlight words, sentences, or both as they're spoken. You can change the highlight color and style.
    - **Typing Feedback**: You can configure typing feedback for the onscreen and external keyboards and choose to have iPhone speak each character, entire words, auto-corrections, auto-capitalizations, and typing predictions.
    To hear typing predictions, you also need to go to Settings > General > Keyboards, then turn on Predictive.
    - **Voices**: Choose a voice and dialect.
    - **Speaking Rate**: Drag the slider.
    - **Pronunciations**: Dictate or spell out how you want certain phrases to be spoken.

Hear iPhone speak

Siri: Say something like: "Speak screen."

Or do any of the following:

- **Hear selected text**: Select the text, then tap Speak.
- **Hear the entire screen**: Swipe down with two fingers from the top of the screen. Use the controls that appear to pause speaking or adjust the rate.
- **Hear typing feedback**: Start typing. To hear typing predictions (when turned on), touch and hold each word.

Hear audio descriptions for video content on iPhone

If you have video content that includes audio descriptions of scenes, iPhone can play the descriptions for you.

1. Go to Settings ⚙ > Accessibility > Audio Descriptions.
2. Turn on Audio Descriptions.

Physical and Motor

Use AssistiveTouch on iPhone

AssistiveTouch helps you use iPhone if you have difficulty touching the screen or pressing the buttons. You can use AssistiveTouch without any accessory to perform actions or gestures that are difficult for you. You can also use a compatible adaptive accessory (such as a joystick) together with AssistiveTouch to control iPhone.

With AssistiveTouch, you can use a simple tap (or the equivalent on your accessory) to perform actions such as the following:

- Open the AssistiveTouch menu
- Go to the Home Screen
- Double-tap
- Perform multifinger gestures
- Perform scroll gestures
- Activate Siri
- Access Control Center, notifications, the Lock Screen, or the App Switcher
- Adjust the volume on iPhone
- Shake iPhone
- Take a screenshot
- Use 3D Touch
- Use Apple Pay
- Use Emergency SOS
- Speak screen
- Adjust dwell settings
- Restart iPhone

Set up AssistiveTouch

Siri: Say something like: "Turn on AssistiveTouch" or "Turn off AssistiveTouch."

Or do the following:

1. Go to Settings ⚙ > Accessibility > Touch > AssistiveTouch.
2. Turn on AssistiveTouch.
3. To customize AssistiveTouch, tap any of the following:
   - **Customize Top Level Menu:** Tap an icon to change its action. Tap − or + to change the number of icons in the menu. The menu can have up to eight icons.
   - **Single-Tap, Double-Tap, Long Press, or 3D Touch**: Assign custom actions that run when you interact with the menu button. 3D Touch is available only on supported iPhone models.
   - **Create New Gesture**: Add your favorite gestures.
   - **Idle Opacity**: Adjust the visibility of the menu button when not in use.
   - **Confirm with AssistiveTouch**: On an iPhone with Face ID, confirm payments with Face ID by using AssistiveTouch instead of double-clicking the side button.

Tip: To turn AssistiveTouch on or off quickly, triple-click the side button.

Add a pointer device

You can connect Bluetooth and USB assistive pointer devices, such as trackpads, joysticks, and mouse devices.

1. Go to Settings ⚙ > Accessibility > Touch > AssistiveTouch.
2. Turn on AssistiveTouch.
3. Below Pointer Devices, tap any of the following:
   - **Devices**: Pair or unpair devices and customize buttons.
   - **Mouse Keys**: Allow the AssistiveTouch pointer to be controlled using the keyboard number pad.
   - **Pointer Style**: Adjust the size, color, and auto-hide settings.
   - **Show Onscreen Keyboard**: Display the onscreen keyboard.
   - **Always Show Menu**: Show the AssistiveTouch menu when a pointer device is connected.
   - **Tracking speed**: Drag the slider to adjust the speed.
   - **Drag Lock**: Turn on to enable dragging.
   - **Zoom Pan**: Choose Continuous, Centered, or Edges.

Set up Dwell Control

iPhone performs a selected action when you hold the cursor still on a screen element or an area of the screen.

1. Go to Settings ⚙ > Accessibility > Touch > AssistiveTouch, then turn on Dwell Control.
2. Adjust any of the following:
   - **Fallback Action**: Turn on to revert the dwell action to the selected fallback action after performing an operation.
   - **Movement Tolerance**: Adjust the distance the cursor can move while dwelling on an item.
   - **Hot Corners**: Perform a selected action—such as take a screenshot, open Control Center, activate Siri, scroll, or use a shortcut—when the cursor dwells in a corner of the screen.

478

- Time needed to initiate a dwell action: Tap – or +.

Move the AssistiveTouch menu button

Drag the menu button to a new location on the screen.

Use AssistiveTouch

Tap the menu button, then choose an action or gesture.

For a multifinger gesture, do the following:

- **Pinch**: Tap Custom, then tap Pinch. When the pinch circles appear, touch anywhere on the screen to move the pinch circles, then drag them in or out to perform a pinch gesture. When you finish, tap the menu button.
- **Multifinger swipe or drag**: Tap Device > More > Gestures, then tap the number of digits needed for the gesture. When the circles appear on the screen, swipe or drag in the direction required by the gesture. When you finish, tap the menu button.

To return to the previous menu, tap the arrow in the center of the menu. To exit the menu without performing a gesture: Tap anywhere outside the menu.

Create custom gestures

You can add your favorite gestures (such as touch and hold or two-finger rotation) to the AssistiveTouch menu. You can even create several gestures with different degrees of rotation.

1. Go to Settings 🔘 > Accessibility > Touch > AssistiveTouch > Create New Gesture.
2. Perform your gesture on the recording screen. For example:
   - **Touch-and-hold gesture**: Touch and hold your finger in one spot until the recording progress bar reaches halfway, then lift your finger. Be careful not to move your finger while recording, or the gesture will be recorded as a drag.
   - **Two-finger rotation gesture**: Rotate two fingers on the iPhone screen around a point between them. (You can do this with a single finger or stylus—just create each arc separately, one after the other.)
3. If you record a sequence of taps or drag gestures, they're all played back at the same time. For example, using one finger or a stylus to record four separate, sequential taps at four locations on the screen creates a simultaneous four-finger tap.
4. If your gesture doesn't turn out quite right, tap Cancel, then try again.
5. When you're satisfied with your gesture, tap Save, then name the gesture.

To use your custom gesture, tap the AssistiveTouch menu button, tap Custom, then choose the gesture. When the blue circles representing your gesture appear, drag them to where you want to use the gesture, then release.

Adjust how iPhone responds to your touch

If you have difficulties with hand tremors, dexterity, or fine motor control, you can adjust how the iPhone touchscreen responds to tap, swipe, and touch-and-hold gestures. You can have iPhone recognize faster or slower touches and ignore multiple touches. You can also prevent iPhone from waking when you touch the screen, or turn off Shake to Undo if you unintentionally shake iPhone.

Adjust settings for taps, swipes, and multiple touches

1. Go to Settings > Accessibility > Touch > Touch Accommodations, then turn on Touch Accommodations.
2. You can configure iPhone to do any of the following:
   - **Respond to touches of a certain duration**: Turn on Hold Duration, then tap − or + to adjust the duration. (The default is 0.10 seconds.)
   - **Prevent unintended swipe gestures**: To increase the amount of movement required before a swipe gesture begins, tap Swipe Gestures, turn on Swipe Gestures, then adjust required movement.
   - **Treat multiple touches as a single touch**: Turn on Ignore Repeat, then tap − or + to adjust the amount of time allowed between multiple touches.
   - **Respond to the first or last place you touch**: Choose Use Initial Touch Location or Use Final Touch Location.

If you choose Use Initial Touch Location, iPhone uses the location of your first tap—when you tap an app on the Home Screen, for example. If you choose Use Final Touch Location, iPhone registers the tap where you lift your finger. iPhone responds to a tap when you lift your finger within a certain period of time. Tap − or + to adjust the timing. Your device can respond to other gestures, such as a drag gesture, if you wait longer than the gesture delay.

Adjust settings for touch-and-hold gestures

The touch-and-hold gesture reveals content previews, actions, and contextual menus. If you have trouble performing this gesture, do the following:

1. Go to Settings > Accessibility > Touch, then tap Haptic Touch or 3D & Haptic Touch.
2. Choose the touch duration—Fast or Slow.
3. On an iPhone with 3D Touch, you can also choose the pressure needed—Light, Medium, or Firm.
4. Test the new setting on the image at the bottom of the screen.

Turn off Tap to Wake

You can prevent touches on the display from waking iPhone. Go to Settings > Accessibility > Touch, then turn off Tap to Wake.

Turn off Shake to Undo

If you tend to unintentionally shake iPhone, you can turn off Shake to Undo. Go to Settings > Accessibility > Touch.

Tip: To undo text edits, swipe left with three fingers.

Tap the back of iPhone to perform actions or shortcuts

You can double-tap or triple-tap the back of iPhone to perform actions such as taking a screenshot, turning on an accessibility feature, running a shortcut, and more.

1. Go to Settings > Accessibility > Touch > Back Tap.
2. Choose Double Tap or Triple Tap, then choose an action.
3. To perform the action you set, double-tap or triple-tap the back of iPhone.

Reach the top of the iPhone screen with one hand

When you use iPhone with one hand in Portrait orientation, you can use Reachability to lower the top half of the screen so it's within easy reach of your thumb.

1. Go to Settings ⚙ > Accessibility > Touch, then turn on Reachability.
2. To lower the top half of the screen, do one the following:
   ○ Swipe down on the bottom edge of the screen.
3. To return to the full screen, tap the upper half of the screen.

Route and automatically answer calls on iPhone

You can automatically direct the audio of phone or FaceTime calls to the iPhone speaker, a Bluetooth headset, or your hearing devices. iPhone can also automatically answer calls after a specific duration.

1. Go to Settings ⚙ > Accessibility > Touch > Call Audio Routing, then choose an audio destination.
2. Tap Auto-Answer Calls, turn on Auto-Answer Calls, then set the duration of time before the call is answered by tapping − or + .

During a call, you can switch the audio routing from your hearing aid to the iPhone speaker by removing the hearing aid from your ear.

Customize iPhone for vibration sensitivities

If you have a sensitivity or intolerance to vibrations, you can customize iPhone to suit your needs.

- Set vibration options for specific alerts: Go to Settings ⚙ > Sounds & Haptics.
- **Turn off all vibrations**: Go to Settings > Accessibility > Touch, then turn off Vibration.

ote: This setting turns off vibrations for earthquake, tsunami, and other emergency alerts.

Change Face ID and attention settings on iPhone

On an iPhone with Face ID, you can adjust Face ID and attention settings if you have physical or vision limitations.

Set up Face ID with Accessibility Options

By default, setting up Face ID requires you to gently move your head in a circle to show all the angles of your face. If you can't perform the full range of head motion, you can still set up Face ID without moving your head.

1. Go to Settings ⚙ > Face ID & Passcode.
2. Position your face within the frame, then tap Accessibility Options.

Face ID is still secure but requires more consistency in how you look at iPhone.

Change attention settings

For additional security, Face ID is attention aware. It unlocks iPhone only when your eyes are open and looking at the screen. iPhone can also reveal notifications and messages, keep the screen lit when you're reading, or lower the volume of alerts.

If you don't want iPhone to check for your attention, do the following:

1. Go to Settings ⚙ > Face ID & Passcode.
2. Turn on or off any of the following:
   o Require Attention for Face ID
   o Attention Aware Features
   o Haptic on Successful Authentication
3. These settings are turned off by default if you turn on VoiceOver when you first set up iPhone.

Note: Requiring attention makes Face ID more secure.

Switch Control

Set up Switch Control on iPhone

If you have physical difficulties, you can use Switch Control to operate iPhone using one or more switches. With switches, you can select, tap, drag, type, and even draw freehand. You use a switch to select an item or location on the screen, then use the same (or a different) switch to choose an action.

Add a switch

You can use the iPhone screen, camera, microphone, or the back of iPhone, or you can add an external adaptive switch.

Before you add an external switch, connect it to iPhone, following the instructions that came with the switch. If the switch connects using Bluetooth, pair it with iPhone—turn on the switch, go to Settings ⚙ > Bluetooth, turn on Bluetooth, tap the name of the switch, then follow the onscreen instructions.

1. Go to Settings > Accessibility > Switch Control > Switches.
2. Tap Add New Switch, then choose any of the following:
   o **External**: Choose a Bluetooth switch or Made For iPhone (MFi) switch that plugs into the Lightning connector on iPhone.
   o **Screen**: Tap the iPhone screen to activate the switch.
   o **Camera**: Move your head left or right while facing the camera.
   o **Back Tap**: Double-tap or triple-tap the back of iPhone.
   o **Sound**: Make voiced and voiceless sounds such as "Oo" or a pop.
3. Assign an action to the switch.

To ensure Switch Control functions correctly, you must assign a switch to the Select Item action and another switch to the Move to Next Item action.

Choose a scanning style and customize Switch Control

You can adjust the behavior of Switch Control in a variety of ways, to suit your specific needs and style.

1. Go to Settings ⚙ > Accessibility > Switch Control.
2. Tap Scanning Style, then choose one of the following:
   o **Auto Scanning**: The focus automatically moves to the next item after a specified duration.
   o **Manual Scanning**: You trigger a switch to move the focus to the next item (requires multiple switches).
   o **Single Switch Step Scanning**: You trigger a switch to move the focus to the next item; if no action is taken with a specified duration, the item with the focus is automatically activated.
3. Customize Switch Control by setting options such as the following:
   o **Switches**: Add switches and specify their function.
   o **Recipes**: Create, edit, and choose recipes to temporarily assign special actions to switches.
   o **Auto Scanning Time**: Adjust the item scanning speed.
   o **Pause on First Item**: Set scanning to pause on the first item in a group.
   o **Loops**: Choose how many times to cycle through the screen before hiding Switch Control.
   o **Move Repeat**: Set the delay before moving to the previous or next item while a switch is pressed.
   o **Long Press**: Set whether a different action occurs when you press and hold a switch, and how long to wait before performing that action.
   o **Tap Behavior**: Choose a tap behavior and set the interval for performing a second switch action to show the Scanner Menu.
   o **Focused Item After Tap**: Choose whether Switch Control resumes scanning at an item you tap or from the beginning.
   o **Hold Duration**: Set whether and how long you need to hold a switch down before it's accepted as a switch action.
   o **Ignore Repeat**: Ignore accidental repeated switch triggers.
   o **Gliding Cursor**: Adjust the point scanning style and speed.
   o **Head Tracking**: Adjust settings for head tracking and assign actions to facial expressions.
   o **Sound Effects**: Turn on sound effects.
   o **Speech**: Speak items as they're scanned.
   o **Menu Items**: Choose the actions shown in the Scanner Menu and the order in which they appear.
   o **Group Items**: Group items for faster navigation.
   o **Large Cursor**: Make the selection cursor larger.
   o **Cursor Color**: Choose a different color.
   o **Saved Gestures**: Create and save custom gestures to the Scanner Menu.
   o **Confirm with Switch Control**: On an iPhone with Face ID, confirm payments with Face ID by using Switch Control instead of double-clicking the side button.

Turn Switch Control on or off

Important: Switch Control changes the gestures you use to control iPhone.

To turn Switch Control on or off, use any of the following methods:

- Go to Settings ⚙ > Accessibility > Switch Control.
- Triple-click the side button.
- Use Control Center.

Use Switch Control on iPhone

After you set up Switch Control, you can use the following methods to select an item on the screen:

- **Item scanning**: The focus moves (automatically or manually) from one item to the next until you select an item; this is the default scanning method.
- **Point scanning**: You select an item on the screen by pinpointing it with scanning crosshairs.
- **Head tracking**: You move your head to control a pointer on the screen. You can also use facial expressions to perform actions.

After you select an item, you can choose an action (for example, tap, drag, or pinch) in the Scanner Menu.

Use item scanning

With item scanning, the focus sequentially moves from one item to the next item on the screen.

1. If you use Auto Scanning, watch or listen as the focus moves. If you use Manual Scanning, trigger your Move to Next Item action to move the focus.
2. When the focus surrounds the item you want, trigger your Select Item switch.
3. In the Scanner Menu, choose an action such as the following:
   - Tap
   - Gestures
   - Scroll
   - Media Controls
   - More (the dots at the bottom of the menu) for more options
   - Home (to return to the Home Screen)
   - Device (for other hardware actions)
   - Gliding Cursor (to use point scanning)
   - Head Tracking (to control the pointer with head movements)
   - Settings (to adjust Switch Control behavior)
4. The available actions in the Scanner Menu depend on the selected item.

To dismiss the Scanner menu without choosing an action, trigger your switch while the original item is highlighted and all the icons in the Scanner Menu are dimmed.

Use point scanning

With point scanning, you select an item on the screen by pinpointing it with scanning crosshairs.

1. Use item scanning to select an item.
2. In the Scanner Menu, choose Gliding Cursor.
3. To position the vertical crosshair, do the following:
   - Trigger your Select Item switch when the wide vertical band is over the item you want.

- ○ Trigger your Select Item switch again when the fine vertical line is over the item.
4. Repeat to position the horizontal crosshair.
5. Choose an action from the Scanner Menu.

To return to item scanning, choose Item Mode in the Scanner Menu.

Use head tracking

You can move your head to control a pointer on the screen. You can also use facial expressions to perform actions.

1. Go to Settings > Accessibility > Switch Control > Switches, then make sure you've set up switches.
2. Go to Settings > Accessibility > Switch Control > Head Tracking, then turn on Head Tracking.
3. Do any of the following:
   - ○ **Assign actions to facial expressions**: Choose actions to perform when you smile, open your mouth, stick out your tongue, or raise your eyebrows.
   - ○ **Choose how the pointer tracks your head movement**: Tap Tracking Mode, then choose With Face, When Facing Screen Edges, or Relative to Head.
   - ○ Adjust the pointer speed: Tap ⁻ or ⁺ .
4. Turn on Switch Control, then access the Head Tracking mode in the Scanner Menu.

Use Voice Control to interact with iPhone

You can control iPhone with just your voice. Speak commands to perform gestures, interact with screen elements, dictate and edit text, and more.

Set up Voice Control

Before you turn on Voice Control for the first time, make sure iPhone is connected to the internet over a Wi-Fi network. After iPhone completes a one-time file download from Apple, you don't need an internet connection to use Voice Control.

1. Go to Settings 🔘 > Accessibility > Voice Control.
2. Tap Set Up Voice Control, then tap Continue to start the file download.

   When the download is complete, 🎤 appears in the status bar to indicate Voice Control is turned on.
3. Set options such as the following:
   - ○ **Language**: Set the language and download languages for offline use.
   - ○ **Customize Commands**: View the available commands and create new commands.
   - ○ **Vocabulary**: Teach Voice Control new words.
   - ○ **Show Confirmation**: When Voice Control recognizes a command, a visual confirmation appears at the top of the screen.
   - ○ **Play Sound**: When Voice Control recognizes a command, an audible sound is played.
   - ○ **Show Hints**: See command suggestions and hints.
   - ○ **Overlay**: Display numbers, names, or a grid over screen elements.

485

    ○   **Attention Aware**: On an iPhone with Face ID, Voice Control wakes up when you look at your iPhone and goes to sleep when you look away.

Turn Voice Control on or off

After you set up Voice Control, you can turn it on or off quickly by using any of the following methods:

- Activate Siri and say "Turn on Voice Control."
- Say "Turn off Voice Control."
- Add Voice Control to Accessibility Shortcuts—go to Settings ⚙ > Accessibility > Accessibility Shortcut, then tap Voice Control.

Learn Voice Control commands

When Voice Control is turned on, you can say commands such as the following:

- "Open Control Center"
- "Go home"
- "Tap item name"
- "Open app name"
- "Take screenshot"
- "Turn up volume"

To learn more Voice Control commands, say "Show me what to say" or "Show commands."

Use a screen overlay

For faster interactions, you can navigate iPhone with a screen overlay that shows item names, numbers, or a grid.

- **Item names**: Say "Show names" or "Show names continuously," then say "Tap item name."
- **Numbers**: Say "Show numbers" or "Show numbers continuously," then say the number next to the item you want. You can also give a command to perform a gesture, such as "Tap number," "Long press number," "Swipe up at number," or "Double tap number."
- **Grid**: To interact with a screen location not represented by an item name or number, say "Show grid" or "Show grid continuously," then do any of the following:
  - ○ **Drill down**: Say a number to show a more detailed grid.
  - ○ **Say a command to interact with an area of the grid**: Say something like, "Tap number" or "Zoom in number."
- **Tip**: To adjust the number of grid rows and columns, go to Settings ⚙ > Accessibility > Voice Control > Overlay, then select Numbered Grid. When Voice Control is turned on, you can also say something like, "Show grid with five rows," or "Show grid continuously with three columns."

To turn off the overlay, say "Hide names," "Hide numbers," or "Hide grid."

Switch between dictation mode, spelling mode, and command mode

When you're working in a text input area—for example, writing a document, email, or message—you can easily switch between dictation mode, spelling mode, and command mode as needed. In dictation mode (the default), any words you say that aren't Voice Control commands are entered as text. In command mode, those words are ignored and aren't entered as text; Voice Control responds only to commands. Command mode is especially helpful when

486

you need to use a series of commands and want to prevent what you say from inadvertently being entered in a text input area.

When you're in dictation mode and need to spell out a word, say "Spelling mode." To switch back to Dictation mode, say "Dictation mode."

To switch to Command mode, say "Command mode." When Command mode is on, a dark icon of a crossed-out character appears in the text input area to indicate you can't dictate. To switch back to Dictation mode, say "Dictation mode."

Adjust settings for the side button on iPhone

You can adjust accessibility settings for the side button.

1. Go to Settings ⚙ > Accessibility, then tap Side Button.
2. Set any of the following:
    o **Click Speed**: Choose the speed required to double-click or triple-click the button—Default, Slow, or Slowest.
    o **Press and Hold to Speak**: Choose whether Siri responds when you press and hold the button.

You can also use AssistiveTouch or use Switch Control to confirm payments with Face ID instead of double-clicking the side button.

Use buttons on the Apple TV Remote on iPhone

On the Apple TV Remote on iPhone, you can use buttons instead of swipe gestures.

Go to Settings ⚙ > Accessibility > Apple TV Remote, then turn on Directional Buttons.

Change the pointer appearance when using a mouse or trackpad with iPhone

If you use a mouse or trackpad with iPhone, you can change the appearance of the pointer by adjusting its color, shape, size, scrolling speed, and more.

Go to Settings ⚙ > Accessibility > Pointer Control, then adjust any of the following:

- Increase Contrast
- Automatically Hide Pointer
- Color
- Pointer size
- Scrolling Speed

To customize the buttons of the pointing device, go to Settings > Accessibility > Touch > AssistiveTouch > Devices.

Adjust the onscreen and external keyboard settings on iPhone

You can adjust the onscreen (software) keyboard on iPhone. If you use an external (hardware) keyboard with iPhone, you can customize keyboard shortcuts and change settings such as the key repeat rate.

Set the onscreen keyboard to display only uppercase letters

If you have difficulty seeing the onscreen keyboard, you can set it to display only uppercase letters.

Go to Settings ⚙ > Accessibility > Keyboards, then turn off Show Lowercase Keys.

Type on a larger onscreen keyboard

Rotate iPhone to landscape orientation to use a larger keyboard for typing in many apps, including Mail, Safari, Messages, Notes, and Contacts.

Control iPhone with an external keyboard

If you have difficulty using the touchscreen, you can control your iPhone using shortcuts on Magic Keyboard (sold separately).

1. Go to Settings ⚙ > Accessibility > Keyboards, tap Full Keyboard Access, then turn on Full Keyboard Access.
2. Control your iPhone using keyboard shortcuts.

Action	Shortcut
Go to the next item	Tab
Go to the previous item	Shift-Tab
Activate the selected item	Space bar
Go to the Home Screen	Command-H
Open the App Switcher	Tab-A
Open Control Center	Tab-C
Open Notification Center	Tab-N
Show Help	Tab-H

3. To customize the keyboard shortcuts, tap Commands.
4. To customize the appearance of the focus, tap any of the following:
a. Auto-Hide
b. Increase Size
c. High Contrast
d. Color

Change how the keys respond on an external keyboard

If you have difficulty using an external keyboard, you can adjust the settings.

Go to Settings ⚙ > Accessibility > Keyboards, then tap any of the following:

- **Key Repeat**: You can adjust the repeat interval and delay.
- **Sticky Keys**: Use Sticky Keys to press and hold modifier keys, such as Command and Option, as you press another key.
- **Slow Keys**: Use Slow Keys to adjust the time between when a key is pressed and when it's activated.

Adjust the accessibility settings for AirPods on iPhone

If you have AirPods (3rd generation), AirPods Pro, or AirPods Max, you can adjust the accessibility settings to suit your motor or hearing needs.

1. Go to Settings ⚙ > Accessibility > AirPods.
2. If you have multiple AirPods, select one.
3. Set any of the following options:
   o **Press Speed**: Adjust how quickly you must press two or three times before an action occurs.
   o **Press and Hold Duration**: Adjust the duration required to press and hold on your AirPods.
   o **Noise Cancellation with One AirPod**: (AirPods Pro) Turn on noise cancellation even when you're using only one of your AirPods.
   o **Spatial Audio Head Tracking**: (AirPods (3rd generation), AirPods Pro, and AirPods Max) When you turn on Follow iPhone, the audio adjusts based on your head movement (for supported audio and video content).
4. To customize your audio, tap Audio Accessibility Settings.

Interact with Apple Watch on your iPhone

Apple Watch Mirroring allows you to see and control your Apple Watch screen from your paired iPhone. You can use touch or assistive features like Voice Control, Switch Control, and more on your iPhone to interact with Apple Watch.

Turn on Apple Watch Mirroring

To turn on Apple Watch Mirroring, use any of the following methods:

- Go to Settings ⚙ > Accessibility > Apple Watch Mirroring.
- Triple-click the side button.

To turn off Apple Watch Mirroring, tap ⓧ .

Hearing

Use hearing devices with iPhone

You can use Made for iPhone (MFi) hearing aids or sound processors with iPhone and adjust their settings.

Pair a hearing device with iPhone

If your hearing devices aren't listed in Settings ⚙ > Accessibility > Hearing Devices, you need to pair them with iPhone.

1. Open the battery doors on your hearing devices.
2. On iPhone, go to Settings > Bluetooth, then make sure Bluetooth is turned on.
3. Go to Settings > Accessibility > Hearing Devices.
4. Close the battery doors on your hearing devices.
5. When their names appear below MFi Hearing Devices (this could take a minute), tap the names and respond to the pairing requests.

Pairing can take as long as 60 seconds—don't try to stream audio or otherwise use the hearing devices until pairing is finished. When pairing is finished, you hear a series of beeps and a tone, and a checkmark appears next to the hearing devices in the Devices list.

You need to pair your devices only once (and your audiologist might do it for you). After that, your hearing devices automatically reconnect to iPhone whenever they turn on.

Adjust the settings and view the status of your hearing devices

- **In Settings**: Go to Settings ⚙ > Accessibility > Hearing Devices > MFi Hearing Devices.
- Using accessibility shortcuts.
- **On the Lock Screen**: Go to Settings > Accessibility > Hearing Devices > MFi Hearing Devices, then turn on Control on Lock Screen. From the Lock Screen, you can do the following:
  ○ Check battery status.
  ○ Adjust ambient microphone volume and equalization.
  ○ Choose which hearing device (left, right, or both) receives streaming audio.
  ○ Control Live Listen.
  ○ Choose whether call audio and media audio are routed to the hearing device.
  ○ Choose to play ringtones through the hearing device.

Use your hearing devices with more than one device

If you pair your hearing devices with more than one device (both iPhone and iPad, for example), the connection for your hearing devices automatically switches from one to the other when you do something that generates audio on the other device, or when you receive a phone call on iPhone.

Changes you make to hearing device settings on one device are automatically sent to your other devices.

1. Sign in with your Apple ID on all the devices.
2. Connect all the devices to the same Wi-Fi network.

Turn on Hearing Aid Compatibility

Hearing Aid Compatibility may reduce interference and improve audio quality with some hearing aid models.

1. Go to Settings ⚙ > Accessibility > Hearing Devices.
2. Turn on Hearing Aid Compatibility.

Hearing aid compatibility ratings aren't a guarantee that a particular hearing aid works well with a particular phone. Some hearing aids might work well with phones that do not meet the FCC requirements for hearing aid compatibility. To ensure that a particular hearing aid works well with a particular phone, use them together before purchasing.

Stream audio to your hearing devices

You can stream audio from Phone, Siri, Apple Music, Apple Podcasts, Apple TV, and more. Tap ⓦ in Control Center, on the Lock Screen, or in the Now Playing controls for the app you're listening to, then choose your hearing device.

You can also automatically route audio calls to a hearing device.

Use iPhone as a remote microphone with Live Listen

You can stream sound from the microphone on iPhone to your Made For iPhone (MFi) hearing devices or AirPods. This can help you hear better in some situations—for example, when having a conversation in a noisy environment.

1. If you're using AirPods, place them in your ears.

   If your AirPods don't automatically connect to iPhone, tap ⓦ in Control Center or on the Lock Screen, then choose your AirPods.
2. Turn Live Listen on or off with one of the following methods:

   ○ Open Control Center, tap 👂, tap your hearing device or AirPods, then tap Live Listen.

   (If you don't see 👂, add it to Control Center—go to Settings ⚙ > Control Center, then choose Hearing.)
   ○ Triple-click the side button, tap Hearing Devices, then tap Live Listen.
3. Position iPhone near the sound source.

Recognize sounds using iPhone

Your iPhone can continuously listen for certain sounds—such as a crying baby, doorbell, or siren—and notify you when it recognizes these sounds.

Note: Don't rely on your iPhone to recognize sounds in circumstances where you may be harmed or injured, in high-risk or emergency situations, or for navigation.

Set up Sound Recognition

1. Go to Settings ⚙ > Accessibility > Sound Recognition, then turn on Sound Recognition.
2. Tap Sounds, then turn on the sounds you want iPhone to recognize.

Tip: To quickly turn Sound Recognition on or off, use Control Center.

Add a custom alarm, appliance, or doorbell

You can also set up iPhone to recognize a custom alarm, appliance, or doorbell if they aren't recognized automatically.

1. Go to Settings 💮 > Accessibility > Sound Recognition > Sounds.
2. Tap Custom Alarm or Custom Appliance or Doorbell, then enter a name.
3. When your alarm, appliance, or doorbell is ready, place iPhone near the sound and minimize background noise.
4. Tap Start Listening, then follow the onscreen instructions.

Set up and use RTT and TTY on iPhone

If you have hearing or speech difficulties, you can communicate by telephone using Teletype (TTY) or real-time text (RTT)—protocols that transmit text as you type and allow the recipient to read the message right away. RTT is a more advanced protocol that transmits audio as you type text.

iPhone provides built-in Software RTT and TTY from the Phone app—it requires no additional devices. If you turn on Software RTT/TTY, iPhone defaults to the RTT protocol whenever it's supported by the carrier.

iPhone also supports Hardware TTY, so you can connect iPhone to an external TTY device with the iPhone TTY Adapter (sold separately in many regions).

Important: RTT and TTY aren't supported by all carriers or in all countries or regions. RTT and TTY functionality depends on your carrier and network environment. When making an emergency call in the U.S., iPhone sends special characters or tones to alert the operator. The operator's ability to receive or respond to these tones can vary depending on your location. Apple doesn't guarantee that the operator will be able to receive or respond to an RTT or TTY call.

Set up RTT and TTY

1. Go to Settings 💮 > Accessibility.
2. Tap RTT/TTY or TTY, then do any of the following:
    ○ If your iPhone has Dual SIM, choose a line.
    ○ Turn on Software RTT/TTY or Software TTY.
    ○ Tap Relay Number, then enter the phone number to use for relay calls using Software RTT/TTY.
    ○ Turn on Send Immediately to send each character as you type. Turn off to complete messages before sending.
    ○ Turn on Answer All Calls as RTT/TTY.
    ○ Turn on Hardware TTY.
3. When RTT or TTY is turned on, ☎ appears in the status bar at the top of the screen.

Connect iPhone to an external TTY device

If you turned on Hardware TTY in Settings, connect iPhone to your TTY device using the iPhone TTY Adapter. If Software TTY is also turned on, incoming calls default to Hardware TTY. For information about using a particular TTY device, see the documentation that came with it.

Start an RTT or TTY call

1. In the Phone app, choose a contact, then tap the phone number.
2. Choose RTT/TTY Call or RTT/TTY Relay Call.
3. Wait for the call to connect, then tap RTT/TTY.

iPhone defaults to the RTT protocol whenever it's supported by the carrier.

If you haven't turned RTT on and you receive an incoming RTT call, tap the RTT button to answer the call with RTT.

Type text during an RTT or TTY call

1. Enter your message in the text field.
   If you turned on Send Immediately in Settings, your recipient sees each character as you type. Otherwise, tap ⬆ to send the message.
2. To also transmit audio, tap 🎤.

Review the transcript of a Software RTT or TTY call

1. In the Phone app, tap Recents.
   RTT and TTY calls have ▦ next to them.
2. Next to the call you want to review, tap ⓘ.

Note: Continuity features aren't available for RTT and TTY support. Standard voice call rates apply for both Software RTT/TTY and Hardware TTY calls.

Adjust the mono audio, balance, and phone noise cancellation settings on iPhone

You can adjust mono audio, left-right stereo balance, and phone noise cancellation to suit your needs.

1. Go to Settings ⚙ > Accessibility > Audio/Visual.
2. Adjust any of the following:
   - **Mono Audio**: Turn on to combine the left and right channels to play the same content.
   - **Balance**: Drag the Left Right Stereo Balance slider.
   - **Phone Noise Cancellation**: Uses air pressure to reduce ambient background noise to help you hear better when you're holding the receiver to your ear on phone calls in certain noisy environments. Phone noise cancellation is available and on by default on iPhone 12 and earlier, and can be turned off for your comfort.

Flash the LED for alerts on iPhone

If you can't hear the sounds that announce incoming calls and other alerts, iPhone can flash its LED (next to the camera lens on the back of iPhone). The LED flashes only if iPhone is locked.

Tip: LED Flash for Alerts is a useful feature for anyone who might miss audible alerts in a noisy environment.

1. Go to Settings ⚙ > Accessibility > Audio/Visual, then turn on LED Flash for Alerts.
2. To prevent LED flashes when iPhone is in silent mode, turn off Flash on Silent.

Adjust headphone audio settings on iPhone

With supported Apple and Beats headphones, you can amplify soft sounds and adjust certain frequencies to suit your hearing. These adjustments help music, movies, phone calls, and podcasts sound more crisp and clear.

Set headphone accommodations

1. Go to Settings ⚙ > Accessibility > Audio/Visual > Headphone Accommodations, then turn on Headphone Accommodations.
2. Tap Custom Audio Setup, then follow the onscreen instructions. Or manually set any of the following:
   o **Tune Audio For**: Choose Balanced Tone, Vocal Range, Brightness, or Audiogram (if available).
   o **Level**: Choose Slight, Moderate, or Strong amplification of soft sounds.
   o **Phone**: Apply these audio settings to phone calls.
   o **Media**: Apply these audio settings to media playback.
   o **Transparency Mode**: (available when you have AirPods Pro connected to iPhone) Turn on Custom Transparency Mode, then adjust the amplification, balance, tone, and ambient noise reduction to help you hear what's happening around you. You can also turn on Conversation Boost to focus on a person talking in front of you.
3. To preview your audio settings, tap Play Sample.

Add an audiogram

You can use an audiogram to customize your audio settings on supported Apple and Beats headphones. You can import an audiogram by taking a photo or importing a saved file.

1. Go to Settings ⚙ > Accessibility > Audio/Visual > Headphone Accommodations, turn on Headphone Accommodations, then tap Custom Audio Setup.
2. Select an audiogram from the list or tap Add Audiogram.

Play background sounds on iPhone to mask environmental noise

You can play calming sounds—such as ocean or rain—to mask unwanted environmental noise and help minimize distractions so you can focus or rest.

1. Go to Settings ⚙ > Accessibility > Audio/Visual > Background Sounds, then turn on Background Sounds.
2. Set any of the following:
   o **Sound**: Choose a sound; the audio file downloads to your iPhone.
   o **Volume**: Drag the slider.
   o **Use When Media is Playing**: Adjust the volume of the background sound when iPhone is playing music or other media.

o   **Stop Sounds When Locked**: Background sounds stop playing when iPhone is locked.

Display subtitles and captions on iPhone

iPhone can provide subtitles, closed captions, and transcriptions so you can follow along more easily with audio and video.

Turn on subtitles and captions in the Apple TV app

When you play video content in a supported app, you can turn on subtitles and closed captions (if available). iPhone usually shows standard subtitles and captions, but you can also choose special accessible captions—such as subtitles for the deaf and hard of hearing (SDH)—if available.

1.   While playing video content, tap 🗨.
2.   Choose from the list of available subtitles and captions.

Customize the subtitles and captions in supported video apps

1.   Go to Settings ⚙ > Accessibility > Subtitles & Captioning.
2.   If you prefer closed captioning or subtitles for the deaf and hard of hearing when available, turn on Closed Captions + SDH.
3.   Tap Style, then choose an existing caption style or create a new style based on the following:
     o   Font, size, and color
     o   Background color and opacity
     o   Text opacity, edge style, and highlight

Show transcriptions for Intercom messages from HomePod on iPhone

If members of your home use HomePod for Intercom messages, iPhone can transcribe Intercom messages for you.

1.   In the Home app, tap 🏠, then tap Home Settings.
2.   Tap Intercom, then choose when you receive notifications.
3.   Go to Settings ⚙ > Accessibility > Subtitles & Captioning, then turn on Show Audio Transcriptions.

Get live captions in real time on iPhone

With Live Captions (beta), spoken dialogue is turned into text and displayed in real time on your iPhone screen. You can more easily follow the audio in any app, such as FaceTime or Podcasts, and in live conversations around you. (Live Captions is available in English (U.S. and Canada)

Important: The accuracy of Live Captions may vary and shouldn't be relied upon in high-risk or emergency situations.

Set up and customize Live Captions

1. Go to Settings ⚙ > Accessibility > Live Captions (Beta).
2. Turn on Live Captions, then tap Appearance to customize the text, size, and color of the captions.
3. By default, Live Captions are shown across all apps. To get live captions only for certain apps such as FaceTime or RTT, turn them on below In-App Live Captions.

See live captions

With Live Captions turned on, iPhone automatically transcribes the dialogue in apps or around you. You can do any of the following:

- Transcribe a conversation near you: Tap 🎤 .
- **Make the transcription window bigger**: Tap ⤢ . To restore the window to the smaller size, tap 🔽 .
- Pause the transcription: Tap ⏸ .
- **Hide the transcription window**: Tap ◀ . To restore the window, tap 💬 .

Use Guided Access on iPhone

Guided Access helps you stay focused on a task by temporarily restricting iPhone to a single app, and allowing you to control which app features are available. You can do any of the following:

- Disable areas of the screen that aren't relevant to a task, or areas where an accidental gesture might cause a distraction
- Disable the iPhone hardware buttons
- Limit how long someone can use the app

Set up Guided Access

1. Go to Settings ⚙ > Accessibility > Guided Access, then turn on Guided Access.
2. Adjust any of the following:
   - **Passcode Settings**: Tap Set Guided Access Passcode, then enter a passcode. You can also turn on Face ID as a way to end a Guided Access session.
   - **Time Limits**: Play a sound or speak the time remaining before a Guided Access session ends.
   - **Accessibility Shortcut**: Turn the shortcut on or off during Guided Access sessions.
   - Display Auto-Lock: Set how long it takes iPhone to automatically lock during a Guided Access session.

Start a Guided Access session

1. Open the app you want to use.
2. Turn on Guided Access using accessibility shortcuts.
3. Circle any areas of the screen you want to disable. Drag the mask into position or use the handles to adjust its size.

4. Tap Options, then turn on or off any of the following:
    o Side Button
    o Volume Buttons
    o Motion (to prevent iPhone from switching from portrait to landscape or from responding to other motions)
    o Keyboards
    o Touch
    o Time Limit
5. Tap Start.

End a Guided Access session

- Double-click the side button, then unlock with Face ID (if enabled). Or triple-click the side button, then enter the Guided Access passcode.

Use accessibility features with Siri on iPhone

Siri is often the easiest way to start using accessibility features with iPhone. With Siri, you can open apps, turn many settings on or off, or use Siri for what it does best—acting as your intelligent personal assistant.

Siri: Say something like: "Turn on VoiceOver" or "Turn off VoiceOver."

Siri knows when VoiceOver is on, so will often read more information back to you than appears on the screen. You can also use VoiceOver to read what Siri shows on the screen.

Set how long Siri waits for you to finish speaking

1. Go to Settings ⚙ > Accessibility > Siri.
2. Below Siri Pause Time, choose Default, Longer, or Longest.

Type instead of speaking to Siri

1. Go to Settings ⚙ > Accessibility > Siri, then turn on Type to Siri.
2. To make a request, activate Siri, then interact with Siri by using the keyboard and text field.

Control voice feedback for Siri

1. Go to Settings ⚙ > Accessibility > Siri.
2. Choose Don't Speak in Silent Mode, Only Speak with Hey Siri, or Always Speak Responses.

Use "Hey Siri" when iPhone is covered or facing down

To allow iPhone to listen for "Hey Siri" when it's covered or facing down, go to Settings ⚙ > Accessibility > Siri, then turn on Always Listen for "Hey Siri."

Hide apps when Siri is active

To hide the current app when you activate Siri, go to Settings ⚙ > Accessibility > Siri, then turn off Show Apps Behind Siri.

Have Siri hang up Phone and FaceTime calls

(Requires download of speech models. Not available in all languages.)

1. Go to Settings ⚙ > Accessibility > Siri, then turn on Call Hangup.
2. To end a call, say "Hey Siri, hang up" (participants on the call will hear you).

Use accessibility shortcuts on iPhone

After you set up accessibility features, you can quickly turn them on or off with any of the methods below.

Use Siri to turn on an accessibility feature

Say something like: "Turn on VoiceOver."

Triple-click the side button

On an iPhone with Face ID, you can turn accessibility features on or off by triple-clicking the side button.

- **Set up Accessibility Shortcut**: Go to Settings ⚙ > Accessibility > Accessibility Shortcut, then select the features you use the most.
- Slow down the double-click or triple-click speed for the side button: Go to Settings > Accessibility > Side Button.
- **Use Accessibility Shortcut**: Triple-click the side button.

Use Control Center

You can also add accessibility features to Control Center and then activate them from there.

1. Go to Settings ⚙ > Control Center, then tap ⊕ next to the accessibility features you use the most.
2. To activate the feature from Control Center, open Control Center, then tap the control.

Customize accessibility settings for specific apps on iPhone

You can choose different display and motion settings for certain apps, the Home Screen, and Settings.

Change the settings for an app

1. Go to Settings ⚙ > Accessibility > Per-App Settings.
2. Tap Add App, then choose an app, Home Screen, or Settings.
3. Tap the app or Home Screen, then adjust the settings.

Security and privacy

Use the built-in security and privacy protections of iPhone

iPhone is designed to protect your data and your privacy. Built-in security features help prevent anyone but you from accessing the data on your iPhone and in iCloud. Built-in privacy features minimize how much of your information is available to anyone but you, and you can adjust what information is shared and where you share it.

To take maximum advantage of the security and privacy features built into iPhone, follow these practices.

Protect access to your iPhone

- **Set a strong passcode**: Setting a passcode to unlock iPhone is the most important thing you can do to safeguard your device.
- **Use Face ID**: Face ID provides a secure and convenient way to unlock your iPhone, authorize purchases and payments, and sign in to many third-party apps.
- **Turn on Find My iPhone**: Find My helps you find your iPhone if it's lost or stolen and prevents anyone else from activating or using your iPhone if it's missing.
- **Control what features are available without unlocking your iPhone**: Disallow or allow access to some commonly used features, such as Control Center and USB connections, when your device is locked.

Keep your Apple ID secure

Your Apple ID provides access to your data in iCloud and your account information for services like the App Store and Apple Music.

Lock down your iPhone if it's facing a sophisticated cyberattack

If you find your iPhone and personal accounts are targeted by sophisticated remote attacks, you can also help protect yourself with Lockdown Mode. Lockdown Mode offers an extreme level of security for the very few users who, because of who they are or what they do, may be personally targeted by some of the most sophisticated digital threats, such as those from private companies developing state-sponsored mercenary spyware. Lockdown Mode automatically protects Safari, Messages, Home, and many other Apple services and apps. Webpages and internet communications continue working, but with reduction in performance and usability.

Protect access to your iPhone

Set a passcode on iPhone

For better security, set a passcode that needs to be entered to unlock iPhone when you turn it on or wake it. Setting a passcode also turns on data protection, which encrypts your iPhone data with 256-bit AES encryption. (Some apps may opt out of using data protection.)

Set or change the passcode

1. Go to Settings ⚙, then do one of the following:
   o Tap Face ID & Passcode.
2. Tap Turn Passcode On or Change Passcode.

To view options for creating a password, tap Passcode Options. The most secure options are Custom Alphanumeric Code and Custom Numeric Code.

After you set a passcode, you can use Face ID to unlock iPhone (depending on your model). For additional security, however, you must always enter your passcode to unlock your

iPhone under the following conditions:

- You turn on or restart your iPhone.
- You haven't unlocked your iPhone for more than 48 hours.
- You haven't unlocked your iPhone with the passcode in the last 6.5 days, and you haven't unlocked it with Face ID in the last 4 hours.
- Your iPhone receives a remote lock command.
- There are five unsuccessful attempts to unlock your iPhone with Face ID.
- An attempt to use Emergency SOS is initiated.
- An attempt to view your Medical ID is initiated

Change when iPhone automatically locks

Go to Settings ⚙ > Display & Brightness > Auto-Lock, then set a length of time.

Erase data after 10 failed passcodes

Set iPhone to erase all information, media, and personal settings after 10 consecutive failed passcode attempts.

1. Go to Settings ⚙, then do one of the following:
   o Tap Face ID & Passcode.

Scroll to the bottom and turn on Erase Data.

After all data is erased, you must restore your device from a backup or set it up again as new.

Turn off the passcode

1. Go to Settings ⚙, then do one of the following:
   o Tap Face ID & Passcode.
2. Tap Turn Passcode Off.

Reset the passcode

If you enter the wrong passcode six times in a row, you'll be locked out of your device, and you'll receive a message that says iPhone is disabled. If you can't remember your passcode, you can erase your iPhone with a computer or with recovery mode, then set a new passcode.

Note: If you made an iCloud or computer backup before you forgot your passcode, you can restore your data and settings from the backup.

Set up Face ID on iPhone

Use Face ID to securely and conveniently unlock iPhone, authorize purchases and payments, and sign in to many third-party apps by simply glancing at your iPhone.

To use Face ID, you must also set up a passcode on your iPhone.

Set up Face ID or add an alternate appearance

- If you didn't set up Face ID when you first set up your iPhone, go to Settings ⚙ > Face ID & Passcode > Set up Face ID, then follow the onscreen instructions.
- To set up an additional appearance for Face ID to recognize, go to Settings > Face ID & Passcode > Set Up an Alternate Appearance, then follow the onscreen instructions.

If you have physical limitations, you can tap Accessibility Options during Face ID set up. When you do this, setting up facial recognition doesn't require the full range of head motion. Using Face ID is still secure, but it requires more consistency in how you look at iPhone.

Face ID also has an accessibility feature you can use if you're blind or have low vision. If you don't want Face ID to require that you look at iPhone with your eyes open, go to Settings > Accessibility, then turn off Require Attention for Face ID. This feature is automatically turned off if you turn on VoiceOver when you first set up iPhone.

Use Face ID while wearing a face mask

On iPhone 14 models, you can use Face ID to unlock your phone while you wear a face mask (or other covering that blocks your mouth and nose).

When you turn on Face ID with a Mask, Face ID analyzes the unique characteristics around

your eyes, and it works with all of the Face ID options you turn on in Settings ⚙ > Face ID & Passcode.

Note: Face ID is most accurate when it's set up for full-face recognition only.

Go to Settings > Face ID & Passcode, then do any of the following:

- **Allow Face ID to work while you wear a face mask**: Turn on Face ID with a Mask, then follow the onscreen instructions.
  Important: If you usually wear glasses, you can improve the accuracy of Face ID by wearing a pair of transparent glasses (not sunglasses) when you turn on Face ID with a Mask.
- Add a pair of transparent glasses (not sunglasses) to your appearance: Tap Add Glasses, then follow the onscreen instructions.
- Don't allow Face ID to work while you wear a face mask: Turn off Face ID with a Mask.

Alternatively, you can use Apple Watch with all models of iPhone that support Face ID to unlock iPhone while you wear a face mask.

Temporarily disable Face ID

You can temporarily prevent Face ID from unlocking your iPhone.

1. Press and hold the side button and either volume button for 2 seconds.
2. After the sliders appear, press the side button to immediately lock iPhone.
   iPhone locks automatically if you don't touch the screen for a minute or so.

The next time you unlock iPhone with your passcode, Face ID is enabled again.

Turn off Face ID

1. Go to Settings ⚙ > Face ID & Passcode.
2. Do one of the following:
   o Turn off Face ID for specific items only: Turn off one or more of the options.
   o **Turn off Face ID for face masks**: Turn off Face ID with a Mask.
   o **Turn off Face ID**: Tap Reset Face ID.

Keep your Apple ID secure on iPhone

Your Apple ID is the account you use to access Apple services like the App Store, Apple Music, iCloud, iMessage, FaceTime, and more. Your account includes the email address and password you use to sign in as well as the contact, payment, and security details you use across Apple services. Apple employs industry-standard practices to safeguard your Apple ID.

Best practices for maximizing the security of your Apple ID

- Don't let others use your ID, even family members.
  To share purchases, subscriptions, a family calendar, and more without sharing Apple IDs, set up Family Sharing.
- Use two-factor authentication. If you created your Apple ID on a device with iOS 13.4, iPadOS 13.4, macOS 10.15.4, or later, your account automatically uses two-factor authentication. If you previously created an Apple ID account without two-factor authentication, turn on two-factor authentication.
- Never provide your password, security questions, verification codes, recovery key, or any other account security details to anyone else. Apple will never ask you for this information.
- When accessing your Apple ID account page in Safari or another web browser, look for the lock icon 🔒 in the address field to verify that your session is encrypted and secure.
- When using a public computer, always sign out when your session is complete to prevent other people from accessing your account.
- Avoid phishing scams. Don't click links in suspicious email or text messages and never provide personal information on any website you aren't certain is legitimate.
- Don't use your password with other online accounts.

Add Account Recovery Contacts

Choose one or more people you trust as Account Recovery Contacts to help you reset your Apple ID password and regain access to your account if you ever forget your password or get locked out.

Go to Settings ⚙ > [your name] > Password & Security > Account Recovery, tap Add Recovery Contact, then follow the onscreen instructions.

For more information, go to Settings ⚙ > [your name] > Password & Security, then tap "Learn more" below Add Recovery Contact.

Add Legacy Contacts

The Digital Legacy program allows you to designate people as Legacy Contacts so they can access your Apple ID account in the event of your death.

Go to Settings ⚙ > [your name] > Password & Security > Legacy Contact, tap Add Legacy Contact, then follow the onscreen instructions.

Generate a recovery key for your account

For additional control over your account security, you have the option to generate a recovery key that helps you reset your account password or regain access to your Apple ID. A recovery key is a randomly generated 28-character code that you should keep in a safe place. You can reset your account password by either entering your recovery key or using another device already signed in with your Apple ID. To ensure you have access to your account, you are personally responsible for maintaining access to the recovery key and your trusted devices.

Restart, update, reset, and restore

Turn iPhone on or off

Use the side button to turn on iPhone. You can use the side button or Settings ⚙ to turn off iPhone.

If your iPhone isn't working as expected, you can try restarting it by turning it off, then turning it back on. If turning it off and on doesn't fix the issue, try forcing it to restart.

Turn on iPhone

Press and hold the side button until the Apple logo appears.

Turn off iPhone

- Simultaneously press and hold the side button and either volume button until the sliders appear, then drag the Power Off slider.
- Go to Settings ⚙ > General > Shut Down, then drag the slider.

Force restart iPhone

If iPhone isn't responding, and you can't turn it off then on, try forcing it to restart.

1. Press and quickly release the volume up button.
2. Press and quickly release the volume down button.
3. Press and hold the side button.
4. When the Apple logo appears, release the side button.

Update iOS on iPhone

When you update to the latest version of iOS, your data and settings remain unchanged.

Before you update, set up iPhone to back up automatically, or back up your device manually.

Update iPhone automatically

If you didn't turn on automatic updates when you first set up your iPhone, do the following:

1. Go to Settings ⚙ > General > Software Update > Automatic Updates.
2. Turn on Download iOS Updates and Install iOS Updates.

When an update is available, iPhone downloads and installs the update overnight while charging and connected to Wi-Fi. You're notified before an update is installed.

Update iPhone manually

At any time, you can check for and install software updates.

Go to Settings ⚙ > General > Software Update.

The screen shows the currently installed version of iOS and whether an update is available.

To turn off automatic updates, go to Settings > General > Software Update > Automatic Updates.

Update using your computer

1. Connect iPhone and your computer with a cable.
2. Do one of the following:
   - **On a Mac (macOS 10.15 or later)**: In the Finder sidebar, select your iPhone, then click General at the top of the window.
   - **On a Mac (macOS 10.14 or earlier) or a Windows PC**: Open the iTunes app, click the button resembling an iPhone near the top left of the iTunes window, then click Summary.
     Note: Use the latest version of iTunes.
3. Click Check for Update.
4. To install an available update, click Update.

Back up iPhone

You can back up iPhone using iCloud or your computer.

Tip: If you replace your iPhone, you can use its backup to transfer your information to the new device.

Back up iPhone using iCloud

1. Go to Settings ⚙ > [your name] > iCloud > iCloud Backup.
2. Turn on iCloud Backup.
   iCloud automatically backs up your iPhone daily when iPhone is connected to power, locked, and connected to Wi-Fi.
   Note: On models that support 5G, your carrier may give you the option to back up iPhone using your cellular network. Go to Settings > [your name] > iCloud > iCloud Backup, then turn on or off Backup Over Cellular.
3. To perform a manual backup, tap Back Up Now.

To view your iCloud backups, go to Settings > [your name] > iCloud > Manage Account Storage > Backups. To delete a backup, choose a backup from the list, then tap Delete & Turn Off Backup.

Note: If you turn on an app or feature to use iCloud syncing (in Settings > [your name] > iCloud > Show All), its information is stored in iCloud. Because the information is automatically kept up to date on all your devices, it's not included in your iCloud backup.

Back up iPhone using your Mac

1. Connect iPhone and your computer with a cable.
2. In the Finder sidebar on your Mac, select your iPhone.
   To use the Finder to back up iPhone, macOS 10.15 or later is required. With earlier versions of macOS, use iTunes to back up iPhone.
3. At the top of the Finder window, click General.
4. Select "Back up all of the data on your iPhone to this Mac."
5. To encrypt your backup data and protect it with a password, select "Encrypt local backup."
6. Click Back Up Now.

Note: You can also connect iPhone to your computer wirelessly if you set up syncing over Wi-Fi.

Back up iPhone using your Windows PC

1. Connect iPhone and your computer with a cable.
2. In the iTunes app on your PC, click the iPhone button near the top left of the iTunes window.
3. Click Summary.
4. Click Back Up Now (below Backups).
5. To encrypt your backups, select "Encrypt local backup," type a password, then click Set Password.

To see the backups stored on your computer, choose Edit > Preferences, then click Devices. Encrypted backups have a lock icon in the list of backups.

Note: You can also connect iPhone to your computer wirelessly if you set up syncing over Wi-Fi.

Return iPhone settings to their defaults

You can return settings to their defaults without erasing your content.

If you want to save your settings, back up iPhone before returning them to their defaults. For example, if you're trying to solve a problem but returning settings to their defaults doesn't help, you might want to restore your previous settings from a backup.

1. Go to Settings ⚙ > General > Transfer or Reset iPhone > Reset.
2. Choose an option:
   WARNING: If you choose the Erase All Content and Settings option, all of your content is removed.

- Reset All Settings: All settings—including network settings, the keyboard dictionary, location settings, privacy settings, and Apple Pay cards—are removed or reset to their defaults. No data or media are deleted.
- Reset Network Settings: All network settings are removed. In addition, the device name assigned in Settings > General > About is reset to "iPhone," and manually trusted certificates (such as for websites) are changed to untrusted. Cellular data roaming may also be turned off.

When you reset network settings, previously used networks and VPN settings that weren't installed by a configuration profile or mobile device management (MDM) are removed. Wi-Fi is turned off and then back on, disconnecting you from any network you're on. The Wi-Fi and Ask to Join Networks settings remain turned on.

To remove VPN settings installed by a configuration profile, go to Settings > General > VPN & Device Management, select the configuration profile, then tap Remove Profile. This also removes other settings and accounts provided by the profile.

To remove network settings installed by MDM, go to Settings > General > VPN & Device Management, select the management, then tap Remove Management. This also removes other settings and certificates provided by MDM.

- Reset Keyboard Dictionary: You add words to the keyboard dictionary by rejecting words iPhone suggests as you type. Resetting the keyboard dictionary erases only the words you've added.
- Reset Home Screen Layout: Returns the built-in apps to their original layout on the Home Screen.
- Reset Location & Privacy: Resets the location services and privacy settings to their defaults.

Made in United States
North Haven, CT
02 November 2022

26233121R00276